Praise for *The Childwise Catalog,* first edition:

"*The Childwise Catalog* does more than point out the potential dangers of products...it also contains suggestions for parents looking for pediatricians or child care facilities, how to travel with children, and safety tips."

UPI

"The book is unusual in both the number of products surveyed and the safety analysis of each product...(it) also gives good advice about services for children."

Trial Magazine

"In this comprehensive guide parents will have at their disposal, for the first time, a complete and up-to-date guide to the products and services that their children, from newborn through age five, will need to be safe and happy."

National Safety Council

"(*The Childwise Catalog*) is as handy to use as a dictionary. If its information is followed carefully, it should make a contribution in preventing children from being harmed by unsafe items."

Los Angeles Times

"This extensive guide covers products and services needed by parents of infants and preschoolers. In addition to many helpful hints and general considerations for parents, Gillis and Fise offer brand-name recommendations for a number of products."

American Library Association

"(It's) chock full of straight-forward information and helpful tips for parents of children age newborn to five."

San Francisco Chronicle

"A veritable shopping mall of information: from brand-specific comparisons of furniture, toys and clothes to health and child care matters. One hopes that this trove of facts will be updated regularly— it could well become a staple on every parent's shelf."

Publishers Weekly

"...is filled with examples of safe and unsafe products, and explanations on how to tell the difference."

New York Daily News

"No topic or item is too big or too small to be included."

Cleveland Plain Dealer

Praise for *The Childwise Catalog,* first edition:

"I'd advise every parent to buy this book. It covers all the conceivable products and services for children, from baby shampoos and adoption services to health foods and unsafe toys—thousands of items! It should prove its value practically. More important, it should prevent many of the serious accidents that harm children every year."

-Dr. Benjamin Spock

"This extremely informative book will certainly give any parent the pros and cons of any article necessary for child care and development, as well as giving excellent child safety guidelines."

-Virginia E. Pomeranz, M.D.,
author of *The First Five Years:
The Relaxed Approach to Child Care* and
The Mothers' and Fathers' Medical Encyclopedia

"I have always viewed the ranking miracle of a child not as the birth, but the fact that most grow up to be healthy, whole adults in spite of the hazards that crowd the way. *The Childwise Catalog* by *Good Housekeeping* columnist Jack Gillis and co-author Mary Ellen R. Fise will go a long way to even the odds for the new parent."

-John Mack Carter,
Editor-in-Chief,
Good Housekeeping

"It's a jungle of baby products out there. *The Childwise Catalog* will be a great help in negotiating it efficiently, economically and safely."

-Stan and Jan Berenstain,
creators of the Berenstain Bears

"As a parent and a legislator, product safety is a vital concern to me. *The Childwise Catalog* will go a long way to helping parents in this complex and sometimes confusing marketplace. I wish I had it when my children were younger."

-Timothy E. Wirth,
U. S. Senator, Colorado

"In my opinion as a battle-scarred parent and writer of parent's books, no parent's library will be truly complete without this book. It is incredibly comprehensive and even fun to browse in. It's good for grandparents, aunts, and other relatives as well as parents themselves."

-Dr. Futzhugh Dodson,
author of *How to Parent* and
Your Child from Birth to Six

THE
CHILDWISE
CATALOG

NEWBORNS
THROUGH
AGE FIVE

THE
CHILDWISE
CATALOG

A Consumer Guide
to Buying the
Safest and Best
Products for Your
Children

JACK GILLIS AND MARY ELLEN R. FISE

Consumer Federation of America

PERENNIAL LIBRARY

Harper & Row, Publishers, New York
Grand Rapids, Philadelphia, St. Louis, San Francisco
London, Singapore, Sydney, Tokyo, Toronto

First PERENNIAL LIBRARY edition published 1990

Library of Congress Catalog Card Number 89-45656

ISBN 0-06-096450-2

90 91 92 93 94 10 9 8 7 6 5 4 3 2

To
Marilyn & Tom
and four very special children
Katie, John, Brian and Peter

C · O · N · T · E · N · T · S

PART **1** ONE

PRODUCTS YOU CAN PURCHASE FOR YOUR CHILD

CHAPTER ONE

Getting Ready: Newborn to 6 Months   9

CHAPTER TWO

CHAPTER THREE

Growing Up: 2 to 5 Years   145

PART **2** TWO

SERVICES YOU PURCHASE FOR YOUR CHILD

CHAPTER FOUR

Child Care, Preschool and Babysitting   223

CHAPTER FIVE

Health Matters   237

CHAPTER SIX

Traveling Together   261

PART **3** THREE

PROTECTING YOUR CHILD

CHAPTER SEVEN

Safety Inside and Outside the Home   279

CHAPTER EIGHT

Protecting Your Child   329

CHAPTER NINE

Resources for Parents   347

INDEX   397

THE
CHILDWISE
CATALOG

ACKNOWLEDGMENTS

Preparing a book like this means sorting through and researching massive amounts of information—in the case of *The Childwise Catalog* the task was so formidable that it would have been impossible without the assistance of many dedicated and bright people. The key factor in bringing everything together was the incredible effort of Karen Fierst, our research associate. Her research, long hours and hard work are a major factor in getting this important information to America's parents.

We would also like to thank Steve Brobeck, Executive Director of Consumer Federation of America, who first brought us together to write this book and for supporting our efforts all along the way.

We are also grateful to Pam Dorman, our first edition editor, who was instrumental in the birth of *The Childwise Catalog* and Stuart Krichevsky our friend, agent and loyal supporter. We hope that, soon, you both will have occasion to use this book!

Our thanks also go to a wonderful group of people that assisted us in preparing this revision. Special thanks are due to Abbie Gerber, Cristina Mendoza and Teri Ginther for their thorough research and for just pitching in; to April Page, Bill North-Rudin, Teresa Talley, Bryan Pratt and Robin Taulton for their dedicated and proficient word processing; to Cathryn Poff, Roy Perkins, Barbara Roper, and Sue Nielsen Perino for extraordinary help in editing and copy editing; and very special thanks go to Susan Cole our talented and creative designer and to Jennifer Barrett our illustrator. As always, Ace typesetter, Ray Weiss came through with a masterful job under incredible pressure.

The staff of the U.S. Consumer Product Safety Commission was particularly helpful, and we would like to especially thank Jim Bradley, Joyce Coonley, Jay DeMarco, Shelley Deppa, Sandra Eberle, Jacqueline Elder, Joel Friedman, Ken Giles, Liz Gomilla, Jim Hoebel, Wendella Holland, Bob Hundermer, Ron Medford, Chris Nelson, Anne Pavlich, Carlos Perez, John Preston, Terri Rogers, Marc Schoem, Jim Sharman, David Thome, Deborah Tinsworth, Elaine Tyrrell, Bill Walton, and Virgina White.

We would also like to thank Ann Brown, Dr. Mark Widome, Phyllis Spaeth, Roseanne Soloway, William MacMillan, Clare Murnane, Marcella Ridenour, John Lineweaver, Jack Walsh, David Snow, Mike Deese, Linda Tracey, Stephanie Wood, and the Arts and Crafts Materials Institute.

In preparing this edition of *The Childwise Catalog* we conducted a survey of parents about their product preferences, child care arrangements, and numerous other matters. These parents, whom we promised confidentiality, each took an hour (or more!) out of their hectic schedules to complete a very detailed survey. Their responses were a tremendous help in making this edition a practical compendium of parenting information. Thanks to your efforts our readers will benefit from the experience and advice of the true experts—veteran parents. Thank you for sharing it with us and them.

Our commitment to improving children's safety and helping parents make wise consumer decisions is the result not only of our consumer advocacy, but our interactions with many parents and children. First among these are our own parents, Ann and Reds Rector and Jean Gillis, from whom we first learned about safety and who have unabashedly encouraged our professional efforts. We also have been significantly affected by the many children who have entered our lives, especially our nieces and nephews—or as they are fondly known in both our families— *The Cousins:* Ray, Stephanie, Lisa, Steve, Megan, Greg, Kenneth, Amy, Matthew, Joe Daniel, Spencer, Thomas, little Whelan, Vicki, Marni, Kara, Andy, Leeanne, Michele, Brian, Amanda, Todd, Kate, Stacey, Megan, Conor, Reid, Kevin and Casey.

Our own children, Katie, John, Brian and Peter have been an inspiration throughout our work on this book. The smiles on their young faces are a constant reminder of the importance of preventing accidents and creating happy childhood memories.

Finally, and most importantly, we would like to thank our spouses, Marilyn and Tom, for their encouragement, interest, suggestions, review and overall understanding and support. They are two great parents!

INTRODUCTION

One of the potential "hazards" associated with a book like this is creating the impression that shopping for your child is like finding your way through a nightmarish maze of unexpected catastrophes. As parents ourselves, we too don't like to hear about the pratfalls and injuries associated with the many fun and exciting purchases we will be making. We also know, however, that it is impossible for the average parent to keep up with the products on the market—knowing what to look for and what to avoid. As a result, most parents are eager for the information necessary to make informed purchases for their most prized possession.

But it is not necessarily easy. As parents, we are being subjected to a marketing blitz unprecedented in the child product industry. Never before has there been such a wide variety of choices in products and services in the marketplace. There are so many items for infants and children that it is difficult to determine which are necessary and, even more important, which are best in terms of performance and safety. New parents find themselves purchasing products and services which they know little about. Yet, these decisions will directly affect the well being of their child.

The good news is that we, as parents, have been part of an era of consumerism that has taught comparison shopping, cost consciousness and a concern for product safety. This buyer awareness and concern about safety and performance has sent us searching for useful, straightforward consumer information.

As both parents and consumers, we are asking many questions: Are we getting the best buy? Is the product safe? What are the alternatives? How do you find a capable, communicative pediatrician? What should we look for in choosing child care and baby products? What about used products, are they safe?

Furthermore, as the number of accidental deaths and injuries among children continues to rise, our concern for child safety grows. Each year nearly 5,000 children die and thousands more are injured due to unsafe products and the unsafe use of products. But even if we want to monitor our children's environment carefully, it is difficult to find out about, let alone remove, all the hazards.

These concerns are what the *The Childwise Catalog* is all about. As both parents and consumer activists, we have compiled what we feel is the most comprehensive guide available for parents who want to be safe and wise consumers.

Why this Book

Buying for your children should not have to be a doom and gloom proposition. While injury statistics can and should be alarming, the odds *are* in favor of your child. However, despite the odds, most of us know of a little person who has been needlessly injured. Tragically, most of those injuries were preventable, "if only the parents had known"—which is why we wrote this book.

As new parents ourselves, we have received toys that, had we not done the research for this book, we may have passed on to our children. For example, we both received a cute little doll and pacifier set. Not only was the pacifier very tiny, sharp and easy to swallow or choke on, it was on a string around the doll's neck, a dangerous practice. We later learned that this doll has been recalled several times by the Consumer Product Safety Commission.

Sometimes the hazards are less obvious, like the potential harm from a *drop-side* mesh playpen, or the incompatibility of child safety seats with certain cars. Hopefully, armed with this book you can anticipate the unexpected, and offer your little one the safest environment possible.

In addition to avoiding the hazardous products, hopefully this book will assist you in finding some of the great nursery products, toys and books that usually only veteran parents know about. By reading our product descriptions and advice on selecting services you'll get a jump start on making the choices that are best for your family.

We have found, as you no doubt have, that few of life's experiences equal the intense joy and satisfaction, or the hard work and anxiety, of childrearing. One of our goals in preparing this book is to help reduce the anxiety associated with the many decisions you will have to make during your child's first years. By using the tips in *The Childwise Catalog*, you will have more time to experience the joy and happiness that children bring.

How To Use This Book

This book is designed to be both read and referred to. It does not dispense medical or psychological advice. We will, however, pose questions and alternatives that you may want to discuss with your doctor.

The first three chapters, *Part One*, follow your child through the first five years and provide specific advice and suggestions on the equipment and toys you will be buying. For each product discussed, we include simple, straight-forward tips to insure that the product you select will be the one best suited to meet your needs. We also discuss important tips that will enable you to use the products safely and efficiently. Where applicable, we warn you about unsafe products *and* recommend brands that are among the best.

Because your consumer challenges as a parent are not just limited to finding the right products, we also provide information on making the best selection of services for your child—be it choosing a pediatrician, selecting child care arrangements or booking the right airline! These are all in *Part Two*, which covers the services you'll buy for your child.

Part Three offers advice on the safety and safe keeping of your little one. Chapter Seven contains the most comprehensive child-proofing information available anywhere and will be helpful to you as your child grows and encounters new challenges. Our discussion of child protection in Chapter Eight is a compilation of the experts' best advice—we hope you'll never need it.

The final chapter is your resource guide—a lead on practically every source of information about children's products, services and health that you could ever want.

If searching for a particular topic, consult our *detailed index* for easy reference to products or safety issues.

A Few Words on Safety

While reading different sections of this book you will see that we often include statistics on children's injuries and deaths associated with a variety of products. Many parents we spoke with about the book were very surprised at the high frequency of injuries and deaths; some said they were lucky to have gotten their child to the age of three or four without major incident! You may feel that way, too.

We have not included these statistics because we are alarmists. Rather, as parents we know that a box of bandages is a staple in the family medicine cabinet and that a trip to the emergency room at least once during a child's formative years is practically inevitable. And as consumer safety advocates we also know that many very serious accidents are the result of circumstances that even the most concerned parent cannot anticipate. The statistics, therefore, are included to educate you. We believe that the more you know, the better prepared you will be to head off an unfortunate and painful event for your child. If these statistics make only one or two parents take the necessary steps to prevent their child's death, then, to us, they are worth including in this book.

While some children's accidents and injuries are the result of poor design or faulty products, many occur because of misuse, lack of parental supervision, or simply because the parent wasn't aware of the potential hazards involved. Throughout the book we have included tips, suggestions and guidelines for using products safely. Obviously, not every suggestion applies to every household. Similarly, we know it is unlikely that you will take *every* step we mention. We simply urge you to heed as many of the recommendations as possible.

We also encourage you to be safety advocates yourselves. If you think a product is unsafe, call the appropriate government agency (they're listed below) and report your findings. Agencies such as the Consumer Product Safety Commission often initiate recall actions because of reports from parents like yourself. Likewise, if a product you have purchased has an inappropriate age label or does not warn parents of possible hazards, let the government and the manufacturer know.

You also should share safety information with other parents. Your child's nursery school or playgroup, neighbors, and friends are all additional networks of parents who can spread the word and protect more children.

Lastly, let us know of any children's safety concerns you have as parents. While we can't promise an individual response to you, your communication serves a very vital purpose. Letters from consumers may, in some cases, point out problems of which we are unaware. They also can serve as evidence that the Consumer Federation of America, the national consumer group we are both affiliated with, can use in its advocacy work before government agencies to show that action is needed. When consumer correspondence illuminates a new area of concern, CFA has the resources to communicate this information to hundreds of thousands of Americans. One of our chief goals is to educate more people, with help from concerned parents and others, and thereby hopefully decrease those alarming death and injury statistics.

Besides becoming safety conscious, we hope that the shopping tips and information on services will make your job as parents easier. Armed with this information you'll be able to spend less time on buying and other decisions and more time enjoying your child during this wonderful time you have together.

Who's Who

Throughout this book we make reference, often by acronym, to several organizations, including both government and private. In order to keep these straight, refer to the descriptions below. Other organizations are listed in Chapter Nine.

Consumer Product Safety Commission (CPSC)

The CPSC is an independent regulatory agency of the United States Government. Its mission is to protect consumers from unreasonable risks of injury associated with consumer products.

CPSC learns about product-related injuries and deaths through a variety of sources, including consumer complaints received through letters and Hotline calls. CPSC has the authority to set mandatory standards, ban a product, order recalls of unsafe products or institute labeling requirements.

If you or your child has been injured by a consumer product or if you believe a product is unsafe, you should call or write:
Consumer Product Safety Commission
5401 Westbard Ave.
Bethesda, MD 20816
Product Safety Hotline: 800-638-CPSC

A teletypewriter for the hearing impaired is available on 800-638-8270, in Marlyand 800-492-8104.

Food and Drug Administration (FDA)

FDA is the federal government agency responsible for the safety of foods, drugs, cosmetics and medical devices.

FDA is able to recall unsafe products and has enacted many regulations regarding the manufacture of the products they regulate. To obtain more information on these products or to report a hazardous one, call or write:
Food and Drug Administration
5600 Fishers Lane
Room 16-85
Rockville, MD 20857
301-443-3170

National Highway Traffic Safety Administration (NHTSA)

NHTSA is the federal government agency in charge of automobile, highway and pedestrian safety. In addition to their regulation and recall of automobiles and other motor vehicles, NHTSA provides information on safety belts and child safety seats, tires, car crash test results, fuel economy and defect recalls. To report a safety defect or to obtain information, call or write:

National Highway Traffic Safety Administration
400 Seventh Street, S.W.
NEF-11-HL
Washington, D.C. 20690
800-424-9393
366-0123 (D.C.)

Consumer Federation of America (CFA)

CFA is a non-profit, consumer group. As the nation's largest consumer advocacy organization, CFA represents consumers before Congress, government agencies and the private sector. CFA works on issues such as product safety, telecommunications, energy, and banking. CFA's membership is comprised of other state, local and national organizations, representing over 50 million consumers.

Consumer Federation of America
1424 16th Street, N.W.
Suite 604
Washington, D.C. 20036

This chapter will give you a basic idea of what you should have on hand before the baby arrives and how you should select those items. You'll find information on how to buy and use the equipment and clothing you will need during your child's first six months. We have listed the products alphabetically, and each entry includes a basic description of the product (including both the good features and potential hazards associated with the item), tips to remember when buying, and guidelines for safe and efficient use. Whenever possible, we list our choices of best products as well as hazardous products to watch out for.

Products You Can Purchase for Your Child Getting Ready: Newborn to 6 Months

You may want to look over the next two chapters (ages six months to two years and two to five years) now, even though your child is a newborn or is expected soon. You'll find that you have a lot more time to shop around now for the products you will need later on than you will after the baby arrives. If you can't afford to make all the purchases you will need now—and most of us can't—consider shopping around to get an idea of prices and what's available. That way you can make a quicker (and smarter) decision later on.

As you prepare for your child, do what we did—ask your friends who are parents to tell you what their most indispensable baby products were. (Don't forget to ask them what they bought or received and never used!) If you suspect someone is planning a baby shower for you, *don't buy anything until after the shower.* If you are a baby gift giver, be sure to consult our lists of "Great Gifts" at the ends of Chapters 1, 2, and 3.

If you have friends with young children at different ages, consider purchasing items together. For example, if you are six months more pregnant than your friend, you could buy a swing and your friend could buy a back carrier. When you are finished with the swing, pass it to your friend and your friend can give you the back carrier. You can return the back carrier when your friend's child is ready to use it. Depending upon the age difference between your children, other products you might consider sharing include front carriers, changing tables, bicycle child carriers, and portable hook-on high chairs.

A Shopping Checklist for Getting Ready

If this is your first child, putting together a layette (an outfit of clothing, furniture, linen, etc. for a newborn) is often a romantic notion. As you await the birth of your child you will see many different suggestions as to what the complete layette should include. One drawback of many of these lists is that they are prepared by publications who depend on advertising for revenue—advertisers of the products on the list.

Here, then, is *our* list of products you will need. This list is based not only on our experience, but also on the suggestions of other parents—people who've been there! It's a realistic list of items you will need during the first year of your baby's life. We have **boldfaced** the absolute necessities to have on hand when you come home from the hospital; the rest are optional items you may want to have on hand before the baby arrives. Later on in this chapter we provide detailed descriptions of how to buy and use most of these items.

What You'll *Really* Need

Bath

- ☐ **Towels—Hooded** (4) [Baby towels are lighter than regular towels and are easy to wrap around child; hood keeps your baby warm while drying off.]
- ☐ **Baby Washcloths** (3) [They are softer and smaller than regular ones.]
- ☐ Baby shampoo [See discussion on baby shampoo.]
- ☐ Baby scrub brush [A soft plastic one keeps the scalp clean and removes dry skin.]
- ☐ Blunt edged scissors or **baby nail clippers**
- ☐ Sterilized cotton balls
- ☐ Cotton swabs
- ☐ Zinc oxide cream [For the inevitable diaper rash.]
- ☐ **Moistened toilettes** [Pop up vs. prefolded—your choice—look for unscented ones with low or no alcohol.]

Clothing

- ☐ **Jump suits**—snap or zip type (6-7) [Buttons will drive you crazy.]
- ☐ Sweater and cap (2) [For summer babies, get a bonnet or cap for sun protection.]
- ☐ **Sleeping sack** (3) [For summer babies, light weight with a bottom drawstring; winter babies need a heavy, zippered bag.]
- ☐ Sweat suits (2)
- ☐ **Six-month sized T-shirts** (8) [You may get a couple of "free" three month versions from the hospital.]
- ☐ Socks or booties (3 pairs)
- ☐ Snowsuit (winter babies) [Avoid the sack type, you can't use them with most car seats.]

What You'll *Really* Need (cont'd.)

Diapers
If using cloth diapers:

- ☐ 4 dozen diapers (at least)
- ☐ Rubber pants (6)
- ☐ Safety pins (6 pairs)
- ☐ Diaper pail
  If using disposable diapers:
- ☐ 90 diapers = 1 week

General Items

- ☐ Bulb syringe [Used to drain clogged sinuses—many times the hospital will send you home with one.]
- ☐ Cloth diapers (6) [For protecting you, your clothes and upholstery—great for general clean-up.]
- ☐ Terry cloth bibs (3) [Look for velcro or snaps for a quick on and off.]
- ☐ Cuddle toy [A stuffed animal in the hospital bassinet identifies your child to visitors and will later become a special toy.]
- ☐ Night light [Protection against things that go bump in the night.]
- ☐ **Rectal thermometer**

If nursing:

- ☐ **Bottles** (3-4) [For storing breast milk and formula.]
- ☐ **Nursing bras** (2)
- ☐ **Breast pads** (box)
- ☐ Breast pump
  If bottle feeding:
- ☐ **Bottles** (8-12)
- ☐ **Extra nipples and nipple cap covers for travel.**

What You'll *Really* Need (cont'd.)

Furniture

- ☐ **Crib and mattress**
- ☐ **Changing table or padded surface**
- ☐ Dresser
- ☐ **Car seat** [Make the first ride a safe ride.]
- ☐ Infant seat
- ☐ Front carrier
- ☐ Stroller
- ☐ Swing

Linens

- ☐ Blanket and zippered quilt (1 each)
- ☐ **Receiving blankets** (4) [The hospital nursery staff will teach you how to swaddle.]
- ☐ **Crib sheets** (3)
- ☐ **Bumper pads**
- ☐ Waterproof mattress protectors (2) [The mattress will likely have a multi-year guarantee for everything but urine.]
- ☐ Mattress pads (2)

Baby Shampoo

There are certain chemical ingredients in no-sting shampoos that can anesthetize a child's eyeball. Ordinarily, this is not a dangerous occurrence. But no-sting is not necessarily no-burn. So be careful not to overlook irritations or injuries to the eye since these baby shampoos can burn the eyes for up to seven hours. You might consider holding a washcloth over your baby's eyes when using any type of no-sting shampoo.

In addition, girls may be more susceptible to vaginal infection when they sit in bath water containing shampoo soap and bubbles. Like bubble bath shampoo can be irritating. If you wash your daughter's hair while she is seated in the bath water, wipe her bottom with a washcloth rinsed with clean tap water before taking her from the bathtub.

Bath Products

Depending upon how old you are, you may remember an ancient contraption your parents used for your first baths—the bathinette. This portable, folding tub for bathing was often part of the changing table apparatus. Thankfully, the days of slopping the water from the bathroom to this type of tub are over. But the concept of utilizing something smaller than the standard bathtub for bathing a tiny infant lives on. Today's **portable bathtubs** are inexpensive, and some models fit conveniently over the standard tub, so there's no problem when baby makes waves. In addition to saving your back, portable tubs make it much easier to handle a slippery baby and help new parents conquer one of the more difficult skills of early parenting—giving baby a bath!

To make certain your child's bath is a safe one, *always* test the bath water temperature before immersing your child. An infant's skin is far more susceptible to burns than yours, so use the inside of your wrist or elbow or, better yet, **a bath thermometer** to test. The "Anti-Scald Bath Thermometer" by Kinder Guard ($2.50) allows you to determine quickly whether the water is too hot. Since many scalds occur when children turn on the hot water while playing, keep a close eye on your child at all times when in the bathroom.

To prevent falls, apply **nonskid appliques** to your bathtub surface or use a **rubber bath mat**. Attach cushioned **spout guards** (shaped like bears, whales and elephants) over the faucet to help guard against bumped heads.

A favorite product of ours is a **sponge pad**, used right in the bottom of the tub. The 24 by 18 inch pad has a scooped out surface to help keep little ones in place. It will keep heads from knocking against the tub and will keep little bodies a few inches above the water level. When bath time is over, simply wring out the pad and let it dry. They are inexpensive (around $5) and available at most children's stores. One will easily last until your little one is ready for regular baths, and they're easy to pack on trips.

WARNING: *You may see some other bath products that allow your child to sit up when bathing. One design is a ring-like device with three legs secured by suction cups. Another is an inflatable soft ring of a similar design. Beware—some versions were recalled as unsafe. We think they make washing your baby's entire body harder and really can't keep an active infant in place. If you use one of these, resist the temptation to leave your child unattended in the tub, even for the few minutes it takes to get your soap or supplies.*

RECALLED PRODUCTS: Bath Accessories

If more than 18 months have elapsed since the recall date, the manufacturer may no longer honor the recall. If the company refuses to comply, you should discard the product to ensure the safety of your child.

Seamore the Action Seahorse Bath Rings
WHICH ONES: Model 2772 sold nationwide from March 1986 to December 1988 with the date code (8812 or less) located on the underside of the seahorse seat, visible through the three holes on the underside of the toy. PROBLEM: The push-nut and neck-pin located on the neck of the seahorse can be removed and swallowed by a child. WHAT TO DO: Call Century Products at 1-800-392-6500 for a free repair kit. RECALL DATE: 6/89

Blankets and Quilts

There are three general types of blankets. While your selection will probably be based on style and price, here are a few notes on each type:

Receiving Blankets

These small flannel or cotton blend covers are what hospitals use to wrap newborns. Wrapped tightly around your baby, they provide warmth and comfort. In addition to swaddling, you will use them frequently to clean up spills, dribbles and other expected events. Keep at least four on hand.

Fleece or Thermal Blankets

These are slightly heavier than receiving blankets and offer more warmth. This type of blanket could very well become your child's "blankie" and an indispensable item in your household.

✔ **TIP:** *If you notice that your child has a particular attachment to one blanket or sheet—go out and buy two more like it. It will save heartache and hassle if "special blankie" gets lost.*

Zippered Quilts

Zippered quilts (or comforters if they have more batting) have become indispensable at home and on the road. Zipped up they look like mini sleeping bags and are great in the baby's bed or for sleeping at a friend's or babysitter's house. Unzipped, they become a full fledged baby's blanket for home, in the car or on a plane. The best feature is that they are instant play areas, providing a soft, clean area for your baby to play at home or visiting.

★ REMEMBER: When Buying A Blanket or Quilt

☐ Look closely at the stitching—there should be no loops or loose threads that could catch on a child's fingernails or clothing.

☐ If a comforter, make sure the stuffing cannot come out. Stray batting can easily be swallowed by your baby.

☐ Avoid blankets with long fringes that could loosen and be swallowed.

☐ Look to see if there is a looped tag on a seam—if so, cut it off. Children have wrapped them tightly around their fingers and cut off circulation. Note washing instructions before discarding.

WARNING: *Never use electric blankets with infants. These blankets can overheat the child, and any moisture (urine) can act as a conductor and cause a shock.*

Bottles and Nipples

Unlike the days when you were a child, there are now several different types of baby bottles. You have two basic choices: bottles with liners or bottles without liners. The size, shape and heat sensitivity are also features to examine. Here are the pros and cons of the different types of bottles.

Bottles with liners are easier to clean up—you simply throw the liner away, and the holder often needs no cleaning. Basically, you have a plastic cylinder into which you drop a soft plastic bag, lipping the top of the bag over the top of the cylinder. After pouring in the liquid, you screw on the nipple like you would on a traditional bottle. Breast milk or other liquids can be frozen in the liner ahead of time for easy preparation.

Liner-style bottles can help prevent gas, because the soft liner allows you to squeeze out any air. This also means that your child can suck without getting air, regardless of the position the bottle is held in. While convenient, this is the most expensive bottle system. But some of the extra cost is offset by the fact that you do not need to buy as many bottles, since they do not get dirty. There is also the problem of making sure you have a supply of liners on hand. Finally, after age one, children can reach inside and squeeze the liner, inevitably learn to squirt the liquid out (like a mini-water gun)—a maneuver that has convinced many a parent that its time to wean!

Plastic and glass bottles without liners are easier to prepare and are goof-proof for a babysitter or others uninitiated in the world of baby matters. Bottles do not need to be sterilized if they are washed in an automatic dishwasher and almost all bottles without liners are dishwasher safe. Bottle brushes are also a great help in clean up.

Bottles now come in a variety of designs, shapes, colors and sizes. Some variations include:

An **oval donut-shaped bottle**, that makes it easy for older babies to hang on to the bottle (even one-handed). Ansa makes one called the "Easy-To-Know" model that changes color when the liquid is too hot.

An **angled bottle** with a bend near the top allows the nipple to stay full and reduces the amount of air swallowed during feeding. The maker of the Degree Baby Bottle claims that neck and throat strain is reduced as baby does not have to crane his neck to get the last few ounces.

✔ **TIP:** *To help decide which type bottle to use, experiment on your own or help a friend prepare a batch of bottles and help clean up to get a clearer idea of which style suits you and your child.*

WARNING: *Do not use a microwave to heat baby bottles. It is possible that heating in a microwave can cause a change in infant formula, including a loss of vitamins, and can destroy some of the protective properties of breast milk. In addition, because the liquid is often heated* *unevenly, it is possible to test the liquid and find an acceptable temperature while portions you haven't tested are scalding hot. Also, because of steam build up, glass baby bottles and some plastic ones can explode after being taken from the microwave oven.*

Tips for Safe, Efficient Use:

1. Never put your child's bottle on a string or cord around their neck or attach it in the same manner to their clothing or baby equipment. The cord could become tangled or caught on equipment or toys and strangle your child.

2. Even if you use bottle liner style bottles, buy a plastic bottle for those inevitable times where you run out of bottle liners.

3. For older bottle users, you *can* reuse a plastic liner if you rinse it out well.

Nipples

Your selection of bottle style may depend on which type of nipple you and your child prefer. Nipples are available in a variety of shapes and materials. The three most prevalent are the traditional shape (like the Evenflo nipple many of us grew up on), the Playtex nurser nipple (designed to simulate a breast) and the orthodontic nipple (intended to reduce incorrect sucking that can later lead to tooth problems).

✔ **TIP:** *If you do not plan to breast-feed, take four to six nipples of the style you wish to use to the hospital with you so the nursery staff can start your child on it right away. But be prepared to switch styles—even newborns can exhibit strong preferences!*

Nipples made of rubber are required by the Food and Drug Administration to contain reduced amounts of nitrosamines. (See *Pacifiers* later on in this chapter for important information on the different materials used in nipples and pacifiers.) Silicone nipples contain no nitrosamines. Fortunately most nipples and nipple holders can be used with most bottles that use a screw-on nipple holder; the Evenflo nipple holder will screw on Gerber juice jars, producing an instant bottle of juice.

Breast Pumps

If you are a breast-feeding mother, chances are you'll need to express milk, for which you'll probably use a pump. You have two basic choices, manual and automatic. Both operate on the same principle—a vacuum draws out the milk, which flows into a container.

Electric pumps are considerably more expensive than manual, so most women rent them. They are usually available from hospital supply stores or large drug stores. An electric pump will allow you to express more milk in less time, but they are cumbersome and noisy. On the other hand, manual pumps are quite portable and easy to clean but slower. There are also battery operated pumps. While they are not as efficient as a regular electric pump, they are faster to use than manual pumps.

✔ **TIP:** *Consult friends who have used breast pumps for advice on which ones are the most comfortable to use. You may even be able to borrow one from a friend.*

Here is a description of the different types of pumps:

Manual Breast Pumps

Piston or cylinder pumps are the most popular manual pumps. The pump consists of two cylinders, one inside the other, with a cup which you place over your nipple. These pumps are easy to use, dishwasher safe and small enough to be easily taken to and from work. They usually come with two adapters for varying nipple sizes, and the cylinder doubles as a baby bottle. Some cylinder pumps have an angled breast shield that allows a more comfortable pumping position.

Cylinder Pump
A common, cylinder-type breast pump.

Bicycle Horn Pumps operate on a very simple principle: the breast shield is connected to a tube with a suction bulb and screwed onto a baby bottle. When the bulb (which is similar to a bicycle horn bulb) is squeezed, suction is created and the milk is pumped into the bottle. The suction pressure is increased or decreased by twisting the lid of the bottle. Pumping the bulb can be less tiring than using a cylinder.

Oral Pumps use the mother's mouth to create a gentle suction that draws the milk out. It is very small and it can be used while the mother is lying down.

Convertible Pumps use a piston-type pumping action and include an adapter for an electric breast pump.

Automatic Pumps

Electric Pumps are easier to use than a manual pump and may empty your breasts more thoroughly. This can be a great help in maintaining your milk supply. Another nice feature of an electric pump is that you can adjust the suction to imitate your baby's sucking patterns. Because most of the institutional style electric pumps are very expensive to buy ($400 to $1,000), most women rent them. They rent for about $60 per month plus a personal starter kit which costs about $15.

Gerber has a new product called **Precious Care Electric Breast Pump** which is much smaller than the institutional style pumps. What these electric pumps sacrifice in suction, they more than make up for in portability. They are available in most mass merchandise and drug stores and retail for between $50 and $70. In addition to the breast pump, the kit comes with a nurser and storage container.

Battery Operated Pumps

These pumps are very transportable. But, because they run on batteries, they don't create as much suction as a regular electric pump.

✔ **TIP:** *Breast-feeding mothers who work together should consider sharing an electric pump. Each mother has her own suction cup which attaches to the pump. This is a good way to take advantage of the speed and efficiency of an electric pump while reducing the rental cost.*

★ REMEMBER: When Buying a Breast Pump

☐ Look for one that is easy to clean.

☐ If your doctor prescribes a breast pump, your insurance company may cover the cost.

☐ Some of the popular cylinder pumps have a breast shield, which is easier to use.

Carriers, Front

There are two basic types of baby carriers, front carriers and back packs. Front carriers are usually soft and form a little nest for the infant. Back carriers are like camping back packs, and most styles have a metal frame to distribute the weight. Front carriers are best for younger infants, while back carriers are best for older children.

We love front carriers. In addition to freeing the hands of a busy mother, they are great for soothing fussy or colicky children. They are also great for helping dads with their little one. In fact, a recent study by Columbia Presbyterian Medical Center in New York found that infants held next to a parent's body form healthier attachments than those carried in infant seats.

✔ **TIP:** *Cost is no indication of how well a particular baby carrier will meet your needs. Before buying a carrier, consider how you will be using it.*

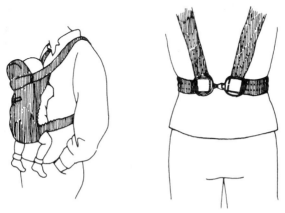

Front Carrier

In addition to giving your baby a very secure resting place, front carriers leave both of your hands free. Look for a carrier that has an easy-to-use catch.

RECOMMENDED PRODUCTS: Front Carriers

Snugli Padded Infant Carrier

This one started the front carrier's popularity. It comes with wide padded straps, a padded seat, and a padded shield to protect the baby's head. It's easy to get in and out of and machine washable.

Evenflo Aviator

This model has padded shoulder straps, two detachable bibs, a nursing zipper and two outer pockets for storage. A removable inner seat allows for growth.

Gerry Cuddle Pack

This model also has padded shoulder straps, a nursing zipper and a removable bib. Its outer pouch opens for easy access and has both back and neck support.

★ REMEMBER: When Buying A Front Carrier

☐ Select a style with wide shoulder straps, so they won't cut into your shoulder.

☐ Straps should be easily adjustable to accommodate both parents and any others who will use the carrier.

☐ Look for sturdy stitching and snaps, zippers and buckles that are secure and easy to use.

☐ Make sure the carrier is easy to put on and take off by yourself.

☐ Watch out for sharp edges or closures that can scratch your baby.

☐ Look for washable carriers.

☐ Buy one that has head and shoulder support for very young babies.

☐ Consider the season in which you are likely to use it. The pouch-type style carriers, particularly those made of corduroy, can be too warm for summer.

☐ You may see a product advertised as a "baby sling." We don't recommend these, because they don't offer very young children enough support, and because they don't adequately restrict older children, who could be able to reach things that could hurt them.

Tips for Safe, Efficient Use:

1. Baby carriers should *never* be used in an automobile. In the event of an accident, your child could be crushed between you and the dashboard. Even if you were wearing your safety belt, the belts of the carrier are not designed to withstand the forces of an accident.

2. When the baby is seated in the carrier, his legs should be spread apart, supported from the knees up, and the knees should be lower than his bottom.

Car Safety Seats

Probably the most important purchase you will make for your child is a car safety seat. To prevent serious injury to a child in the event of a car accident, there is no substitute for a good-quality car safety seat. Every state now requires their use, even for newborns. There are three major types of child safety seats: Infant, Convertible and Toddler. Infant and Convertible seats are described below, and information about toddler seats can be found in Chapter 3. Before buying any seat, read *Remember When Buying* (below) for some potentially life saving tips.

According to the American Academy of Pediatrics, buying a car seat before birth is a must in order to make "the first ride a safe ride." We agree.

How many times have you gone out of your way to prevent your children from being injured, taken special care to keep household poisons out of their reach, or watched carefully while they swam? Yet, despite our concern about our children's welfare in these situations, many parents plunk their children in the back of a station wagon or let them roam around in a moving car. Ironically, of all hazards, it is the automobile that poses the greatest threat to your children's welfare. In fact, after the first weeks of an infant's life, car accidents are the single leading cause of death and serious injury for children. Yet, nearly 80 percent of the children who died in cars could have been saved by the use of child safety seats or safety belts.

Being a safe driver yourself is no excuse not to have everyone buckled up. Quite often crashes or sudden swerves are caused by the recklessness of others. You simply can't protect children by holding them on your lap. Even in low-speed crashes, a child can be hurled against the inside of the car with a violent impact. At 30 mph, a crash or sudden braking can wrench your child from your arms with tremendous force. Your child will continue to fly forward at the speed the car was traveling until he or she hits something. At this speed, even a tiny 10-pound infant would be ripped from your arms with a force of nearly 300 pounds.

To demonstrate the actual forces present even in low-speed crashes, the University of Michigan set up a study using adult volunteers. Both male and female adults were given 17-pound dummies to represent the average six-month-old baby. Sitting in a seat, with safety belts on, each adult held one of the "babies" in tests simulating 15 and 30 mph crashes. Even knowing when the impact would occur and holding on with all their strength, none of the volunteers was able to keep the "baby" from being torn from his or her arms.

If you aren't wearing a safety belt, your own body will be an additional hazard to a child in your lap. You will be thrown forward with enough force to crush your child against the dashboard or the back of the front seat.

The best and only way to protect your child in an automobile is by using a safety seat. If no seat is available, buckle the child in the back seat with a conventional seat belt.

By getting into the habit of always using a child safety seat, you will be on the way to establishing the habit of regular safety belt use when your children get older. As lifelong wearers of safety belts, your children will reduce their chances of being killed or seriously injured in an accident by 50 percent.

It's difficult to judge the adequacy of a safety seat. In fact, the federal government conducted a small study in which parents were asked to select and use a seat from among eight popular models. Only three parents kept the seats they originally picked. This stresses the importance of understanding how a seat works, how it fits in your car, and how comfortable it is for your child before you buy. If the seat is difficult to use, your child might not get the protection he or she needs.

WARNING: *When buying, renting, or borrowing a used child safety seat make certain it has not restrained a child in an accident. If it has, its structure may be weakened, and it should no longer be used. If your own seat has restrained your child in a serious accident, it should be replaced immediately.*

Currently, one of the biggest concerns of car safety experts is the failure of the government to implement effective safety seat recalls and the complexity of some seats which often cause parents to use them incorrectly. Furthermore, car seat manufacturers and auto manufacturers have done nothing to insure compatibility between the car's seat belt system and the child safety seat. Some seats simply can't be installed in certain cases.

Incorrect installation of a child safety seat can deny the child the lifesaving protection offered by the seat and may even contribute to further injuring the child. It is very important to read the installation instructions carefully. If you have any questions about the correct installation of your seat in your particular car, contact the National Highway Traffic Safety Administration.

WARNING: *After an accident, rescue experts suggest that the entire seat be removed from the car, rather than unbuckling the child first.*

Do You Need a Locking Clip?

Most parents don't realize that a substantial number of car seat belts simply cannot restrain a safety seat unless you attach a locking clip. Typically, the problem occurs in imported cars with safety belt latches that slide along the belt. Study the diagram below to see which type of belt you have. Typically locking clips are not packed with every seat and car seat manufactures rarely supply them to stores for purchase. If you need a locking clip and don't have one, you will most likely have to contact the company that made your child's seat.

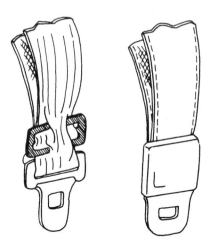

LOCKING CLIP

These are typical buckles on front seat safety belts. The one on the right, with a large buckle, does not require a locking clip in order to be safely used with a child car seat. The one on the left, with a buckle that easily slides along the belt, does require a locking clip (shown). Locking clips are not packed with every child seat. Not using the locking clip on car belts that need it could render your safety seat useless.

✔ **TIP:** *If you own a 1987, 1988, or 1989 GM car equipped with door-mounted, automatic safety belts, you can get a free belt to attach to the seat that allows you to put a child safety seat in the front seat.*

Infant Car Safety Seats

The infant seat can be used from birth until your baby is able to sit up, usually at 6 to 10 months, or at a weight of 20 pounds. This seat can only be installed facing the rear of the car, keeping the baby in a semi-reclining position. In an accident, the crash forces are spread as gently as possible over the baby's back. A harness keeps the baby in the seat, which is anchored to the car by the car's safety belt. Infant seats with more than one harness position will fit the baby better as he or she grows.

One of the benefits of purchasing an infant seat, as opposed to a convertible seat which can be used for infants and toddlers, is that you can easily remove and install the seat with the baby in place. Another benefit is that most infant car seats can be used as indoor baby seats.

WARNING: *Some indoor baby seats look remarkably similar to infant safety seats. These are not crashworthy and should never be used as car safety seats.*

Infant Safety Seat
Infant seats are very convenient and can be used until the child reaches 20 lbs.

Infant Safety Seats

Name	Price	Harness Style	Notes
Century 560, 580	$30-60	Straps only, manual	Locks in shopping cart; 580 - separate base stays belted in car.
Century Infant Love Seat	Bulk	Straps only, manual	Bulk purchase only.
Cosco Dream Ride	$77-82	Straps only, one-step	Unique car-bed position for infants lying flat; converts for semi-reclined rear-facing use.
Cosco TLC	$30-42	Straps only, one-step	
Evenflo Dyn-O-Mite	$20-30	Straps only, manual	Should belt wraps around front of seat.
Evenflo Infant Car Seat	$30-40	Straps only, manual	
Evenflo Joy Ride	$30-60	Straps only, manual	One model has sun shade.
Evenflo Travel Tandem	$60-70	Straps only, manual	Separate base stays belted in car; can be used in second car without base; locks in shopping cart.
Fisher-Price Infant Car Seat	$45-55	Straps plus shield, manual	Locks in shopping cart; no locking clip; sun shade.
Kolcraft Rock 'N Ride	$35-45	Straps only, manual	

Based on data collected by the American Academy of Pediatrics

Convertible Seats

The Convertible Seat can be used from birth until the child reaches 40 pounds. When used for an infant, the seat faces rearward in a reclining position. Once the baby is able to sit up, the frame can be adjusted upright and the seat turned to face forward. The safety harness should also be moved from the lower to the upper slots as the child gets taller.

Buying a convertible seat can save you the expense of buying both an infant *and* a toddler seat. One of our favorite easy-to-use seats is made by Fisher Price.

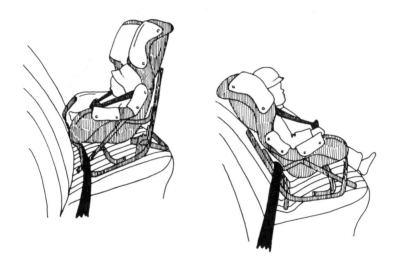

Convertible Seat

This seat can be used with both infants and toddlers. It is very easy to use and install. When using any seat, make sure you follow the manufacturer's instructions on proper installation.

Convertible seats come in three basic types:

Straps only models which consist of two shoulder and lap straps converging at a buckle connected to a crotch strap. These straps are adjustable, allowing for growth and the child's comfort. The best models have adjustable crotch straps that allow you to pull the lap straps down across the child's thighs.

Convertible Safety Seats

Name	Price	Harness Style	Notes
Babyhood Mfg. Baby Sitter	$89	Straps only, one-step	
Century 1000 STE	$50-60	Straps only, manual	
Century 2000, 3000 STE	$50-80	Straps plus shield, one step	2 positions for crotch buckle.
Century 5000 STE	$90-120	Straps plus shield, one-step	Adjustable shield; back pads for infant comfort.
Cosco Commuter	$69-82	Straps plus shield, manual	Back pads for infant comfort; easy shoulder strap conversion.
Cosco 5-Point	$50-70	Straps only, one-step	Back pads for infant comfort.
Cosco Soft Shield	$60-75	Straps plus shield, one-step	High back pads for infant comfort.
Cosco Soft Shield Autotrac	$80-95	Straps plus shield, automatic	High back pads for infant comfort.
Evenflo Convertible	$45-50	Straps only, manual	
Evenflo One-Step	$50-80	Straps plus shield, manual	
Evenflo Seven Year Car Seat	$95-120	Straps plus shield, one-step	Converts to booster seat (see Evenflo Booster).
Evenflo Ultara I, II	$80-95	Straps plus shield, one-step	I - wide shield; II - T-shaped shield.
Fisher-Price Car Seat	$75-85	Straps plus shield, automatic	No locking clip.
Gerry Guardian 643, 653, 655	$55-85	Straps plus shield, automatic	655-back pads for infant comfort.
Gerry Guardian 654	$90	Straps plus shield, automatic	Broad T-shaped shield; back pads for infant comfort.
Kolcraft Dial-A-Fit	$65-85	Straps plus shield, one-step	
Kolcraft Playskool Carseat	$65-85	Straps plus shield, one-step	Like Kolcraft Dial-A-Fit, but with wide shield.
Little Cargo Safety Vest	$30-40	Straps only, manual	Padded shoulder, hip and crotch straps fastened to auto lap belt through padded aluminum stress plate. For children 25-40 lbs.
Nissan Infant/Child Seat	$100	Straps plus shield, automatic	
Prodigy Kiwi, Kiwi Plus	$129-169	Straps only, one-step	Plus - sun shade and fold-down back.
Prodigy Shuttle	$299-329	Straps only, one-step	Converts into stroller.
Renolux GT 2000	$64-76	Straps only, manual	Previously sold by Strolee.
Renolux GT 4000, 5000, 7000	$88-250	Straps only, manual	High headrest; 5000 - swivel base; 7000 - remote-control recline feature.

Based on data collected by the American Academy of Pediatrics.

Straps with shield pad designs are generally more convenient than the straps only models. In fact, many parents find this to be the simplest and easiest type of convertible seat to use. It has a small pad joining the shoulder belts and requires only one buckle to secure the child. The only drawback with this type of seat is that, in the infant position, it is sometimes difficult to get the harness over the child's head.

Shield models offer a third choice. The safety harness is attached to a large safety shield. As the shield comes down in front of the child, the harness comes over the child's shoulders. The shield in this type of seat is designed to provide some safety protection and is an important part of the restraint system. An additional feature is that the child has a place to rest her arms or a toy.

WARNING: *Child safety seats should never be used in the front seat of cars equipped with two-point automatic safety belts unless you have an additional manual lap belt. If your new car has a two-point automatic belt, the manufacturer must offer the means to install a manual belt or provide the additional equipment necessary to secure a child safety seat. Contact the manufacturer of your car if you have questions about the compatibility of the car's belt system with a child safety seat.*

★ REMEMBER: When Buying a Child Safety Seat

☐ Make sure the seat you buy can be properly installed in your car. Some car seats cannot be properly buckled into certain cars. Also, make sure the ceiling of the car is high enough to allow you to completely raise the armrest or safety shield.

☐ Shop around; the same car seat may sell at a wide range of prices in local stores. Put a car safety seat on your baby shower list—it is an excellent gift of love.

☐ Determine how many straps need to be fastened to use the seat. The easy-to-use seats only require one.

☐ Look for a seat with easy-to-use retracting belts—they retract snugly like the safety belts on your car.

☐ Make sure your child will be comfortable. Can he or she move his or her arms freely, sleep in the seat, if older, see out the window and over the armrest/shield?

☐ Will the armrest/shield block the driver's rear view when it's upright?

☐ Is the seat light and easy to install if you have more than one car?

Considering these guidelines, most consumers have found that seats with a three-point harness and a body or safety shield are the easiest to use.

If friends or family pass on a used safety seat to you, be sure to note the date the seat was manufactured to ensure the best protection for your child. Only use seats made after January 1, 1981.

✔ **TIP:** *It may be possible to obtain a child safety seat through a "loaner" program in your community or through your car insurance company. This is a low-cost way of obtaining the latest in safety seats as well as proper instructions on their use. For the name of a loaner program in your area, write the National Highway Traffic Safety Administration. Their address is in Chapter 9 under auto safety.*

Tips for Safe, Efficient Use:

1. The safest seating location for the car seat is buckled in the center of the rear seat.

2. Periodically check the seat's safety harness and the car's safety belt for a tight secure fit.

3. Be sure all doors are locked, and teach children not to play with door handles or locks.

4. Do not permit a child to suck on a lollipop or ice cream on a stick while riding. A bump or swerve could jam the stick into the child's throat.

5. Set a good example for your child, buckle up your seat belt, every time you travel in your car.

6. If your car safety seat has a vinyl pad, hot weather travel can be very uncomfortable for your baby. Buy or make a fabric cover ($11.00 to $22.00). Cover the seat with a light-colored blanket when you leave the car. This will keep the metal parts from getting too hot.

Tips for Safe, Efficient Use: (cont'd)

7. In the winter, try to warm up the car and the safety seat before taking your baby out. Dress a baby in a legged suit. Drape an extra blanket over the seat after baby is buckled in. It can be removed if the car gets too warm.

8. Don't leave sharp or heavy objects loose in the car. Put groceries in the trunk. Anything loose can be deadly in a crash.

9. Make the car seat a child's "own special place," by having the child pick out some special toys (preferably no sharp edges) or books that can be used only in the car seat.

10. On long trips, stop more frequently (about every two hours) to offer your child a little exercise. This extra time is a small price to pay for a tremendous amount of additional protection for your precious cargo.

11. If the baby is very small, you may want to roll up a towel or blanket (or purchase an infant head support) and place it around the baby's head for extra comfort.

12. Do not dress the baby in clothes that will prevent you from using the seat properly. Instead, cover the child with a blanket after he is properly secured.

Car Seats For Premature Infants

More and more babies are leaving the hospital weighing less than five pounds, and many infant car seats are unsafe for premature babies.

The Journal of Pediatrics reports that the crucial dimension is the distance from the seat back to the crotch strap. If that distance is greater than 5 ½ inches, the baby may tend to slouch forward, and you must wedge a blanket between the baby and the strap.

Even seats with the right back-to-crotch measurement need blanket rolls along the sides to support the head. The report says larger infants can also benefit from supporting blankets.

Seats with lap pads or shields were "uniformly unacceptable," because the shields hit the baby in the face or neck. NOTE: This study used live infants because no dummies of that size are currently made, so the crash worthiness of the seats for premature infants is unknown.

Buckled Up = Better Behavior

According to the American Academy of Pediatrics (AAP), a safety seat will not only offer children life-saving protection, but it can also be instrumental in improving their behavior in the car.

In studies done at the University of Kansas Medical School, researchers concluded that "buckled up" equals better behavior. When not buckled up, children squirmed around, stood up, complained, fought, and pulled at the steering wheel. When buckled into car safety seats, however, there were 95 percent fewer incidents of bad behavior.

The Academy says that children behave better when buckled up because they feel secure. In sudden stops and swerves, they are held snugly and comfortably in place. In addition, most car safety seats lift children high enough to see out of the window, which allows the child to enjoy being in the seat. Also, children are less likely to feel carsick and more likely to fall asleep in a car seat.

Safety Seat Warning

The National Highway Traffic Safety Administration (NHTSA) is warning owners to be cautious in using certain child safety seats made by the Strolee Company of California, which is no longer in business.

NHTSA said that the Strolee GT-3000 convertible child seat, manufactured and distributed in 1987 and 1988, did not meet Federal safety requirements when used in the rearward-facing (infant) position. When used in the forward-facing (toddler) position, the seat passed. *NHTSA recommends that you not use the GT-3000 seat in the rearward-facing (infant) position.* The agency estimates that there were approximately 12,000 of these seats sold to the public.

In a separate problem, the agency has received reports that some Strolee Model 609 and 610 seats have developed cracks in the plastic shell. NHTSA tests of these seats seats in 30 mph crash simulations produced limited additional cracking but the structural integrity of the seats was not compromised. The cracks could, however, cut or pinch the child. NHTSA recommends that parents replace them with another child safety seat if any shell cracking is evident. The Strolee Company is no longer in business, and therefore cannot provide replacement units.

Finally, in response to a petition from the Center for Auto Safety, NHTSA is investigating a problem with over 4 million Evenflo One Step child seats for "false latching" that permits children to fly out of the seat in crashes. The false latch condition results when consumers follow the instructions Evenflo provides with the seat, which say to push in and hold the buckle release button while fastening the buckle. By depressing this button, parents cannot hear the click that tells them the latch is properly engaged. You must exert from 6 to 38 pounds of force to detect the false latch.

Important Information from the Center for Auto Safety

The Center for Auto Safety in Washington D.C. is a non-profit public interest organization representing consumers in Washington. Recently they uncovered some serious problems regarding child safety seats.

They found that manufacturers do very little to notify consumers when a safety seat is recalled and that the government is investigating a number of safety seats for potential hazards.

To find out if your seat has been recalled you can check the list of recalled seats below or call the Auto Safety Hotline at 800-424-9393, (in DC call 366-0123). In addition, the Center has published a list of seats under investigation as well as those with no history of safety problems. To get a copy of the list send a stamped, self-addressed, business size envelop to Childwise, c/o Center for Auto Safety, 2001 S Street, NW, Suite 410, Washington, DC 20009.

RECOMMENDED PRODUCTS: Car Safety Seats

We think convertible seats are the most versatile and we strongly recommend buying one with an automatic safety belt. One of the biggest mistakes parents make is having the shoulder straps too loose. This is often because they are difficult to adjust. With the automatic style safety seat, the belts automatically adjust to changes in your child's growth or changes in what they are wearing. These belts work on the same principle as your car's safety belt—once you put it on, it retracts to fit you snugly. A belt that fits comfortably over a bulky snow suit, may be dangerously loose over a jacket, unless it's an automatic belt. Another benefit of automatic belts, is that they readily adjust to children of different sizes, which is very handy if you have more than one child using a car seat or you transport different children in car pools.

The convertible seats that we like are the **Fisher Price, Gerry Guardian** (series) and the **Nissan Safety Seat.**

RECALLED PRODUCTS: Car Safety Seats

If more than 18 months have elapsed since the recall date, the manufacturer may no longer honor the recall. If the company refuses to comply, you should discard the product to ensure the safety of your child.

Century 100, 200, 300 and 400XL

WHICH ONES: Lot numbers 8504 through 8602 which have "mold #1" engraved on the back of the seat above the top bar. PROBLEM: Plastic shell may fracture in crash. WHAT TO DO: To obtain a free plastic reinforcing device, call 800-222-9825. RECALL DATE: 6/86

Century 2000 STE

WHICH ONES: Models 4253, 4263, and 4265. The model number is on the side the seat. PROBLEM: The loop on the end of the shoulder strap is only glued together. WHAT TO DO: Call Century at 800-222-9825 for instructions on how to check your seat and, if necessary to order a free replacement harness. RECALL DATE: 6/89

Century 3000 STE

WHICH ONES: Model numbers 4365DT and 4366 BH with fabric shield pads. Model numbers are on the side of the seat. PROBLEM: Removable fabric pad on the front tray may have exposed foam which a child could ingest and choke on. WHAT TO DO: Call Century at 800-222-9825 for a free replacement shield pad. RECALL DATE: 1/90

Century 400XL Car Seat

WHICH ONES: Model numbers 8604 and below. The model number is on the back of the seat. PROBLEM: The design makes it difficult to determine if the restraint is properly locked. WHAT TO DO: Call

Century at 800-222-9825 and ask for a free orange LOCKED/UNLOCKED sticker label and instructions. RECALL DATE: 5/87

Cosco Safe & Easy, Safe & Snug

WHICH ONES: Safe & Easy model number 02-313 and Safe & Snug model numbers 02-323 and 02-423 made between January 3, 1984 and June 30, 1985. Model numbers and dates are stamped on the back of each seat. PROBLEM: Cracks can develop in the plastic shell where the frame is riveted. WHAT TO DO: Discontinue use. RECALL DATE: 1/88

Cosco Safe-T-Shield

WHICH ONES: Models 02-081A, 02-081B, 02-181A, 02-181B made between 10/80—6/83. PROBLEM: Push pin holding safety shield may break off, making it difficult to remove child from seat. WHAT TO DO: Mail your telephone number to Cosco, Customer Service, 2525 State St., Columbus, IN 47201 and they will call you with information regarding returning the seat. Or call 812-372-0141, (Cosco will not accept collect calls). RECALL DATE: 5/86

Evenflo 410 Safety Seat

WHICH ONES: Seats sold between June 1988 and April 1989 through hospitals and loaner programs. The model number is on the side of the seat. PROBLEM: The strap slide on the system may slip, preventing protection in a crash. WHAT TO DO: Call Evenflo at 800-233-5921 (in Ohio call 800-233-5920) for a free replacement harness. RECALL DATE: 6/89

Evenflo Dyn-O-Mite Infant Safety Seats

WHICH ONES: Model numbers 441 through 446, 448, 456, and 458 sold between 1985 and January 1989. The model number and dates are on the side label. PROBLEM: The seat did not pass the government test for back support in the most reclined position. WHAT TO DO: Do not use the seat in the most reclined position unless you secure it with a combination shoulder-lap belt threaded through the built-in plastic clip on the back of the seat. If the seat belt is not self tightening, you'll need to use a locking clip. For a warning label and information on purchasing a locking clip, call Evenflo at 800-233-5921 (in Ohio call 800-233-5920). RECALL DATE: 4/89

Evenflo Ultara I

WHICH ONES: Seats made from 9-22-88 to 7-1-89. The manufacture date is on the side of the seat. PROBLEM: In the event of a crash the release buckle is too hard to open after impact. WHAT TO DO: Call Evenflo at 1-800-962-7730 for a free repair kit. RECALL DATE: 7/89

Fisher Price Safety Seats

WHICH ONES: All seats made before January 26, 1989. The date is on the back of the seat. PROBLEM: A foam piece between the plastic seat shell and the cloth seat cover does not meet government flammability requirements. WHAT TO DO: Call Fisher-Price at 1-800-334-5439 to get a free replacement pad. RECALL DATE: 2/89

Fisher Price Car Seats

WHICH ONES: All Fisher Price car seats sold before July 1986. PROBLEM: These seats were manufactured without a stop which would prevent the shield from retracting. This could cause the shield to retract up to the child's neck when unbuckled and cause a child to choke. WHAT TO DO: Call Fisher Price at 1-800-334-5439 and they will send you the proper stop. RECALL DATE: 10/88

Graco GT 1000 Safety Seat

WHICH ONES: Model #69985 made between 1-85 and 1-86. The date is on a white sticker on the seat. PROBLEM: Seat failed government crash test in the infant (rear facing) position. WHAT TO DO: Call toll-free at 800-345-4109 (in Pennsylvania call collect 215-286-5951) for a free guard which prevents vehicle seat back from interfering with the latching mechanism. RECALL DATE: 4/86

Kolcraft Rock 'N Ride Car Seat

WHICH ONES: Those made between February and June 1985. The date is on the seat back. PROBLEM: Seat failed government crash tests. WHAT TO DO: For free replacement, call 800-453-7673 (in Illinois call 312-458-3200 collect). RECALL DATE: 5/86

Volvo Child Safety Seat

WHICH ONES: All Volvo Child Safety Seats. PROBLEM: Buckle which does not meet federal standards may not protect child in the event of a crash. WHAT TO DO: Return seat to any Volvo dealer for a full refund. RECALL DATE: 5/89

Changing Tables

A changing table, or at least a convenient, safe place to change your little one, is a must for your nursery. You have three basic choices: the open shelf, traditional-style; the new dresser/

changing table combination; or a modified top of a standard dresser.

Changing table and dresser combinations are a new variation on the scene. Several juvenile furniture manufacturers now offer chests with a fold out top that converts the dresser top to a changing table. In its folded-up position the dresser top has a small shelf. When it's changing time, a flip of the top reveals a padded area for diaper duty. A variation on this concept, from Simmons, consists of a wooden, padded box with short sides that attaches with screws to the dresser top. When a changing area is no longer needed the box can be permanently removed from the dresser.

Another option for diaper changes is using a flat padded surface. The top of a waist-high chest can work nicely and can be outfitted with the machine washable "Rolled Bumper Changing Pad" by NoJo or a standard 17 x 35-inch pad that you can find in most baby supply stores. The NoJo pad has soft rolled bumpers on all four sides. Beware, however, these bumpers won't restrain your child. A restraining strap can easily be tacked or screwed into the front and back panel of the dresser.

Don't forget to use and install the safety strap. The Consumer Product Safety Commission (CPSC), estimated that in 1988 there were 2300 injuries requiring hospital emergency room treatment associated with the use of changing tables. The majority of these injuries were due to falls from the changing tables. CPSC reports nine deaths resulting from such falls.

✔ **TIP:** *To prevent falls, look for a changing table that has a restraining strap.*

Tips for Safe, Efficient Use:

1. If your changing table does not have a strap, purchase and install one. Always use the strap even for quick changes. If the doorbell or phone rings during a diaper change, never leave your baby on the changing table while you tend to the door or phone.

2. Be sure to place all ointments, oil, powder and safety pins out of your baby's reach.

3. As your baby gets older, make sure the changing table is not positioned in a way that allows your child to push off with his legs from a wall or other piece of furniture.

Clothes

Baby clothes are a common gift, so it's best not to buy too many at first. When you do buy, here are some general guidelines.

We recommend that you skip the three-month size. They are very small, and your baby will quickly outgrow them. The six-month sizes will be a bit too big at first, but they won't cause any discomfort and will probably shrink. You'll be amazed at how quickly your child will fill them out.

Baby clothes come in varying degrees of quality. If you expect to have more children, it definitely pays to buy high quality. If this is your last child, it doesn't make sense to pay for quality that will last long after the child outgrows the garment. Also, consider unisex or primary colors if you expect to have more than one child.

Baby clothes are subject to lots of washing. Buying fabric blends (cotton/polyester) rather than all cotton will help avoid shrinkage. If you want the softness of cotton, be sure to consider the shrinkage factor when deciding on the size. (See the clothing section in Chapters 2 and 3 for more clothing tips as your child gets older.)

✔ **TIP:** *Snaps, zippers and Velcro are the best types of fasteners. Buttons may look cute, but they are often difficult to use and you will be changing your baby's clothes very frequently!*

Baby Clothing Size Guide

There are no industry standards for children's clothing sizes. You'll find, as most parents do, that the age indicated on the clothing label never seems to match the actual age of your child and is generally smaller than what your child could wear at the prescribed age/size. Here's one guide for the first year that is more generous in size recommendations than what you would find if you followed the label age/sizes. When in doubt, always go with the weight over the age guidelines. See chapters Two and Three for clothes size information for older children.

Age	Weight	Clothing Size
up to 3 months	up to 10 lbs.	6 months size
3 to 6 months	up to 14 lbs.	12 months size
6 to 9 months	up to 18 lbs.	18 months size
12 months	up to 24 lbs.	24 months size

Tips for Safe, Efficient Use:

1. When washing children's sleepwear, avoid using soap products (including Ivory Snow), since these will leave a residue on clothes that is flammable and hence reduces the flame resistance of the sleepwear.

2. Wash new sleepwear before your child wears it to remove impurities on the garment which result from the manufacturing process and which can reduce flame resistance. (See the clothing section in the next chapter for more on children's sleepwear).

T-Shirt Tips

Because your child will use almost as many t-shirts, or undershirts, as diapers in the first few months, some special tips about this particular garment are in order. We recommend buying at least eight. (It is not uncommon to go through three in one day!) Our size advice given above certainly applies here—skip the three month size because shortly after birth the six-month size will fit just fine.

T-shirts come in three basic types—slip-on, snap-close and tie close. We found the snap-close to be the best for newborns. They're easy to slip on and off a child who hasn't yet learned to hold his or her head up. The slip-on variety are often difficult to get over an infant's head and the tie-close type are a nuisance. When buying T-shirts:

☐ Look for extra tape reinforcing along all sides of the snap, to keep the snap from loosening.

☐ Look for seams that have been folded over and reinforced with an over-edge stitch. These are usually more comfortable than the zigzag seams, which may rub and irritate a baby's sensitive skin.

☐ Because of the many launderings that these shirts— and all baby's clothes, for that matter—will undergo, choose fabrics that are preshrunk, or Sanforized.

T-Shirt Tips (cont'd)
☐ T-shirts are not required to be flame resistant even though they are commonly used as sleepwear. Since cotton is *more* flammable, look for reduced cotton blends. (See the clothing section in the next chapter for information on flame resistant sleepwear).

Cradles & Bassinets

The cradle or bassinet is a product that, unless you have received one as a gift or on loan, is not essential and more likely falls into the luxury nursery product category. A cradle or bassinet can only be used for the first three to four months, depending upon its size and your child's size and her ability to move and push up.

Even tiny babies need sturdy well-built equipment and this is especially true for cradles and bassinets. The most frequent accident involving these items occurs when the bottom of the cradle or bassinet breaks or when it tips over or collapses. The CPSC estimates that during one year 640 children were treated in hospital emergency rooms for cradle or bassinet injuries.

★ REMEMBER: When Buying a Cradle or Bassinet

☐ Many cradles and bassinets are intended only for very young children. Check the manufacturer's guidelines on the appropriate weight and size of child who can safely use the product.

☐ Look for a cradle or bassinet that has a wide, stable base and contains a sturdy bottom.

WARNING: *Avoid using a large basket not specifically designed for child use. However pretty it may look dressed up with ribbons, lace and padding, loose wicker can pose a poking danger, and the stability of the basket may be inadequate to hold your child safely.*

Tips for Safe, Efficient Use:

1. Be sure to check the cradle or bassinet periodically to see that screws and bolts are tight.

2. If your cradle or bassinet has legs that fold for storage, make sure each time you use the product that the locks have been secured to avoid accidental collapse of the legs while in use.

Cribs

In the first two years of life, your child will spend about a year in his or her crib. While comfort and durability certainly are important buying considerations, safety should be of paramount concern when buying and using the crib. (See the section on mattresses that follows later in this chapter.)

CPSC reports that more infants die every year in accidents involving cribs than any other product intended for children—on average 54 deaths per year. Additionally, thousands of infants are injured seriously enough to require hospital emergency room treatment. Unfortunately, these tragedies can not be blamed on freak occurrences, but rather are related to the crib itself, the crib mattress, crib toys, or combinations of the crib and other products, such as pacifier cords. Thus, your job is really only half done when you have selected and assembled your child's crib. Crib safety should be an everyday concern.

★ REMEMBER: When Buying a New Crib

The law requires that cribs have no more than 2-⅜ inches of space between slats or spindles, that the sides be a certain height, that drop-side latches be safe from accidental release or release by a baby inside the crib, and that crib mattresses be of a certain size. Because of continued death and injury reports associated with cribs since the passage of the crib requirements, we recommend you keep these additional factors in mind when purchasing a new crib:

☐ Buy a crib that has no cornerpost extensions or protrusions. Cornerpost extensions, protrusions or decorative knobs on crib corners pose hazards since clothing, pacifiers cords and necklaces can become entangled as the child moves about the corner areas of the crib or attempts to climb out. The knobs or posts have been implicated in two cases of brain damage and nearly 50 deaths due to strangulation. Even cornerposts as tiny as ⅝ of an inch have been involved in strangulation deaths. Because of this hazard, we recommend Fisher Price and Simmons cribs. Fisher Price cribs have never had cornerposts. Simmons has recently eliminated cornerpost protrusions from their cribs. Because retail inventory can remain in stock for a long time (several years), make sure any Simmons crib you purchase is one of the newer models without any cornerpost protrusions. See the following diagram labeled *Head Entrapment and Cornerposts*.

☐ Examine the stability of the crib. Look for adequate strength in the frame and headboard and a securely fitting support structure for the mattress. Here's a test you can perform to check the mattress supports on the crib you're considering (and the one you may already have). To be sure the mattress hangers (see diagram) do not lift easily out of the mattress support hooks, place your fingers under the mattress support and lift upwards; you should have to exert some force to lift the hanger out of the hooks. If the mattress support hanger can pop out easily, it is more likely to pose an entrapment hazard.

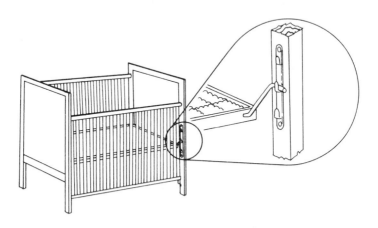

Mattress Support
Always be sure all four mattress hangers are securely attached to the hooks.
Check the supports each time you move the crib or change sheets.

☐ If you purchase a crib after May 1991, make sure that the crib complies with the new ASTM/JPMA voluntary safety standard for full-size cribs. This standard addresses the crib's structural integrity, including its mattress support system, the latching and drop side mechanisms, the strength of the plastic teething rail and other requirements.

☐ For additional safety, convenience, and ease of use, consider the following features:
  —Adjustable mattress support that allows you to lower the mattress as your child gets older.
  —The greatest distance possible between the top of the side rail and the mattress support, making it more difficult for your child to climb out.
  —Steel stabilizing bars on both sides of the crib to enhance stability and rigidity.
  —Drop-sides on both sides allow easy access when either side of the crib is placed along a wall.
  —Casters that make the crib easy to move.
  —A crib that later converts to a regular bed. They're more expensive, but they could save in the long run.

Tips for Safe, Efficient Use:

1. Check to see that all four mattress support hangers are securely held in the hook attached to the cornerpost (See diagram). Failure to attach even one hanger can cause the mattress to sag in the corner and pose an entrapment hazard capable of killing a child. Whenever you move the crib or flip the mattress, be sure to check all four of these hangers to see that they are resting properly in the hooks. Check the hooks regularly, particularly those made of plastic, to be sure none are broken or bent. Be sure the bracket for the guide rod of the drop-side is securely fastened.

2. Check crib hardware before using the first time *and* periodically thereafter, to see that:
  —All nuts, bolts and screws are properly tightened. Promptly replace any missing screws, nuts or bolts. If screws into wood components cannot be securely tightened, replace them with ones that can be.
  —Check to see that plastic teething guards along the

Tips for Safe, Efficient Use: (cont'd)

top rail are adequately secured so that babies won't catch their fingers, lips or tongues under loose teething rails.

3. Be sure that there are no venetian blind or drapery cords within your child's reach. CPSC has reports of more than 40 children who have strangled on such cords.

4. Always keep the side rail locked in its top raised position when your child is in the crib.

5. When your child can pull to a standing position, adjust the mattress to its lowest position and remove toys, bumper pads and other objects that can be used as steps to climb out.
    —When your child is 35 inches in height, she has outgrown the crib and should begin sleeping in a bed. If your child is persistent in attempting to climb out before reaching 35 inches, then the switch to a regular bed should be made. Climbing out incidents have resulted in death and serious injury.

6. Never use thin plastic cleaning or trash bags as mattress covers. The plastic can cling to your child's face and cause suffocation.

7. Never hang any stringed object such as a crib gym toy, laundry bag, or other toy on a string on the cornerpost or nearby where a child could become caught in it and strangle. (See following Crib toys.)

8. If using a mesh-side crib, never leave the drop-side down, no matter how young your child is. The mesh forms a pocket that is a suffocation hazard. (See discussion of this hazard under Playpens.)

9. Do not use a water mattress unless the crib is specifically intended to be used with such a mattress.

10. Write to the manufacturer of your crib for replacement parts rather than using odds and ends from around the house.

Safety Checklist for
second-hand, borrowed or *older* cribs

1. Avoid using a crib with a head- and/or footboard design that might allow a child's head to become caught in the openings between the cornerpost and the horizontal rail along the top of the crib, or in other openings in the headboard structure. These openings pose strangulation hazards because of their rigid, noose-like design. In fact, don't purchase a secondhand crib that has crib cornerpost extensions, including decorative knobs, finials or even very short cornerposts (see discussion above under new cribs). If you have such a crib, unscrew the cornerposts or saw them off and sand them to a smooth finish to make them flush with the top of the head- and footboards.

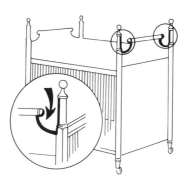

Head Entrapment/Cornerposts
Never use a crib that has places where a child's head or neck could become stuck. This diagram also illustrates dangerous cornerposts.

2. Never use a crib that has missing slats. Make sure that the slats are securely attached and are no more than 2-⅜ inches apart. If you *must* use a crib that fails this requirement, install bumper pads around the entire crib and snap or tie them firmly in place with at least six straps.

Safety Checklist for
second-hand, borrowed or *older* cribs (cont'd)

3. Only use a crib whose mattress fits snugly. If you can fit more than two fingers between the edge of the mattress and the crib side, the mattress is too small. A baby can suffocate if its head becomes wedged between the mattress and crib sides. If you *must* use a mattress that does not fit snugly, place rolled towels between the mattress and crib sides to remove the extra space. Each time you place your baby in the crib, check the towels to make sure they are secure.

4. If you paint or refinish an older crib, only use high quality household enamel paint and be sure to let the paint dry thoroughly so that there are no residual fumes. Before painting, check the paint label to make sure that the manufacturer does not recommend against using the paint on items such as cribs. *Never use a paint manufactured before February 1978, since these paints contain a high percentage of lead.*

5. See the *Tips for Safe, Efficient Use* of new cribs, above, as these guidelines also apply to used cribs.

✔ **TIP:** *For an excellent free publication on used crib safety, contact The Danny Foundation, a non-profit organization dedicated to crib safety. Write: P.O. Box 680, Alamo, CA 94507; or call: 1-800-83-DANNY.*

RECALLED PRODUCTS: Cribs

If more than 18 months have elapsed since the recall date, the manufacturer may no longer honor the recall. If the company refuses to comply, you should discard using the product to ensure the safety of your child.

The cribs listed below are those that CPSC have found to be hazardous. Some of these cribs were manufactured several years ago, yet we include them here because many are probably still in use. In addition, despite recall attempts, we continue to hear stories of unsafe cribs that remain in retail stores for years before being sold. So check both new and second-hand crib purchases carefully.

Baby Line Cribs Questor
WHICH ONES: Recall of brackets used on 29 models of cribs date coded from June 1977 through September 1978. Codes 677, 777, 877, 977, 1077, 1177, 1277, 178, 278, 378, 478, 578, 678, 778, 878, and 978 are found on bottom of crib headboard. PROBLEM: Plastic hangar brackets have broken or bent causing mattress and spring to drop. WHAT TO DO: Write to Questor Juvenile Furniture Co. Baby Line Furniture, 6235 South Street, Andrews Place, Los Angeles, CA 90047 Attn: Corrective Program RECALL DATE: Pre-1986

Bassett Company Cribs
WHICH ONES: Candlelite Crib model 5127, 5028 manufactured from December 1975 to October 1977. Mandalay Crib model 5621, 5225, 5216 manufactured from February 1984 through October 1976. Model numbers are on underside of the headboard. PROBLEM: Head and footboard cutouts are situated next to the four cornerposts, creating a dangerous enclosure area. WHAT TO DO: Unscrew the four cornerposts and contact the Bassett Company at 703-629-6000 for a free repair kit. RECALL DATE: Pre-1986

Corsican Furniture Cribs
WHICH ONES: All PROBLEM: Banned crib failed to meet basic federal safety standards. WHAT TO DO: Discontinue Use. RECALL DATE: Pre-1986

Des Camps Crib
WHICH ONES: All PROBLEM: Banned crib failed to meet basic federal safety standards. WHAT TO DO: Discontinue Use RECALL DATE: Pre-1986

French Style Crib; Corrado
WHICH ONES: All PROBLEM: Head entrapment hazard. WHAT TO DO: Contact Corrado Nursery Furniture, 140 West 22nd St., New York, NY 10011 RECALL DATE: Pre-1986

George Marciano Crib
WHICH ONES: All PROBLEM: Banned crib failed to meet basic federal safety standards. WHAT TO DO: Discontinue Use RECALL DATE: Pre-1986

HBLA Baby Crib
WHICH ONES: All HBLA non-full size baby cribs imported in January 1985 which have a picture of children and rabbits on both

sides of each end panel. PROBLEM: The crib has been banned because it fails to meet federal safety requirements. WHAT TO DO: Discontinue use and return to point of purchase for a full refund. RECALL DATE: 11/87

Kantwet Trav-L-Cribs

WHICH ONES: Model 320 manufactured from January to June 1979. PROBLEM: Bottom of portable crib may separate from sides allowing baby to fall to floor. WHAT TO DO: Contact Questor Juvenile Furniture Co., Trav-L-Crib, 1801 Commerce Drive, Piqua, OH 45456. RECALL DATE: Pre-1986

Questor Brackets and Mattress Support

WHICH ONES: Questor Crib Brackets and Mattress Support Hangers PROBLEM: If slotted hangers become unhooked or plastic bracket bends or breaks, the child can get caught between the mattress and the side rail or end panel of crib. WHAT TO DO: Write to Baby Line Furniture Co. (division of Spalding and Evenflo Companies), Los Angeles, CA 90054. Firm provides free replacement kits for the slotted hangers and plastic brackets. RECALL DATE: Pre-1986

Sears Portable Crib Floorboard

WHICH ONES: Maple stained model 29-30691 and varnish finished model 29-30692 distributed between March 1986 and December 1986. PROBLEM: The floorboard can dislodge while in the changing table position, allows the child to fall. WHAT TO DO: Discontinue use and call North States Industries collect at 612-522-6505 for a free repair kit. RECALL DATE: 9/87

Small Wonders Baby Cribs

WHICH ONES: "Precious Metals" metal baby cribs, models 504, 704 and 904; Wood crib styles include "Colonial" models 2001, 3700, 3707, and 282; "Jenny Lind" models 2002, 2004, 3302, 4302, and 281; "Wicker" model 2207; "Brentwood" models 2003, 283, 284 and 285; "Gay Nineties" model 2005. All imported by Baby Furniture Outlet Inc. between 1981 and 1986. PROBLEM: Cribs do not meet safety standards. WHAT TO DO: Discontinue use call CPSC toll-free at 800-638-CPSC for information regarding your particular model's hazards, and if any corrective measures can be taken. Company is bankrupt, so no recall available. RECALL DATE: Pre-1986

Starlighter

WHICH ONES: (non-full-size cribs) Made between 1975 and 1978. PROBLEM: Neck entrapment hazard. These cribs were never recalled because company was in bankruptcy when hazard was discovered. WHAT TO DO: Discontinue use, no recall available. RECALL DATE: Pre-1986

Portable Cribs

Portable cribs, those less than full size cribs that fold up easily, are very popular. Some of these cribs meet the same safety requirements as full-size cribs, such as those regulating slat spacing and drop-side latches. However, if they have mesh sides, these small cribs are entirely exempt from these regulations! Additionally, there are currently no requirements for structural stability, the mattress support system, or teething rails for *any* type of portable crib.

Some portable cribs may advertise that they meet the play yard (playpen) voluntary safety standard. While this offers some protection, keep in mind that playpens are not intended for unattended nighttime sleep (as a crib is) *and* playpens are not intended for children older than 18 months. Furthermore, the playpen standards are not as rigorous as crib standards.

Because of all these factors, we believe that portable cribs, whatever their construction, should not be used for children over 18 months, and use should be discontinued earlier if your child shows a propensity for climbing out.

Crib Bumper Pads

In addition to adding a special decorating touch to your nursery, bumper pads protect your baby's head from the crib's side slats or spindles. They also can take up space that may exist between the crib sides and the crib mattress.

★ REMEMBER: When Buying Bumper Pads
Make sure any bumper pads you purchase:

☐ fit around the entire crib;

☐ tie or snap into place; and

☐ have at least six straps;

Tips for Safe, Efficient Use:

1. Trim off excess length on the straps to prevent your child from chewing on or becoming tangled in them.

2. Bumper pads should be used only until your child is capable of pulling himself to a standing position. After that, remove them, along with other toys and objects, so that your child cannot use them as steps to climb out of the crib.

Crib Mattresses

Like regular mattresses, crib mattresses come in a variety of firmnesses, constructions and prices. Retail prices range from approximately $30 to $90. At least you don't have to worry about size since the majority of crib mattresses are standardized at 27 ¼ inches by 52 inches.

There are four major types of crib mattress construction:

Urethane Foam Mattresses are made from either polyester or polyether and contain bubbles in the foam to supply resiliency and firmness. These mattresses are available in varying thicknesses, but thicker is *not* necessarily better. The density of the foam is the important factor. One obvious advantage of these mattresses is their lightness and urethane foam mattresses are typically non-allergenic.

Pocketed Coil Innerspring Mattresses have coils that are compressed and individually pocketed under tension. This means that each coil responds as pressure is applied.

Wire-tied Innerspring Mattresses have a number of coil springs joined by special locks. Thus the coils do not operate completely independently. Most experts recommend getting a coil crib mattress that has 88 or more coils per mattress.

Water mattresses for cribs are usually enclosed in a zippered vinyl cover, which is placed on a plywood support deck that fits inside a crib specially designed to hold such a mattress. A foam mattress inside the mattress cover provides firm support around the edge of the mattress. Internal insulation barriers on all four sides provide a firm sleeping surface and, in most cases, eliminate the need for a heater. At least one manufacturer offers a system that includes a low wattage heater. The vinyl mattress covers on these mattresses are generally treated with an antibacterial agent. Crib water mattresses are designed to be used in conjunction with a standard crib mattress pad and fitted crib sheet. Because of the added weight, crib water mattresses should be used only in cribs designed for their use.

Given everything we know about crib mattresses, and considering price, safety and convenience we think that urethane foam mattresses are the best choice.

★ REMEMBER: When Buying Crib Mattresses

☐ California law requires that crib mattresses be fire retardant. In order to ship nationally, major manufacturers of crib mattresses have made all of their crib mattresses fire retardant. A manufacturer that only ships to one region (outside of California) may not meet the fire retardant requirement. Therefore, we believe it best to purchase from a major crib mattress manufacturer to ensure that your crib mattress is fire retardant—a safety feature that's very important during a nighttime fire.

☐ In addition to making fire retardant crib mattresses, three major crib mattress manufacturers—Century/Gerber, Child Craft, and Simmons—also feature crib mattresses that are non- allergenic, stain resistant, non-absorbent, and anti-static. These are features we recommend you look for in any crib mattress.

☐ Crib mattress warranties vary in length, but most include splitting of seams and firmness. However, the most likely source of damage—urine—is usually not included.

☐ If your child is a crib climber or unusually tall and you are concerned about her ability to climb out of a crib at an early age (before age 2), you might consider decreasing the thickness of your crib mattress to provide more depth. The extra inches gained by converting to a 3 or 4 inch foam mattress, may allow you to keep a very young toddler in the crib longer. The disadvantage in using thinner foam mattresses is that they wear out more quickly. This advice does not apply to children age 2 and older who should be sleeping in regular beds.

Tips for Safe, Efficient Use:

1. In using a mattress that has coils as part of the interior construction, check the outside cover periodically to be sure no coils have popped through that could cut or scratch your child.

2. Use a waterproof mattress protector between the mattress and sheets. Crib mattress warranties usually don't include damage from urine.

Crib Toys

Crib toys have been popular for years, but we believe they are very dangerous. Crib toys include crib gyms, that stretch across or are suspended from the crib, mobiles, activity boxes, suspended stuffed toys, music boxes, mirrors and other toys marketed for use in cribs and playpens. Between 1973 and 1987 at least 49 incidents involving crib toys—including 30 deaths, one case of severe brain damage, and 18 near-misses—were reported in the United States.

These toys are particularly hazardous for infants five months of age and older or those who, when lying on their stomach, can push up on their hands. In many cases of death and other near misses, infants have strangled when the toy cord or something worn by the child (such as clothing, bib, pacifier cord) caught on the crib toy. Babies have also strangled, particularly on crib gyms, after they pushed up on their hands and knees and then fell onto the crib toy. In these cases, the child, who is too young to be able to get off the toy, strangles when the child's own body weight creates enough pressure on the neck to cut off air supply.

We give you these details not to horrify, but rather to impress upon you the extreme importance of keeping these toys out of your child's crib. Unless you sit and watch your child continuously while they are using a crib toy and remove the toy from the crib at all other times, we strongly recommend against their use.

WARNING: *Never hang any stringed object, such as a play gym toy, laundry bag or other toy on a string on the cornerpost or nearby where a child could become caught in it and strangle. (See following* *section on crib toys.) Also, as a reminder, never put a loop of ribbon, cord or chain around your child's neck to hold a pacifier or religious medal or for any other reason.*

RECALLED PRODUCTS: Crib Toys

If more than 18 months have elapsed since the recall date, the manufacturer may no longer honor the recall. If the company refuses to comply, you should discard using the product to ensure the safety of your child.

Blue Box Crib Gyms

WHICH ONES: Those distributed in 1987-1988 with a blue plastic bar about 15-inches long and several infant toys suspended from it. PROBLEM: The gym could cause a strangulation hazard if it is not removed from the crib or playpen when the infant begins to push up on his hands and knees and is inappropriately labeled as appropriate for children "ages 3 months and up." In addition, the gym will not fit a standard full-size crib. If parents tie strings or ribbons on the straps to make it fit a standard crib, there is even a greater risk of strangulation. WHAT TO DO: Return to store for refund. RECALL DATE: 2/89

Blue Box Play Mirror

WHICH ONES: Crib toys sold in 1988 with an 11-inch mirror is framed in yellow plastic. PROBLEM: Pieces of plastic may break off and pose a choking hazard. WHAT TO DO: Return to the store where purchased for a refund. RECALL DATE: 3/89

Bright Reflections Crib Mirror

WHICH ONES: 12x16 mirrors for cribs and playpens sold between December 1987 and October 1988 and a decal with a yellow bear and the words "Bright Reflections." PROBLEM: The flexible edging may separate from the mirror and could present a strangulation risk to infants. WHAT TO DO: Return to store where bought for a refund. For a new mirror, return old mirror to G. Pierce Toy Manufacturing Company, 4420 S. Wolcott Street, Chicago, IL 60609 RECALL DATE: 3/89

Chicco Pram Mobiles

WHICH ONES: Those imported in 1987 and 1988 and sold mainly by Toys R Us stores. The toy has four pastel-colored hard plastic bird and flower figures, separated by three small balls. PROBLEM: The package inappropriately recommends that it be used from birth to 18 months of age. This type of toy should be removed when the child begins to push up on hands and knees or by the time they are five months old. WHAT TO DO: Return toy to the store where you bought it for a full refund or send the toy to Artsana of America, Inc., 200 Fifth Avenue, #910, New York, NY 10010. The firm will refund the purchase price and postage. RECALL DATE: 7/88

Crib Activity Play Doggie

WHICH ONES: Those sold in 1988 shaped like a dog dressed in a coat and tie and has a detachable horn and telephone receiver. PROBLEM: Small pieces of the horn and phone receiver may break off, posing a choking hazard. WHAT TO DO: Return to the store where purchased for a refund. RECALL DATE: 3/89

Crib Soft Playground

WHICH ONES: Those sold as the Shelcore Crib Soft Playground, beginning in 1982, and Winnie-the-Pooh Crib Soft Playground sold by Sears in 1982 and 1983. PROBLEM: If strings are not tied tightly enough, or loosen over time, the toy may present a strangulation hazard. WHAT TO DO: Discontinue use immediately and return to Shelcore, Inc., 3474 S. Clinton Avenue, S. Plainfield, NJ 07080. Shelcore will send a free, redesigned activity center which uses velcro attachments and reimburse you for shipping costs. RECALL DATE: 10/87

Playskool Color 'n Contrast Busy Boxes

WHICH ONES: Item number 5388 distributed from the end of March 1989 through the beginning of May 1989. PROBLEM: The printed red logo on the product may exceed government established safety levels for lead. WHAT TO DO: Return to store where purchased for a refund or send it to Playskool, Inc., 110 Pitney Road, Lancaster, PA 17602, for a refund of $15.00. RECALL DATE: 6/89

Red Calliope Crib Kickers

WHICH ONES: Sold between 1980 and 1985, they consist of a series of polyester-filled figures such as animals or flowers, with two long ribbons attached at each. **PROBLEM:** Children who can push up on their hands and knees may become entangled on the loops formed by the ribbons or could fall across the toy and asphyxiate. WHAT TO DO: Take the toy down when the baby is five months old and dispose of it. Because the toy does not contain a warning label, it poses a safety hazard if stored away for future use. RECALL DATE: 6/89

Walt Disney Mickey Mouse Baby Crib Gyms

WHICH ONES: The free-standing activity center for infants sold from March to April 1987, with Mickey Mouse, Donald Duck or a disc-shaped baby rattle hanging down. PROBLEM: The buckles and loops may come off and pose a choking hazard. In addition, the mirrored rattle could break and present a choking hazard. WHAT TO DO: For replacement straps, buckles, and rattles, write to the Consumer Service Department, Illco Toy Company, 200 Fifth Avenue, New York, NY 10010. RECALL DATE: 11/88

Diapers

During the two and a half years after your child is born, you will change more than 5,600 diapers! Your decision between the three alternatives—disposables, cloth or diaper service—is not without consequences. But fear not, it is certainly a non-binding decision. In fact, most parents choose some combination of the three alternatives.

For most parents, disposables are the diaper of choice. In fact, in 1988 American parents used over 18 billion disposable diapers. While industry sources reveal that nearly all households use disposables, 75 percent use a combination of cloth and disposable diapers. This section will review the costs and benefits of the diaper alternatives.

Disposable Diapers

Obviously, the overwhelming reason for the popularity of disposable diapers is convenience. In addition to being very easy to put on, disposables eliminate loads of wash and the diaper pail. In short, disposables save time—something most new parents find themselves short on.

Disposable diapers come in four basic sizes: newborn (0-12 pounds), medium (12-24 pounds), large (23 pounds and over) and extra large (over 27 pounds). The cost per diaper increases with the size. (While there are obvious reasons for paying more for a larger diaper, the cynic in us cannot help but think the user is getting hooked on the cheaper diapers during the newborn stage and thus becoming a willing market for the more expensive larger diapers).

The most popular diapers on the market are Pampers, (a Proctor and Gamble product), followed by Huggies (by Kleenex) and then Luvs (another Proctor and Gamble product). Our survey of parents found that most people developed strong personal preferences.

Disposable diapers are not biodegradable. Even the casual environmentalist should be concerned about dumping 18 billion synthetic diapers—or over 600,000 tons—into the environment each year! In fact, Nebraska has banned non-biodegradable diapers, and Vermont is considering such a law as this book goes to press.

In response to environmental concerns, Proctor and Gamble has started a diaper recycling and composting initiative, and some companies are working on truly biodegradable disposable diapers. Made from natural ingredients—non-woven cotton—these biodegradable disposable diapers would be better for the environment (one catalog that sells biodegradable diapers is listed in Chapter 9). For now, however, the environmental impact remains a big problem.

In addition to the environmental problems, the biggest disadvantage of disposables is the cost. At an average of 25 cents per diaper, you can easily spend $1,414 on the 5,600 diapers you will buy for your child. Suddenly, diapering (especially with two in diapers) becomes a major household expense.

To combat this expense, many parents use cents-off coupons and buy by the case. Another way of reducing disposable diaper expenses is to purchase store brand and generic diapers. While many of these diapers are acceptable, most are not up to the quality of the Proctor and Gamble products. However, it pays to experiment. A few years ago, Proctor and Gamble sued Montgomery Ward for allegedly copying their diapers. The less expensive Montgomery Ward brand may actually have had the same quality of Luvs.

Cloth Diapers

While disposables have some tremendous advantages, cloth diaper services also have their pluses. Some parents prefer the natural fibers up against their baby's skin.

Your first decision with cloth diapers is gauze or birds-eye weave. The best type is a gauze weave, which uses fuzzy, finely spun yarns to make a soft, absorbent diaper. The bird's-eye weave wears longer, but is not as soft. Next you must choose between prefolded diapers and the traditional flat style. Four dozen prefolded gauze diapers will cost about $50, while the same amount unfolded cost about $30. You can also get models with Velcro or snap closures ($68-$80 for 48) eliminating the need for pins, and cloth diapers with a middle layer of sponge material sandwiched into the center panel ($60.00 for 48.)

You'll also need diaper pins (the best are stainless steel pins with plastic safety-locks), rubber pants and a diaper pail. Make sure your diaper pail has a lock top and carrying handle. (See Diaper pails.)

In addition to an initial investment of almost $100 in cloth diapers and associated paraphernalia, you will also spend between $500-$600 (depending on your cost of utilities) caring for the diapers over the 30-month period you'll be using them.

Also, until you get the knack of it, cloth diapers will take longer to change.

Diaper Service

A diaper service is the third option and one that many parents combine with do-it-yourself and disposable use. Diaper service eliminates much of the hassle of caring for diapers.

A diaper service is usually less expensive than disposables, averaging around $25 per week.

✔ **TIP:** *If friends or family ask you what you'd like as a shower gift, suggest a diaper service.*

Comparing the three alternatives on cost alone (for two and a half years): disposables will be approximately $1,414; diaper service, approximately $1200; and do-it-yourself, approximately $700.

Diaper Pails

As surprising as it may seem, there are two serious hazards associated with diaper pails: poisoning and drowning. Several children have been poisoned when they ate the diaper pail cake deodorizer and a number of children have fallen into diaper pails and drowned.

☐ Buy a diaper pail with a locking lid and keep it closed securely.

☐ If possible, keep it in a place to which your child does not have access.

Diaper Bags

Choosing a diaper bag is like choosing a purse or wallet. First of all, the term "diaper bag" is a misnomer—you will use this item for nearly *everything*—not just transporting diapers!

You have two basic options: a cleverly designed carry-all that is filled with pockets, velcro closures and creative multiple use features—or your basic *L.L. Bean or Land's End* canvas bag.

If you are looking for one that doesn't look like a diaper bag, we recommend one of the canvas style tote bags from companies such as L.L. Bean or Lands End. Both have a medium size canvas tote that has a zipper on the top. This will be useful when you find yourself juggling a number of items and the bag suddenly tips over, as it inevitably will—you won't lose all of its contents!

If your preference is the more standard bag that is designed to carry diapering paraphernalia, we recommend one that has bottle holders on the outside, at least two if possible. They're great for getting out milk or juice quickly when traveling. Some of the more sophisticated bags have roll-out changing pads, perfectly sized pockets for wipes, bottles and a few toys. Also look for zipper or velcro compartments on the inside to help keep things organized. We like diaper bags with longer straps so that they can be slung over your shoulder.

WARNING: *Don't hang a diaper bag on a stroller handle. It could easily cause the stroller to tip over backwards.*

Food

One could easily write volumes on the subject of food for children. Because the *Childwise Catalog* is meant to be a guide to purchases and safe use, we've limited our discussion to some important tips and techniques.

Breast Milk

The storage of breast milk is an important issue. Although there is continuing research in the area of storage and handling, the La Leche League advises that breast milk can be stored in the refrigerator for up to 24 hours, and in the freezer for up to six months. When one is needed, put the bottle under warm water or slowly warm it on the stove until it comes to body temperature. Don't overheat the milk, since boiling will destroy its protein. La Leche also suggests that you shouldn't re-refrigerate and reheat unused milk. Remember though, *never let the bottle warm at room temperature, since that encourages bacterial growth.*

If you are a breast-feeding mother who uses a breast pump at work, freshly pumped breast milk can be left unrefrigerated for up to six hours. Breast milk contains agents that help a newborn's developing immune system fight infections and allergies. Freezing protects milk longer but may impair it's bacteria-fighting ability.

WARNING: *Do not use a microwave to heat breast milk. You might alter some of its living properties, depleting important antibodies that fight intestinal infections and allergies.*

If you are breast-feeding, keep in mind that everything you ingest, including alcohol, drugs and cigarette smoke, passes into the breast milk. Although small amounts of alcohol are not known to have ill effects on babies, chemicals in cigarette smoke *are* known to be harmful. Even being around others who are smoking cigarettes may be harmful to the infant.

Avoid drugs and medications as much as possible. You should check with your doctor regarding even an occasional dose of an over-the-counter medication. If you must regularly take medications, it's *essential* for you to talk to your pediatrician.

Formula

The alternative to breast milk is formula. Most pediatricians recommend formula because cow's milk is difficult for infants to digest and doesn't offer the same digestible nutrients as breast milk or formula. Also many infants are prone to milk allergies.

When buying formula, you have three basic choices: powdered, concentrated liquid, or pre-mixed liquid. Powdered is the least expensive and pre-mixed is the most expensive. While cost may be a factor in your ultimate choice, convenience will also play a role. Pre-mixed is not necessarily the most convenient. Powdered saves you the hassle of storage since a 16 oz. can of powdered formula makes numerous bottles. Also, unused premixed or open cans of concentrate have a far shorter life than opened powdered formula. Finally, powdered formula is great for traveling.

★ REMEMBER: When Buying Formula

☐ Store infant formula cans in a cool place. If you find *any* problem with a can of infant formula, notify the store and the FDA immediately.

☐ Consider buying *cases* of liquid concentrate or the largest container of powder to save money. Some large discount toy stores sell formula at prices markedly below supermarket prices.

Tips for Safe, Efficient Use:

1. Infant formula will curdle when stored improperly at high temperatures. Curdled infant formula separates into a yellow fat/oil layer on top and a water/protein layer on the bottom, and these layers will not remix entirely. If you suspect that an infant formula has curdled, do not use it and return it to the store. Ingestion of curdled formula can cause mild upset stomach and diarrhea or vomiting.

2. Never use damaged containers of infant formula; either dispose of them or return them to the store. Serious illness can result if the formula has become contaminated with airborne microorganisms.

3. When purchasing infant formula, always check the expiration date of the cans.

4. Newly made formula may be refrigerated and saved up to 48 hours.

Infant Botulism

Although most infants, older children and adults regularly inhale Clostridium botulinum spores—found in house dust (especially in and under beds), soil, honey, syrup and a variety of raw and cooked foods including fresh fruits and vegetables—the intestinal tracts of some infants are susceptible to infant botulism from these spores. Symptoms include constipation, sucking problems, irritability, lethargy and "floppy-baby syndrome." Often, however, the symptoms are not recognized by parents, and the babies are not taken to a doctor until the illness is advanced.

Because of the risk of infant botulism, the FDA warns against the use of such nutritionally nonessential foods as honey and corn syrup in infant feeding. Commercially sterilized low-acid canned foods, including infant formula, do not contain the Clostridium botulinum spore or toxin.

RECALLED PRODUCTS: Food

If more than 18 months have elapsed since the recall date, the manufacturer may no longer honor the recall. If the company refuses to comply, you should discard the product to ensure the safety of your child.

Gerber Rice Cereal

WHICH ONES: Eight ounce boxes which were sold from September 1989 to October 1989. Each box says " Best used by date code 24 Aug 91 S-." PROBLEM: Product is contaminated with metal fragments. WHAT TO DO: Return to store where bought for refund or replacement. RECALL DATE: 12-89

Infant Beanbag Pillows

Infant beanbag pillows or cushions are a new category of infant product that we strongly recommend against. In fact, we believe they should be banned. Made like a beanbag, these pillows or cushions, typically 24 inches long by 12 inches wide, have a soft quilted exterior that is loosely filled with plastic foam (polystyrene) beads. This product poses a suffocation hazard to young babies since the pillow can easily mold around the child's face and cut off air. In the 15 month period between December 1987 and February 1990, 11 infants (3 months of age or younger) suffocated and died on this type product. Manufactured by at least 10 different companies, more than 1.8 million of these products have been sold nationwide. As we went to print, CPSC and the manufacturers had not reached an agreement on a recall of these pillows. Don't buy this product and if you already have one, discard it immediately. Remember, suffocation is a quick and silent killer—don't take any chances.

Infant Seats

These seats are intended for newborns through infants approximately six months old (or when your child can sit unassisted). They make convenient feeders, carriers or play seats, while providing head and back support.

Infant seats (sometimes called carrier seats) include several different designs. The more traditional infant seats are made of plastic with a padded seat and a support stand. Another popular design is a sling seat composed of fabric stretched over a metal frame. The advantage of this type of seat is that it bounces gently as the child waves his arms and legs. One version of the sling-type infant seat that we particularly like is the **Cradle Bouncer by Sassy, Inc.**

Other features on infant seats might include: a carrying handle; a two-way rocker attachment; a footrest; a canopy; and a toy bar holding objects to amuse baby.

Although these handy seats can make life easier, parents often fail to realize that very young infants are strong enough and active enough to move the seat by pushing against other objects with their feet. Children have also been known to fall out of the seats. In fact, the CPSC estimates that in one year 3,700 children were injured seriously enough to require hospital treatment in infant seat accidents. In most cases, either the child fell out of the seat or the infant seat fell with the child in it.

★ REMEMBER: When Buying An Infant Seat

☐ Look for an infant seat that has a wide sturdy base for stability and non-skid feet.

☐ Make sure the seat comes with a crotch and waist safety belt.

☐ Cloth seats are cooler in summer months. Look for those that can be removed for machine washing.

Tips for Safe, Efficient Use:

☐ When your child is seated in an infant seat placed on a table, couch, chair or other elevated surface, always stay within an arm's reach, and never turn your back. Remember that infant seats slide more easily on smooth or slippery surfaces such as glass table tops. Place the seat away from objects your child could push off of.

☐ *Always* use the safety belt. If your seat does not have a restraint system, purchase one.

☐ Attach rough surfaced adhesive strips to the underside of your infant seat if it does not have non-skid feet.

☐ If your infant seat has wire supporting devices that snap on the back, check them regularly. They can pop out and cause the seat to collapse.

WARNING: *Never (Never!) use an infant seat as a substitute for an automobile restraint system.*

Medicine Chest

Children's illnesses seem to have a way of striking after doctor's regular hours. In those instances, a carefully stocked medicine chest can be a life saver. Be sure to follow your doctor's recommendations in administering any prescription or over-the-counter drug and in treating any medical emergency.

✔ **TIP:** *The cost of electronic thermometers is now low enough ($5-$20) that many people are buying them for home use. Electronic thermometers are used like mercury thermometers, but with the benefit of much faster temperature readings.*

Your Medicine Chest

Every medicine chest should include:

☐ thermometer (rectal design for infants)

☐ acetaminophen (Tylenol) for infants

☐ infant nail clipper

☐ nasal aspirator

☐ hot water bottle (always test the temperature of a hot compress before applying—too cool is better than too hot)

☐ ice bag or ice pack (These are useful for sprains, bruises, athletic injuries and tooth extractions because cold reduces swelling and speeds healing.)

☐ adhesive strips

☐ ipecac

☐ teething relief medicine

WARNING: *Child resistant caps don't always work. Recently, the CPSC contacted the families of over 2,000 children under five who took medicine accidentally. All of these families had called poison control centers. Remarkably, 75 percent of the containers which the* *children were poisoned from had child-proof caps. The study cited two reasons for the failure of the child resistant caps: liquid medicines that left a sticky residue around the rim, preventing the top from closing properly; and "push and turn" type bottle caps that appeared to be worn out from use. The report also revealed that the poisoned children found half of the medicines in the kitchen, most frequently in the refrigerator.*

Night Lights

Night lights can and should be certified to insure safe, trouble-free use. This is important because an old or poorly constructed light can be a real hazard. CPSC data shows that night lights have been responsible for a wide variety of personal injuries and property damage, including house fires. These occurred when the night light melted or short circuited, igniting pillows, pillowcases, sleeping bags or mattresses. Night lights also can explode and scatter small pieces of glass or give electrical shocks to children. We like the photo electric lights, such as **Hemco's Baby Room Night Light**; it turns off automatically as the morning light approaches and likewise turns on as the room darkens in the evening. This is a good feature if you are inclined to forget to turn the night light off each morning.

If you are purchasing a light to allay a preschooler's fear of the dark, and his room does not have outlets in accessible locations that will allow a night light to function properly, consider using a flashlight instead. We recommend the **Playskool Flashlight**. It shuts off automatically if the handle is not squeezed, and its battery storage is very child resistant.

★ REMEMBER: When Buying A Night Light

☐ Check to see that it has a UL (Underwriters Laboratories) certification mark.

☐ Look for a light that has no sharp edges or points.

☐ Purchase a light on which the bulb is shielded from access to prevent choking, electrocution or laceration hazards. Young children are capable of unscrewing a small night light bulb.

Tips for Safe, Efficient Use:

1. Avoid placing night lights in a socket where bed linens or other material could drape over them.

Nursery Monitors

We consider the nursery monitor—one of the most popular gadgets for today's nursery—a necessity. Most of us, as new parents, find it difficult to leave an infant alone in a room (sleeping) without regularly checking on them. A nursery monitor provides regular radio contact with your youngster from virtually every room in the house. So we think they are a must!

These remarkable devices will allow you to stay in touch with your child from anywhere in your home. In fact, most of the better models will even work out in the yard. The transmitter is set up in your child's room and the receiver travels with you. Monitors range in price from $30 to $60 and, as with any electronic gadget, come with a slew of different features. Most models have a belt clip for the receiver and operate off of AC current or batteries. What is truly amazing about these products is that most are so sensitive that you can actually hear your child breathing!

Before you buy, however, check with your neighbors to see if they have the same product. Not only can this prevent your monitor from doing its job—but it can provide some embarrassing moments if your neighbor's can inadvertently tune in on you! To avoid this problem, buy a monitor that has at least two channels and coordinate use with your neighbor, or buy a different brand.

Some of the brands we like include the **Fisher Price Nursery Monitor** ($47.00), which has a light that displays the sound level. The louder the sound, the more it lights up. This is especially useful if you're in a room with loud noises (a dishwasher or TV) that might drown out sound from the receiver. A glance at the light can alert you to your baby's cries. A nice added feature of the **Gerry Deluxe Two-Way Nursery Intercom and Baby Monitor** ($60.00) is that you can communicate back to your child via the intercom. This is especially handy when your child is a little older and you need to answer a question or issue a command!

The **Sassy Baby Monitor** operates on a slightly different principle. You plug the unit into electrical wall outlet and tune the monitor to a clear frequency on an FM radio. You then tune in an FM radio to the frequency. This is a relatively complicated procedure and we don't think the savings are worth the effort. In addition, you'll need an FM radio in each room in which you'll want to hear your baby.

✔ **TIP:** *Pack your nursery monitor when you go on vacation. They are a great way to keep track of your little one in unfamiliar surroundings.*

While we think that a nursery monitor is a must, installing a TV monitor is a little much! There are a number of companies offering products that allow you literally to keep an eye on your child as he sleeps. Unless you have some special health reasons for such close contact, we don't think such surveillance is healthy for either of you!

Pacifiers

The law requires that all pacifiers be strong enough to resist breaking up into small pieces and have guards or shields to prevent the pacifier from being drawn entirely into a baby's mouth. These guards or shields must also have ventilation holes to allow a baby to breathe even if the pacifier shield gets into the mouth. Pacifiers may not be sold with a ribbon, cord, or yarn attached.

Despite this regulation, CPSC still receives *many* reports of babies who have strangled on pacifier cords or ribbons tied on by parents or others. This is done so the pacifier can hang from the cord placed around the child's neck. The hundredth time you pick up a dropped pacifier, this may seem like a convenient arrangement, but the risk is just not worth it. The cord can easily get caught on crib cornerposts, pieces of furniture and even door knobs.

With nearly a hundred styles of pacifiers for sale (made by some 25 manufacturers) there are many kinds to try. Your own choice may be irrelevant, since your young pacifier tester will probably indicate her preferences quite fiercely. There are three types of materials used in pacifier nipples: vinyl, latex rubber, and silicone. In the past, some vinyl pacifiers contained DEHP [di(2-ethylhexyl)phthalate], a chemical that causes cancer in animals. CPSC reports that, while some pacifiers still contain DEHP, it is present at low levels that do not pose a risk to children.

Rubber pacifiers contain nitrosamines, chemicals that have caused cancer in animals and are suspected of causing cancer in humans. As with DEHP, CPSC monitors pacifiers to see that they do not contain more than a specified amount of nitrosamines.

★ REMEMBER: When Buying Pacifiers

☐ Smaller sizes are available for newborns.

☐ Try silicone pacifiers, they last longer than rubber and can be washed in the dishwasher.

The following products have been deemed unsafe by the CPSC. Problems include breakable small parts, improperly designed shields, weak nipples and other hazards. In most cases the problem description is quite technical, so we have simply listed these as "unsafe pacifiers."

RECALLED PRODUCTS: Pacifiers

If more than 18 months have elapsed since the recall date, the manufacturer may no longer honor the recall. If the company refuses to comply, you should discard the product to ensure the safety of your child.

Mikey Pacifiers

WHICH ONES: Two of three styles of baby pacifiers sold off of 11 by 13 ½ inch display cards are banned. The banned pacifiers have the words "Mayee" and "Hong Kong" on either side of the handle and come in a variety of colors. Over 72,000 of these pacifiers were distributed before 1987. PROBLEM: One style of pacifier has no ventilation holes and the shield is small enough to enter and infant's mouth and block its throat. The ventilation holes on the other pacifier are too small. WHAT TO DO: Discontinue use and return to point of purchase for a refund. RECALL DATE: 11/87

Mother's Helper/Pacific Holder

WHICH ONES: Pacifier holders sold between October 1987 and August 1988. The holder consists of various-shaped, two-inch plastic discs, each with a swivel metal clip attached for fastening the holder to the infant's shirt, sleepwear, blanket, etc. The words "Mother's Helper 1986 Steven Barrie & Co., Inc., Ivyland, PA. U.S.A." are embossed on the back and raised, multi-colored designs and letters on the front of the disc read " I'm a 10," "I'M A BOY," or "Hot Stuff." PROBLEM: The metal clip could come loose from the disc and pose a choking hazard to infants. WHAT TO DO: Return to the store where bought for a full refund or send the holder to Steven Barrie & Company, 1055A Louis Drive, Warminster, PA 18970 for a refund of the purchase price and postage. RECALL DATE: 5/89

Tips for Safe, Efficient Use:

1. *NEVER fasten a pacifier (or other item) around your baby's neck, and never tie cords, ribbons, or yarn on to a pacifier, even if you do not plan to place it around your child's neck. In fact, never put a loop of ribbon, cord or chain around your child's neck to hold a pacifier or religious medal or for any other reason.*

2. Since pacifiers can deteriorate with age or exposure to food and sunlight, you should inspect them frequently to determine if there are any changes in the texture, such as rips, holes, or other signs of weakening. If any of these signs are present, immediately throw the pacifier away. Such weakenings in the pacifier may allow your child to bite off a portion of the nipple, which then poses a choking hazard. You can hold silicon pacifiers up the light to inspect for tears.

Teething Relief

During teething, when the primary teeth gradually push up through the gums and they can become swollen and tender. This is especially true when the upper and lower front teeth and first back teeth are erupting (usually between the fourth and fifteenth month). Your baby may react by becoming restless and irritable as well as tearful and wakeful. One way to comfort your baby during teething is to try rubbing his gums gently with your finger (after washing your hands). A bottle of water, juice or milk or a pacifier or cold teething ring may also ease his pain. Certain over-the-counter products, such as Orajel or Num-Zit, carefully used, can provide soothing relief in seconds.

Powder, Oils and Ointments

Baby powder containers, seemingly innocuous items, can be hazardous because they often resemble a bottle. Babies have been known to put a powder container to their lips, pucker up and suck. When the top is open, powder can be sucked in or inhaled. In one New York study, 25 of the 40 such cases occurred while the child's diapers were being changed. A Canadian study reported 25 additional cases of talcum powder aspiration, with five of these resulting in death.

Even though only a small percentage of the infant patients studied required hospitalization, talcum is closely related to the carcinogen asbestos and may contain microscopic asbestos particles. Experts have urged the baby powder industry to change the appearance of containers and use a safety device on the cap to control dispensing of the powder.

According to the American Academy of Pediatrics, baby powder, oil and lotion serve no medical purpose. The AAP says baby powder is a product looking for a disease. There's no scientific evidence that it does anything to prevent diaper rash or any other kind of infant dermatological problem. The AAP cites the inhalation hazard and adds that "in some cases, when the powder gets into the cracks and crevices of a baby's skin, it serves as an irritant."

Because babies are born with a fully developed set of oil glands, most physicians feel there is no need to grease them up with oils and lotions. While there is no physical benefit to the skin, many parents (and babies) enjoy the contact of a nice massage and a slight amount of oil will allow your hands to move smoothly over your baby's skin.

One of the best things you can do for your baby's skin is to leave his or her diaper off from time to time, so air can get to the skin the diaper covers. Fresh air and mild soap and water are really the only products you'll need to take care of a healthy baby's skin.

WARNING: *Never give your child the powder container to play with while changing diapers, and keep the container (and other products such as ointments and baby oil) out of reach of a crawling or toddling child.*

Finally, a group of scientists and health activists have petitioned the FDA to take ointments and lotions containing iodocholr-hydroxyquin off of the market. Animal studies were conducted using creams containing this ingredient as you would to treat diaper rash. All of the animals suffered severe side effects, including liver damage, lethargy and weight loss. Some of the products on the market that contain this ingredient include: Vioform, Vioform-Hydrocortisone, Pricort Cream and Lotion, HCV Creme, Nystaform Ointment, and Pedi-Cort V Creme. While the product has not been banned by the FDA, you may want to check the ingredients on the ointment you use for treating diaper rash to make sure iodocholrhydroxyquin is not present.

Rattles

Even the classic baby's rattle can be a potential problem if it is too small. An infant's mouth is extremely flexible and can stretch to hold larger shapes than you'd expect. According to CPSC records, a rattle as large as 1-⅝ inches in diameter has become lodged in a baby's throat. In light of this hazard, the CPSC has issued regulations requiring that infant rattles be large enough so that they cannot be swallowed and constructed so that they will not separate into small pieces. Check older rattles which may have been manufactured or sold before the regulations became effective in August 1978 for parts or ends that are small enough to fit in a baby's mouth.

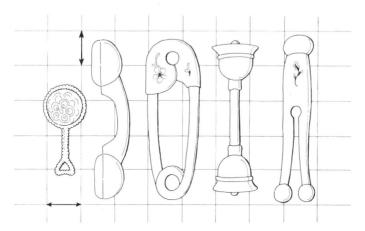

Rattles

These rattles are dangerous because of their size. All of these rattles were banned, because they could easily become lodged in a child's throat. Often small rattles are part of flower bouquets or fancy wrapping on a child's present. If you receive any of these small rattles, your best bet is to throw them away. In the diagram, one square equals one inch.

RECALLED PRODUCTS: Rattles

If more than 18 months have elapsed since the recall date, the manufacturer may no longer honor the recall. If the company refuses to comply, you should discard the product to ensure the safety of your child.

Baby Mirror Rattles

WHICH ONES: The rattles sold at K-mart stores from November 1987 to June 1989, are in the shape of a man with a hat came in blue and yellow or red and yellow. The package was labeled "Baby Mirror Rattle" K-mart code #28-17-62 or #1300. PROBLEM: The rattle may present a choking or suffocation hazard. WHAT TO DO: Return to any K-mart store for a refund. RECALL DATE: 6/89

Baby Wheel Rattles

WHICH ONES: The snail-shaped rattle sold at K-mart stores since October 1987, comes in white, blue, and yellow and has red and yellow wheels. The package was labeled "Baby Wheel Rattle" K-mart code #28-17-60 or #1303. PROBLEM: The antenna may break off the snail and pose a potential ingestion, choking, or suffocation hazard. WHAT TO DO: Return to any K-mart store for a refund. RECALL DATE: 6/89

Crib Pals Play Shapes

WHICH ONES: Approximately 15,000 sets. The sets sold at Toys R Us during 1988 and 1989 have four plastic pieces; a cone with a whistle, a cube with a mirror, a cylinder, and a ball that rattles. Each piece is a different color. The sets were packaged in blister packs and labeled "Crib Pals Play Shapes, SKN 157198, Ages 1 and up, Lucky Star Enterprises, Made in Taiwan" PROBLEM: The product fails to meet government baby rattle standards and may cause choking. WHAT TO DO: Return to Toys R Us for a refund or call Toys R Us at 800-548-0364; in NJ, 599-7897. RECALL DATE: 11/89

Flower Rattles

WHICH ONES: The rattle, which was sold from October 1987 to October 1988, is six inches long and made of white plastic with a sphere on one end of the handle and a circle on the other. Inside the sphere is a blue, pink, or yellow plastic flower with colored beads inside its petals. The model number M6588 is found on the package and on a slip of paper inside the package. PROBLEM: The rattle could break and the small pieces pose a choking hazard. WHAT TO DO: Return to store where bought for a full refund. RECALL DATE: 2/89

Helicopter Rattles

WHICH ONES: Baby rattles sold by Toys R Us in 1988 individually and as part of a three-piece rattle set. They were sold singly as "Crib Pals Tiny Tinkers Rattle Copter." The three-piece "Crib Pals Tiny Tinkers" included two other rattles, a carry-along clock and a dial-and-spin rattle which are not choking hazards. The helicopter rattle is 3-½ inches tall and made of white, red and blue hard plastic. "Royal Co. Ltd, Japan 1987" is imprinted on the bottom. PROBLEM: The tail section is long enough to reach the back of an infant's throat, and the small yellow caps at the top of the copter may come off—both pose a choking hazard. WHAT TO DO: Return the rattle to a Toys R Us store for a refund or call Toys R Us toll-free at 1-800-548- 0364. RECALL DATE: 3/89

Mini Togs Baby Bib #200 Rattles

WHICH ONES: Rattles shaped like a bear face, butterfly, bell or train engine sold as a set through J. C. Penney from January 1988 to March 1989. PROBLEM: The rattles can easily break and small parts could present a choking hazard. WHAT TO DO: Take the rattles to the store where purchased for a $1.00 refund. In case of a problem, call Mini Togs toll free at 800-551-4914; ask for Lisa. RECALL DATE: 10/89

Para Mi Bebe Bottle Cap Rattles

WHICH ONES: Screw-on bottle caps of both soap and cologne for infants designed as rattles which were sold from November 1987 through October 1988. The containers come with ball-shaped "rattle" caps in blue and pink, with a gold band around the diameter and small beads inside. PROBLEM: The plastic caps could shatter, releasing small beads and plastic pieces, which pose a choking hazard. WHAT TO DO: Return to the store where purchased and exchange for non-rattle caps. RECALL DATE: 6/89

Playskool Shake N' Sort Rattles

WHICH ONES: The rattles sold between 1986 and August 1988 in the shape of a plastic hour glass and are five inches long, with an orange handle and yellow plastic caps sealing each end. "Playskool" is printed on one of the yellow caps. PROBLEM: Some rattles made prior to 1988 may separate, releasing small beads which could choke a child. WHAT TO DO: Return to store where purchased for full refund or send the rattle to Playskool, 450 Division Street, Pawtucket, RI 08262. For questions, call Playskool at 800-237-0063 (in RI call 401-431-8697). RECALL DATE: 10/88

Playtime Pals Crib Rattles

WHICH ONES: Toys-R-Us sets of seven rattles sold from November 1987 to July 1988. Each set includes: Musical Chime, Li'l Fish Bath Toy, Dial "N Rattle, Squeaky Rattle, Star Rattle, Happy Horn, and Trumpet Time. Each rattle is made of yellow, red, blue and white plastic, with "Royal" and/or "Japan" printed on it. PROBLEM: Two of the rattles, Star Chime and Musical Chime, have small parts and may pose a choking hazard. WHAT TO DO: Return to nearest Toys-R-Us for a full refund. For more information, call Toys-R-Us at 800-548-0364. RECALL DATE: 11/88

Rainbow Bell Baby Rattles

WHICH ONES: These rattles were sold between July 1987 and January 1988. One is multi-colored with a handle of beads at one end and four bell shaped noise makers at the other. It is labeled "CT made in Taiwan." The other model, has two bulbs shaped like chicks' heads and an oval bulb between them. The bulbs are attached to the handle by flexible stems and each has a metal bell inside. PROBLEM: The handles of the rattles are small enough to enter a child's mouth and long enough to reach the back of the throat and the metal bells can come off posing a choking hazard. WHAT TO DO: Discontinue use and discard. RECALL DATE: 8/88

Spinning Windmill Baby Rattle

WHICH ONES: The plastic baby rattle, which has a rubber suction cup, four balls fastened to a hub which spins on a shaft has label on the hub of the toy which says "Made in Italy". The suction cup is labeled "Chicco". The package indicates that the toy is appropriate for infants age 3 months to 24 months. PROBLEM: Small parts on this toy could present a choking hazard. WHAT TO DO: Discontinue use and return to point of purchase for a refund. RECALL DATE: 9/87

Telephone Rattle

WHICH ONES: "Plastic Telephone Receiver Rattles" shaped like a telephone receiver which were sold at K-Mart stores from December 1987 to October 1988. PROBLEM: Rattles present a choking hazard or could cut infants. WHAT TO DO: Return to any K-Mart store for a full refund. RECALL DATE: 10/88

Tips for Safe, Efficient Use:

☐ Be certain the rattle is constructed of one piece that will not break apart.

☐ Check over your baby's rattles. If you feel that an older rattle may be too small for safety, or have ends that could extend into a baby's mouth, break the rattle and throw it away.

☐ Watch carefully when your baby is playing with a rattle or other small object.

☐ Take rattles and other small objects out of the crib or playpen while your baby sleeps.

Strollers and Carriages

A stroller or carriage is another very useful baby product that can make getting out and about with your child much simpler. A variety of options are available in a broad price range. At the bottom of the price scale are folding strollers, also known as umbrella strollers (because they resemble an umbrella). These strollers are generally lighter than others. Some will even fit in the overhead storage compartment of an airplane.

Convertible strollers are a combination of carriage and stroller. They recline to a flat area for napping. With the seat upright, they are a stroller. Most convertible strollers fold up flat and boxy (as opposed to upright and lengthwise like the umbrella stroller) but are compact enough to fit in car trunks.

Double strollers for twins or two siblings come in side by side or tandem models (children seated one behind the other or face to face). The former are more difficult to maneuver through doorways, so keep this in mind if you plan to use the stroller for shopping that requires lots of entrances and exits. Also make sure the stroller's weight limits can accommodate the combined weights of your children as they grow.

Carriages are for infants, newborn through six months. Providing a ready napping area for babies, some parents use them inside as an extra little bed. The usefulness of carriages declines with each month, since your child will seek more visual stimulation on her outings as she ages, (usually between four and six months) and will be less satisfied lying flat. Also, the increased ability of your child to push up on her hands or roll over reduces the safety and, hence, usefulness of these vehicles.

In 1988 some 13,000 children required a trip to the hospital emergency room as a result of stroller-related injuries. Many of these occurred when the child was not securely strapped in. Try to make buckling up in the stroller a habit just as it should be with your car seat and other baby products. Other stroller and carriage injuries can also be avoided if you pay careful attention to where small hands and feet are placed.

As with high chairs and playpens, there is a voluntary safety standard for strollers and carriages. In order to be certified to meet the ASTM/JPMA standard, the stroller or carriage must have a locking device to prevent accidental folding and a child restraint system. The carriage or stroller must be able to hold sufficient weight, remain stable while a child is seated or climbing in, and not have any hazardous edges or protrusions. In addition, the manufacturer must provide instructional guidelines. Be certain they are included.

★ REMEMBER: When Buying A Stroller or Carriage

☐ Purchase a stroller or carriage that meets the ASTM/JPMA voluntary safety standard. Because a manufacturer may *not* have *all* of the different carriage and stroller models in his line certified, you should look for the ASTM/JPMA Certification seal on the floor model or on the box or other packaging, rather than relying on the manufacturer's name alone. Look for this seal:

☐ Look for a stroller or carriage with a base wide enough to prevent tipping, even when your child leans over the side.

☐ If the stroller seat can be adjusted to a reclining position, make sure that the stroller does not tip backward when your child lies down.

☐ Make sure the stroller or carriage comes with seat belts that seem durable, fit snugly around your child, and are easily fastened and unfastened.

□ Check to see that the brake actually locks the wheels and operates easily. Brakes on two wheels provide more safety.

□ Check out the various optional features available and decide which you are willing to pay extra for. Some of these include:
—a reversible handle that allows you either to face your child or push your child from behind.
—a one-hand folding mechanism that makes it easier to fold the stroller while you hold your child. (Test this out in the store—some are easier than others.)
—a stain-hiding color—at a minimum; better yet, look for a removable, machine-washable cover.
—swivel wheels for increased maneuverability.
—weight—when we spoke with parents about their strollers' different features, this is the one feature they commented on the most. Some strollers are extremely heavy and cumbersome to use. Again, "test drive" the stroller in the store before purchasing.
—an attachable shopping basket or bag to hold purchases and for diaper bag storage. Look for one positioned low on the back of the stroller and directly over or in front of the rear wheels (under the seat) to prevent tipping.
—a canopy for sun protection.
—a front bar that swings open or is removable, a helpful feature when using the stroller for toddlers.

RECALLED PRODUCTS: Strollers

If more than 18 months have elapsed since the recall date, the manufacturer may no longer honor the recall. If the company refuses to comply, you should discard the product to ensure the safety of your child.

Hedstrom Li'l Steeler Strollers

WHICH ONES: Over 100 different models are affected. The model number can be found on the identification label attached to the frame of the stroller. Affected strollers also have the word "Hedstrom" sewn into the safety strap. PROBLEM: Some strollers have unexpectedly collapsed while a child was sitting in them. Children with fingers in the side hinges of the stroller may suffer serious lacerations and, possibly, amputations. WHAT TO DO: Contact Hedstrom for a free safety lock to prevent unexpected collapse. Identify model number of your stroller and call Hedstrom toll-free at 800-233-3271 (in Pennsylvania call 800-242-9034) for instructions on obtaining a free safety lock. RECALL DATE: 2/86

Perego Avanti Stroller

WHICH ONES: Strollers distributed 11,344 January 1, 1986 and December 15, 1986. A label which says "Avanti Made In Italy" appears on the front bumper of the model being recalled (the name Avanti was used on two stroller models). PROBLEM: A child's chin can get caught in the one-inch space between the metal wire guide (which guides the reversible handle back and forth) and the arm rest. This can result in lacerations to the mouth, and in some cases loosening or loss of teeth. WHAT TO DO: Write to Peg Perego, USA, Inc. 3625 Independence Drive, Fort Wayne, IN 46818 and request a free repair kit. RECALL DATE: 5/88

PRT Umbrella Stroller

WHICH ONES: Umbrella strollers purchased at Service Merchandise stores from August 1986 through March 1987. The strollers are navy blue with red trim. The model number, 1601, is on a tag attached to the top of the fabric seat. PROBLEM: Each stroller has end plugs on the end of the aluminum tubes which form the frame. If the end plugs come out, small children could choke on them. In addition, sharp edges would be exposed at the end of the aluminum tubes. WHAT TO DO: Contact Service Merchandise toll-free at 800-251-1389 (in Tennessee call 800-251-1212) for a free modification kit. RECALL DATE: 5/88

Strollers

WHICH ONES: Three models of imported strollers sold at McCrory, Britt's, Elmore, H.L. Green, Kittinger, Kress, McLellan, Newberry, Silver, TG&Y, and some independent stores. The affected strollers were sold between May 1983 and May 1988. Affected model numbers are Model AT410, Item #129098 umbrella stroller; Model PHT438, Item #128942 umbrella with canopy stroller; and Model PHT417, Item #129007 canopy stroller. Stroller Item #128942 is labeled, "Made in Taiwan Expressly for McCrory Corp., York, Pa 17402." Strollers Item # 129007 and Item #129098 are labeled, "YDC. 2955 E. Market St. York, Pa. 17402 U.S.A." All of the strollers are labeled "Baby World Industries, Inc. Taiwan." PROBLEM: The tube ends of the strollers were sealed with plastic plugs, which can be removed and are small enough to present a choking or ingestion hazard for young children. Also, if the plugs are removed, the sharp exposed metal ends of the tubes could cut a toddler's fingers, hands or arms. WHAT TO DO: Send the stroller's item number and style to McCrory Stores, Dept. #06-Mail Stop #0512, 2955 East Market Street, York, PA 17402 for a free modification kit. RECALL DATE: 6/89

Twin Totliner Strollers

WHICH ONES: These strollers with a two piece footrest were sold under three different brand names. Those under the Hedstrom name include model numbers 15-063, 15-5623, 15-862, 15-163, 15-662, 15-963, 15-562, 15-763. Sears Roebuck model 36494 and Simpson Sears model 66068 are also included. The model number can be found on the label attached to the metal frame. PROBLEM: Child could wedge a foot or leg between the two pieces of footrest, which could result in a broken leg. WHAT TO DO: Call Hedstrom toll-free at 800-233-3271 (in Pennsylvania call 800-242-9034) for free protective guard for footrest. RECALL DATE: 3/86

Tips for Safe, Efficient Use:

1. Never leave your child unattended in a carriage or stroller.

2. Never hang pocketbooks, shopping bags or other items on the back of a stroller. This could cause tipping.

3. Always use the restraint system.

4. When folding or unfolding a stroller, keep your child's fingers away.

5. Do not let your child treat the stroller or carriage like a toy.

6. When pushing a stroller or carriage, remember that it reaches traffic and/or a possibly dangerous situation before you do. Drivers are often unable to see a stroller that is very close to the front of their car. It's always good to exercise caution when pushing your child in a stroller or carriage in traffic or crowded places.

7. Thoroughly read the instructions that accompany your stroller. Some strollers require you to set locks or push down on certain parts of the strollers to lock the stroller into the correct position. If you do not follow these instructions, it is possible that, even though the stroller may appear to be ready to use, it could collapse or fold up while in use.

8. When you first get your stroller, we recommend practicing the set up and fold up of your stroller several times in a row to get down the sequence of steps needed to accomplish this task quickly. Later, when struggling with your squirming child in a busy mall or airport, you'll appreciate your mastery of this skill.

Sun Protection Products

Many people mistakenly believe that young children are immune to the potential dangers of skin cancer. Although one is more likely to develop skin cancer later in life, prolonged exposure at an early age can increase the probability of skin cancer later. Many of us identify a tan with good health. Unfortunately, it is really a sign of injury to the skin.

Infants, whose skin has a very low concentration of melanin (the skin's color-producing chemical) are particularly susceptible to the ultraviolet rays of the sun. These rays can cause painful burning and inflammation. In addition, excessive or prolonged exposure may lead to skin cancer. Because the tender skin of infants and small children can burn so easily, excessive unprotected exposure should be avoided. And even for older, more active children, protection from the sun is important.

The American Academy of Pediatrics and the Skin Cancer Foundation recommend keeping infants and young children out of the sun during their first year. A severe burn can be serious for an infant. If you plan to be in the sun with your child, try to avoid the peak hours of intense sunlight—between 10:00 a.m. and 2:00 p.m. (11:00 a.m. to 3:00 p.m. Daylight Savings Time). If your child must be in the sun during these times, make efforts to cover the child, and always use a sunscreen. Many suntan lotions now come with a sun protection factor (SPF) of 22.

Harvard researchers have found that regular use of sunscreen during the first 18 years of life reduces a person's lifetime risk of developing skin cancer by 78 percent.

Some children are likely to suffer more than others. Very fair-skinned children may get severe sunburn from a half hour of exposure in hot summer sun. In general, people who freckle and sunburn easily are most vulnerable to skin cancer. Children who are taking certain types of drugs are also at greater risk, since the sun combined with the drugs can bring on photosensitive or phototoxic effects. Among such drugs are certain tranquilizers, anti-emetics (to prevent vomiting), antihypertensives, diuretics, tetracycline antibiotics, sulfa drugs, oral diabetic drugs and quinidine. If your child is taking any medication, prescribed or over-the-counter, check with your physician or pharmacist for possible reactions to strong sunlight.

While over-the-counter sunscreens do not offer absolute prevention of sunburn, they can extend the time it takes for the sun to cause a burn.

American manufacturers of sunscreen products have adopted a numerical system used in Europe, called "sun protection factor" (SPF), to designate the relative effectiveness and limitations of sunscreens. When selecting a sunscreen, the higher the number, the greater the protection.

Some sunscreens are waterproof or water resistant, an important consideration for active children since the sunscreen doesn't have to be reapplied each time the child perspires heavily or comes out of the water. However, most experts recommend liberal reapplication every two hours.

To best understand SPF ratings, consider this: a product rated SPF 5 means your child can stay in the sun five times longer than if he had no protection and receive about the same amount of sun.

The SPF rating values are as follows:

SPF 2 to 3: minimal protection from sunburning; permits sun tanning; recommended for people who rarely burn and who tan easily and deeply.

SPF 4 to 5: moderate protection from sunburning; permits some sun tanning; recommended for people who tan well with minimal burning.

SPF 6 to 8: extra protection from sunburning; permits limited sun tanning; recommended for people who burn moderately and tan gradually.

SPF 9 to under 14: maximum protection from sunburning; permits little or no sun tanning; recommended for people who always burn easily and tan minimally.

SPF 15 or greater: offers the most protection from sunburn, permits no sun tanning; recommended for people who burn easily and never tan.

✔ **TIP:** *Some high SPF sunscreens come in a stick form which makes them easier to apply to lips, cheeks and noses.*

For a free *Guide to Sun Protection for Children* send a self-addressed, stamped business size envelope, with 25 cents postage to the American Academy of Pediatrics, P.O. Box 927, Elk Grove Village, IL 60009.

Swings

One of our favorite baby products (and most necessary) is the swing. The swing's back and forth action very often will lull a newborn off to sleep or calm a fussy baby, giving parents some "hands free" time. Portable baby swings are free-standing units that either wind up and swing for set periods of time or are battery operated and swing for hours.

Few products endear themselves more to parents than the swing. Motion is a great tranquilizer for children. Most of our parents tell stories of donning the bathrobe for midnight car rides to settle down crabby children. And most of us have developed our own "patented" rocking motion that uniquely quiets our fussy child. Thankfully, there are now a great number of indoor swings that also do the job beautifully.

Most baby swings are portable and free-standing, with a wind-up or motorized mechanism that allows them to swing independently for set periods of time. They are best for babies from birth to nine months or 25 pounds and range in price from $20 to $100. The range reflects the many different available options that are available beyond the simple to and fro swing action.

The basic models are wind-up and swing for about 10 to 15 minutes. The wind-up mechanism can be a little noisy, and the seat is of the no-frills variety, but they do the job quite adequately. Additional dollars buy additional swing minutes, an upgraded swing seat, and, in some products, play dials or other small toys to amuse the swinger.

Some more expensive models use a battery-powered mechanism that allows your child to swing for much longer. Since getting your baby in and out of the swing is the trickiest aspect of this product, some companies have simplified their designs to make them easier to use.

✔ **TIP:** *Some swings have seats that convert to baby carriers or change positions, allowing the swing to be used as a cradle for the very young baby.*

CPSC estimates that each year in the U.S. there are 1300 cases requiring hospital emergency room treatment for injuries related to the use of portable baby swings. The most commonly reported incident is entrapment of the head, which can occur when a baby's neck gets caught between the edge of the backrest and the bars from which the seat hangs. Other accidents include falls that occur when the back of the swing seat collapses or when the swing becomes dislodged from the door frame, and scraping or bumping of the child's head while he is being taken out of the swing.

RECOMMENDED PRODUCTS: Baby Swings

Graco Swyngomatic
A wind up model that does the job, if you don't mind winding it up. It's a great buy at $20.

Graco Non-Stop Swyngomatic
Operates on batteries that will power the swing for up to 150 hours!

Graco Easy Entry Swyngomatic
Has a tray that swings up, allowing for an easy exit.

Cosco Vista Swing
Has an innovative open top frame that eliminates the possibility of bumping your child's head when lifting him out of the swing. It's also battery powered and converts to a carrier.

Doorway Jumpers

A product somewhat similar to the swing is the doorway jumper. Designed to be hung in a doorway, most versions are portable and consist of a soft, swing-like seat attached to elastic or spring cords that allow the child to bounce up and down. These products are not designed for newborns. We don't recommend jumpers at all. First of all, there is a relatively short period of time (two to three months) between when your child is old enough to use them and when she is too old to use them. Secondly, they can come loose when your child really starts to bounce around. Finally, because they are generally designed to be hung on door frames, it's quite possible that your child can get carried away and bounce into the side of the doorway. If you already have one, be careful when using it.

★ REMEMBER: When Buying a Portable Baby Swing

☐ Follow the manufacturer's suggested guidelines for size and weight and select a swing that is compatible with your child's size.

☐ Look for swings that have safety straps to keep your child from climbing out.

☐ If the swing comes with small toys attached to it, make sure these toys are safe and contain no small parts.

☐ Check to see that there are no support tubes with open ends into which your child could put his fingers. Be sure there are no sharp edges or rough surfaces.

☐ Look for seat materials with strong stitching and heavy-duty snaps.

☐ If you plan to purchase a swing with a spring apparatus for automatic wind-up, make sure that no parts of the mechanism are exposed.

Tips for Safe, Efficient Use:

1. Do not leave your child unsupervised in a swing. It's not a babysitter, so set it up where you can maintain eye contact with your little swinger.

2. Carefully follow all manufacturer assembly instructions. Make certain that nuts, bolts and screws are securely tightened. If there are any sharp edges, cover them over with tape.

3. When setting up a free-standing swing, be sure that all four legs are properly set and that the swing is stable and balanced.

4. Prop a young baby in the seat so that his head cannot slump over and get trapped between the backrest and suspending bars. Try using rolled up towels to support a newborn's head.

5. Always use a restraining system with your portable swing. When the swing is not in use, tighten straps securely to avoid creating a noose that could become looped around a child playing near the swing.

6. Make sure your child cannot kick or push off any furniture, walls, or other obstacles. Also, to reduce the risk of your child falling out, remove any objects your child might be tempted to grab while swinging.

Tips for Safe, Efficient Use: (cont'd.)

7. When placing your child in or out of the swing, be careful not to scrape or bump her head or catch fingers or arms in the swing chains, straps, or bars.

8. When not using your portable swing, place it in an out-of-the-way location.

Toys

Here are some tried and true ideas for great baby toys.

Toys for Newborns to Three Months:

Mirror
PURPOSE: A great toy that will amuse for hours. GOOD CHOICES: Be sure to use smooth-edged unbreakable mirrors and securely attach them with *very short* straps.

Rattle
PURPOSE: Early experience with grasping and making sound. A small dumbbell or telephone rattle is easy to grab. GOOD CHOICES: Make sure it is not small enough to be swallowed nor too large to be comfortably held.

Soft Doll
PURPOSE: Fun to look at and feel the clothes. Babies often follow faces if you move them slowly from side to side. GOOD CHOICES: A small lightweight colorful doll with simple facial features will be most interesting.

Toys for Three to Six Months:

Bath Toy
PURPOSE: Makes bath time fun. GOOD CHOICES: Bright floating toys that have different parts are fun. Also, common household items make great tub toys. Try some plastic cups, for instance.

Rattle
PURPOSE: Fun to shake, watch, and hear, and to transfer from hand to mouth and mouth to hand. GOOD CHOICES: Choose

rattles with handles, mirrors and faces. Rattles with holes are fun to explore. Rattles that attach to the wrist or feet are also fun.

Squeak Toy

PURPOSE: Encourages grabbing and demonstrates cause and effect. GOOD CHOICES: Make sure they are easy to squeak and too big for the mouth.

Great Gifts for New Babies

We surveyed parents and reviewed hundreds of baby products to come up with a list of great baby shower and newborn presents. While there are many products that are useful, they may not have made our list because they are so frequently given. Many of these items are described in greater detail in other sections of this book, including features to look for when shopping and other important buying information. (Also see our list below of Gifts to Avoid.)

When selecting gifts, you should also consider the family's life style. A family that eats out a lot may appreciate a hook-on high chair; if they are involved in outdoor activities, a back carrier may be just the right thing! When in doubt, practicality should be your prevailing consideration. Unless you know the parents very well, it may be best to avoid gifts that reflect a certain style or taste, such as wall decorations, lamps and other decorative gifts.

Baby Calendar or Baby Book

While not all parents like these, if you suspect the new parents are collectors of memories, this can become a treasured gift years later. We like the new baby calendars that come with stickers to note big events (first food, first Halloween, etc.) In addition to keeping track of first year events, some calendars can serve as a wall decoration for baby's room.

Baby Swing by Graco

This is one of our favorite baby products.

Baby Bath Tub and Sponge Bathtub Insert

These miniature hard plastic tubs assist parents in bathing wiggling newborns. The bathtub insert is essentially a large sponge with a scooped out section that your child sits on in the bathtub to prevent her from slipping and sliding.

Books for Parents and Children

For new parents, we recommend: *Working and Caring* (and other books) by T. Berry Brazleton, M.D.; *The Read Aloud Handbook* by Jim Trelease (publisher). For the new baby's library: *Pat the Bunny*, *Goodnight Moon*, and other classics. We believe children's books are *the* fail-safe gift!

Car Seat

This is clearly a gift of love.

Children's Tape Player and Tapes

A cassette player to keep in baby's room, that later can be child-operated (we like the Fisher Price Cassette Player), and a Raffi or lullaby tape are a great gift combination. See page 00 for tape suggestions.

Crib Sheets

An extra set is always useful.

Diaper Bag

While this is already a popular new baby gift, most parents will need more than one before their need for a diaper bag ends.

Diapers

Whether the parents plan to use cloth or disposable diapers, this is the gift that will always be used! Combine with a book on toilet training!

Dust Buster by Black & Decker

These hand-held mini vacuums are excellent for quick clean up jobs. It will be used *daily* when the baby starts to eat finger food.

Front Carrier

This is a great way for dads to bond with their little ones.

Handmade Blankets

Although time-consuming to make, these "gifts from the heart" are much treasured by new parents.

Help

A meal prepared for one of the first nights home or three hours of babysitting are gifts any new parents would welcome.

Depending upon the family, there may be many other services that would be greatly appreciated during the baby's first month (car pooling older children a few hours of yard work, etc.).

Infant Seat Bouncers

This seat is a variation on the traditional hard back infant seat. The seat consists of fabric stretched over a metal frame, allowing your baby's weight and movement to cause her to gently bounce and rock. We recommend the Sassy Cradle Bouncer.

Large-size Clothes

Consider an outfit, such as a sweat suit or play outfit, in a 24-month or 2T size. Parents told us again and again that looking back on gifts they received, large-size clothes were the some of the most practical and appreciated!

Mini Food Processor

Great fun for making baby food. These gadgets allow parents to make up a small baby food portion of what they are eating for dinner, rather than making baby food up in bulk or using prepared baby food.

Nursery Monitor

This "must have" item lets parents keep track of baby sounds from anywhere in the house.

Safety Products

Help new parents childproof their home by giving them cabinet door drawer latches, outlet guards, corner cushions and other child-proofing products.

Stretchies

Also known as stretch suits and sleepers, these one piece snap or zip up suits are indispensable during baby's first year. The summer version has short sleeves and snaps at the crotch for cool and easy comfort. Don't be tempted to buy newborn sizes; parents recommend 12, 18 or 24 month sizes.

Stroller

This is an expensive gift, but a must!

Toys

Consider keys on a ring, a large rattle, or Fisher Price "Rock-A-Stack" stacking rings or "Foot Jingles" rattle socks by Playskool—these and other toys for *non-crib* use.

Zip Quilt Sleeping Bag

This is one of only two types of blankets we recommend giving (see handmade blanket above). These quilts which fold in half and zip up to form baby sleeping bags are extremely useful when visiting.

Little Items

Individually these don't seem like very important gifts, but these will often be the items that send parents to the store in the first few months after birth. Combine two or more of these for a very appreciated gift: extra undershirts, parents like one-piece shirts with snap crotch; Rectal thermometer, (an overlooked item that's a necessity for the first case of the flu); a mesh bag to hang in the bathtub to hold bath toys; baby nail scissors or clippers; an extra seat belt (safety strap) if a hand-me-down high chair or stroller is going to be used; a night light; a "Splat Mat" for use under baby's high chair to protect against the invariable spills and tosses; disposable bibs by Playtex.

Gifts to Avoid Giving

Baby Walkers

We do not recommend the use of baby walkers because of the frequency and severity of injuries associated with their use.

Bath Seats

This product is intended to assist babies to sit upright in the bathtub. We recommend against this product because it may encourage parents to let go of children in the bathtub or, much worse, leave them unattended.

Bath Sacks

Several parents told us, and we agree, that these zip-up terry-lined suits with hoods are very impractical. They are intended to be put on after baby's bath to keep her warm. But most parents prefer to dry their babies and dress them in play clothes or sleepwear, something they would eventually do after placing their child in a bath sack. What parents of newborns don't need is one more clothes change!

Blankets

There are a few exceptions to this rule: Zip quilt sleeping bags and handmade blankets (see Great Gifts chart) or, if you plan to spend a lot of money, a blanket/quilt that you know the new parents are sure to love. Otherwise, avoid blankets. From our experience and what other parents have told us, blankets are one of the most over given presents.

Humidifiers

Unless prescribed by the baby's pediatrician, this product is not necessarily helpful.

Newborn-size Clothing

While these itsy-bitsy clothes are cute to look at, they are really more appropriate for dolls. Babies outgrow newborn size clothes within months or very often within weeks!

Polyester Clothing

With the exception of children's sleepwear that is flame resistant to prevent tragic burns, parents dislike polyester clothing for their children. They want natural fibers (or at least blends with lower polyester content) that are comfortable and more stain forgiving.

Right Size but Wrong Season Clothing

Guessing how big a baby will be next winter or summer is a very tricky calculation. A 12-month size snowsuit isn't much use to a baby who is 12-month size in June. If you opt for this type of gift, make sure the clothing is returnable, so that the parents of a newborn who weighs in at five pounds or nine pounds can do their own calculating as to whether the next season clothing will fit.

Stuffed Animals

It's not that we don't like stuffed animals, but again these fall into the over given present category. Children continue to receive them for birthdays and other holidays, so that by the time they are four, their menagerie has started to take over the household!

C H A P T E R   T W O

This can really be a fun time for you and your child. He or she has probably settled into a routine and become an "explorer." This new mobility means that your child will be coming in contact with all kinds of products. As such, buying carefully and monitoring activities closely will never be more important.

With this new age, you will have graduated into buying all kinds of products and equipment that correspond with your child's development. Of particular importance are the gates, playpens and childproofing products that you will need to keep your little one safe. We've listed these and most of the items you will need, alphabetically with our usual buying tips and recommendations. Because toys, and soon books, will become the main focus of enjoyment and learning, we have also included a list of excellent books and more tips on toys for this age group. The chapter ends with our *Great Gifts* section.

**Products You Can
Purchase for
Your Child
The Early Years:
6 Months to 2 Years**

Bicycle Child Carriers

A good bicycle child carrier offers your child an exciting opportunity to participate in your two-wheel adventures. Most children love riding on the back of a bike. To make sure your child is safe and sound as you whiz down the road, here are some tips on buying a bicycle child carrier and using it safely.

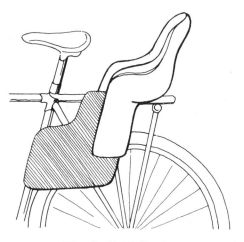

Bicycle Child Carriers

The best child carriers have a seat with a high back. Be sure to buy a carrier that comes with a safety shield to prevent your child's feet from getting tangled in the spokes. The diagram shows the proper positions of the seat on the bike.

★ REMEMBER: When Buying a Bicycle Child Carrier

☐ Make sure the seat comes with a safety restraint. We recommend safety belts that restrain both the upper and lower body (waist). Upper body or shoulder restraints will help keep your child upright should she fall asleep (as many children do) while on the ride. Also look for a restraint that has a crotch strap, as this will protect against your child sliding feet first out the bottom.

☐ A high back seat will offer a younger child a place to rest his or her head.

☐ Purchase only a rear bicycle child carrier; front carriers make it far more difficult to control your bicycle.

✔ **TIP:** *Helmets save lives and little ones learn by your good example. (See Chapter 3 for separate section on Bicycle Helmets.) New York and California laws requires children in bicycle carriers to wear helmets; Florida, Pennsylvania and Washington are considering similar requirements.*

Tips for Safe, Efficient Use:

1. Always buckle up your child in the safety restraint. The grab bar or cross bar that the child sits behind is *not* a restraint and will not protect him adequately in the event of a sudden stop or fall.

2. Never leave your child in the seat while the bike is on its kickstand.

3. Always use a bicycle helmet for both your child and yourself.

4. Never use a bicycle child carrier without a safety shield to protect your child's feet and legs.

WARNING: *Nighttime riding with a child is not recommended. If you ride alone on your bike at nighttime (with the carrier empty), install a reflector on the back of your carrier for nighttime visibility. The reflector on your bike is often obstructed by the child carrier.*

RECALLED PRODUCTS: Bicycle Child Carriers

If more than 18 months have elapsed since the recall date, the manufacturer may no longer honor the recall. If the company refuses to comply, you should discard the product to ensure the safety of your child.

Championship Deluxe Bicycle Child Carrier

WHICH ONES: Those sold between February 1986 and July 1986 through Sears with stock number 82595 on the box. PROBLEM: Plastic buckle may come loose, allowing a child to fall. WHAT TO DO: Discontinue use and call D & R Industries, 1-800-323-2852, (Illinois, Hawaii, Alaska may call 312-677-3200 collect) for a new shoulder harness. RECALL DATE: 5/86.

Books

"Read me a story" is probably one of the first phrases your child will learn. Night after night good books will help you take your children on adventures into other lands! Since young children love repetition, "adventure" may mean the same old book each night. As any parent knows, reading the same stories over and over can get old quickly. If you are tired of the books you are reading, your child will surely sense your attitude. Chances are that neither one of you will have a good time. So, when you're looking for a change, go to the library (or bookstore) and bring home some of the books on the list below. Our list is based on what parents report their children most enjoy and includes some of the perennial best sellers. In addition to offering some reading treats, many of these are books that have held the attention of hundreds of thousands of parents and children.

Great Books for 1 - 2 Year Olds

Adelaide to Zeke, by Janet Wolf (Harper & Row). Each letter of the alphabet is represented by a different character who introduces the next letter.

Are You My Mother?, by P.D. Eastman (Random House). Baby bird searches high and low for his mother.

Big Book of Mr. Small, by Lois Lenski (Derrydale Books). Six classic stories about Mr. Small.

Dad's Back, by Jan Ormerod (Lothrop, Lee & Shepard Books). Baby and dad have fun together!

Drummer Hoff, adapted by Barbara Emberley (Treehouse Paperbacks). Repetition and rhyme are the key to this Caldecott Medal award winner.

First Little Golden Books, (Western Publishing) are just the right size and length for toddlers. A variety of titles, are available such as, **Goodnight, Moon**, by Margaret Wise Brown, illustrated by Clement Hurd (Harper & Row). Sweet dreams to our crescent friend.

Let's Play Peek-A-Boo, by Joan Webb (Golden Book by Western Publishing).

The Little Engine That Could, retold by Watty Piper (Platt Munk/Putnam). Many versions are available of this lesson in perseverance.

The Little Mouse, the Red Ripe Strawberry and the Big Hungry Bear, by Don and Audrey Wood (Child's Play). The little mouse will do anything to save his strawberry from the big hungry bear.

Pat the Bunny, by Dorothy Kunhardt (Golden Press). A warm and fuzzy friend for little folks.

Pat the Cat, by Edith Kunhardt (Golden Press). In the tradition of Pat the Bunny.

The Peter Rabbit Pop-Up Book, by Beatrix Potter (Frederick Warne). The better to see him hop, hop, hopping along.

Quick as a Cricket, by Audrey Wood (Child's Play). A celebration of self-awareness with beautiful illustrations by Don Wood.

The Real Mother Goose, illustrated by Blanche Fisher Wright (Rand McNally). The 78th printing of Old King Cole and friends.

Spot's Birthday Party, by Eric Hill (Putnam). A pop-up celebration.

Ten in the Bed, by Penny Dale (Walker Books and Discovery Toys). There were ten in the bed and the little one said, "Rollover, rollover!"

The Very Hungry Caterpillar, by Eric Carle (Philomel/Putnam). How much and what a caterpillar eats to become a butterfly.

Where's Spot, by Eric Hill (Putnam). A pop-up game of hide-and-seek.

Bubble Bath

Bubble baths and sudsy bath oils contain detergent ingredients that strip away natural skin oils and increase the chance of rashes, particularly in cold weather. These bath products also can affect the mucous membrane of the urinary tract, and this may lead to infection (see Baby Shampoo in Chapter 1). To steer clear of these problems, avoid too frequent and prolonged exposure to bubble bath products for your child.

Carriers, Back

When your child gets too old for the front carriers we discussed in Chapter One, a back carrier will enable you to keep your walking and hiking regime intact. Like a camping style back pack, back carriers have a light weight metal frame and padded shoulder straps that distribute your child's weight evenly over your shoulders and hips. Back packs are best used for children over six months and until they reach 35 pounds.

✔ **TIP:** *Here's a back-saving rule of thumb—most people can comfortably carry a child who weighs up to one-fourth of their own weight.*

Back Carrier
Most back carriers will stand on their own, so you can put your baby in before putting the carrier on your back.

There are several types of back carriers. Most have metal frames; some will stand on their own; and others have frames that resemble a chair, with you and the child back-to-back. Typically, back carriers are used for hikes and other outdoor activities. They are also great when you are in very busy places, such as train stations or airports—you can move much faster and easier than with a stroller (and carry luggage too).

✔ **TIP:** *Before buying, try the carrier on and place your baby in it. Do not buy one that does not have enough depth to support the baby's back. Look for leg openings that are small enough to prevent your baby from slipping but large enough to avoid chafing his legs. When the baby is seated in the carrier, his legs should be spread apart, supported from the knees up and the knees should be lower than his bottom.*

★ REMEMBER: When Buying A Back Carrier

☐ Select a style with a waist strap that goes across your lower back and wide, padded shoulder straps, (so they won't cut into your shoulder).

☐ Look for a lightweight model.

☐ All straps should be easily adjustable.

☐ The design should allow you to put the carrier on and take it off easily by yourself.

☐ Make sure frame packs have a stand.

☐ Be sure to select a carrier that is washable.

☐ Check the carrier for possible finger traps and watch out for sharp points, edges, or rough surfaces.

☐ Look for soft, padded covering over the metal frame near the baby's face to cushion your baby from bumps.

☐ Buy a carrier that matches your baby's weight and size.

☐ Make sure the carrier has a restraining strap. Simply being in the carrier is not enough to hold a child who tries to climb or push himself out.

☐ Look for materials with strong stitching and large heavy-duty snaps.

RECOMMENDED PRODUCTS: Back Carriers

Gerry Carrier

This is a stand-type carrier with a removable cotton seat for easy care. It has adjustable padded shoulder straps and folds flat for storage. The frame is lightweight and has a back bow that goes across the adult's lower back for support. Support of child ends at mid-back.

Pak-Seat (by Gram)

This is also a stand-type carrier that folds flat for storage. It has padded shoulders, as well as a padded back and headrest and a strap that goes across the adult's lower back. When used as a child chair, it reclines for a resting or napping child.

Snugli Framed Backpack

This is not a stand-type carrier. It has a light solid frame with padded shoulders, back and headrest. The seat is adjustable, and there is an accessory pouch for storage.

Tips for Safe, Efficient Use:

1. *Never* leave a child unattended in a back carrier with a stand.

2. *Never* use a framed back carrier before your baby is four to five months old. At this age the baby's neck is able to withstand minor jolts without sustaining an injury to the neck.

3. Always use a restraining strap with the carrier.

4. When you lean over or stoop while wearing the carrier, always bend from the knees rather than from the waist to prevent your baby from falling out.

5. When folding the carrier, make sure your baby's fingers are clear of the frame joints.

6. Periodically check your carrier for ripped seams, frayed seats or straps, and missing or loose snaps.

Childproofing Products

We call the six months to two years age the "mobile years"— the time when your little one begins to move about. In your child's natural search for adventure, the home that you now take for granted will become a virtual mine field of obstacles and dangers. With a little planning and the right stuff, you can easily give your child the freedom to roam without having to anticipate every move. While safety is your prime concern, your sanity is also a factor. Repeatedly putting the entire contents of your kitchen cabinets back in place gets old, fast!

In Chapter Seven we set out a comprehensive childproofing roadmap detailing the hazards contained in each room of your house. Here we discuss the products that will assist in making your home a safe one. *Most of the child-proofing products mentioned below can be found in a wonderful and unique catalogue called "Perfectly Safe." For a free copy, write to Perfectly Safe, 7245 Whipple Avenue, N.W., North Canton, Ohio 44720 or call 800-262-2376 (in Ohio call 216-494-4366).*

✔ **TIP:** *Take a crawl through your home. Even the most scrupulous housekeeper will be amazed at the variety of things imbedded in rugs and hidden under furniture. Seemingly innocuous items, like lamp cords and pet food bowls, take on new meaning when your child is on the crawl.*

In the Kitchen

Childproof latches on cabinets and drawers within your child's reach add a measure of safety *and* help prevent some messy clean-up jobs. There are three basic types of cabinet locks: **Gerber Drawer Latches** are opened by pressing on the spring-loaded latch as you open the drawer. **Safe Lok Cabinet Latches** offer two-way security. In addition to keeping curious children out, they won't fully close until released by an adult helping to prevent pinched fingers! Both of these latches must be installed with screws. Less convenient to use than standard drawer and cabinet locks, but far simpler to install, are the "u-shaped" cabinet slide locks.

Appliance latches will prevent small children from opening oven doors, dishwashers, and microwaves. A slightly different device for refrigerators will automatically lock the door when it is closed. With a little practice, you can easily open it, but your toddler cannot. If your stove knobs are easily accessible, you can buy covers which make it difficult for children to turn the knobs. They're easy to install and work on many different makes of stoves.

✔ **TIP:** *To avoid totally frustrating your children and help them feel a part of the kitchen, keep a bottom drawer filled with play cups, plates, spoons, and other safe non-breakable objects specially earmarked for kitchen play.*

In the Bathroom

Most bathroom injuries come from slips and falls. To avoid bumped heads, you can put **nonskid appliques** on the bottom of the tub or use a rubber bath mat and slide a **cushioned spout guard** over the faucet. There are a number of soft faucet guards in animal shapes that fit securely over tub spouts and protect children from possible gashes and bruises in a slippery tub.

Toilet seat locks can prevent entrapment between the seat and bowl and drowning. Lid Loc and Potty Lock are two products which will do the job.

The step stool that provides access to the sink may also invite exploration of the medicine cabinet. First, make sure everything in the cabinet has childproof tops, and keep the medicines you use on a regular basis only on the highest shelf.

WARNING: *One out of three childhood poisonings occurs at the home of a child's grandparents, in part because older people often buy medicines without child-resistant caps. While this is a convenience to grandparents, they should be aware that it could pose dangers for their grandchildren.*

To safeguard against accidental poisonings you can buy locking **medicine cabinet inserts** or small locks and latches designed to keep medicine cabinet doors closed. One tamper proof container, half the size of a tissue box, is Medi-Safe. It fits in a medicine cabinet, drawer, or suitcase and has its own combination lock.

Another must for the medicine chest is a measuring device for dispensing medicines. Remember all teaspoons are not created equal, and even small differences from the recommended dosage for your child can have adverse effects. One of our favorites is a spoon-like device that has a hollow handle with dosage markings. Simply fill to the correct dosage and your child can take exactly the right amount from the spoon.

In the Living and Dining Room

Fireplaces can be dangerous, even if no fire is burning. One way to keep an explorer from inhaling and swallowing soot is to install a **glass fireplace screen**. These are popular as energy savers, and great for keeping the fireplace off limits. Remember they do get very hot when the fire is burning.

To decrease the chance of your child being involved in a furniture-related accident, apply **cushioned corner covers** to coffee tables and other sharp corners in heavy traffic use.

If your toddler sticks a hand in the front loading slot of a VCR and pushes the buttons, the internal VCR mechanism may seriously cut and damage fingers. Your best bet is to keep these machines out of reach. If you can't move the VCR, you should buy a **VCR LOCK** which goes in the front (like a tape) and prevents your child from reaching inside.

✔ **TIP:** *If you can't perfectly secure a room, consider a playpen or play enclosure.*

Throughout the House

To most children, electrical cords are irresistible. They love to chew on and pull them. A **cord shortener** will shorten and secure electrical cords making them less of a hazard. You can buy **clamps** that attach to the furniture and will prevent a lamp from toppling over if the cord is pulled. Make sure, however, that the table the lamp sits on is very secure, or the whole thing might fall over. There are also **spring type cord shorteners**, which automatically coil up excess cords, and simple rods with hooks on either side to wrap the cord around the rod and keep it out of reach.

Electrical wall outlets, which are typically close to the floor, are another obvious hazard to young children. Inexpensive **plastic safety caps** will help prevent this disaster. Because removing and remembering to replace outlet caps on frequently used outlets is difficult for even the most conscientious parent, consider installing a **safety outlet plate**. You insert the plug into the slots in the safety plate, turn the plug clockwise until it stops and then push it into the outlet. When the plug is removed, the plate automatically snaps back and prevents access to the outlet. This is also a great feature if your child accidentally pulls the plug out. An **outlet guard** completely covers the outlet, plugs and all, and prevents a child from pulling out the electrical cord or inserting objects into the outlets.

✔ **TIP:** *Buy some extra outlet caps to use when you travel.*

Clothes

As your child grows bigger, chances are your need to guess at clothes sizes and styles (and sometimes even color) will become more frequent. Buying children's clothes doesn't always have to be a hit or miss experience. But matching the sizes, fabrics, and styles of children's clothes to your child takes some getting used to. Here are some pointers to ease the selection process.

✔ **TIP:** *Buy clothes based on your child's size and anticipated growth, rather than the age on the label. See chart below.*

Clothing Sizes		
Age	**Weight**	**Size**
6 to 9 months	up to 18 lbs.	18 months
12 months	up to 24 lbs.	24 months
18 months	up to 28 lbs.	2T (toddler)
24 months	up to 34 lbs.	3T

When we recently asked parents what brand of children's clothes they like and dislike, we found some clear favorites! It is interesting to note, however, that several of the favorite brands were also on the parents' disliked list. This dichotomy of preferences is related to factors such as fit, comfort, material and style appeal—all of which are subject to individual tastes and the variety of children wearing the clothes. The following are the favorite brands among the families we surveyed: Absorba, Buster Brown, Carter, Healthtex, Oshkosh B'Gosh, Lands' End (mail order, see Chapter Nine) Izod, and Sears.

We offer some guidelines below and in Chapters One and Three under *Clothes*.

Tips for Safe, Efficient Use:

Many veteran parents have their own methods for attacking the tough stains that children incur with ease. Here are a few for your experimentation—with no guarantees promised!
1. Wash or soak clothes as soon as possible after stain occurs.
2. Before washing, rinse protein stains in cold water and sugar or fruit stains in warm water.
3. Presoak and wash clothes in stain loosening solution. We recommend Clorox II, Biz, Spray & Wash, or GOOP.
4. Anticipate the stain. If the child is wearing a pale yellow

---

Tips for Safe, Efficient Use: (cont'd.)

outfit, give her apple juice or lemonade to drink, not grape juice. And carry extra old playclothes in the car so that the unexpected messy play activity can be enjoyed to the max.

Sleepwear Safety

Each year, many children are burned while wearing sleepwear. The CPSC requires that all children's sleepwear through size 14 (and all fabric intended to be made into sleepwear) be made of flame-resistant material. These materials must stop burning after the fire source is removed. Sleepwear is not required to carry a label indicating compliance with the standards, but it must carry a label if its flame resistance is affected by laundering. Today, virtually all U.S. manufacturers meet the standard by using inherently flame-resistant fibers or through fiber construction, rather than by adding flame-retardant chemicals to the fabric. The flame-retardant TRIS, suspected of causing skin cancer, has been banned by CPSC and has not been used on children's sleepwear for over eight years. Daywear for infants and children, including diapers and underwear, are *not* required to meet the sleepwear standards, even though children may sleep in this clothing.

✔ **TIP:** *When washing sleepwear, check the label for any special washing instructions. Some flame-resistant sleepwear cannot be washed with soap products (such as Ivory Snow), since the soap can build up on the product and decrease the effectiveness of the garment's flame resistant properties.*

Keep Kids' Clothes Safe

We were disturbed to learn recently of an effort by some clothing retailers, most notably Hanna Anderson mail order company, to have the federal flammability standards for children's clothes repealed. The CPSC has determined that any clothing that will be used as sleepwear must meet the flammability safety requirements (see discussion above). Because of the growing popularity of cotton

Keep Kids' Clothes Safe (cont'd.)

clothing and the fact that 100% cotton cannot be made to meet the fire safety standards without chemical treatment, the Hanna Anderson Company is distributing a newsletter with their orders encouraging parents to write to their Congressional representatives urging a repeal of the children's sleepwear standard.

We believe their position is misguided and irresponsible. Since the children's sleepwear standards went into effect in the early 1970s, clothing fire deaths of children newborn through age 14 have decreased from 60 to less than five per year. Anecdotal evidence from hospital emergency room personnel who treat child burn victims also supports the benefits of these regulations. Having personally witnessed the CPSC flame tests that demonstrate the burning time difference between cotton and flame resistant materials (in this test cotton garments ignite and burn up in mere seconds), we are further convinced of the need for this standard.

As parents, we understand the desire for soft pajamas; we too want sleepwear for our children that is comfortable. But we also want it to be safe. While some children's sleepwear material is more stiff, we know that brands are available that are soft, comfortable and similar in feel to cotton. Most importantly, they could prevent a death or the pain, suffering and scarring for life that an unexpected nighttime fire could inflict.

We encourage you to support continuation of the children's sleepwear standard and to make your views known to your Representative (his or her name, Washington, D.C. 20515) and Senator (Washington, D.C. 20510). If you are a customer of Hanna Anderson or other companies opposing this life-saving safety standard, we urge you to let them know your views.

Special Clothes

A unique collection of adaptive clothing for children with special clothing needs is offered by a company called *Special Clothes*. Aimed at providing attractive, comfortable, and practical clothing for children with disabilities, these garments contain special adaptations, such as Velcro closures, full snap crotches, bibs, and gastrostomy-tube access openings. The special features are designed to be inconspicuous, helping to preserve the child's dignity and self-confidence. *Special Clothes* will even work with parents to create a special adaptation to solve a particular problem. See Chapter 9, Mail Order Catalogues, for more information.

RECALLED PRODUCTS: Clothing

If more than 18 months have elapsed since the recall date, the manufacturer may no longer honor the recall. If the company refuses to comply, you should discard the product to ensure the safety of your child.

Hush Puppies Sweat Suits

WHICH ONES: 100% acrylic two-piece sweat suits sold at Montgomery Ward stores from August to December 15, 1988. The sweatshirt has a Hush Puppies dog on it. PROBLEM: The decal of the Hush Puppies dog can come loose, releasing a small squeaker, which poses a choking hazard. WHAT TO DO: Return suits to Montgomery Ward store for a full refund or send them to The Haddad Group, Ltd., 90 East 5th Street, Bayonne, NJ 07002 for a full refund plus postage. Write "Recall" on the package. RECALL DATE: 8/89

Mullins Square Baby Bibs, Pants and Panties with Santa Claus or Animal Faces

WHICH ONES: Baby pants and panties distributed during 1988 with a label which read "Mullins Square *** Austin, Texas *** ." Sleeved and non-sleeved bibs distributed before 1989 with no label, and sold for about $9.50 each. PROBLEM: Small plastic eyes pose a choking hazard. WHAT TO DO: Return to point of purchase for a refund. If you have no receipt, the manufacturer will replace the hazardous eyes with safe fabric ones and return the garment to you. RECALL DATE: 5/89

Enclosures

An alternative to the playpen is a portable fence that corrals your child. Enclosures usually don't have a bottom, can be used indoors or out, and offer more space than a playpen. Some enclose up to 37 square feet—a space about six feet by six feet—compared to a typical playpen, which offers nine square feet. In addition to being portable, enclosures can be fun for two or three toddlers. Because they can be used outdoors, they're great for giving the child a feel for the ground at the beach or park. When buying one, try it out first to see how stable it is and how easy it is to set up. These corrals are usually made of plastic or of a combination of wood and wire mesh.

WARNING: *Never, never use an expandable accordion-style enclosure made from criss-crossed slats riveted together to form a continuous circular enclosure. When in use, the slats cross one another and form a series of V-shaped angles at the top and bottom of the enclosure. (See diagram). Deaths and injuries occur when a child's neck becomes trapped in one of the V-shaped angles at the top of the enclosure. Accidents can also result when children put their heads through a diamond-shaped opening formed by the criss-crossed slats of the enclosure. If you own an accordion-style expandable enclosure, do not use it. Throw it away so that others who are unaware of the serious hazards it poses will not be tempted to use it for their children.*

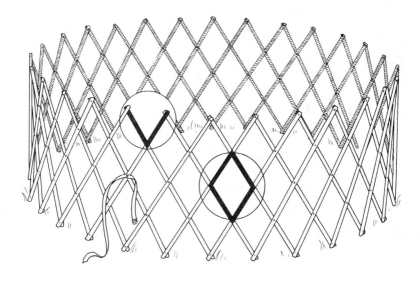

Baby Enclosure
Highlighted areas pose hazards to children, who can easily get their necks trapped in these enclosures.

★ REMEMBER: When Buying an Enclosure

☐ Buy an enclosure that meets the ASTM/JPMA voluntary standard for expandable gates and enclosures to ensure that the spacing of any openings will not entrap your child's head. Look for JPMA seal:

Enclosures

☐ Never purchase or use a *second-hand* wood expandable enclosure.

☐ Carefully review the packaging and instructions to learn whether there are any limitations in installation that will affect your intended use. For example, many models require the use of stakes to anchor the enclosure outdoors.

☐ Check the age guidelines for each model—some enclosures are for children up to 18 months and others for children up to two years of age.

☐ Examine different models to determine how easy they are to set up and transport.

RECALLED PRODUCTS: Enclosures

If more than 18 months have elapsed since the recall date, the manufacturer may no longer honor the recall. If the company refuses to comply, you should discard the product to ensure the safety of your child.

Crawl Space Portable Mesh-Sided Enclosure

WHICH ONES: Gerber Furniture Group model number 14-816 sold from September 1985 to late 1988. The model number is on the instruction sheet and the words "Crawl Space" appear on the vinyl. PROBLEM: Crawl space must be assembled with the metal legs on the outside of the mesh and away from the child, otherwise the child may become caught between the leg-tube and the netting and could suffocate. WHAT TO DO: For more information, warning labels and an instruction sheet showing proper assembly, call Gerber, 1-800-222-9825 or write to Gerber Furniture Group, Inc., 9600 Valley View Road, Macedonia, OH 44056. RECALL DATE: 10/88

Enclosures Made of Wood

WHICH ONES: Enclosures made of criss-crossed wooden slats, which are riveted together and expand to form a corral for baby. They were made by a number of manufacturers and have not been sold for some years. PROBLEM: Children can get their heads trapped in the openings and strangle. WHAT TO DO: Discontinue use and contact Nu-Line Industries at 1-800-558-7300 (in Wisconsin call 414-842-2141 collect) for free pickup and to receive a $10 cash refund or $15 coupon for new products made by Nu-Line, Paris and Northstates Industries. RECALL DATE: 5/86

Tips for Safe, Efficient Use:

1. Be sure to follow the manufacturer's instructions for assembly.
2. An enclosure should never be used for a child older than two years of age, since it may not be capable of withstanding the child's pulling or attempts to climb out. Some enclosures are intended only for children up to 18 months.
3. Do not use an enclosure as a gate. If the ends of the enclosure are not fully connected, your child may be able to push over the enclosure or could become trapped between the enclosure and the furniture or a wall.
4. If you own an accordion-style expandable enclosure, *do not use it* and discard it so that others who are unaware of the serious hazards it poses will not be tempted to use it for their children.

Food

In this era of natural foods, exercise and high fiber diets, parents are reconsidering some of the traditional foods that have been the mainstay of kid's diets. More and more we are concerned about ingredients, toxic reactions and the long term effect of diet on our children's lives. This section will review some of the food issues that you may be concerned about.

Allergies

Experts suggest breast feeding may minimize a child's chance of developing allergies. Toward that end, it is also wise to postpone introduction of solid foods until after the first four to six months. Introduce only one new food at a time and wait five to seven days to check your baby's tolerance. If your baby has a bad reaction to a food, consult your pediatrician or wait one to two months and try the food again. You may also delay introduction of common allergenic foods (wheat, egg white, corn, citrus, fresh milk, chocolate) until after the first year.

Aspartame

As a result of the growing aprehension about food additives, many parents are concerned about the sugar substitute, aspartame. Its brand names are NutraSweet and Equal, and it is showing up in many children's foods.

The Food and Drug Administration officially maintains that the product poses no risks for children. However, some FDA officials believe that aspartame should not be fed to infants.

One problem with aspartame is that it contains a harmful component called phenylalanine. Children who have the inherited disorder phenylketonuria, or PKU, are unable to process foods containing phenylalanine. It is well documented that a high level of phenylalanine can cause irreversible brain damage.

Another hazard associated with aspartame is the fact that it decomposes into diketopiperazine (DKP), methyl alcohol and other chemicals when exposed to heat or after sitting in acidic liquids (such as soft drinks). These chemicals can have toxic, and possibly carcinogenic, effects on humans, especially children. Consumer advocates in Arizona are concerned about the problem, since soft drinks containing aspartame are often left in very warm warehouses before shipping to stores.

It is wise to store any products containing aspartame in a cool place. Parents should consider limiting their children's intake, particularly if any adverse effects, such as headaches, dizziness, hyperactivity, or rashes occur.

Baby Food

The sales of prepared baby food have been growing rapidly. Part of the increase is due to the introduction of convenience foods for toddlers. Gerber calls its version *Chunky Foods* and aims them at children one to three years old.

Beech-Nut has a line of foods, which come in stages, starting with single ingredient foods, going to mixed foods and ending up with mini-bites.

H.J. Heinz Co. offers a line called *Flakes* that sounds like the equivalent of back pack food for babies. Heinz's *Flakes* come in a number of flavors, including mixed vegetables or chicken noodle dinner, and all you do is add water. According to Heinz, they introduced *Flakes* because the company's market research showed that processed baby food buyers don't like jarred products because of waste. Baby food in jars has a refrigerator life of about three days after opening, while the dried instant can be mixed in whatever amount is needed, and the remainder can be stored for two weeks.

There is relatively little price competition on baby foods. The best way to save money is by using coupons and stocking up during sales. The relative similarity in prices allows you to experiment with different brands to see if your infant has any preferences. Don't be afraid to taste the food yourself. If you like the taste of Heinz pears better than Gerber's, chances are your baby will too.

★ REMEMBER: When Buying Baby Food

☐ Examine the top. If the button in the center is curved downward, the jar is vacuum-sealed. The food will stay safe and wholesome on the shelf as long as this seal is intact. If the seal is broken, the circle or button will curve upward, warning you not to use the food.

☐ Check the date printed on the sides of packages of cereal and bakery items, and on top of the cap on baby food jars.

Tips for Safe, Efficient Use:

1. Unopened jars of baby food and strained juices should be stored in a dry, cool place away from steam or heat. Avoid freezing or storage in very cold or warm places.
2. Rotate the jars and packages of baby foods stored at home, using those that have been on hand the longest first.
3. Keep packaged baby cereals away from heat and moisture, and away from soaps, cleaners, drugs and strongly flavored vegetables to prevent them from absorbing strange odors.
4. Just before opening a jar of baby food, check to make sure the circle on the cap is curved downward and the seal has not broken since the jar was brought home. When the cap is removed for the first time, listen for a definite "pop" sound as the vacuum seal is broken.

Tips for Safe, Efficient Use: (cont'd)

5. After opening, baby foods should be refrigerated and used within two to three days.
6. Do not feed your child out of the jar or return leftovers to the jar. Saliva from the baby's spoon contains enzymes that begin to break down starches.
7. When only part of a jar's content is to be used, do not heat the food in the jar. Reheating can spoil the taste and texture and lower the nutritive value of baby food.
8. Beware of heating food in a microwave oven. Uneven heating of these thick products may cause splattering.
9. Test all warmed foods for a comfortable eating temperature before serving.

Baby Food—Homemade

Homemade baby food can save money and give your child an early start on enjoying "grown-up food." During the seventies it was popular to prepare your own baby food. It seems to be less popular now, but if you want to try to prepare your own baby food, keep the following tips in mind:

Tips for Safe, Efficient Use:

1. Use a mini food processor to make quick baby meals from the same foods you will be eating.
2. Select fresh foods and don't overcook them or you will lose nutrients.
3. Do not add salt or seasonings; offer single flavors; avoid mixing foods together, such as two vegetables or two fruits.
4. As with adult food, check the food in the refrigerator regularly to be sure it remains fresh.

Bone Meal

Bone meal is used primarily as a calcium and/or phosphorus supplement. All bone-meal products contain lead because of the diet of the cattle or horses from which the bone is taken. The animal's bone tissue retains lead, which is then passed on to the person consuming the bone-meal product. The FDA has warned that infants, young children and pregnant or nursing mothers should avoid ingesting bone meal in products such as hot dogs and luncheon meat because they often contain substantial amounts of lead.

Another source of calcium is dolomite, a mineral deposit. Dolomite can also contain lead and should be avoided by infants, young children and pregnant or nursing mothers.

Unless specifically recommended by your doctor, bone meal and dolomite should be avoided. Lead is absorbed more efficiently by children than by adults and, when consumed in excess, can produce central nervous system damage, anemia, and abdominal pains, as well as learning disabilities. In large quantities it can cause death.

Choking

Food is a significant cause of choking among children. In fact, the Journal of the American Medical Association published the results of a study that found hot dogs as the food most likely to cause a child to choke. In commenting on the study, one medical expert said the shape of a hot dog is the perfect design for blocking a child's throat.

Every year as many children die of choking on food as do from accidental poisoning, yet many people do not realize how serious the problem is. One study found that over 65 percent of the choking deaths involve children under two. Researchers at the Johns Hopkins University have recommended that warning labels be placed, whenever possible, on the foods most likely to cause choking. According to their research, the ten foods most likely to cause choking are listed in the following table.

Foods That Choke	
Food	**Incidence**
Hot dogs	17
Candy	10
Peanuts/Nuts	9
Grapes	8
Cookies	7
Meat	7
Carrot	6
Apple	5
Popcorn	5
Peanut butter	5
Journal of the American Medical Association	

✔ **TIP:** *Be very, very careful when giving your child little meat sticks or "baby" hot dogs from a jar. They are very easy to choke on.*

The Food and Drug Administration offers the following tips to prevent choking:

☐ Do not give small, hard foods to young children.

☐ Children should eat or drink only in an upright sitting position.

☐ Avoid propping a baby's bottle to enable them to drink by themselves.

☐ Use caution when feeding children who have just been given a topical anesthetic for teething, as it may impair the child's ability to swallow solid foods.

☐ Cut foods into small, **well-cooked** pieces for small children.

☐ Don't leave young children alone when snacking or at mealtime.

WARNING: *After a choking incident, it's important to monitor a child, because tiny fragments of the choking item may remain in the lungs. Except for a faint wheezing noise when the child breathes, there are often no indications of any respiratory problems. If something is trapped in the lungs, they can become inflamed in a few days. Any child who chokes should be examined by a physician to ensure that no fragments remain trapped in his upper respiratory tract.*

Fat

Even though obesity is a growing problem among children, limiting foods with fat and cholesterol for babies may not be the best thing to do. Babies need fat to absorb the fat-soluble vitamins; they need cholesterol to form body and nervous system cells; and they need calories to grow.

Minerals

Some minerals, such as calcium, phosphorus, sodium, chloride, potassium, magnesium and sulfur, are necessary in relatively large amounts in our diet, while others are needed only in trace amounts. Lead, mercury and cadmium, which often are found in our diet, are regarded as harmful. But, even minerals needed by the body are harmful if we absorb too much of them.

If all the potassium required by the body in one day were taken in a single concentrated dose, severe illness could result. Many children under five years of age are hospitalized each year due to iron poisoning caused by accidental ingestion of multiple daily dietary supplements.

Taking too much of one essential mineral may upset the balance and function of other minerals in the body and can contribute to such health problems as anemia, bone demineralization and breakage, neurologic disease and fetal abnormalities. The risks, according to the FDA, are greatest for very young children, pregnant and breast-feeding women, the elderly, and those with inadequate diets or chronic disease.

Gates

Baby gates are used in open doorways and at the bottom and top of stairs to prevent a crawling or walking child from leaving a room or from climbing up or down stairs. Although not a substitute for child-proofing, baby gates are extremely useful in keeping your child from getting "out of bounds."

There are three basic types of gates: accordion style (made of criss-crossed wood slats—see diagram); mesh style (with mesh or netting stretched tightly over frames); and steel-framed swinging style (a two-panel swinging gate made of metal bars or mesh).

WARNING: *Never, never use an expandable accordion style model where a child's head and neck can become trapped if they attempt to crawl through or over the gate. There have been at least eight deaths and 23 near misses involving this type of gate.*

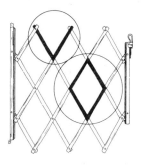

Baby Gate
Avoid using this type of gate. Your child's neck could easily be trapped in the highlighted areas.

The manufacturers of accordion style baby gates halted distribution of this hazardously designed gate in early 1985. In 1987 a voluntary safety standard was developed to address the strangulation hazard posed by these gates. The standard prohibits openings along the top edge of a gate that would admit a child's neck. Openings in the side and under the gate also must prevent entry of a child's head. Gates that meet this standard have a seal on the box, on the in-store display model, or on the product itself. When purchasing a baby gate, make sure it complies with the ASTM/JPMA voluntary safety standard. Because this is a voluntary standard, the manufacturer may not have all of its models certified—make sure the gate you buy bears a seal. Look for this seal:

Baby Gate

★ REMEMBER: When Buying a Gate

☐ *Never* purchase a second-hand accordion style baby gate or use one lent to you. Because these gates were never recalled, there are about 15 million of the hazardous type in use or stored in attics and garages.

☐ Consider where you will be placing the baby gate. Taller models will help keep your child from reaching over the gate to touch something "off limits."

☐ Gates that open to allow you to pass through can make your room to room movement easier and safer.

☐ If purchasing a gate to place at the top of a staircase, make sure it can be anchored into the wall.

Tips for Safe, Efficient Use:

1. Do not use a gate if your child is older than two.
2. Do not use a gate at the top of a stairway, unless it is screwed to the wall. Never use a pressure gate at the top of stairs or any place where a falling hazard may exist.
3. Install the gate according to the manufacturer's installation instructions. Don't improvise.

Tips for Safe, Efficient Use: (cont'd.)

4. Only use the gate with the lock, latch, or pressure bar securely fastened.
5. Never leave your child unattended. The gate will only restrain him and is not intended as a babysitter.
6. If your gate is retained by means of an expanding pressure bar, install it so that this bar is on the side away from your child. Otherwise the child can use the bar to climb over the gate.
7. Before each use check to see that your gate is securely anchored in place.
8. When it is not in use, store the gate away from your toddler's play area.

High Chairs

After the crib, the high chair is probably one of the most used baby products you will buy. This seat will become very important to your little one as he associates it with his daily sustenance, and eventually learns to feed himself. In the past 30 years, high chair styles have gone full circle, from wood to metal to plastic and back to wood. Today's models are constructed of a mixture of materials and feature larger wrap-around trays.

High chair safety is important since mishaps are surprisingly common—each year more than 8000 injuries require hospital emergency care. Most of these injuries occur when children are not securely strapped in and fall from the high chair. The chair can also fall or collapse on the child. While pinching and entrapment might not sound very serious, they can be for tiny hands, feet, and fingers. This piece of equipment must bear three years of tough daily use, so it's worth some careful thought before you buy. Luckily, high chair manufacturers themselves are helping out, by setting their own safety standards.

In order to be certified to meet the ASTM/JPMA voluntary safety standard, a high chair *must* meet general requirements (such as not containing any hazardous edges), and it must pass several tests, including drop tests of the tray, and load and stability tests of the chair. The standard also requires that dangerous coil springs be inaccessible and offer protection from pinching and scissoring. Each chair must have a restraint system and complete label and instructions.

✔ **TIP:** *If your child slips around on the seat of the chair, try attaching rough-surfaced adhesive strips to the seat.*

★ **REMEMBER: When Buying a High Chair**

☐ Purchase a highchair that meets the ASTM/JPMA voluntary safety standard for high chairs.

☐ Because a manufacturer may *not* have *all* of its different high chair models certified, you should look for the seal on the box, in-store display model or product itself when shopping. Look for this seal:

JUVENILE PRODUCTS MANUFACTURERS ASSOCIATION

CERTIFIED

THIS MODEL TESTED BY AN INDEPENDENT LABORATORY FOR COMPLIANCE TO ASTM F-404 SAFETY STANDARDS FOR HIGH CHAIRS

☐ Look for a high chair that has a wide base for stability.

☐ Make sure the high chair has some system for restraining your child. Pull on these straps and their buckles to test their sturdiness. Remember that the restraint system will be used several times a day. We prefer safety restraints that use a plastic quick-fasten buckle rather than the more difficult D- rings, which require threading the restraint strap for each use. The restraint should also have a crotch strap that can help prevent your child from sliding out the bottom of the chair.

Tips for Safe, Efficient Use:

1. Never leave your child unattended in a high chair.
2. A high chair should be used only for children who are capable of sitting upright unassisted.
3. Always secure your child in the restraint system. The tray is *not* intended as a restraint. Children have strangled and died when, secured by the tray alone, they slipped down in the seat catching their head on the tray. This is sometimes called submarining entrapment and has resulted in numerous deaths.
4. If you are using an older chair without a restraint, purchase one with a crotch strap.

Tips for Safe, Efficient Use: (cont'd.)

5. Be sure that the tray is locked properly each time you place your child in the chair.
6. If you have a folding high chair, make sure the locking device is secure each time you set it up.
7. Place the high chair on a level surface and away from any tables, counters, walls or other obstructions your child could push off against.
8. To avoid pinching, check to see where your child's hands are before you attach or detach the tray.
9. Do not let children play around the high chair, climb into it unassisted, or allow older children to hang onto a high chair while a baby is in it.
10. When not using the high chair, place it out of the way. If it folds up, put it someplace where it can not be knocked over.
11. Periodically clean the chair, its restraint system and other parts. Liquid and food particles can interfere with the locking mechanisms and cause deterioration of the restraint system.
12. It is important to check older model high chairs to see that restraint straps, locks, and trays are still sturdy and work properly.

WARNING: *Observe these precautions in restaurants. A study in one metropolitan area found that only 60 percent of the high chairs in restaurants had a restraining system. Carry your own safety harness to use when away from home and encourage the proprietors of restaurants you visit to provide restraints. (See hook-on chairs following.)*

Hook-On Chairs

A hook-on chair is a portable, legless high chair that hooks directly onto a table. The child's weight helps holds the chair in place. Because of the seats' clever design, the child is actually seated at the table and thus is more involved in the family meal. Because they are so convenient and portable, they are great for travel and restaurants.

There should be no problem using these chairs as long as the chair itself and the table are strong and sturdy and the restraint system is used. Injuries associated with this product occur when the chair falls because the child pushes off the table, chair components detach or break, or the table to which the chair is attached tips over.

As with a regular high chair, a hook-on chair should be used for children who are capable of sitting upright unassisted. Two hook-on chairs that we particularly like are the Sassy Seat Executive and the Graco Tot-Loc Chair.

There are different designs of hook-on chairs: some seats are permanently assembled and fold up for storage; others have cloth seats attached to a metal frame; and still others have plastic and metal parts that snap together.

★ REMEMBER: When Buying a Hook-on Chair

☐ Only buy a chair that has locks or clamps that tighten to the underside of the table and *does not* snap together. Both of these criteria are critically important!

☐ Make sure the chair has some system for restraining your child. Most chairs have some type of waist belt, but should also have a crotch bar or strap to prevent the child from sliding out the bottom of the chair.

✔ **TIP:** *A voluntary safety standard for hook-on chairs has been developed that requires an adequate safety belt and will help prevent the chair from easily being pushed off the table or coming apart. Manufacturers are expected to begin certifying that their products comply with that standard in May 1991. When purchasing a hook-on chair after that time, look for the ASTM/JPMA seal to assure that the chair meets this important safety standard.*

WARNING: *Older chairs that only have a crotch bar type of restraint can be dangerous, since they do not prevent your child from climbing out the top.*

Tips for Safe, Efficient Use:

1. Never leave a child unattended and always use the restraint strap.
2. Do not use on glass, loose top or pedestal tables. Also, do not use on card tables nor hook chair onto the leaf of a table.
3. Do not use with placemats and tablecloths—they can significantly reduce the holding power of the tips or suction cups.
4. Check the stability of your table before seating your child. If your child is able to rock the table once seated, don't use the seat on that table.
5. Do not use without all four tips (or suction cups) attached securely and resting on the table surface. Removal of just one can cause the chair to slide and move and may cause the chair to cut or pinch your child's fingers.
6. If your chair has set locks or clamps, be sure they are firmly set before placing your child in the chair. Always remove your child before releasing the locks or clamps.
7. If your chair snaps together, be sure that all parts of the seat are fastened firmly. If your child is capable of unsnapping chair parts, discontinue use.
8. Never place an ordinary chair under the hook-on chair. Your child could attempt to stand on the chair and push the hook-on chair away from the table.
9. For similar reasons, do not place the hook-on chair on counters or near other obstructions that could be used by your child to push away from the counter or table.
10. Do not allow other children or animals under the hook-on chair while it is in use. Either could cause the chair to lift upward and fall off the table.
11. Discontinue use if child can bounce or move the chair up and down or move the chair arms on the table top when sitting in it.
12. To avoid twisting your child's legs, check to see that his legs are free from the chair supports before removing him from the chair.

Tips for Safe, Efficient Use: (cont'd.)

13. While the chair may be tested by the manufacturer to withstand loads of 65 pounds or more, you probably should discontinue use of the chair when your child reaches 30 pounds. Most hook-on chair accidents investigated by the CPSC involved children weighing 20 pounds or more.
14. Check your hook-on chair periodically to see that it is clean and dry, that any clamps or locks still function properly, that all the suction cups or tips still are securely in place, and that any assembly screws are fully tightened.
15. Discontinue use if the chair is broken. Contact the manufacturer for replacement parts or service.

Humidifiers

Portable humidifiers increase moisture in the air. While they are traditionally used to relieve congestion, it's important to realize that experts differ on the benefits of using humidifiers. There is evidence that improper use may actually exacerbate your child's condition by exposing him to microbiological agents and particulates being spewed forth in the mist. Many pediatricians agree that a humidifier may help a child with croup, but children with allergies, asthma and the common cold may be at increased risk as a result of exposure to "dirty" humidifier mist. Some doctors advise letting a cold run its course without a humidifier. Since this may be a product you can very well do without, we recommend that you consult with your pediatrician before purchase.

There are three types of portable humidifiers:

Electric steam vaporizers heat water and release steam into the air. These are the least expensive of the three, but they are risky products to use around young children. If the container of boiling water is accidentally tipped over or a child gets too close to the steam port, severe burns may result. These steam vaporizers are noisy and may make the room uncomfortably warm.

Cool-mist humidifiers use a motor to force water droplets into an aerosol. Although cool-mist humidifiers do not present a potential burn hazard, the container of water can serve as a reservoir for bacteria, fungi, and molds. These germs are dispersed throughout the room in the aerosol mist emitted from the humidifier. Scum on the tank, on exposed motor parts, or on the filter is a sure sign that the unit is contaminated and in need of a thorough cleaning.

Ultrasonic humidifiers create mist using high-frequency vibrations. They do not disperse living germs in the mist, because the droplets created by this type of unit are much smaller than those dispersed by the cool-mist humidifiers. These tiny droplets can contain minerals that are present in the water, as well as bacteria and molds, which could cause problems for persons sensitive to molds. A fine white dust on surfaces in the area near the humidifier is evidence of this problem. Although most minerals in water are non-toxic, there is concern that breathing these particulates may aggravate existing respiratory conditions. Some scientists are also concerned that this humidifier dust may contain lead, asbestos, and radon present in the water. Finally, some physicians believe ultrasonic humidifiers increase the risk of pneumonia, since the tiny droplets can be drawn into the lungs.

Portable humidifiers range in price from $15.00 for cool mist humidifiers to $150.00 for ultrasonic humidifiers. Beware of the ultrasonic humidifiers designed for children's rooms (some look like trains or have little ducks swimming in the reservoir). *This product is not intended to amuse your child!*

★ REMEMBER: When Buying A Humidifier

☐ Look for units with a "humidistat" that automatically turns the machine on and off to keep humidity at desirable levels.

☐ Purchase a unit that can be easily cleaned. Check to see that you can easily reach into the reservoir to scrub the insides.

☐ Examine the filters—are they easily cleanable, removable for replacement; how often do filters have to be replaced, and how much do they cost?

Tips for Safe, Efficient Use:

1. Read the instructions carefully for use before operating.
2. Change the water in the humidifier tank daily, emptying the tank before you refill it.
3. Use bottled distilled water or demineralized water to fill the humidifier tank. Tap water contains more minerals than distilled or demineralized water. If the manufacturer provides demineralization filters, use them and replace them as necessary.
4. Clean the humidifiers often, following the manufacturer's instructions. Unplug the unit before cleaning it. The CPSC recommends that portable humidifiers be emptied *daily*. All surfaces that come in contact with water should be scrubbed, using a three percent solution of hydrogen peroxide. Rinse the tank thoroughly after cleaning. If you use a diluted solution of household chlorine bleach to clean the tank (one half cup bleach to one gallon water), as some manufacturers recommend, be sure to rinse it thoroughly. Avoid using other chemical cleaners. To avoid respiratory irritation, which could result from incomplete rinsing after chemical cleaning, some experts recommend scrubbing the inside surfaces of the humidifier with a pot scrubber and rinsing thoroughly afterwards.
5. Clean sponge filters or replace them when dirty.
6. Before storing a humidifier, make sure it is thoroughly cleaned and dried. When using a humidifier, leave your child's bedroom door open, particularly if it's an ultrasonic humidifier.

Playpens

Attitudes towards playpens vary. In the fifties and sixties they were a fixture in every home. In the seventies they fell out of fashion for being too confining and "prison like." The eighties saw them come back, as busy parents needed to buy a little time to get things done without fear of having their child get into trouble.

If you want to use a playpen during the crawling age, it is almost imperative to begin using it when your child is very young. If she becomes accustomed to the playpen as a special resting or play area, your child won't feel "jailed" when you need to cut off her roaming and exploring for safety's sake. Favorite toys saved just for playpen time also help make it a fun place and distract an unwilling occupant.

Playpens come in three basic sizes: 36-inch and 40-inch squares and rectangular shapes. Many of the rectangular playpens, which are also advertised as portable cribs, offer considerably less playing space. Square playpens (both 36 inch and 40 inch) range in price from $50 to $70; rectangular playpens/portable cribs cost up $100 and some fit through a doorway. If you have the space, the extra inches provided by the 40-inch model will give your child more play space and less of a feeling of being cooped up.

We recommend that you only buy playpens certified to meet the ASTM/JPMA voluntary safety standard for play yards. This means the top rail height is high enough to contain an 18 month old child; there are no sharp edges or protrusions; there is a locking device to prevent accidental folding; the drop-side cannot be lowered by a child; caps and plugs must be difficult for a child to pull off and must be able to hold sufficient weight to sustain hard and active use.

The playpen safety standard does not take into account the fact that the product may also be used as a crib, as many of the rectangular models advertise. Cribs are designed to meet standards for unsupervised use (at night when your child is asleep), whereas the playpen, as described in the safety standard, is intended for use by a supervised child no more than 18 months old.

WARNING: *The most crucial safety factor to keep in mind when using a mesh-sided playpen is* never *to leave your child in it with the drop-side down. The folded drop-side creates a suffocation hazard for any baby who may roll into the space between the pad or mattress and loose mesh side. Also, never tie any item across the top of the playpen, including crib gyms, as these can pose a strangulation hazard.*

Meshsided Playpen
Never leave the drop-side of a mesh playpen down. An infant could easily roll into the space between the pad and mesh and suffocate.

If using an older, used playpen, check mesh sides to see that the mesh has a small weave and that there are no holes. These can easily stretch and catch a child's buttons and strangle her. On older wooden playpens, make sure the slats are no more than 2-⅜ inches apart to avoid head entrapment. Check the vinyl or fabric-covered top rail of the playpen for holes and tears— your child could chew off pieces and possibly choke. Make sure the pad can not be easily lifted allowing a child to catch fingers or hands in holes in the floorboard.

★ REMEMBER: When Buying a Playpen

☐ Look for a playpen that meets the ASTM/JPMA voluntary safety standard for playpens (playyards). Because a manufacturer may *not* have *all* of the different playpen models in its line certified, you should look for this seal on the product, its packaging or the display model.

☐ If you plan to buy a wooden playpen, look for one that has spaces between slats no more than 2-⅜ inches in wide.

☐ If purchasing a mesh side playpen, look for mesh netting with a very small weave (less than ¼ inch by ¼ inch) that will not be able to catch on small children's buttons or other decorative features on children's clothing.

Tips for Safe, Efficient Use:

1. *Never* leave an infant in a mesh playpen with the drop-side down. Even when you're not using the playpen, keep the drop-side up and locked into position. Your child may try to climb back into the playpen and can cut or pinch his fingers on the unlocked hinge mechanism.

2. Unlike a crib, this product is not intended to be used without supervision. Do not leave your child unattended in a playpen.

3. Do not place boxes, bumper pads or large toys in the playpen. Your child can use them as steps for climbing out.

4. Never tie any item across the top of the playpen as it can be a strangulation hazard. Any toys attached to the playpen's sides should have very short straps (six inches or less) so that they can not wrap around your child's neck.

5. Regularly check the vinyl or fabric-covered rails for holes and tears since this is a favorite chewing spot for teething children. The vinyl or the padding below it can be bitten off and cause children to choke. Recover or repair these holes and tears with non-toxic materials, such as plastic tape.

6. Make sure all staples used to attach the mesh side to the floor plate of the playpen are not missing or loose. Check the stitching frequently and repair loose threads.

7. Also check for holes in the mesh sides. Never use a playpen whose mesh sides contain holes, as these could entrap a child's head and cause strangulation. Because mesh stretches, even small holes can be dangerous.

Tips for Safe, Efficient Use: (cont'd.)

8. Carefully remove the "law tag" found on the playpen pad. The consumer (in every state) is allowed to remove this tag, which is required by some state laws to be placed on bedding products. These tags pose a choking hazard to children who pull them off and put them in their mouths. As children attempt to tear these tags off, they can also tear the vinyl or cloth of the mattress pad.
9. Discontinue use of the playpen when your child is 18 months old, or sooner if she is persistent in trying to climb out.
10. Day care providers should check the safety of their playpens (including items above) on a regular basis, since the wear and tear on these products is significantly greater than in home use.

RECALLED PRODUCTS: Playpens

If more than 18 months have elapsed since the recall date, the manufacturer may no longer honor the recall. If the company refuses to comply, you should discard the product to ensure the safety of your child.

Circus America Playpens

WHICH ONES: Meshside playpens distributed since November 1984, with a label on the floorboard which says "Art.585, Circus America Ex.". PROBLEM: These playpens present a suffocation hazard if the drop-side is left down, a finger crushing hazard in the folded drop-side locking system, and a choking hazard in the removable plastic feet. WHAT TO DO: Call C & T International at 201-896-2555 (C & T will not accept collect calls) for a free modification kit. RECALL DATE: 5/88

Small Wonders Play Yards

WHICH ONES: Playpen Models 286 and 391. PROBLEM: Playpen could trap a child's arms or legs if the floor collapses, and staples could cut or choke children. WHAT TO DO: Discontinue use and destroy playpen. It should not be used again. Company is bankrupt, so no recall available.

Riding Toys

Learning to scoot around on a riding toy is a delightful experience for a young toddler and helps them develop their gross motor skills. In addition, after a few falls and bumps, they'll get some valuable lessons in cause and effect! Riding toys are four and three-wheeled vehicles that children straddle or sit on and propel with their feet. Once a child learns to walk she is capable of learning to push with her feet from a straddling position.

Riding toys come in all shapes, sizes and materials. Some look like animals and others resemble cars, fire engines or other vehicles. They range in price from $15 to over $100.

A word of caution about riding toys. The Consumer Product Safety Commission (CPSC) reports that riding toys have been involved in numerous fatalities—primarily when children ride them into the paths of vehicles or into pools. In fact, riding toys are associated with more injuries than any other type of toy.

Another category of riding toys are electric- powered vehicles. These can range from the "D" cell battery-powered cars and trucks from Combi ($30-33) to the fully featured dream machines found in F.A.O. Schwartz which can cost up to $500! We believe these should be last on your list of riding toy purchases. As one parent said, "These are riding toys for couch potato kids." The models we've observed at friends' homes seem prone to breakdowns and after the initial thrill wears off, they are often shunted aside.

WARNING: *Battery-powered cars that go 2-5 mph may seem like they would be a lot of fun for your child, but they can be "unsafe at any speed." Tipping over at these relatively low speeds could result in severe injuries to little ones. We don't recommend these products.*

RECOMMENDED PRODUCTS: Riding Toys

The Cozy Coupe by Little Tikes

This two-seater coupe with its bright yellow roof is the BMW of the two- to three-year-old set! It has the unique quality of being one of the few toys that kids love at other children's homes *and still love* when you buy one for your family!

The Little Clang Along Fire Engine by Combi Industries.

This is another great rider for the younger set. This red plastic fire engine has a steering wheel that beeps, a phone, a bell that rings, and a seat that lifts up to reveal a storage compartment for blocks, small stuffed animals and other treasures. A key feature of the Combi fire engine is the grab bar at the back which helps early walkers take their first stroll. This versatile toy costs less than $20!

RECALLED PRODUCTS: Riding Toys

If more than 18 months have elapsed since the recall date, the manufacturer may no longer honor the recall. If the company refuses to comply, you should discard the product to ensure the safety of your child.

Big Wheel Ride-On Toys

WHICH ONES: Battery-operated toys sold from 1986 through 1988 called Kawasaki KLT 250 Prairie Big Wheel (item numbers 1215, 1220 and 1223) and Sweet-Tee-Nuff Big Wheel (item number 1221). PROBLEM: The "ON" switch, located on the handlebar, can overheat and may burn a child's hand or become stuck, causing loss of control, (the toy should stop when the button is released). WHAT TO DO: Call Empire of Carolina 800-334-5666 (919-823-4111 in North Carolina) for a free replacement switch and handlebar. This repair is necessary even for a previously replaced switch. Have the model name and number when calling. RECALL DATE: 6/89

CBS "Wonder" Spring Ride On Horses

WHICH ONES: Clippety-Clop, Comanche and Colt ride-on toy horses with a plastic body suspended by four springs from a metal frame, sold from March 1984 to May 1986. Model number 86206 or lower is stamped the horses' belly. PROBLEM: The body of the toy may break without warning. WHAT TO DO: Discontinue use and call Service Concepts International at 800-227-3378 for return and replacement instructions. (714-836-4981 in California) The firm will not accept collect calls. RECALL DATE: 10/87

Schaper Speed Wheels Ride-On Toy

WHICH ONES: Model number 61106 sold in 1986. The model number is only on the box. PROBLEM: This model has no pedal bar guard, leaving the shaft from the pedal to the steering shaft exposed, presenting a severe laceration hazard. WHAT TO DO: Call Tyco at 800-257-7728 (800-322-8011 in New Jersey) to request a free protective pedal guard. RECALL DATE: 4/88

Shoes

Purchasing your child's first pair of shoes is a momentous event! Somehow shoes on your little one make her look like a "big person" and it's often difficult to tell who is more excited about the event, you or your child! Here are the facts, as well as some veteran parents' opinions, about children's shoes.

Pediatricians generally agree that your child should begin wearing shoes when he begins walking. Some qualify this recommendation by saying that shoes should be worn when children begin walking on surfaces that hurt their feet. So unless your youngster is going to walk only indoors on surfaces that are always clean, shoes are a necessity when walking begins. Going barefoot on carpet or sand, however, is good for muscle development and strengthening ankles.

It's not really important if your child's first shoes are high *or* low tops or leather, *or* even sneakers. What is important is the shoe's flexibility. Hightop leather shoes were the standard in the fifties and sixties because they were thought to provide more support, but now they are just one of many available choices. They are more difficult than other shoes for your child to take off, and many parents see that as an advantage.

Obviously you'll want to have your child's feet measured in a children's shoe department or in a store experienced in measuring children's feet. The shoes should not fit too snugly and should allow room for growth. Check to see that they are half an inch longer than the longest toe (not always the big toe). If you can't feel toes, then the shoe is too hard. The shoe should fit the heel and should be wide enough so that sides are not bulging.

In the early years your child may outgrow shoes as often as every two to four months! Ignore the temptation to buy shoes too big, as they'll cause tripping and allow the foot to slide in the shoe, causing blisters. When your child outgrows his shoes, discard them. Each person's foot is different, and shoes mold to each child's feet. The expensive truth about children's shoes is that they are more often outgrown than outworn.

They may be small, but they're not inexpensive. Be prepared to spend between $25 and $50 per pair of shoes. Like adult shoes, cheaper children's shoes may not wear as well. However, we know some parents that think that "Balloons" from Thom McCann are comparable to some of the pricier sneakers available. If price is a concern, do your own shoe test! Most parents find they can get by with one pair of shoes at a time (per size). A pair of low-top all white sneakers (touched up occasionally with white shoe polish) can get you through with most outfits, for dress or play. If party shoes are a must, consider a more inexpensive pair if they will not be used very often.

When we asked parents what kind of children's tennis shoes they preferred, several parents responded simply, "Anything with velcro!" We're sure there are probably tie shoe aficionados out there too. One advantage of velcro—your child can put on their shoes all by themselves. But what they can put on, they can usually take off too. The "putting on" advantage probably outweighs the "taking off" disadvantage, particularly as your child enters her twos and threes. A child's ability to tie shoes varies, but certainly, on average, not before age four or five. This is probably an area where you'll develop your own preference.

There were some clear brand favorites among the parents we asked about children's tennis shoe/sneaker preferences. Stride Rite (including their sneaker "Zips") is clearly a popular choice; as are Reeboks (and Weeboks), Nike and Keds. (See our reference above about Thom McCann.)

★ REMEMBER: When Buying Shoes

☐ Avoid shoes that are stiff and do not permit the foot muscles to move naturally.

☐ Avoid shoes with slipper soles, pointy toes, raised heels, or that are plastic and prevent air circulation.

☐ Check to see that the shoe is about a half inch longer than the largest toe.

WARNING: *Before buying corrective shoes, talk to your pediatrician. She or he will be able to assess your child's feet and will refer you to a specialist if needed. Be extremely skeptical of salespersons who try to point out problems in your child's feet and recommend a corrective shoe. Leave this judgment to the expert and professional you trust.*

Tableware

In the past few years hundreds of knives, forks, spoons, cups, bowls, and plates designed specifically for children have come on the market. This cutlery is designed to fit tiny hands, and the dishware is often crafted to minimize spills and prevent food from sliding off the plate.

We recommend plates with high rims that will help your child capture his food as he chases it to the side of the plate. Good bowls for the very young will have suction cup bottoms and lips that turn inward to help push food onto the spoon.

The best cups have large handles, large or weighted bases and a removable, screw on cover that minimizes spills when the child is just learning to use a cup. Look for lids with only an opening for the child to drink out of. Some lids have an additional small hole to allow air in as the child is drinking. Unfortunately, this design also allows the liquid to pour out if the cup is tipped over or dropped on the floor—as it will be thousands of times! Without the extra hole, your child will still be able to get a mouthful and not get too much if he is just learning to drink from a cup.

For everyday use, look for heavy plastic plates, bowls and cups with a colorful design. They will last until you're ready to use regular tableware and are durable enough to be passed on.

✔ **TIP:** *When purchasing these items, check to see that they are dishwasher safe and that they are the appropriate size for your child's hands.*

Toy Chests and Boxes

Toy chests are an ideal way to control the chaos and simplify clean up, but since kids often use them when no one is watching, they also conceal some surprising hazards. Most dangerous are the particularly large, often cumbersome lid's of many older chests. Accidents typically occur when a small child attempts to open the lid himself or use the chest to pull himself up. The lid then falls from the upright, open position, causing a bump or bruise. Sadly, these lids have also caused some extremely serious injuries and have even resulted in death. A tragic accident could also occur if a child climbs into an airtight chest to hide or sleep.

All these problems can be avoided with a little foresight and common sense. We like the toy chests from Little Tikes. They are made of tough plastic and have a lightweight, removable lid.

★ REMEMBER: When Buying a Toy Chest

☐ Look for open chests or bins that have no lids, chests with lightweight, removable lids, or chests with sliding doors or panels.

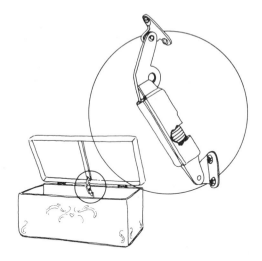

Toy Chest Hinge
Make sure your toy chest has a lid support which will prevent the lid from falling and hurting children or trapping them inside the chest.

☐ If the chest has a hinged lid, be sure that it is lightweight and has a special hinge that will hold it open and not slam shut under its own weight. *How the lid functions is the most important toy chest consideration, since more than 20 children have died as a result of hazardous free-falling chest lids.* The lid support should prevent the lid from falling and pinching your child.

☐ Look for a lid with a flat inner surface. There is some evidence that a lid with protrusions or recessed areas on the inner side may make it more difficult for children to get free should the lid close on them.

☐ Avoid metal chests with sharp edges and check for splinters on wooden boxes. Rounded and padded edges and corners are desirable features.

☐ Look for ventilation in the lid and at least one side or a lid that cannot close completely.

☐ Do not buy a toy chest with a lock or latch.

Tips for Safe, Efficient Use:

1. Carefully select where you place the toy chest in your home. Avoid heavily travelled areas, and don't push it flush against the wall, blocking ventilation.

2. Don't place the chest near stairways.

3. Keep the area around the chest clear to avoid falls.

4. Make sure the surface under the toy chest is secure. For example, do not place the chest next to a throw rug or on a waxed surface.

5. Don't allow children to run around or jump off of the toy chest.

6. If you install a lid support device, it should be periodically checked to make certain that it is clean and functioning properly.

7. Examine the toy chest regularly to see if protective padding has worn away or if rough or sharp areas have developed.

8. If you already own a toy chest with a free falling lid, you should either completely remove the lid or install a lid support to hold the lid open in any position.

You can order the safety lid support hinge from the following companies: Carlson Capitol Manufacturing Company, P.O. Box 6165, Rockford, Illinois 61125 ($6.50 per lid support); and Counter Balance Support Company, 4788 Colt Road, Rockford, Illinois 61125, (815) 874-7211 ($4.50 per lid support plus $2.00 shipping/ handling charges.)

You must inform the company of supply the length, width and weight of your toy chest lid. Rather than guess the weight, remove the lid and place it on your bathroom scale for a good estimate. The support hinges come with instructions and require installation.

Toys

Toy safety *is* a major problem. Government statistics report that each year over 125,000 children are injured seriously enough by toys to require an emergency room visit.

The following are the typical causes of toy related injuries to children under five:

Small Parts

Toys with small, removable parts may pose a serious hazard to the curious toddler. These parts may cause choking, aspiration, or ingestion injuries. Pieces of toys should not be small enough to be swallowed, or should be securely attached, especially on toys for children under three. (See Chapter Three for more on the small parts hazard.)

Sharp Points and Edges

Toys with sharp points or edges, or those which will have such edges if broken by foreseeable misuse, should not be given to children under eight.

Loud Noises

Toys that produce loud noises, such as caps or toy guns, may permanently impair a child's hearing.

Propelled Objects

Propelled objects, such as toy darts and projectiles, should have soft, non-removable rubber or cork ends to prevent eye injury.

Electric Toys

In general, children under eight should not have sophisticated electric toys. Other items, like tape recorders and battery operated toys should be checked regularly for loose or exposed wires.

See Chapter Three for more on toy safety.

Toy Tips for Six to Twelve Month Olds

Balls

Good for bouncing, kicking, rolling and chasing. GOOD CHOICES: A large ball is good for rolling back and forth, and teaching the game of catch. Soft balls are easy to grab. Avoid any ball smaller than an adult fist.

Books

Provide visual and audio enjoyment as well as time together. GOOD CHOICES: Interactive books that have different activities on each page are good as are heavy cardboard or cloth books with simple, bright pictures. Books with simple rhymes are also favorites.

Doll or Stuffed Animal

Serves as both a friend and companion. GOOD CHOICES: Buy washable ones that don't have small parts that can be chewed or pulled off. A doll that can go in the bath is also an excellent choice.

Playboard

Teaches cause and effect and motor skills. GOOD CHOICES: Make sure it is sturdy and has components of varying difficulty. Look for one with short straps for attachment.

Rolling toys

Gives practice making things go. GOOD CHOICES: Look for a toy that is colorful, moves easily, stays upright, and makes noise.

Roly-poly toys

Teaches cause and effect and the realization that baby can make things happen. Best used when child can sit up. GOOD CHOICES: Find a toy that is large, visually interesting, and has a pleasant sound. Bright colored musical clowns are good.

Toy Tips for Twelve to Twenty-Four Month Olds

Blocks

Provide the fun of building, teaches differences in size and—the best part—gives baby a chance to knock things down (cause and effect). GOOD CHOICES: To help teach sizes and shapes, buy blocks that have a uniform color for each shape. Also, blocks that fit together help teach size relationships.

Books

Help teach new sounds and words. GOOD CHOICES: All-time favorites are colorful, with simple, familiar pictures. Books that rhyme are fun to listen to.

Fit-together toys

Provide a sense of accomplishment and teach relationships between sizes and shapes. GOOD CHOICES: Pegboards, building blocks, and puzzles that do not contain small parts. Designs should offer varying degrees of difficulty so the toy will hold interest longer. Duplo blocks by Lego are great for 18- to 24-month-old children and will hold their interest for a number of years.

Pounding toys

Pounding is fun and helps relieve frustration. GOOD CHOICES: Make sure pounding toys are well made. Finished wood is better than plastic; it lasts longer, and won't break as easily. Avoid pounding toys that use balls, as this size ball poses a choking hazard.

Push-and-pull toys

Make walking more fun. GOOD CHOICES: Push-toys that make noise or play music are more fun than pull-toys for beginning walkers. They are easier to use and can be watched. Pull-toys are harder to get the knack of and the string can get wrapped around a child's neck.

Ride-on toys

Helps develop balance and a sense of self control. GOOD CHOICES: Look for sturdy ride-ons that have a grab bar for pushing. Steering wheels, gas caps, and places to carry other toys will add to the fun.

Shape toys

Children love to put one thing inside another. GOOD CHOICES: Stacking cups can also be used to empty and fill with sand or water.

RECALLED PRODUCTS: Toys

If more than 18 months have elapsed since the recall date, the manufacturer may no longer honor the recall. If the company refuses to comply, you should discard the product to ensure the safety of your child.

Animal Squeeze Toys

WHICH ONES: Animal shaped squeeze toys with long handles and flared ends. The initial recall was instituted in 1982, however the recent death of a five month old infant from one of these toys has spurred the Consumer Product Safety Commission to alert the public again to the danger. The animal shapes include a pink elephant, a yellow bear and an orange lion. The toys have long handles and built in squeekers. PROBLEM: The handle can lodge in an infant's throat and cause choking. WHAT TO DO: Destroy the toy. RECALL DATE: 4/89

Animal Voices Musical Toys

WHICH ONES: Model number 670508B packaged in pairs on a pink card labeled 2 PC animal voices 1986 Summco International Ltd.

PROBLEM: Small parts present a choking hazard. WHAT TO DO: Return to Toys-R-Us for full refund. RECALL DATE: 4/89

Baby's First Squeeze Toy

WHICH ONES: Toys shaped like a telephone receiver, barbell, dumbbell, baseball, basketball, or soccer ball. PROBLEM: The squeakers may come out and could cause young children to choke. WHAT TO DO: Return to any K Mart store for a full refund. RECALL DATE: 10/88

Calderon Stuffed Animal Mobile

WHICH ONES: Mobiles in the shape of toucans, giraffes, pelicans, elephants, ducks and penguins. PROBLEM: When hung within the reach of an infant, the nylon cord could cause strangulation. One death has already been reported. WHAT TO DO: Take the mobile away from children and cut the nylon cord and springs off. Send them to Calderon Co., Inc. 480 Forest Avenue, Locust Valley, NY 11560 for a free plush toy in return. RECALL DATE: 9/87

First Years Squeaky Ducky Toy

WHICH ONES: Sold between April 1985 and March 1987 with item number 2096 on the front of the package. The 5x2-inch toy has a yellow baby duck on a blue background. PROBLEM: The vinyl which covers the soft foam toy can separate from the foam causing a choking hazard. WHAT TO DO: Return toy to Consumer Relations Manager, Kiddie Products, Inc., One Kiddie Drive, Avon, MA 02322, for a replacement. For further information, call the company toll-free at 800-225-0382 (in MA call 508-588-1220 collect). RECALL DATE: 9/88

Sesame Street Cookie Monster

WHICH ONES: 28-inch toys are made of blue plush fur with model number 14087. Sold from May to December 1988 and with Made in Korea attached to the derriere. PROBLEM: The large eyes of the toy shatter easily, allowing small pellets to fall out and cause a choking hazard. WHAT TO DO: Return to store where purchased for a full refund or call Applause 1-800-777-3998 between 8:30 a.m. and 4:30 p.m. (Pacific time). RECALL DATE: 8/89

Slinky Pull Toys

WHICH ONES: Those sold from 1986 to May 1989 with red and white cords. Recalled models include white trains; green frogs; red and yellow worms; pink or blue kittens; and blue seals. PROBLEM: The red paint used on these products contains lead at levels which exceed government regulations. WHAT TO DO: Return to store where purchased for a replacement or refund or return to James Industries Inc., Beaver Street Extension, Hollidaysburg, PA 16648. The company will reimburse shipping costs. RECALL DATE: 11-89

Stuffed Teddy Bear

WHICH ONES: Bears in assorted colors measuring 26 inches tall and nine inches wide with tag on the side that reads "Toycraft Industries, Inc., Brooklyn, NY, Stuffed Toys for Tots and Teens." PROBLEM: The eyes and nose come off the bear and present a choking hazard. WHAT TO DO: Return bear to point of purchase for a full refund. For questions, call Toycraft 718-788-2900. RECALL DATE: 6/88

Toy Stuffed Bears

WHICH ONES: Imported by Superior Toy & Novelty Corp and distributed by Nike through Mervyn's Department Store (AZ, CO, CA, LA, NV, NM, OK, OR, TX, UT, WA). PROBLEM: The toy violates the small parts standard and could be a choking hazard. WHAT TO DO: Return bear to Mervyn's to receive credit on next purchase of Nike footwear or call Mervyn's customer service collect at 415-786-7000. RECALL DATE: 11/86

Walkers

The walker is probably the most controversial of baby products. The problem is the astonishingly high number of injuries associated with baby walker use. Each year more than 20,000 children are treated in hospital emergency rooms for injuries received in walker accidents. This product is associated with more injuries than any other baby product. The most typical accident is a fall down the stairs. Other hazards include tipping over when the walker rolls over an uneven surface (such as a door threshold or rug), pinched fingers, and increased access to other household dangers, such as plants and heaters. On top of this, experts agree that a walker will not hasten your child's ability to walk.

The American Academy of Pediatrics (AAP) recommends that parents and others not use walkers. Dr. Mark Widome, Chairman of the AAP Committee on Accident and Poison Prevention, explained the pediatricians' position: "Because of the high incidence of injuries associated with walkers, and the lack of evidence that they hasten the onset of walking, we recommend that parents not use walkers for their children."

Fractures and/or concussions, are some of the more serious

consequences of walker accidents, typically result when the walker falls down a stairway. Other injuries result from tipping over (when a child attempts to move onto an uneven surface, like over a door threshold or from a floor to a rug), or finger entrapment. Canada feels strongly enough about the risks associated with walkers that the Canadian voluntary standard requires that a walker be constructed so that it cannot go through a door or opening less than 36 inches wide. Since no walker is this wide, the Canadian standard is the equivalent of a ban of the product in that country.

While we subscribe to the AAP position, we advise parents who *do* choose to buy walkers to select only those that meet the ASTM/JPMA voluntary safety standard for walkers. The voluntary standard requires that the walkers be stable enough to prevent tipping; have a latching device to prevent accidental folding; be constructed so as to minimize scissoring, shearing and pinching injuries; have holes or openings that do not catch fingers, toes or buttons; and have a conspicuous warning label.

Walkers range in price from approximately $27 to $65 but tend to be very similar in design. Some are adjustable, which allows for some growth. Others have a feature that allows them to bounce and be used as a jumper. A few models have a wheel release which allows you to retract the wheels (like an old typewriter stand) in order to keep the child from scooting around. (Immobilized, walkers make good feeding stations or places to play with blocks and rattles.) Hanging toys and front trays are other walker options.

The Cosco "Sure Step" walker incorporates a newly designed rubber base that grips the floor whenever a wheel crosses a step or an uneven surface in order to help stop the walker's forward motion. While this design certainly won't prevent all falls down steps, the gripping action of the walker base may give parents a few extra seconds to catch a falling child.

Walkers are appropriate for babies age five to 15 months, or until they begin walking. Make sure your child is in constant view when he is in the walker and be sure to close off stairways and clear other obstacles on which a walker-bound child could stumble. Remember, house plants, hot radiators, ovens and other hazards which are out of reach to your crawling child may be easy to get at when they're upright and mobile in their walker.

★ REMEMBER: When Buying a Walker

☐ Select a walker that is certified to meet the ASTM/JPMA voluntary safety standard for walkers. Look for the certification seal on the box, the display model, or the unit you are purchasing.

☐ Look for a walker with a wheel base that is both wider and longer than the frame of the walker itself to ensure the greatest degree of stability and reduce tip overs.

☐ If you are considering purchasing a second-hand x-frame walker, look for one with protective covers over the accessible coil springs, spacers between scissoring components, and locking devices to prevent the frame from collapsing.

☐ Make sure that metal parts are free of sharp edges and points.

☐ Look for a walker that can be locked into a stationary position; this will allow you to restrict your child's movement at those times when you want him in one place. In the stationary position, your child can be fed or just have a seat from which to watch you and your family.

RECALLED PRODUCTS: Walkers

If more than 18 months have elapsed since the recall date, the manufacturer may no longer honor the recall. If the company refuses to comply, you should discard the product to ensure the safety of your child.

Century Roadster Walkers

WHICH ONES: Walkers in the shape of a car manufactured before January 1989. The manufacture date can be found on a sticker located underneath the left rear "fender." PROBLEM: These walkers have a horn that can be torn or bitten off by a child and cause a choking hazard. WHAT TO DO: Remove the horn immediately from the steering wheel with pliers. For a free replacement horn, call Century Products Company at 800-922-6700. RECALL DATE: 12/88 (CPSC)

Hi-Back Kidde Kare Infant Walkers

WHICH ONES: Model number 106 FLP sold in Service Merchandise Stores. The model number is located on the ID tag of the seat. Affected models have white vinyl binding tape on the edges of the crotch strap. PROBLEM: The crotch strap could slip through the buckle which secures the front of the walker's seat to its deck and cause the child to fall out or become trapped and suffocate. WHAT TO DO: Discontinue use. For a free replacement seat, call Service Merchandise Co. at 800-251-1389 (in Tennessee call 800- 251-1212) RECALL DATE: 3/87

Perego Walkie Baby Walker

WHICH ONES: "Walkie" walkers with a plastic height adjustment mechanism displaying the number 997 inside the plastic handle of the locking mechanism (which can be seen if the walker is turned upside-down). PROBLEM: The plastic height adjustment mechanism can fracture, causing the walker to collapse and the child to fall. WHAT TO DO: For a free repair kit call Perego Products at 800-553-5000. RECALL DATE: 4/87

York Baby Walker

WHICH ONES: Those sold at McCrory, T.G. & Y., J.J. Newberry, McLellan, H. L. Green, Kress, Silver, Elmore, Britts, Kittinger and some other retail stores. They are round with a silver metal frame, yellow tray with three play dials, and a silver sticker under the tray with number PHT417 and York Distribution Co. printed on it. PROBLEM: Crotch strap may slip causing an infant to fall out or become trapped and suffocate. WHAT TO DO: Discontinue use and return to point of purchase for a full refund. RECALL DATE: 5/87

Tips for Safe, Efficient Use:

1. Never leave your child unattended in a walker. Maintain eye contact at all times while the child is in the walker.

2. Never allow the walker to be used near stairs, steps and other thresholds. Close doors and put guards at the top of all stairways. Do not use a pressure gate at the top of stairs as a means of protecting against walker falls; the force of the child in the walker could be enough to dislodge the pressure gate.

3. Check that floor surfaces are flat and free of obstacles, including rug edges or raised thresholds that might cause your child to trip or tip over.

Tips for Safe, Efficient Use: (cont'd.)

4. To prevent burns, never allow your child to use a walker near a range, radiator, space heater, fireplace or other heat surface.

5. Never carry the walker with your child in it.

6. To reduce the chance of your child slipping out of the seat, make sure that both feet touch the floor.

7. Exercise extra care when using the walker outdoors, since there are many additional obstacles, and surfaces are not as flat as those typically found indoors.

8. Discontinue use of the walker when your child is able to walk unassisted. Walkers should not be used by children older than 15 months, even if they have not begun to walk.

Great Gifts for Six Months to Two Years Old

Busy Beads - By Playskool. Sliding beads move along twisting and turning curved wire attached to a sturdy base. Several sizes are available—from Mini Busy Beads ($12) to Deluxe Action Busy Beads ($50). (age 1 ½ and up)

Clang Along Fire Engine by Combi - A great first ride-on toy. This hard plastic fire engine has a grab bar in back (great for pushing), a toy phone, horn, bell and a seat that lifts up to reveal a storage area for important treasures. (ages 12 months to three years)

Corn Popper - By Fisher Price. As its pushed, balls strike the plastic dome making a popping sound. (1 to 3 years)

Cozy Coupe by Little Tikes - An all-weather, rustproof, indoor/outdoor foot powered coupe. (age 18 months to five years)

Interlocking Blocks - Tyco and Duplo brands are interchangeable. The Tyco line is less expensive than Duplo, but Duplo has the most creative accessories. In either case, buy a base plate.

It gives two year olds a much needed anchor for their buildings. (age 18 months and up)

Poppin' Pals by Playskool - Available with Sesame Street or Disney figures. Your child will spend hours learning how to make his favorite character appear. (age 18 months to three years)

Raffi tapes - Raffi is to children's music what the Beatles or Springsteen are to rock! (age 1-up)

Rock 'N Stack Rings - By Fisher Price. Five colorful plastic rings fit over a cone with a rocking base. (6 to 36 months)

See 'N Say - By Mattel. This popular toy, now 25 years old, has been updated with a new pull-lever that replaces the previous hard-to-operate pull-string mechanism. Youngsters point the selector and listen to animal sounds, alphabet sounds, counting and Mother Goose.

Sort 'N Stack Mailbox - By Fisher Price. A portable mailbox with six plastic post cards that are great for sorting, stacking and dumping. (age 9 to 36 months)

Stack and Dump Truck by Johnson & Johnson - This large sturdy truck has squares and circles that can be dropped through a slot, attached to the wheels, or stacked on the truck bed. (age 1-up)

Stack'em Up Cups by Discovery Toys - They stack, they store, stamp imprints and teach size relationships. (age 1-up)

Toy Chest - By Little Tykes. The lid comes off completely as a special safety feature.

Developmentally, these are important years for a child: mobility will increase dramatically as will skills in numerous areas. You will experience the blossoming of a new little person—someone with likes and dislikes and a unique personality.

During this time, your child will be ready for a whole new range of products and toys. Art projects, bike riding, and more sophisticated games and puzzles will become daily activities. Toys will become a major attraction, so this chapter contains a detailed listing of some of the best and worst toys on the market. In addition, we have included a special section on art supplies and popular books, and we finish up with product descriptions of the items you are likely to purchase for your two- to-five-year-old child.

Because the toy section is so large, we diverged from our usual alphabetical format and put *Toys* at the end, just before *Great Gifts*.

Products You Can Purchase for Your Child Growing Up: 2 to 5 Years

Art Supplies

As you know, or will soon find out, art supplies have a habit of ending up in your child's mouth. Licking paste off their hands, moistening paint brushes with tongues, chewing on crayons, and inhaling chalk dust are not uncommon experiences for children. Therefore, it is important to provide your child with *non-toxic* art supplies. Toxic art supplies are a serious threat to children because their lower body weights and developing nervous systems make them more susceptible to toxicity. Many manufacturers voluntarily place warning labels on their *toxic* products, which parents should heed. Look for a products that have been *certified* as non-toxic.

✔ **TIP:** *Make sure that your child's nursery school, day care center or playgroup also purchases certified non-toxic items.*

★ REMEMBER: When Buying Children's Art Supplies:

☐ Look for products marked with a CP (certified product) or AP (approved product) or HL/NT (Health Label/Non-Toxic) seal. These seals mean they have been certified by a medical expert as not containing materials in sufficient quantities to be toxic or injurious.

WARNING: *According to The Art and Craft Materials Institute, the word "non-toxic" on the label does not necessarily mean the product is safe. A "non-toxic" designation may relate only to acute or short term adverse effects and not take into account whether the product may have adverse chronic or long-term effects on your child. The quantity of substances ingested over time is the key factor. The certified products in the list that follows take this distinction into account in their assurance of safety.*

Approved Non-Toxic Art Supplies

These products all carry a CP or AP seal. They are listed by manufacturer brand name and organized by material.

Adhesives

Polymers

Binney & Smith/Crayola Art & Craft Glue
Ceramichrome, Inc./Ed's Glue
Delta/Shiva/Ceramcoat Gold Leaf
Duncan Enterprises/Foil 'N Accent
Plaid Enterprises/Mod Podge Gloss
Plaid Enterprises/Mod Podge Matte
Rich Art Color Co./Rich Glu White Glue
The Slomons Group/Drape 'N Shape
The Slomons Group/Quik
The Slomons Group/Sobo
The Slomons Group/Stitchless
The Slomons Group/Thik 'N Tacky
The Slomons Group/Velverette
The Slomons Group/Woodwiz

School Paste

Binney & Smith/Crayola White
Lindow Manufacturing/Lindco
Rich Art Color Co./Rich Art School Paste

Glues

American Tombow/Tombow Adhesive Sticks
American Tombow/Tombow Liquid Glue
Artis, Inc./Aleene's Fabric Stiffener
Artis, Inc./Aleene's Tacky Designer Glue
Artis, Inc./Aleene's Tacky Glue

Artis, Inc./Aleene's White Craft Glue/School Glue
Delta/Shiva/Delta Rainbow
Dixon Ticonderoga/Prang Roll-On
Lindow Manufacturing/Lindco School
Lindow Manufacturing/Lindco White
Omega Chalk Factory/Omega White
Plaid Enterprises/Stiffy

Chalks

Charcoal

Berol USA/Berol Charcoal Pencil
Dick Blick Co./Dick Blick

Extruded Colored
(for Chalkboard)

Binney & Smith (Canada)/ Crayola Sanigene
Dixon Ticonderoga Co./Hyga-Color
J. L. Hammett Co./Hammett's
NationArt, Inc./3B Blackboardbest
NationArt, Inc./Omyacolor
NationArt, Inc./Robercolor
Omega Chalk Factory/Omega
School Mate, Inc./School Mate
Weber Costello/Omega
Weber Costello/Ritebrite

Extruded Sightsaving
(for Chalkboard)

Binney & Smith/Crayola Anti-Dust
Binney & Smith/Crayola E-Z-Syte
Binney & Smith (Canada)/ Crayola Sanigene

Approved Non-Toxic Art Supplies (cont'd.)

Dixon Ticonderoga Co./Forsythe
Dixon Ticonderoga Co./Velvatex
J. L. Hammett Co./Hammett's
NationArt, Inc./3B
  Blackboardbest
NationArt, Inc./Omyacolor
NationArt, Inc./Robercolor
School Mate, Inc./School Mate
Weber Costello/Alphasite
Weber Costello/Ritebrite

Extruded White (for Chalkboard)
Binney & Smith/Crayola An-Du-
  Septic
Binney & Smith/Crayola Anti-
  Dust
Binney & Smith (Canada)/
  Crayola Sanigene
Dixon Ticonderoga Co./Hygieia
J. L. Hammett Co./Hammett's
NationArt, Inc./3B
  Blackboardbest
NationArt, Inc./Omyacolor
NationArt, Inc./Robercolor
Omega Chalk Factory/Omega
School Mate, Inc./School Mate
Weber Costello/Alpha
Weber Costello/Ritebrite
Weber Costello/Webco

Extruded Color
(for Paper & Crafts)
Binney & Smith/Crayola Colored
  Art
Dixon Ticonderoga/Prang
  Pastello
Dixon Ticonderoga/Prang Poster
  Pastello
Weber Costello/Alphacolor
Molded Colored (for Chalkboard)
Binney & Smith/Crayola Colored
Chemitron USA Corp./Colorup
Dixon Ticonderoga/Prang
  Sidewalk

Molded White (for Chalkboard)
Binney & Smith/Crayola
Binney & Smith (Canada)/
  Crayola Swan
Chemitron USA Corp./Colorup
Coloron, Inc./Avalon/Coloron
  Nu-Chalk
Dixon Ticonderoga/Colorart
Dixon Ticonderoga/Waltham
Montrose Products/Futura

Molded Colored
(for Paper & Crafts)
Binney & Smith/Crayola Colored
  Drawing
Binney & Smith/Crayola Colored
  Poster
Binney & Smith (Canada)/
  Crayola Colorex
Binney & Smith (Canada)/
  Crayola Goodhue
Coloron, Inc./Avalon/Coloron
  Nu-Chalk
Dixon Ticonderoga/Ambrite
Dixon Ticonderoga/Freart
Dixon Ticonderoga/Lecturers
Dixon Ticonderoga/Prang Color
  Chalk
Dixon Ticonderoga/Prang Fluo-
  rescent Lectures

Clays

Modeling (Permanently Plastic,
  Non-Hardening)
American Art Clay Co./Amaco
  HBX-2
American Art Clay Co./Amaco
  Plast-I-Clay
American Art Clay Co./Artone
  Venus A-18
American Art Clay Co./
  Permoplast
Binney & Smith/Clayola
Binney & Smith/Clayola
  Claytime Clay

Approved Non-Toxic Art Supplies (cont'd.)

Binney & Smith/Silly Putty
Coloron, Inc./Avalon/Coloron
Coloron, Inc./Color Craft
Dixon Ticonderoga/Prang
J. L. Hammett Co./Hammett's
Havo, B.V./Creatherm
NationArt, Inc./Plasticolor
Sargent Art/Sargent
School Mate, Inc./Schoolmate
Van Aken Int'l./Leisure Clay
Van Aken Int'l./Van Aken

Modeling Dough
American Art Clay/Amaco
American Art Clay/Super Dough
Tree House Toys/Granny's
Dabblin' Dough

Paper Mache
American Art Clay/Claycrete

Crayons

Hard Molded
Binney & Smith/Artista II
Binney & Smith/Crayola Color
Works

Molded
Binney & Smith/Crayola
Binney & Smith/Crayola Easy Off
Binney & Smith/Crayola Fabric
Binney & Smith/Crayola So-Big
Binney & Smith/Peacock
Chemitron USA Corp./Colorup
Coloron, Inc./Color Craft
Dixon Ticonderoga Co./My First
Crayon
Dixon Ticonderoga Co./Prang
Colorart
J.L. Hammett Co./Art Utility
Havo, B.V./Creall
Pentel of America/GL 1-16 Plastic
Pentel of America/PTC 2-25 Soft
Plymouth, Inc./Fisher-Price
Sargent Art/Gothic

Sargent Art/Sargent
Winsor & Newton/Reeves Giant
Wax

Pressed
Berol USA/Chinamarker
Berol USA/Prismacolor Art Stix
Dixon Ticonderoga/Color
Classics
Dixon Ticonderoga/Crayograph
Dixon Ticonderoga/Kantroll
Dixon Ticonderoga/Kindograph
J.L. Hammett Co./Art Utility
Sargent Art/Sargent

Water Color
Dixon Ticonderoga/Prang Payons
Weber Costello/Alphacolor
Winsor & Newton/Reeves
Paintstix

Paints

Acrylics, Artists
Binney & Smith/Crayola
Binney & Smith/Crayola
Permanent
Binney & Smith/Liquitex
Binney & Smith/Liquitex Acrylic
Basecoats
Dick Blick Co./Blickrylic
Dick Blick Co./Strokemaster
Cardinal School/Cardinal acrylic
Ceramichrome, Inc./Deco Art
Ceramichrome, Inc./Decoart
Americana
Ceramichrome, Inc./Decoart
Softees
Charvoz/Maimeri/Brera
Chroma Acrylics/Jo Sonja
Color Craft/Createx Poster/Fabric
Daler-Rowney/Rowney System 3
Delta/Shiva/Aqua Stain
Delta/Shiva/Delta Liquid Lead
Delta/Shiva/Delta Liquid Pewter
Delta/Shiva/Embossart

Approved Non-Toxic Art Supplies (cont'd.)

Delta/Shiva/Shiva Signatex
Demco Manufacturing/Demcryl
Duro Art Industries/Duro
Golden Artists Colors/Fluid
Golden Artists Colors/Golden
M. Grumbacher, Inc./Hyplar
  Colors
Hunt Manufacturing/Speedball
Lefranc & Bourgeois/Polyflashe
Martin/F. Weber Co./Permalba
Martin/F. Weber Co./Priscilla's
  Basecoat
Martin/F. Weber Co./Weber
  Acrylic Base
NASCO International/Bulkrylic

Acrylics, Washable
Chroma Acrylics/Chromacryl
Delta/Shiva/Ceramcoat
Duncan Enterprises/Doll Composition Primer
Duncan Enterprises/Iridescent
  Scribbles
Duncan Enterprises/Natural
  Touch Drybrushing
Duncan Enterprises/Shiny
  Scribbles
Duncan Enterprises/Prep Coat
Duncan Enterprises/Ultra
  Metallics
Koh-I-Noor/Pelikan Top-Color
  Metallic
Koh-I-Noor/Pelikan Top-Color
  Non-Metallic
Rich Art Color Co./Rich Cryl

Finger Paint, Liquid
Binney & Smith/Crayola
Binney & Smith/Crayola
  Washable
Dick Blick Co./Strokemaster

Dixon Ticonderoga Co./Prang
J.L. Hammett Co./Art Utility
Havo, B.V./Creall
Lake Shore Curriculum/Best Buy
Omega Chalk Factory/Omega
Palmer Paint Products/Palmer
Rich Art Color Co./Rich Art
Sargent Art/Sargent
Sax Arts & Crafts/True Color
Weber Costello/Alphacolor

Pastels

Oil Pastels
Dixon Ticonderoga/Sketcho
Pentel of America/PHN-36
Pentel of America/PTA-50
Pentel of America/PTS-15 Dye
  Sticks
Sakura of America/Chubbies
Sakura of America/Cray-Pas
Sakura of America/Deluxe Sticks
Sakura of America/For Artists'
  Use
Sakura of America/Jumbo
Sakura of America/Junior
Sakura of America/Large Size
Sakura of America/Square Sticks
Sakura of America/Square Type
Sakura of America/Super
Sanford Corp./Jumbo
Sanford Corp./Regular
Sanford Corp./Square Sticks
Winsor & Newton/Reeves
Winsor & Newton/Reeves
  Greyhound

Soft Pastels
Royal Talens/Rembrandt
Weber Costello/Alphacolor

NOTE: The products listed above were certified by the Art and Craft Materials Institute, Inc., November, 1989. For updates of this list, contact the Art and Craft Materials Institute, Inc., 715 Boylston Street, Boston, MA 02116.

Beds

Moving from the crib to a bed is a rite of passage that many parents often view with mixed emotions. Your little one will look so tiny in that first "big girl" or "big boy" bed, and access to their room and the rest of the house is significantly increased.

For safety's sake it is important to make the "big move" when your child is 35 inches tall or two years of age, whichever comes first. If she is persistent in her attempts to climb out of the crib, you may have to make the change sooner.

To make the move easier for your child, provide plenty of advance notice. Discuss it or read a story about moving to a bed *before* disassembling the crib. If the move to a bed is due to the arrival of a new baby, do it a few months ahead so that the baby's arrival is not associated with the loss of the crib. Encourage your child to make a gift of his crib to the little one and let him help you get it ready!

WARNING: *The risk of strangulation increases as the child becomes bigger and has the physical ability to try to climb out of a crib. More than 33 children have died, and 2 were severely brain damaged, when their clothing, pacifier cord, religious necklace or other string caught on the crib while they were attempting to climb out.*

Safety in the new bed should also be a concern, since small children can become trapped between the bed and wall, footboard or headboard, and suffocate or strangle. For this reason, we strongly recommend the use of guardrails on your child's first bed. In addition to protecting against these hazards, they will prevent frightening falls to the floor in the middle of the night. Purchase two guardrails, one for each side of the bed—even if one side of the bed is up against the wall, since children can become fatally caught between the bed and wall. Look for guardrails that are solid or contain vertical rails. Most adjust to any bed and are held in place by slipping the guardrail arms under the mattress. After your child is asleep check to see that the guardrails are snug up against the side of the bed and that no space is created that could entrap a head, arms or legs.

The **Sleeper Keeper** is an innovative new product that stops children from rolling out of bed, with inflatable plastic bolsters slipped inside a specially designed sheet. Write to Sleeper Keeper, Springs Industries, Inc., 295 Fifth Ave., New York, NY 10016, for information.

Youth beds, which are shorter and narrower in width, are one option. Some come with their own guardrails, and their smaller size may accommodate your child's room better if space is minimal. While a youth bed's size is an advantage, it is also its biggest disadvantage, since your child will definitely outgrow it and will eventually need a regular size bed.

Bunk Beds

Bunk beds are a popular bedding option—kids love them and parents appreciate their space-saving design. However, the CPSC reports numerous deaths from bunk bed accidents. These accidents have occurred when the bunks were being used in both the stacked configuration and as single twin beds. In fact, each year over 31,000 children are injured seriously enough to require hospital emergency room treatment.

While bunk bed injuries are usually associated with falls from the bed, bunk bed deaths involving children most often occur one of three ways:

Entrapment and strangulation between the guardrail and the mattress. Deaths have resulted when the sleeping child slid out, feet first, through the space between the guardrail and the mattress. Because the child's head could not fit through this space, the child hung suspended from the guardrail and strangled, ironically on the safety device that is supposed to prevent deaths and injuries.

Entrapment and suffocation between the bed and wall. Here the young child, asleep in a bunk bed against the wall, fell into a small space between the bed and the wall and suffocated.

Mattress support dislodgment and suffocation. In these cases there were either no cross ties or the cross ties became dislodged and the mattress fell on the child below. Such deaths have resulted when the beds were stacked as bunks or in the twin bed configuration.

★ REMEMBER: When Buying a Bunk Bed

☐ Children under 6 years of age should not sleep on the top bunk. Do not purchase bunk beds for two siblings under age 6 unless you plan to use the bunks as twin beds.

☐ When purchasing a new set of bunk beds, look for a label on the beds to make sure it complies with the Revised Voluntary Bunk Bed Guidelines. Earlier guidelines did not include all of the recommended safety measures from CPSC and consumer advocates. Compliance with the revised voluntary measure means that the bed comes with two guard rails. If using both beds, you should get another set of guardrails for the bottom or second twin.

☐ We recommend against buying a secondhand set of bunk beds since it may be difficult to determine whether the beds pose the strangulation hazards discussed above (particularly without a mattress in the bed). See our advice below on secondhand bunk beds.

☐ Bunk beds are generally not sold with mattresses, so be sure. To purchase the right size mattresses. Bunk beds take either Twin or Twin Extra Long mattresses. Extra long mattresses are 5 inches longer than regular mattress. If you place a regular size mattress in a bed that is extra long, this creates a gap where a child could become entrapped and strangle.

Tips for Safe, Efficient Use:

1. Never allow a child under age 6 to sleep on the top bunk.

2. For older children, if the upper bunk is not against a wall, use guardrails on both sides. No matter how old your child is, keep the guardrails in place on the top bunk since children roll during sleep. For younger children, it is advisable to use guardrails on both sides of the bed in the twin bed configuration (even if up against a wall) to prevent entrapment between the bed and wall.

3. If you are not sure whether your bunk bed complies with the Revised Industry Guidelines (see above) or *if you are using a second hand bunk bed*:

   —Check to see that the space between the bottom of the guardrail and the top of the side rail is no more than 3 ½ inches, to prevent a child from rolling or sliding feet first under the guardrail and becoming entrapped. If this space is more than 3 ½ inches, use screws or nails to affix another rail or board to close the space. Also check to see that guardrails are screwed, bolted or otherwise firmly attached to the bed structure.

Tips for Safe, Efficient Use: (cont'd.)

—Be sure that there are cross ties under the mattress foundation of each bed and make sure they are screwed into the bed frame or otherwise securely attached to each bed (even if beds are being used as twin beds).

—Make sure the ladder is secured to the bed frame so that it does not slip when the child climbs on it. Replace loose or missing rungs on the ladder.

4. Make sure the mattress is the correct length. A regular size mattress on a twin extra long size bed creates a dangerous gap where a child could become entrapped.

5. Teach your child that a bunk bed is not a play gym for climbing and rough play. Keep an eye on younger children who may view an older sibling's bunk bed as a wonderful climbing challenge.

6. Instruct your child to always use the ladder and not to use other furniture to climb into or out of the top bunk.

7. If your child is sleeping on the top bunk, consider keeping a night light on (and out of contact with any bed linens) so he will be able to safely climb down the ladder if he gets up during the night.

RECALLED PRODUCTS: Bunk Beds

If more than 18 months have elapsed since the recall date, the manufacturer may no longer honor the recall. If the company refuses to comply, you should discard the product to ensure the safety of your child.

Sears Brawny Bunk Bed

WHICH ONES: Brawny bunk beds without the cross wire mattress assembly screwed into side rails. PROBLEM: Mattress assembly can come loose, trapping or suffocating small children playing under the bed. WHAT TO DO: Call Sears for a free modification kit at 800-831-5551 (800-323-0366 in Illinois), or go to your nearest Sears. RECALL DATE: 3/86

United Bunk Beds

WHICH ONES: Models #500, #600, and #700. Sold east of the Mississippi since 1984. The firm's name is found only on the state law tag attached to mattresses. For specific identification information call the CPSC at 800-638-CPSC and ask for the United Bunk Bed Press Release 11/87. PROBLEM: No problems involving these beds have been reported. However, three children have died in incidents involving bunk beds with mattress supports and foundations similar to those manufactured by United. Each bed should have two cross wires securing it to the side rail to prevent the mattress assembly from being displaced. WHAT TO DO: Company went out of business. RECALL DATE: 11/87

Bicycles and Tricycles

Riding a bicycle or tricycle will provide hours and hours of fun for your child. In addition to the exercise and development of gross motor skills, your child will delight in the mastery of this new skill. The age at which your child is ready for a tricycle or bicycle will depend mostly on your child's size, pedalling and balancing skills, and, for bicycles, comprehension of the use of brakes.

Tricycles

Starting at about age two, your child may be interested in and capable of using a simple tricycle, although mastery of tricycle pedalling may not occur until age three. Tricycles provide lots of fun for pre-schoolers and help motor development and coordination. In addition to actually riding the trike, your young child will have fun pushing it or climbing on and off. As with any moving product, keep safety in mind; the CPSC estimates that last year over 12,000 persons received tricycle-related injuries serious enough to require hospital emergency room treatment. Accidents can occur as a result of collisions, entanglement of a child in the tricycle's moving parts, inability to stop the tricycle (usually because tricycles don't have brakes), instability (causing the tricycle to tip over when the rider turns or speeds up suddenly) and poor construction or design.

You have two basic tricycle choices: the standard trike, which has remained virtually unchanged for years, and the "Big Wheel" style, low-slung tricycles, with seats very close to the ground. These trikes offer more stability than a traditional trike, but because most of the weight is on the rear wheel, children will find them difficult to ride up small hills. Beware, because these vehicles are so stable, your child's increased confidence may lead him to try out a hill or two and it is very easy to lose control and zoom out into traffic.

★ REMEMBER: When Buying a Tricycle

☐ Match the size of your child to the size of the tricycle. If a child is too large for the tricycle, it will be unstable. If the child is too small, the tricycle may be difficult to control.

☐ For extra stability, look for wheels that are widely spaced.

☐ Avoid tricycles with sharp edges, particularly on or along fenders.

☐ Look for pedals and handgrips with rough surfaces to prevent the child's hands and feet from slipping.

Tips for Safe, Efficient Use:

1. Teach children safe riding habits, and check on them frequently.

2. Caution your child against riding double. Carrying a passenger on a tricycle greatly increases its instability.

3. Try to teach your child that riding down hills is dangerous. A tricycle can pick up so much speed that it becomes almost impossible to stop without brakes.

4. Advise your child to avoid sharp turns, to make all turns at low speed, and not to ride down steps or over curbs.

5. Advise your child to keep hands and feet away from moving spokes.

6. Purchase a bicycle helmet for use with your child's tricycle. This will get her accustomed to riding with a helmet and will make it easier to get your child in the habit of always using a helmet on a two-wheel bicycle. (See section below on Bicycle Helmets).

Tips for Safe, Efficient Use: (cont'd.)

7. Keep the tricycle in good condition. Check regularly for missing or damaged pedals and handgrips, loose handlebars and seats, broken parts and other defects.

8. Cover any sharp edges and protrusions with heavy, waterproof tape.

9. Don't leave tricycles outdoors overnight—moisture can cause rust and weaken metal parts.

RECOMMENDED PRODUCTS: Tricycles

Fisher-Price Trike

This all-plastic trike is a safer alternative to the low-slung "big wheel" style plastic tricycles. The seat is raised a little above the wheels and pedals, making it easier for a younger child to push down on the pedals. It also features a neat underseat storage compartment and is very resilient to hard use.

The Safety Cycle

This West German tricycle is sold through the *Perfectly Safe Catalog* (See Chapter Nine for address) and is designed to overcome many of the hazards associated with tricycles. It has a hand brake, a seatback to help prevent backward falls, and a particularly useful (and removable) parent's guide bar which allows you to use the trike as a stroller (or to slow down your speedster)! The pedals move only in the forward direction, which allows the child to rest his feet on them if coasting or strolling. Unfortunately, this makes backing up impossible and prevents the child from using his feet on the pedals to slow down. But we like this bike.

Bicycles

Learning to ride a two-wheel bicycle has become a rite of passage in American childhood akin to a baby's first step and leaving for college! Some 40 million children ride bicycles. Most children are ready to learn to ride a two-wheeler (without training wheels) by the time they're six or seven years old.

The first decision you'll have to make is choosing the right size—

which depends on your child's size. For tips on getting just the right size, see *Remember When Buying* below. Remember that children's bike sizes relate to wheel diameter and not frame height. The most common wheel diameters for children's bikes are 12, 16, 20, and 24 inches, and, although buying a new bike each time your child grows would be ideal, it's not practical. Be prepared, however, to buy more than one bike.

Bicycle prices vary tremendously ($45 to over $150). Prices will be lower at department and children's stores, but you'll have to put the bike together yourself unless you pay for assembly. Most bike shops are required by manufacturers to sell bikes assembled.

Watching your child take that first wobbly ride on a two-wheel bicycle is a proud parenting moment! Shopping for and using a bicycle requires more attention than many of the purchases you make for your child. Following the tips below could help avoid some nasty injuries and ensure that your child's first bike is the right bike. The importance of safe bicycling is critical, since this activity is associated with thousands of hospital-treated injuries each year. Be sure to get your child a bicycle helmet and insist that it be worn (see section below on Bicycle Helmets).

✔ **TIP:** *Experts recommend that a child not be pushed to ride a two-wheel bicycle. Children will be ready at different ages, with most showing an interest between five and seven. Be sure to read the size information included below, since bicycle size can greatly affect the safety and your child's enjoyment of bicycling. Happy riding!*

★ REMEMBER: When Buying a Bicycle

☐ It is very important to purchase the correct size bicycle for your child. Don't be tempted to buy a bike your child "will grow into." A bike that is too big will be hard to mount and dismount, hard to control and unsafe. There should be about one inch of clearance between your child's crotch and the horizontal bar of a boy's bike when your child straddles the bike with both feet flat on the ground. For girl's bikes, use a yardstick to simulate the horizontal bar. Typically, 16-inch bikes are suitable for children aged 4-6 (inseam 17-22 inches), while kids aged 7-15 (inseam 23 inches or larger) move up to 20- to 24-inch bikes.

☐ Children under age eight should only have bikes with coaster or foot brakes; older kids can safely operate hand brakes.

☐ Look for a bicycle that comes with training wheels—more likely than not your child will need them for a little while.

☐ Children under 10 should only have single-speed bikes.

☐ Wheels with spokes are better than plastic wheel rims; the latter have been known to crack. Also, the greater the number of spokes the better. Less expensive models have 20 spokes per wheel whereas better children's bikes have 28 spokes.

☐ Bike warranties offered by bike shops and department stores differ. Bike shops generally service the bikes they sell, unlike most department stores. Some bike shops even give a free tune-up. With these considerations in mind, shop around for a good sale; in the long run the expensive bike shop may not be that expensive.

☐ Inspect the foot pedals to ensure that they offer a good grip and do not have sharp metal teeth.

Tips for Safe, Efficient Use:

1. Your child should always wear a bicycle helmet when cycling. (See the section below on Bicycle Helmets).

2. Children under age 6 should always ride under the direct supervision of an adult, even on sidewalks. Teach your child about traffic hazards; explain that even on sidewalks there are intersections with driveways and drivers may not be watching out for him.

3. Periodically check your child's bicycle to make sure there are no loose nuts, bolts or screws. Check the brakes and make sure the front wheel is straight. Examine the chain; there should be no caked grease or dirt and it should not be dry or rusty.

4. Check the tires by pushing them against a curb; if you can flatten them, more air is needed. Inflate to the pressure shown on the tire's side wall.

5. Make sure the seat does not rock or turn in any direction and the handlebars are not loose. Check for broken spokes and make sure the wheel's axle nut is tight.

Tips for Safe, Efficient Use: (cont'd.)

6. Young children should not ride bicycles at night or dusk. Riding at night is 20 times more dangerous than riding during the day, and most children lack the experience and ability necessary for safe night riding.

7. As your child gets older, expand your instruction on bicycle safety, including how to safely ride on streets and the importance of obeying traffic signals.

Bicycle Helmets

You may have noticed that bicycle helmets have received a lot of attention lately and that more and more riders are wearing them. This change relates to the increase in evidence that helmets save lives and prevent serious head injuries. Helmet design has also vastly improved—gone are the days of the clunky, heavy, ugly helmets. Helmets today are colorful, lightweight and easy to wear.

If you are still not convinced about bicycle helmets, consider this: each year 500-600 children die and 300,000 require hospital treatment for injuries as a result of bicycle crashes. Many of these are attributable to skull and brain injuries. The National Head Injury Foundation estimates that each year nearly 50,000 bicyclists suffer serious head injuries leaving them with permanent disabilities. Fortunately, the good news is that bike helmets can help turn this tragic tide. A recent study in Seattle found that bicycle helmets reduced the risk of head injury by 85 percent.

Purchasing a bike helmet and getting your child to wear it on each ride is one of the most important things you can do for your growing child. Like childproofing your home or making sure she is buckled into a car safety seat, making bike helmet use a habit is a critical safety measure. Below are some important tips from the Head Smart Coalition, a national campaign to reduce head injuries by promoting the use of bicycle helmets. For more information, contact the National Head Injury Foundation at 1-800-444-NHIF.

★ REMEMBER: When Buying a Bicycle Helmet

☐ Only buy a helmet that meets the American National Standards Institute (ANSI) or the Snell Memorial Foundation standards. In either case there will be a sticker in the helmet signifying that the helmet passes the applicable standard. While helmets made in compliance with either of these standards will protect the head in a crash, the Snell standard is considered more rigorous.

☐ Let your child help pick out the helmet. Helmets now come in a variety of colors and patterns, and being involved in the selection process will help in getting your child to wear the helmet.

☐ Have your child try on the helmet in the store, to make sure you get the right size. Helmets come in child and adult sizes. The helmet should fit snugly but not too tightly. It should not rock side to side nor front to back. Most helmets come with sizing pads, often foam pads attached with Velcro, which can be adjusted as your child grows.

☐ Try to get a helmet included in the deal when you buy your child a bike. This is probably easier to accomplish if buying from a bike shop rather than a large department store.

Tips for Safe, Efficient Use:

1. A bike helmet should be worn on each and every ride. Serious accidents can happen close to home on short rides.

2. Until your child is old enough to put the helmet on correctly each time, help her make sure the straps are properly fastened and the helmet covers the top of her forehead.

Tips for Safe, Efficient Use: (cont'd.)

3. Praise your child for wearing his helmet. When you ride with him, wear a helmet yourself to set a good example. Make it a game to point out other riders that do or do not wear helmets. Explain to your child in simple terms why it is important to wear a helmet. For older children, point out helmeted riders who bike often, such as couriers and racers.

4. Encourage other parents, particularly those of your child's friends, to purchase bicycle helmets for their children to help eliminate the discomfort of being different.

5. Before applying paint or stickers to the helmet surface, make sure that these will not damage the bicycle helmet. Bright reflective stickers for bike helmets are often sold in bike shops.

6. Clean your child's bike helmet with gentle soap and warm water. Cleaning solvents may damage the helmet, even though the damage is not visible.

7. Teach your child not to throw or kick the helmet around. Such actions could damage the helmet or weaken its ability to protect your child's head. If your child is particularly hard on toys and equipment, consider a hard shell helmet.

8. If your child and helmet are in a crash, discontinue use of that helmet and obtain a new helmet for your child. The helmet may be damaged even though you may not see any visible evidence of such. Experts always recommend replacement after a crash.

Books

Your child is now at the age where books truly are "windows on the world." In addition to offering your child wonderful adventures, books offer something else—time for the two of you to be together. We often hear that parents are concerned that TV is supplanting the time they would like their children to be spending with books. Sometimes this happens because children haven't been shown how much fun books are. One way to do this is to take an active interest in reading to your child; in doing so, you'll be spending special time together and joining him on wonderful trips through the imagination.

Following is a list of some of our favorite books to get you started on what we think will be a marvelous adventure. We strongly recommend that you and your child become regulars at the children's section in your local library. Soon you'll both develop particular favorites. One of the best books on the subject is *The Read Aloud Handbook* by Jim Trelease. In addition to offering tremendous insight on the benefits of reading to your children, Trelease provides detailed reviews of the best in children's reading.

Remember, the more you enjoy the books you read to your children, the more they will too.

RECOMMENDED PRODUCTS: Great Books for Toddlers

Alexander and the Terrible, Horrible, No Good, Very Bad Day by Judith Viorst, illustrated by Ray Cruz (Atheneum). Here's an experience that you *and* your child can identify with! (Ages 4 and up)

Amelia Bedelia by Peggy Parish, illustrated by Fritz Seibel (Harper & Row). Kids love to take directions literally and Amelia is no exception. (Ages 4 and up)

Bedtime for Frances by Russell Hoban, illustrated by Garth Williams (Harper & Row). Here's all the reasons not to go to bed, many of which you both will recognize, woven into a humorous tale. (Ages 3 and up)

The Berenstain Bears and Too Much Junk Food, by Stan and Jan Berenstain (Random House). A family of bears exchanges sweets for good food. (Ages 3-6)

Blueberries for Sal by Robert McCloskey (Viking, Puffin). A warm story about a mixup between a little girl, her mother and some bears. (Ages 3-6)

Brown Bear, Brown Bear, What Do You See? by Bill Martin, Jr., illustrated by Eric Carle (Holt). A great first reader, this school book will capture a toddlers attention as well. (Ages 2-7)

Cloudy With a Chance of Meatballs by Judi Barrett, illustrated by Ron Barrett (Atheneum). When it rains, it pours—in this case, meatballs, a really funny story. (Ages 4 and up)

Corduroy by Don Freeman (Viking, Puffin). A wonderful story of friendship and love between a teddy bear and a little girl. (Ages 3 and up)

The Country Bunny and the Little Gold Shoes by DuBose Heyward, illustrated by Marjorie Hock (Houghton Mifflin). The trials and tribulations of struggling to reach your goal, in this case a little country bunny's dream to be the Easter Bunny—a story of courage and persistence. (Ages 4-8)

Curious George by H. A. Rey (Houghton Mifflin). George is a monkey whose curiosity always gets him in trouble—no wonder children identify so well with him. (Ages 4 and up)

An Evening at Alfie's by Shirley Hughes (Lothrop). When the babysitter comes, catastrophe strikes and Alfie copes wonderfully. (Ages 4-7)

The Giving Tree by Shel Silverstein (Harper & Row). What could be more important than friendship, love, and sharing? (Ages 4 and up)

Harry the Dirty Dog by Gene Zion, illustrated by Margaret B. Graham (Harper & Row). Harry doesn't like baths and once in a while he gets into trouble—as a result, children like Harry. (Ages 4-8)

The House on East 88th Street by Bernard Waber (Houghton Mifflin). Who would have know that a giant crocodile could be such a great guy! (Ages 4-10)

If I Ran the Zoo by Dr. Seuss (Random). Just one of the timeless Seuss classics—an adventure into the imagination. (Ages 3 and up)

Katy and the Big Snow by Virginia Lee Burton (Houghton Mifflin). When the blizzard strikes, Katy, a persistent tractor, saves the snowbound city of Geoppolis. (Ages 3-7)

Little Bear by Else Holmelund Minarik, illustrated by Maurice Sendak (Harper & Row). Tremendous Sendak illustrations and tenderly poignant stories depicting the important events in a child's life—playing, birthdays, making wishes, clothes. (Ages 3 and up)

The Little House by Virginia Lee Burton (Houghton Mifflin). Life's changes are portrayed in a classic story about a little country house that ends up surrounded by skyscrapers. (Ages 4 and up)

Little Toot by Hardie Gramatky (Putnam). One of America's most famous boats shares life in the shadow of his powerful parents. (Ages 3-8)

Madeline by Ludwig Bemelmans (Viking, Puffin). A series of books about the daring antics of an impish personality and her extended family and friends at a convent school. (Ages 4- 10)

Make Way for Ducklings by Robert McCloskey (Viking, Puffin). A Boston classic—mother Mallard and her eight ducklings make a heart stopping journey through the city to their home on the Common. (Ages 3-8)

Mike Mulligan and His Steam Shovel by Virginia Lee Burton (Houghton Mifflin). An age old and heartwarming classic about a now extinct machine. (Ages 4-8)

Miss Nelson Is Missing by Harry Allard, illustrated by James Marshall (Houghton Mifflin, Scholastic). What a surprise for the worst children in the school. (Ages 4-8)

Moses the Kitten, by James Herriot, illustrated by Peter Barrett (St. Martin's).. An orphaned kitten finds his home on a farm, and a pig for a foster mother. (Ages 3-8)

Nice Little Girls by Elizabeth Levy, illustrated by Mordicai Gerstein (Delacorte). A must read for parents who are working to avoid sexual stereotyping—tool boxes and trains are for everyone. (Ages 4-8)

The Poky Little Puppy by Janette S. Lowrey, illustrated by Gustaf Tenggren (Golden). A well told lesson about what can happen to a "slow-poke." (Ages 3-5)

The Random House Book of Poetry for Children, selected by Jack Prelutsky, illustrated by Arnold Lobel (Random House). Verse for the video generation. (Ages 4-12)

The Red Balloon by A. Lamorisse (Doubleday). Pictures from the classic film recount the loyalty of the red balloon. (Ages 4 and up)

Regards to the Man in the Moon by Ezra Jack Keats (Four Winds). With a little creativity, anyone can go to the moon. (Ages 4-8)

The Rose In My Garden, by Arnold Lobel, illustrated by Anita Lobel (Greenwillow). Life in the garden, with a rose, a bee, flowers, a mouse and a cat that topples it all. (Ages 3-8)

The Story of Ferdinand by Munro Leaf, illustrated by Robert Lawson (Viking, Puffin). The great Spanish bull who, quite sensibly prefers flowers to fighting. (Ages 4-8)

The Stupids Step Out by Harry Allard, illustrated by James Marshall (Houghton Mifflin). Stupid behavior always gets a laugh and this case, it comes with a lesson. (Ages 4 and up)

The Tale of Peter Rabbit, by Beatrix Potter (Arne). Adventures in Farmer McGregor's garden patch. (Ages 3 and up)

Thy Friend, Obadiah by Brinton Turkle (Viking, Puffin). A series of books about honesty, friendship and other important values told through the colonial life of a six-year-old boy who lives on Nantucket Island. (Ages 4 and up)

The Velveteen Rabbit, by Margery Williams, illustrated by William Nicholson (Doubleday). A charming tale about how a toy rabbit becomes a real rabbit. Many versions of this story are available. (Ages 3-6)

Where the Wild Things Are, by Maurice Sendak (Harper & Row). Little Max, sent to bed for misbehaving, becomes king of the wild things. (Ages 3 and up)

When the New Baby Comes I'm Moving Out by Martha Alexander (Dial). Classic new baby jealousy provides a background for a story that will help siblings deal with a new arrival. (Ages 3-7)

William's Doll by Charlotte Zolotow, illustrated by William Pene du Bois (Harper & Row). A poignant lesson in fatherhood that can help conquer sexual stereotypes. (Ages 4- 12)

Winnie the Pooh, by A.A. Milne (Dutton). Meet Christopher Robin, his teddy bear and their friends who dwell in the Three Acre Wood. (Ages 4-up)

Car Safety Seats - Booster

To prevent serious injury to a child in the event of a car accident, there is no substitute for a good-quality car safety seat. Every state now requires their use, even for newborns.

There are three major types of child safety seats: Infant, Convertible and Booster. See Chapter One for information about convertible and infant seats.

The booster seat can be used for children between 40 and 60 pounds, depending on the type of seat purchased. Note: The manufacturers claim that these seats can be used for children weighing as little as 20 pounds. The American Academy of Pediatrics, however, recommends waiting until your child reaches 40 pounds.

A booster seat provides much better protection than a poorly-fitting lap belt. But it offers much less protection than convertible seats for children under 40 pounds.

Some models are called *belt positioning boosters* and are designed to make a lap/shoulder belt fit a small child correctly. Used with the lap/shoulder belt, this type of booster provides better upper-body protection than one with a small shield.

★ REMEMBER: When Buying a Booster Seat

☐ A booster with a large shield provides more protection than one with a small shield.

☐ Small shield boosters provide more protection than lap belts alone if the lap belt does not fit properly (very low on the hips) or if the child slouches so the belt moves up dangerously high onto the tummy.

WARNING: *Never use a booster seat with a lap belt alone unless the booster has a shield.*

Sheild Type Booster Seat

Booster Seats

Name	Price	Belt Position	Notes
Century Commander	$25-35	Wrap-around	
Century CR-3	$25-40	Wrap-around	Belt-positioning booster.
Cosco Explorer	$23-32	Wrap-around	2 seat heights
Evenflo Booster Car Seat	$40-45	Through base or wrap-around	Split shield opens in middle; belt through base for short child; internal crotch strap.
Evenflo Sightseer	$25-30	Wrap-around	
Ford TotGuard	$65	Wrap-around	Large shield; 2 seat heights.
Gerry DoubleGuard	$45-55	Through base when used with lap belt	Belt-positioning booster; internal self-adjusting lap belt built into shield.
Kolcracft Tot Rider Quik Step	$20-45	Wrap-around	Shield pivots down on crotch post for seating child.
Virco/Pride-Trimble Click 'N Go	$30-45	Wrap-around	

Based on data collected by the American Academy of Pediatrics.

RECALLED PRODUCTS: Booster Seats

If more than 18 months have elapsed since the recall date, the manufacturer may no longer honor the recall. If the company refuses to comply, you should discard the product to ensure the safety of your child.

Kolcraft Flip 'N Go and Flip 'N Go II Car Booster Seats

WHICH ONES: All PROBLEM: If the padding is removed, the rough surface could injure a child in a crash. WHAT TO DO: Call Kolcraft, at 800-453-7673 (708-458-3800 in Illinois) to receive a snap-on fix-it kit. RECALL DATE: 3/87

Pride Trimble Click 'N Go Car Booster Seat

WHICH ONES: Models 890, 891, and 892 sold nationwide between February 1986 and October 1987. PROBLEM: Seat design allows the child's head to move beyond the standard limit which could result in head injury in the event of a collision. WHAT TO DO: Contact manufacturer at 800-347-8909 ext. 225 (213-532-3570, collect in California) for a free replacement. RECALL DATE: 6/88

Strolee Quick-Click Booster Seat

WHICH ONES: Model 605 with April 1985 stamped on the bottom. PROBLEM: Seat failed government crash test and child may sustain head injury in an accident. WHAT TO DO: Return to point of purchase for free exchange. RECALL DATE: 5/87

Child Identification Products

Most parents are now aware of the importance of maintaining records to help identify their children in the event of an accident. Sometimes these means of identification are associated with efforts to prevent child abduction. While it is certainly important to be able to identify your child if she is abducted, remember that child identification procedures will not prevent child abduction. Here are some methods of identification that many parents have used successfully.

Dental Technology

Forensic dentistry has produced some child identification methods that can assist in recovering abducted children.

The MC-MD, Inc. program involves bonding a micro-disk, no larger than the letter "O", to the back side of a natural tooth or dentures. The disk contains the wearer's name, birthdate, city and state of residence, medical problems and religious preference. It is invisible from the outside but can be easily seen by an examining dentist, physician or police official as a tiny black square covered by clear bonding material. When this is removed from the mouth, it can be viewed under simple magnification to reveal the vital information.

Another dental identification method is Exact-I-Dent, which involves bonding a stainless steel data wafer to a child's tooth. The wafer contains a 10-character alphanumeric code, assigned to the child upon insertion of the wafer by a dentist. The code, which can be read with a convex dental mirror, corresponds to a number-coded statistics sheet that the parents fill out and retain. The code number can be easily transmitted to law enforcement agencies along with other information on the missing child.

Fingerprinting

Almost everyone agrees that fingerprinting is a valuable means of identifying a missing child. This is particularly true when a child is too young to talk, has been badly injured, is uncooperative or afraid to communicate, or has died. Fingerprints are also valuable to police, who may be able to pick up a child's prints in an abductor's car or house.

The controversy surrounding fingerprinting has to do with what method should be used to take the prints and who keeps the prints once they have been taken.

In order for the child's fingerprints to be of help, they must meet the FBI's standards. Many do-it-yourself fingerprint kits currently on the market may not meet these standards and it is difficult for an amateur to get good prints. For more information on getting good fingerprints of your child, contact your local law enforcement agency.

Once you have your child's fingerprints, you should decide if you want someone other than yourself to store them. Many experts strongly recommend that parents keep the prints themselves rather than turning them over to a fingerprint bank that stores them for a fee. Similarly, the American Civil Liberties Union does not believe that police departments should retain children's fingerprints because of their concern about future misuse of the records. If you are at all concerned about privacy, keep the prints yourself and store them in an easily accessible, fire-safe place.

✔ **TIP:** *When fingerprinting, have two sets of prints made and store them in separate places.*

I.D. Cards

I.D. cards are more useful if your child has been in an accident than if he has been abducted. In the case of an abduction, it is likely that the child will be searched for identification. It's important that any form of identification be hidden, so that a potential abductor cannot lure a child by using his name.

For a list of additional organizations that provide child identification cards see Child Identfication in Chapter Nine.

Radio Transmitters

The National Center for Missing and Exploited Children (NCMEC) is concerned about the use of these devices. According to NCMEC, they will not prevent a child from being taken, and a child can still be molested within the protected area. The organization feels the device provides a false sense of security for parents and fosters the notion of a society where children are raised as victims.

One such product is called "Kiddie Alert". It's a tiny (two inches square) radio transmitter worn on a child's belt that sends an alarm to the parents' receiver when the child is more than 100 feet away. It also has a panic button for the child to use if he or she feels threatened in any way. "Kiddie Alert" is also designed to work under water. While these devices have the potential to offer some protection, we don't recommend them.

RECALLED PRODUCTS: Child Identification/Protection

If more than 18 months have elapsed since the recall date, the manufacturer may no longer honor the recall. If the company refuses to comply, you should discard the product to ensure the safety of your child.

Playskool Baby Hand Holder

WHICH ONES: Hand holders sold between June and November 1987 and called Baby Guards Disney Hand Holder No. 9590 with Mickey Mouse on the wristband, and Baby Guards Sesame Street Hand Holder No. 9562 with Big Bird on the wrist band. PROBLEM: The painted characters may contain excess levels of lead which could pose a lead poisoning hazard. WHAT TO DO: Return to point of purchase for a full refund or return product to Playskool Baby, Inc., 108 Fairway Court, Northvale, NJ 07647 for a full refund. If you have questions call 800-526-0371 (201-767-0900 in New Jersey) and ask for Irene Wittels. RECALL DATE: 8/88

Clothes

When shopping for your growing child's wardrobe, look for clothes that are easy to put on and take off. This becomes even more important as your child is toilet trained and learns to dress himself. Look for elastic waists and front zippers. Buttons are difficult unless they are large; snaps are preferable.

The cost of clothing a growing child is not surprising, particularly when they grow so fast and need to be changed so often. To save on clothes, trade clothes with friends who have different-aged children. To avoid misunderstandings, make it clear if you expect the clothes to be returned for a future baby. It will also help if you find out where the consignment and used children's clothing shops are. Most larger cities have many used clothing stores for children. Consignment shops are an excellent way to recycle those clothes that are too good to throw away, but which you know you will no longer need. Buying at used clothing stores does not mean second-quality merchandise—you will be surprised at the generally good condition and quality of clothes offered. You will also save 50 to 70 percent on the cost of your child's clothes.

Here is one set of guidelines for sizes 2T through size 6x (girls) and 7 (boys). Since there are no standards that all manufacturers follow for children's clothing, not all clothes will follow this guide.

Clothing Sizes				
Size	Height	Chest	Waist	Hip
		Girls & Boys [2T-4T and 4-6]		
2T	33	21	20	21
3T	36	22	20.5	22
4T	39	23	21	23
4	39	23	21	23
5	42	23.5	21.5	24
6	45	24.5	22	25
		Girls 6X		
6X	47	25.5	22.5	26
		Boys 7		
7	49	25.5	22.5	26

WARNING: *Apply reflector tape to your child's clothes if they will be outside in the evening hours. This can reduce their chances of being hit by a car by 50 percent. Also avoid letting your child wear a poncho if playing on playground or other equipment where the poncho might get caught and strangle her.*

See Chapter Two for more information on clothing brands, cleaning clothes, children's sleepwear, and special clothes.

Computer Software

There are now over 10,000 computer programs designed for children, and finding a good one is often a matter of luck. Educational Products Information Exchange (EPIE), a nonprofit agency which evaluates educational software, is concerned that most of the so-called educational software on the market today is simply drill-and-practice programs dressed up to look like arcade games. Children talk their parents into buying them because they look fun, but then they quickly get bored.

EPIE estimates that only about three or four of every 100 programs they review are educationally challenging.

Some of the problems associated with "educational" software include: the simple transfer of workbook exercises to a computer program; programs that don't give an explanation of mistakes; confusing directions; and, programs that fail to keep records of progress. Finally, because software manufacturers seek the largest possible market, programs suited to a small group (grades six to eight, for example) may be mislabeled for a wide grade range (kindergarten to nine).

Experts suggest that the best programs are those that teach problem-solving strategies, rather than giving only drills.

✔ **TIP:** *Because the letters on a regular keyboard follow no apparent pattern, young children learning the alphabet find standard keyboards difficult to master. Muppet creator Jim Henson has joined forces with some computer whizzes to produce a keyboard designed especially for kids. The new keyboard has letters in alphabetical order and the familiar muppets aid in improving the "friendly interface" between young operators and their computers.*

Food

Volumns have been written on food issues and the impact of diet on children. In this section we highlight some important issues that we, as consumer advocates and parents, thought you should know about.

Caffeine

Caffeine is a drug and, like most drugs, affects the nervous system when ingested. While most parents know that caffeine is in coffee and chocolate, they don't realize that it is also present in many soft drinks and drug products. In fact, caffeine is an ingredient in more than 1,000 nonprescription drug products as well as numerous prescription drugs. Most often it is used in weight-control remedies, alertness or stay-awake tablets, headache and pain relief remedies, cold products and diuretics. When caffeine is an ingredient, it is listed on the product label.

Caffeine often has a greater stimulant effect on young children than on adults, so you should avoid giving your child foods that contain caffeine.

The tables represent the caffeine content of various foods, beverages and drugs. The data on coffee, tea and other foods are based on the studies using the largest number of samples and reflecting consumer taste preferences.

Caffeine Content of Beverages and Foods

Item	Milligrams Average	Caffeine Range
Coffee (5-oz. cup)		
Brewed, drip method	115	60-180
Brewed, percolator	80	40-170
Instant	65	30-120
Decaffeinated, brewed	3	2-5
Decaffeinated, instant	2	1-5
Tea (5-oz. cup)		
Brewed, major U.S. brands	40	20-90
Brewed, imported brands	60	25-110
Instant	30	25-50
Iced (12-oz. glass)	70	67-76
Cocoa beverage (5-oz. cup)	4	2-20
Chocolate milk beverage (8 oz.)	5	2-7
Milk chocolate (1 oz.)	6	1-15
Dark chocolate, semi-sweet (1 oz.)	20	5-35
Baker's chocolate (1 oz.)	26	26
Chocolate-flavored syrup (1 oz.)	4	4

Source: Food and Drug Administration

Soft Drinks	Milligrams Per 12 oz serving
Sugar-Free Mr. PIBB	58.8
Mountain Dew	54.0
Mello Yello	52.8
TAB	46.8
Coca-Cola	45.6
Diet Coke	45.6
Shasta Cola	44.4
Shasta Cherry Cola	44.4
Shasta Diet Cola	44.4
Mr. PIBB	40.8
Dr. Pepper	39.6
Sugar-Free Dr.Pepper	39.6
Big Red	38.4
Sugar-Free Big Red	38.4
Pepsi-Cola	38.4
Aspen	36.0
Diet Pepsi	36.0
Pepsi Light	36.0
RC Cola	36.0
Diet Rite	36.0
Kick	31.2
Canada Dry Jamaica Cola	30.0
Canada Dry Diet Cola	1.2

Source: Institute of Food Technologists, based on data from the National Soft Drink Association

Fat-Fighting Strategies for Kids

Few parents consider a child's potential for obesity a health hazard. Yet some children are truly in need of a weight reduction program. In addition, medical research shows that the roots of heart disease—clogged arteries and unhealthy eating habits—often begin to develop in childhood.

One study has found that 80 percent of kids overweight as young children were overweight when they reached their teens and early 20s. Overall, about 20 percent of kids were at least 10 percent over a normal, healthy weight. In addition, about half of those with high cholesterol levels as children had elevated levels later, too.

Deciding if a child needs to go on a diet, say experts, depends on several factors:

- ☐ Start with height and weight tables. Children 20 percent over the norm for their age, height and sex are considered obese.

- ☐ Look at your own weight. Children with heavy parents are often predisposed towards obesity.

It is crucial that you check with your child's doctor before starting any weight loss program. To help children lose weight, University of Pittsburgh psychologist Leonard Epstein offers this advice drawn from his years of research on overweight youngsters:

- ☐ Record what your child eats for one week. Figure the number of calories per day. Then cut out 500 calories a day, never going below 1,000 total calories per day. This will allow the child to lose about a pound a week.

- ☐ Make sure children eat a balanced diet.

- ☐ Show youngsters how to use a calorie counter. Have them help you shop for groceries, and when they request high calorie foods, ask them to look up the calorie count so they know why they can't have it. Likewise, show them which foods are allowed.

- ☐ Decrease sedentary activities. Among the least active: watching television, playing video games and working on computers. Put time restrictions on these activities.

- ☐ Increase aerobic exercise. Suggested activities: walking, swimming, jogging. Promote active lifestyle changes, such as using the stairs instead of the elevator.

☐ Keep daily records of what children eat and how much they exercise.

☐ Reward children for losing weight, but don't offer food, money or material possessions. Instead, give them new privileges or spend more time with them.

Food Color

Artificial colorings are added to foods to make them look more appealing. Rarely do these additives contribute to nutrition. Color additives are used in beverages, candy, cereals, ice cream, butter and cheese, sausage casings and meats, baked foods, snack foods, gravies, jams and jellies, nuts, salad dressings and many other foods.

There are two major areas of concern with regard to the health implications of artificial colorings. One is their possible effect on the behavior of children; the other is their toxicology, as revealed by experimental testing.

A connection between diet and hyperactivity in children has been suggested by Dr. Benjamin Feingold, a San Francisco allergist. His theory, implicating many food additives, has prompted numerous experimental studies. Results have been inconclusive, although hyperactive youngsters have shown improvement in their behavior when additives were eliminated from their diets. If you suspect that additives may be affecting your child's behavior, discuss the problem with your family doctor in order to decide if an additive-free diet would be wise.

Studies of the safety of artificial colorings contained in products already on the market have been underway for more than 20 years. The FDA allows these additives to be used by the food industry while testing continues. Completed studies indicate that some of the colors may be harmful, but they have not been removed from the market. In fact, many children will consume up to three lbs. of food dyes by the time they are twelve.

Several consumer groups charge that the FDA has permitted the testing to continue for too long and is reluctant to remove certain artificial colors from the market even if evidence of their danger exists. The following is a list of artificial colorings, still on the market, which may be unsafe.

FD&C Blue No. 2. Industry studies have shown an increase in brain tumors among rats fed this additive, which is used in baked goods, pet foods and beverage powders.

Citrus Red No. 2. This is restricted to coloring the skins of oranges sold in produce departments, and has induced cancer in animals.

Orange B. This coloring is restricted to casings and surfaces of frankfurters and sausages, and has a chemical structure similar to that of amaranth, which was banned because it was found to be unsafe.

FD&C Red No. 3. Some evidence exists that this additive may be harmful, but clear evidence is lacking. It has shown adverse effects on blood and may also cause mutation of the genes. Its use is now banned in cosmetics.

FD&C Yellow No. 5. This additive has been found to cause allergic reactions. As of July 1, 1982, manufacturers are required to list this additive on labels of food that contain it. It is used mainly in candy, desserts, cereals and dairy products.

FD&C Blue No. 1, FD&C Green No. 3 and FD&C Yellow No. 6. No evidence of hazard has been found in these last three additives. However, they may cause an allergic reaction and products containing them may be required to be labeled in the future.

WARNING: *Food manufacturers are not required to list artificial colors on the ingredient label and they seldom do so. But the color of a food may suggest that an artificial color has been used.*

Health Foods

As concerned parents who want to offer our children the best food possible, we will often buy "health foods." Food safety experts are beginning to challenge claims that "health," "organic" and "natural" foods are safer and more nutritious than conventionally grown and processed foods. These terms are often used interchangeably, are difficult to define and often are not supported by scientific evidence. To add to the confusion, the FDA has dragged its feet in taking a position on legal definitions of these terms for food labels. One thing all "health," "organic" and "natural" foods seem to have in common is that they cost the consumer more than conventional foods.

Of course, the mere absence of chemicals is claimed as an advantage for such foods, but the claim is often false. Many of them do contain pesticide residues: even if no pesticide was used on a particular crop, residues may remain in the soil from a prior application or drifting sprays from nearby areas. Since chemically and organically grown foods do not differ in appearance, it is difficult to be sure if a label "organically grown" is accurate.

Many people buy "health" foods because they incorrectly believe that "natural" products are safe. Many poisons occur naturally in foods. Sassafras tea, for instance, has been banned by the FDA because it contains safrole, which produces liver cancer in laboratory animals. Kelp, a seaweed, can have a high arsenic content. Aflatoxin, a known cancer-causing mold, can grow on improperly stored peanuts, corn and grains.

Parents concerned about their child's diet may find it easier to concentrate on "healthy foods" (carrots, apples, raisins, fresh fish, vegetables, etc.) as snacks and at mealtime than trying to buy "health foods."

Pesticides

Many parents are concerned about the harmful effects that pesticide residues on vegetables and fruits can have on both themselves and their children. It's helpful to know that many of the pesticides on foods are topical and can be washed off. The National Coalition Against the Misuse of Pesticides (NCAMP) recommends that you wash all produce in mild soapy or vinegar water and rinse thoroughly. Soap and vinegar cut through the chemicals that keep the pesticides on the plant when it rains.

Washing will not remove systemic pesticides—those that actually enter the plant during growth. The following are some recommendations from the NCAMP for making food safer for your children.

Tips for Safe, Efficient Use:

1. When squeezing homemade juice, remove the rind first. Citrus rinds absorb pesticides.

2. Remove and discard the outer leaves from leafy vegetables, such as cabbage, brussel sprouts, and lettuce, and wash the inner ones.

3. Peel thin-skinned produce, such as peaches and tomatoes. Also peel foods such as cucumbers and apples because fungicides are often used in the wax that covers them.

4. Blanching or cooking thin-skinned produce, such as beans, peas, and carrots, can reduce the levels of many pesticides.

RECALLED PRODUCTS: Food

If more than 18 months have elapsed since the recall date, the manufacturer may no longer honor the recall. If the company refuses to comply, you should discard the product to ensure the safety of your child.

Chilly Bang Bang Fruit Drink

WHICH ONES: Drinks packaged in containers which look like plastic toy guns sold from April through May 1989. PROBLEM: The opening tab at the end of the gun barrel can separate and pose a choking hazard. WHAT TO DO: Return to point of purchase for a full refund. RECALL DATE: 8/89

Pacifier Candy

WHICH ONES: Soft gelatin candy sold under a number of names in various package sizes and in bulk, shaped like a pacifier. PROBLEM: The candy's name and shape imply that it is suitable for young children and babies. When it becomes wet it could lodge in the throat, posing a choking hazard to infants and toddlers. WHAT TO DO: Return to point of purchase for refund or exchange. RECALL DATE: 1/89 and 3/89

Insect Repellents

When it comes to protecting children from insect bites, safety experts are concerned that some of the ingredients in insect repellents may be more harmful than the itchy bites themselves. Diethyltoluamide (DEET), an ingredient found in most insect repellents, has been found to cause toxic reactions in some children after repeated applications.

This chemical can irritate the skin and be absorbed into the bloodstream. If absorbed, DEET can be carried to internal organs and can even affect the child's nervous system, resulting in slurred speech, headaches, and convulsions.

Toxic reactions have occurred when an insect repellent containing DEET was applied to a child's skin for as few as three nights in a row. Experts advise using such products sparingly, preferably not more than one or two consecutive days. If your child really needs the repellent, try putting a very small amount on his clothing or hat instead.

The medical community has not confirmed that DEET is the cause of reactions such as headache, mood changes (crying, irritability), confusion, nausea, and, in severe cases, muscle spasms, convulsions, or unconsciousness, but the EPA is concerned that a small segment of the population may be sensitive to DEET.

Tips for Safe, Efficient Use:

1. Only use products that bear an EPA-approved label.

2. Each time you use the product, read the label and follow the directions carefully. Make sure the product is recommended for the insect you are having trouble with.

3. Always keep the container out of reach of children.

4. Repellents should be applied only to exposed skin and/ or clothing (as directed on the product label). Do not use under clothing.

5. Never use repellents over cuts, wounds, or irritated skin.

6. Don't use near the eyes and mouth or on the hands of young children.

7. When returning indoors, wash the repellent off with soap and water.

8. If your child is reacting to an insect repellent, wash the treated skin and call your local poison control center. If you go to a doctor, take the repellent with you.

You can get specific medical information about the active ingredients in repellents and other pesticides by calling the National Pesticide Telecommunications Network at 800-858-7378. NPTN operates 24 hours a day, 7 days a week.

Life Jackets

Federal regulations require boats less than sixteen feet long, canoes, and kayaks to carry U.S. Coast Guard-approved throwable (a cushion or ring) or wearable "personal flotation devices" (PFDs) for everyone aboard. For safety, the wearable PFDs are preferable.

★ REMEMBER: When Buying a Life Preserver

☐ Check the label for Coast Guard approval and look for any weight limitations.

☐ Have your child try it on to see if he or she is comfortable. Bib-style vests sometimes dig into the neck and certain vests may be too bulky for a toddler to sit down in.

Tips for Safe, Efficient Use:

1. Before you get into a boat, have your child get accustomed to his life jacket by trying it out in the water.

2. Remember that a life jacket doesn't necessarily prevent drowning. It's not hard for a child to overcome a life jacket's stability. In fact, it may be difficult for him to float in a safe position because his body weight is distributed differently than an adult's, and a child is more apt to panic if thrown into the water.

3. A life preserver is not a substitute for supervision by an adult who can swim.

4. A life jacket can't save a life unless it is worn. Coast Guard figures indicate that most people who drown in boating accidents have life jackets aboard but aren't wearing them.

Play Gyms and Slides - Indoor

Play gyms for indoor use offer practice for gross motor skills and, more importantly, are just plain fun! They are intended for children between 18 months and three years. Play gyms are usually made of wood or plastic. A typical wood play gym consists of a hollow box, made of either fiberwood or masonite, and wood that supports a two-step ladder on one side and a short slide on the other. The top of the box, or "platform," serves as a bridge between the ladder and the side and is bordered on both sides by wooden railings (see diagram). Molded plastic indoor play gyms, such as the popular models made by Little Tikes, consist of a climbing platform or slide. Some include a covered canopied platform or added climbing features. One advantage of these molded plastic models is that they generally can also be used outdoors during mild weather months. We prefer the plastic models by Little Tikes over the wood models because we believe they can withstand heavy use and have surfaces that are more forgiving than wood points and edges when little folks trip and fall.

Individual slides of varying heights, for indoor use by young children, are also available in molded plastic from Little Tikes.

★ REMEMBER: When Buying a Play Gym

☐ Make sure the space between the top rung of the play gym ladder and the platform is at least 7.5 inches wide (too wide to entrap a small head).

☐ If constructed of wood, check all pieces to ensure that the wood surfaces are sanded smooth.

☐ Check instructions to determine how difficult the product will be to put together and whether any special tools are needed.

RECALLED PRODUCTS: Play Gyms

If more than 18 months have elapsed since the recall date, the manufacturer may no longer honor the recall. If the company refuses to comply, you should discard the product to ensure the safety of your child.

Mini Gym
WHICH ONES: Model 337 made by Halbrook-Patterson. PROBLEM: Spacing between rungs of ladder could trap a child's head. WHAT TO DO: Discontinue use. RECALL DATE: Pre-1986

Play Gym
WHICH ONES: Model 1601 made by American Toy and Furniture Co. PROBLEM: Spacing between rungs of ladder could trap a child's head. WHAT TO DO: Discontinue use. RECALL DATE: Pre-1986

Timber Form 4000 Series Play Platforms
WHICH ONES: 1,500 sold before 1/86. PROBLEM: Children can get trapped between the metal ladder rungs and wooden platform. WHAT TO DO: Call Columbia Cascade Timber Co. at 800-547-1940 to request a repair kit. RECALL DATE: 1/87

Toddler Gym

WHICH ONES: Those made by Joint Craft. PROBLEM: Spacing between rungs of ladder could trap a child's head. WHAT TO DO: Discontinue Use. RECALL DATE: Pre-1986

Tips for Safe, Efficient Use:

1. When constructing the gym, follow instructions and remember to tighten all nuts, bolts and screws thoroughly.

2. Check for sharp edges and overall stability.

3. The play gym should be checked periodically for loose screws and slippery or sticky surfaces that could cause a child to fall.

4. When deciding where to place the gym, keep in mind that it should not be stationed in a place where a child could use it as a climbing apparatus to reach dangerous things, such as electrical outlets or breakable objects. If using a play gym or slide outdoors on grass, move the equipment periodically as grass becomes worn and packed, in order to provide a more cushioned surface for falls.

5. As always, small children should be supervised when playing on this type of gym.

6. This apparatus is built for toddlers. Older, heavier children should not be allowed to play on it, as they may render it unsafe for younger children.

7. If you have any reason to believe that a play gym you have acquired secondhand was manufactured before 1980, measure the distance between the upper rung of the ladder and the platform. If this space is less then 7.5 inches, do not use it.

Scooters

One of the hottest trends in riding toys is the scooter. They've been revived from the 50's, but they barely resemble the scooters we used as kids. Hand brakes are the biggest difference. For the junior set, Little Tikes and Playskool have models that offer stability. The Little Tikes version has three wheels, with two in the back, and the Playskool two-wheel version has detachable training wheels.

Unfortunately, the increase in scooter popularity has also meant an increase in injuries. The CPSC reports that the number of scooter-related injuries has skyrocketed from approximately 1,000 in 1986 to 18,400 in 1988! Active scooter riders should wear helmets and knee pads. Also, remind children to pay special attention on hills.

Sleds

It's sometimes hard to tell who's having more fun at a neighborhood hill in the winter, the parents or their children! For many of us the first snowfall is a chance to relive the thrill of sledding under the guise of "making sure the kids get some fresh air."

Sledding is great exercise and fun for children of all ages. The very young love being pulled or riding down a not-too-steep hill with Mom or Dad. And two- and three-year-olds can experiment with appropriately sized sleds (slightly shorter than the child's height) on gentle hills too boring for the older sledders (i.e. they're not around.)

There are several different types of sleds, toboggans and disks. Sleds come either with or without runners. A recent study of six- to 12-year-olds determined that the wooden platform sled with flexible metal runners was more steerable than any other style tested. The least steerable was the circular-disk (saucer) sled with no runners.

When purchasing a sled, look for sturdy construction and secure handholds. If using an older, traditional sled, watch for split or splintered wood and metal parts bent out of shape. Check sleds for easy steering without jamming and avoid equipment with sharp, jagged edges and protruding rivets. Do not purchase or use sleds with runners that end in sharp-edged hooks.

Because there are more than 50,000 serious sledding injuries each year, parental supervision is imperative. Changes in terrain, obstacles, and sled steerability are risk factors that children do not necessarily appreciate. Early sledders should stick to short, gradual, uncluttered slopes. Explain how to stop, and teach your child to roll sideways off a sled that goes out of control and to move quickly to the side of the hill. Teach them to walk back up along the side of the hill and not to slide down a slope until all is clear. Sledding is definitely a heads-up activity!

Swing Sets and Outdoor Play Equipment

When you think about it, there are few childhood pleasures more lasting or enjoyable than swinging. In fact, the memories of that sensation are so lasting that few of us can stand idly by an empty swing without being tempted to try it out. Even those of us who won't admit to such temptation would probably confess to enjoying a porch swing, hammock, or rocker.

Most swing sets are shipped directly from the factory and take two to four weeks to arrive. And don't forget you'll have to put it together! (Don't let the idea of assembling the set deter you from buying.) Most kits are designed to be assembled by amateurs in two to four hours. In addition to being good therapy, putting together your child's swing set will give you the satisfaction of actually building what will likely become your child's most used and favorite toy!

If you're still not convinced that you need a swing set, consider this: During good weather most children will want to spend the majority of their free time outside. Good, sturdy play equipment can make outside play even more enjoyable and lets your youngster practice the gross motor skills utilized in climbing, swinging, jumping and sliding, as well as acting out the fantasy of swinging through the "jungle" or keeping watch over the territory from a "pirate ship" or "castle tower."

Today's swing sets are far, far better than the rusty, rickety tubular models you may remember from the backyards of your youth. While you will no doubt be shocked by their price ($400-$1500), these new models represent substantial improvements in design and safety and are built to make their high initial cost a truly good value. Here's what you need to know to select and install the best play equipment for your children.

You have two basic decisions to make when buying backyard play equipment. The first is metal vs. wood and the second is the design.

Metal vs. Wood

Wooden play equipment is fast becoming the more popular option for home use. One reason is that these sets are sturdier, more attractive, and last longer than the thin-gauged, candy striped, metal sets of the past. However, it is possible to purchase metal equipment for home which is much like that found in parks and school playgrounds.

In addition to overall design, the key factor in buying wood equipment is how well the material will withstand moisture and resist decay. Redwood is more expensive and does not need special treatment to naturally resist decay and insect infestation. However, it usually doesn't come with the 10, 15, or 25 year guarantees that pine, Douglas fir and yellow cedar have when they have been pressure treated to withstand moisture and termites. (Look for the term "pressure treated" wood on the label.) This guarantee is generally limited to the wood and not to the equipment itself. When looking over the guarantee, make sure the manufacturer will honor any problems with the wood.

Wood equipment may splinter, so it is best to look for completely sanded equipment. If finishing wood play equipment yourself, avoid using wood preservatives that contain creosote, a carcinogen, or pentachlorophenol, a highly toxic chemical that may be contaminated with the carcinogen dioxin.

If you decide on metal equipment, be sure to look for hot-dipped galvanized tubing for the best rust resistance. Also, check to see that the metal used is a thick-gauge steel (the top bar should be as thick as a nickel and a dime) and has a sealer to help further protect the equipment from the elements.

There are relatively few high-quality metal swing and playsets suitable for home use. If you like the strength and durability of metal, a good choice is a set from Florida Playground and Steel in Tampa, Florida. The company's products look like and are of the same quality you would find in a park, but are specially designed for residential use. For a complete brochure, call 800-444-2655; they also sell wood equipment.

While we're on the subject of materials, you may see some equipment made from white plastic PVC tubes. While it doesn't rust or get splinters, the material can be subject to ultraviolet sunlight degradation and may not withstand as many users because of its limited strength.

Regardless of the material used to make the equipment, check for the following: caps or other protection over exposed nuts and bolts; climbing and gripping parts with slip-resistant surfaces;

plastic or lightweight rubber swing seats; tire swings with a hole for water drainage and no metal-to-metal rubbing parts. You'll also want to know how the equipment is attached to the ground. Metal sets should be anchored in concrete, and most wood sets require metal or wood stakes pounded into the ground and attached to the base to keep them from tipping over. Sets made by some companies such as Woodset Inc. (pressure treated wood) 301-843-7767, and Woodplay (redwood) 919-832-2920 have very wide legs that eliminate the need for an anchor. This makes it easier to move the swing set around your yard to even out the wear and tear on your grass, or to just change things around. If the equipment you choose requires anchoring, make sure the devices for anchoring, or information on concrete footings, are provided along with adequate instructions. If wood stakes are used, they should be pressure treated and not easily loosened. To ensure stability, experts advise using concrete footings for any equipment requiring anchoring.

Choosing the Right Design

After you've selected the material, you must decide what type of equipment you'll choose. A typical basic set includes two swings, a trapeze, and a glider or swing horse. Nearly all the companies offer numerous add ons. If you have the space (and budget) you may want to add some type of climbing gym.

Typically, a climbing gym is attached to one end of the swing set and comes with slides, rope ladders, platforms, and even tents. Further additions include sand boxes, fire poles and tire swings. Adding a climbing gym increases the stability and strength of the swing set, as well as the cost. If you have space limitations, you can purchase the climbing gym separately from the swing set. Shop around—you might find that you like the features of a swing set from one company and that of a climbing gym from another.

✔ **TIP:** *One way to determine which additional features to choose is to watch what your children like when they go to the park or a neighbor's house.*

Other features to look for include: soft seats that keep little fannies in place and won't cause serious injuries if they hit someone; swings that adjust at the top bar so children won't be encouraged to disassemble seats; a slide wide enough to accommodate older children (12 inches is a good width); and a trapeze bar wide enough for older children (12-14 inches).

Finally, make sure you ask about delivery charges and whether or not the set will be dropped off in your yard or out in the street. Tailgate delivery means that you have to lift the cartons off the back of the truck. Many companies offer set-up for an additional charge if you're not feeling adventurous.

WARNING: *We do not recommend swing sets which have an overhead ladder because a child using the overhead ladder may drop or fall onto a swinger or the apparatus below.*

Using Your New Swing Set

As you might suspect, falls are the major hazard with play equipment. In fact, about 60 percent of injuries associated with playground equipment are a result of falling to the ground. The best way to reduce the chances of injury is to carefully select the surface below your playset.

Play equipment should never be placed on asphalt or concrete surfaces. Likewise, packed earth or worn out grass areas are also potential problems. One of the best surfaces for play equipment is shredded mulch. Four to six inches of mulch provides a good cushion for inevitable falls and is easily maintained with a rake. Sand is another alternative, but it can become hard-packed, is kicked up easily, and is attractive to animals. Pea gravel, often found at public playgrounds, offers a less cushioned impact and can cause abrasions. Finally, if you set up your play equipment on grass, add mulch when the grass begins to wear down.

WARNING: *A four-foot fall onto packed earth, or even a one-foot fall onto concrete or asphalt, can be fatal if the child lands on his head. When 4-6" of mulch cover the ground around outdoor play equipment, the likelihood of a serious head injury diminishes significantly.*

Play equipment should be installed at least six to eight feet from fences, walls, trees, bushes and other equipment to avoid injury if (and when) children fall.

Particularly in warm climates, try to face slides to the north or east or in the shade to minimize heat build up. Teach your children to test how hot the slide is before using it.

For safety's sake, it's very important to periodically inspect the equipment. Make sure all nuts, bolts, and clamps are tight and free of rust. Sand and repaint any rusted equipment or surface where protective coatings have worn away. Check for splinters and sand if necessary. Check ground stakes for security and inspect all wood contact points with the ground for rotting.

RECOMMENDED PRODUCTS: Swings and Outdoor Equipment

The following are just a few of the many companies that sell home play equipment. All will send catalogs and price information upon request. Your local toy store, hardware store, lawn and garden supplier or nursery are other good sources for this type equipment.

Child Life Play Specialties, Inc.

This company sells a full line of swings, climbing equipment, tree houses, slides, and more, constructed from pressure treated Douglas fir and yellow cedar. Call 800-462-4445 (508-429-4639 in Massachusetts)

Florida Playground & Steel Co. Inc.

This company sells a full line of swings, climbers, merry-go-rounds, see-saws, slides, and balance beams constructed of thick-gauge tubular, hot-dipped galvanized steel. Call 800-444-2655.

Woodplay Inc.

This company sells equipment made of redwood. They have a full line of swings, climbing equipment, slides, treehouses and more. Call 800-982-1822.

Woodset, Inc.

This company's products are made from pressure treated Southern yellow pine, hand rubbed and sealed with dark brown stain. They sell a full line of swing sets, climbing equipment, slides, sky lodges, chalets and more. This manufacturer also has a Disability Department that will discuss and help customers select equipment for disabled children. Call 301-843-7767.

Limited Space?

City dwellers with tiny backyards or no back yards at all, take heart. There is some play equipment that takes up less space and can easily be moved around as other demands for your family's play area dictate. Generally, these are for toddlers and preschoolers.

Fisher Price

The new Teeter-Round has a seat in the middle so one child can play on it alone or with two friends. It also spins like a merry-go-round. Call 716-652-8402

Little Tikes

We haven't met a child yet that can resist this manufacturer's Play Slide or Indoor Climbing Sets. Little Tikes offers slides in three heights, a Toddler Swing, a Tike Treehouse, an Activity Gym and a Junior Activity Gym, plus picnic tables, sandboxes and play houses. All are made of heavy duty polyethylene that won't chip, rust or splinter. 800-321-0183.

Lillian Vernon

If you're looking for a single swing or rope ladder, consult this popular catalog. Lillian Vernon's old-fashioned wood swing and five-rung rope ladder can be attached to a beam or tree branch and are inexpensive. 914-633-6300.

Today's Kids

They have a Slide-Out Hide-Out that will keep kids climbing and sliding—without even realizing they're exercising! 800-258-TOYS.

★ REMEMBER: When Buying a Swing Set

☐ Choose durable materials. When selecting a metal set, make it is galvanized or painted to prevent rust. Cedar, redwood and pressure treated lumber are recommended in areas where the wood comes in contact with soil or in humid climates, because they tend to resist deterioration. Avoid using wood preservatives that contain creosote, a carcinogen, or pentachlorophenol, a highly toxic chemical that may be contaminated with the carcinogen dioxin. These wood preservatives often ooze to the surface long after application and are more hazardous to young children because of their still developing respiratory and nervous systems.

☐ Look for equipment that comes with its own anchoring device.

☐ Don't buy equipment with open ended hooks, particularly S-hooks. Avoid moving parts that could pinch or crush fingers, rings with a diameter of more than 5 inches but less than 10 (they tend to entrap children's heads) and sharp edges or rough surfaces.

☐ Avoid swing sets with wooden or hard plastic seats. These can injure standing children more easily than soft plastic seats.

☐ Determine the dimensions of the equipment before you buy. You will need at least 6 feet of clearance from walls, fences and other objects. Swing sets take up a deceptively large amount of room.

☐ Only buy equipment that has detailed assembly instructions. Follow instructions for proper assembly, including specifications for tightening nuts and bolts and spacing and anchoring equipment. Make sure that any exposed screws or bolts are capped. If there are no caps available, tape over these protrusions.

RECALLED PRODUCTS: Swing Sets and Outdoor Play Equipment

If more than 18 months have elapsed since the recall date, the manufacturer may no longer honor the recall. If the company refuses to comply, you should discard the product to ensure the safety of your child.

Big Toys Cablewalk Playground Structure
WHICH ONES: Models SB-9B, SB-1 SB-100, and SB-500 made by Northwest Design. PROBLEM: Overhead cables could trap a child's head. WHAT TO DO: Discontinue use. RECALL DATE: Pre-1986

Blazen-Flexible Flyer, Inc. Gym Sets and Horse Attachments
WHICH ONES: Gym sets manufactured between November 1986 and May 1987. Models include 30002, 30012, 41000, 41001, 41121, 41122, 41129, 42021, 42112, 42131, 42132, 42139, 42334, 45131, 61221, 62231, 62431, 62439, 62541, 62624, 62631, 62739, 69231, 69233, 69432, 69461, 69541, 69567, 87538, 99597, 99565. PROBLEM: The brackets which connect the Teeter Totter, Lawn Swing and Horse Attachments to the top support bar could break. WHAT TO DO: Call Blazen-Flexible Flyer, Inc. at 800-521-6233 (601-494-4732 collect in Mississippi) for a free repair kit and installation instructions. RECALL DATE: 7/88

Bounce Around Whirl Playground Equipment
WHICH ONES: Those made by Miracle Recreation Equipment Co. PROBLEM: Children's arms and legs can hit stationary metal supports while riding on the equipment, causing injuries such as broken bones and lacerations. WHAT TO DO: Discontinue use. RECALL DATE: Pre-1986

Empire Super Slide
WHICH ONES: Those made by Carolina Enterprises. PROBLEM: Spacing between rungs of ladder could trap a child's head. WHAT TO DO: Discontinue use. RECALL DATE: Pre-1986

Flying Wheels Tire Swing
WHICH ONES: Those made by Miracle Recreation Equipment Co. PROBLEM: Weld may fail, causing hub assembly to fall and strike user or bystander. Firm offers a choice of two repair options, plus $50 to pay for labor since certified welder is required. WHAT TO DO: Discontinue use. RECALL DATE: Pre-1986

Hedstrom and Sears Wooden Baby Swings
WHICH ONES: Wooden swings sold between April and December 1987 with model numbers Hedstrom 4-789 and Sears 512.70907. Model numbers are on a label on the swing side or seat. PROBLEM: The glue joining the slats frame may fail. WHAT TO DO: Return to point of purchase for a free replacement, or call Hedstrom at 800-233-3271. RECALL DATE: 4/88

Hedstrom Gym Sets
WHICH ONES: Gym sets with model numbers 4-277, 4-377, 4-677, 4-777, 4-778, and 4-877 and Sears brand Gym Sets model numbers 72226, 72026, and 72066, sold from 1982 through July 1988. Model numbers are on a label on the top bar of each set. PROBLEM: The unprotected top bar bracket on glide ride could possibly sever fingertips or cause severe lacerations. WHAT TO DO: For a free Glide Guard Kit, call Hedstrom at 800-233-3271 (800-242-9034 in Pennslyvania), or write Hedstrom Corporation, Department 100, P.O. Box 432, Bedford, PA 15522-0432. RECALL DATE: 11/88

Playground Equipment & Tricycle Seat
WHICH ONES: Those made by PCA Industries. PROBLEM: Lead in paint. WHAT TO DO: Discontinue use. RECALL DATE: Pre-1986

Tips for Safe, Efficient Use:

1. Teach your child not to twist swing chains, swing empty seats, walk in front of moving swings or climb up the wrong side of a slide.

2. Regularly inspect your swing set for loose screws, nuts and bolts.

3. See Chapter Seven for additional playground safety tips.

Television

You may be shocked to learn that American children watch 27 hours of television a week—almost four hours daily. Establishing a pattern for good television viewing habits is a priceless gift any parent can give their child. Action for Children's Television (ACT), a non-profit membership organization dedicated to improving the quality of children's TV experiences, has lots of good advice on children and TV. Here are some of their tips for parents, which apply to the under age five set:

☐ Help your child learn to make good TV selections and plan their viewing ahead of time.

☐ Watch TV with your child; ask questions, explain actions and enjoy the experience together.

☐ If your child chooses programs you prefer he not see, don't hesitate to say no and explain your reasons.

☐ Decide on the number of hours you'll allow on weekdays and weekends; try to limit your children's viewing to 2 hours per day or less.

☐ Don't use TV to punish or reward. Good behavior should not be equated with more television.

If you are concerned about the quality and availability of children's television, ACT suggests that you express your views to broadcasters, your congressional representatives and the Federal Communications Commission (FCC, 1919 M St., N.W., Washington, DC 20554).

These suggestions and more are contained in ACT's "The TV-Smart Book for Kids," which is accompanied by a Parents' Guide. To order this publication and obtain more information on ACT, write to: Action for Children's Television, 20 University Rd., Cambridge, MA 02138.

Toothbrushes

The major difference between a child's toothbrush and yours is, of course, size. In addition, a child's toothbrush tends to have softer fibers. We think the best toothbrushes are the ones your kids are going to use! One way to encourage use is to let your the child help pick one out. Suggest that they choose one with their favorite color or character. The ownership that comes with selecting their own toothbrush will often encourage more frequent use. The same goes for toothpaste. All the popular brands are perfectly adequate in terms of doing the job. However, the key is which ones taste and look the best to your child. There are now a number of flavor selections, (including bubble gum) and styles (sparkle, stars, etc.) that are fun to use and may encourage brushing.

Playskool has introduced a unique toothbrush for children called **Baby's Hugger**. The toothbrush has a three-sided design that wraps around the child's teeth to, theoretically, clean the top, bottom and sides at once. Playskool claims that it's also designed to fit the contour of a child's mouth. It is unquestionably a different design; if it works for your child, go for it!

Videotapes

Explaining to your child that the video cassette recorder (VCR) had not been invented when you were a child is very much akin to your own parents' revelation that they didn't have television when growing up! The VCR is quickly becoming standard equipment in most American homes.

Statistics show that people rent adult videos and buy children videos. This probably is due to the fact that young children like to watch a video over and over again, just as they want to hear that favorite storybook read again and again. While movies such as "Lady and the Tramp" may lose much of their appeal for parents after the fifth showing, kids are still enthralled. Children's videotapes generally retail for $9 to $30, so the purchase of a real favorite can be cost-effective.

★ REMEMBER: When Buying or Renting Children's Videotapes

☐ What is the tape about? You know your child's preferences, fears, and dislikes. You know, too, what values you want imparted. Look for videos that stimulate your child's imagination, entertain or educate. Keep in mind that this advice is sometimes easier given than followed successfully— what is entertaining to you may not catch your youngster's attention and vice versa. Patterns in viewing preference do emerge, and our list of favorites (see below) is a good starting point.

☐ Does the length of the tape match your child's attention span? Some videotapes (such as some of the Golden Book videos) contain three separate stories on one tape so the entire video does not have be viewed in one sitting.

☐ Check out your local library—many libraries today have extensive video collections for loan. This is probably the most inexpensive way to try out a number of videos before purchasing one.

☐ If your child has a particular interest in one subject, consider renting instructional or educational videos prepared for adults on that topic. We know one three-year-old boy who loves airplanes and anything about flying; his favorite video—a professional pilot tape on flying. Previewing any adult tape is always recommended, regardless of the subject matter.

☐ Taping your child's favorite TV programs is an easy and inexpensive alternative to buying or renting. Taping favorites include Sesame Street, Mister Rogers, Charlie Brown specials, Zoobilee Zoo, Wonderful World of Disney, holiday specials (most young children will watch Christmas specials any time of the year!), National Geographic and other learning specials, and Winnie the Pooh.

We culled the video reviews and surveyed parents to find the favorite videotapes for children. Ages listed are approximate and, as with adult tapes, individual preferences will vary! A comprehensive collection of videotapes available for sale by mail order catalogue is offered by Parent Care, 2515 E. 43rd St., P.O. Box 22817, Chattanooga, TN 37422; 800-334-3889.

Great Videotapes for Children

Ages 1-2 (and older)

Hi-Tops' Baby Songs (Media Home Enterprises)
Jim Henson's Mother Goose Stories (Warner Home Video)
Jim Henson's Peek A Boo (Warner Home Video)
Kidsongs (Warner Home Video)
Raffi Concerts (A&M, Several titles available)
Sesame Street's Count It Higher (Random House/Children Television Workshop
Wee Sing (Several titles available)

Great Videotapes for Children (cont'd.)

Ages three and up

Alice in Wonderland (Disney)
American Tale
The Animal Alphabet (Scholastic/Lorimar)
Barney & the Backyard Gang (Several titles available)
Care Bears
Charlotte's Web (Paramount)
Chip and Dale (Disney) (Several titles available)
Cinderella (Disney)
Clifford's Fun With Numbers, Fun With Sounds, Fun With Shapes, Fun With Opposites, Fun With Rhymes, Fun With Letters (Family Home Entertainment)
Digging Up Dinosaurs (Children's Video Library)
Dumbo (Disney)
ET (Contains scary scenes for viewers under five)
I'd Like to Teach the World to Sing (View-Master Video)
Lady and the Tramp (Disney)
Mary Poppins (Disney)
Maurice Sendak Library (CC Studios)
Morris Goes to School (Churchill)
The Mother Goose Video Treasury (J2 Communications)
Mr. Rogers (Several titles available)
Peter Pan
Pinnochio (Disney)
Raffi in Concert With the Rise and Shine Band (A&M)
Sesame Street
Sleeping Beauty (Disney)
The Tale of the Frog Prince (Playhouse)
Wee Sing (Several titles available)
Wee Sing Together (Price Stern Sloan)
Wind in the Willows (HOB)
Winnie the Pooh (Disney) (Several titles available)
Wizard of Oz (Contains scary scenes for viewers under five)

Wagons

Like all children's toys, the "Little Red Wagon" comes in many versions—wood, metal, molded plastic, or combinations thereof, each with various advantages and disadvantages. The standard red metal wagon is probably the most economical choice. Make sure it comes with a rust guarantee. Wooden wagons are very durable and often have added features such as removable sides. Typically, wood will be your most expensive choice—so examine the quality carefully, look for a good paint job and smooth, finished edges on all the parts. Wooden wagons are strong, but heavy.

We like some of the new and colorful plastic wagons (Little Tikes, for example). They are relatively lightweight, their softer surfaces mean potentially fewer cuts and bruises and they will not rust or splinter—very practical indeed, but not for the traditionalist!

Wagon size can vary as much as price—from small inexpensive one-seaters ($20-$40) to large wooden wagons ($95- $250) that can accommodate three toddlers. An added advantage of a wagon is that you can use it for hauling stuff around the yard, toting groceries home, or relieving tired legs at the zoo.

Toys

Many parents and grandparents mistakenly believe that if a toy is labeled for a specific age, the label is accurate and always bears a relationship to the physical or intellectual development of the child. More often than not the manufacturer's motivation for providing an age label may be related to marketing goals or avoidance of government requirements. There are currently no regulations that require an age label. However, items intended for children under three must present no danger of choking, aspiration, or ingestion due to small parts. To avoid meeting this requirement, the manufacturer can simply label his product for ages three to five. While the CPSC can intervene if the toy is commonly understood to be for children under three, there is no way the government can adequately review the thousands of toys on the market.

There are four major problems associated with current age labels:

Toys labeled for children three and older with no additional information. Manufacturers often fail to include *informative* age labeling. By labeling the toy for three years and up, the manufacturer can avoid the CPSC small parts rule and provide no information to alert parents that this product may have small parts or other dangerous components that could injure a three or four year old. As many parents know, a child who is three years old can just as easily be harmed by small parts as a child who is two years and 11 months. Additionally, it is often difficult to determine whether these hazards exist before taking the toy home.

Toys labeled inaccurately. Many times toys are too advanced, complicated or dangerous for the recommended age.

Toys that have no age labeling at all. This is often the case with unpackaged toys, like stuffed animals. But even packaged toys, both domestic and imported, frequently lack any age information. Consumers often mistakenly believe that if a toy is not labeled, it is appropriate for all ages.

Parents ignore age labels. Sometimes parents buy toys for children who are younger than the age stated on the label. Labels stating "not recommended for children under 3" may imply that there are some children under three who might be able to handle the toy. Parents are often tempted to give children advanced toys either because they believe the child is ready, or they hope the toy will serve as a challenge. If more age labels were accompanied by *information* on potential safety hazards, however, this practice might be reduced.

A review of toy complaints filed by parents with CPSC revealed a number of injuries due to missing or incorrect age labels, including:

☐ Battery toys for young children who could remove and chew on the batteries;

☐ Small trucks or dolls causing injuries when children under 2 put them in their mouths; and

☐ Riding toys incorrectly labeled for children age 1-3 when children under 2 were injured because the toys tipped over easily.

Because of the lack of adequate age and safety labeling, parents must all too often fend for themselves and their children in the marketplace. While current age labeling practices are not perfect, *some* companies take it seriously, so remember that *safety* as well as developmental skills could be a factor in the age recommendation.

If you purchase a toy that you believe has an inaccurate age label, contains no age label or does not have sufficient information to accompany the age label, let the CPSC know about it. The agency has many toys to keep an eye on, and your call or letter may alert them to a problem they can alleviate.

The following table provides some guidelines for selecting a toy in the right age bracket.

The Right Age

Up to 2 years

Dangerous Toys	Safe Toys
Those small enough to swallow	Sturdy Rattles
Flammable objects	Brightly colored beads on strong cord
Toys with small removable parts	Washable squeak toys (with squeaker removed)
Those with poisonous paint	Stuffed animals
Stuffed animals with glass or button eyes	Large, soft balls
	Blocks with rounded corners
	Push- and pull-toys

2 to three years

Those with sharp edges	Large peg boards
Objects with small removable parts	Wooden animals
Poisonous paint	Large crayons
Marbles, beads, coins	Rocking horse
Flammable toys	Sturdy cars and wagons

3 to 6 years

Sharp or cutting toys	Nonelectrical trains
Highly flammable costumes, unless treated	Building blocks
Electrical toys	Dolls and doll equipment
Shooting games that endanger eyes	Blackboard and dustless chalk
Poisonous paint sets	Modeling clay
Ill-balanced tricycles or wagons that may topple	Simple construction sets
	Paints and paint book
	Small sports equipment

Toy Tips for 18 Months to three Years

Building blocks and construction toys

Help develop dexterity and creativity and are good for individual and group play. Look for items that are easy to stack and fit together. Giant cardboard blocks are great for stacking and building forts. Plastic blocks that fit together easily should not contain small parts. Pick one type of set and add to it rather than buying different sets with parts that don't fit together. Tinkertoys and Lincoln Logs are difficult and might be frustrating, and contain too many small parts. Save them until the child reaches four or five.

Dolls and stuffed animals

Help act out different relationships and provide comfort and friendship. Dolls with different outfits are fun. Make sure the outfits are easy to change. Accessories like cribs, carriages, and feeding equipment help with role playing.

Playhouses

Provide children with their own special place. Most good sets are expensive, but built to last a long time. Look for kitchen appliances, play cars, and shopping carts that can be used indoors and out and that have accessories like play telephones and desks.

Trucks and cars

Boys and girls like to make pretend noises, destinations, and drivers. Small cars that can be pushed without easily tipping over are good. Large working trucks like dump trucks and tractor/trailers are good for "carrying things around." Look for trucks and cars that will be good inside and out.

Balloons

Of all children's products, balloons are the leading cause of suffocation death, according to CPSC injury data. Balloons are made to hold air inside. Therefore, if a balloon or piece of a balloon is drawn into the throat, it will be just as effective in holding air in the throat. Furthermore, balloons easily mold to the throat's contours and adhere, increasing the danger of suffocation.

Accidents involving balloons tend to occur in two ways. Some children have sucked uninflated balloons into their mouths, often while attempting to inflate them. Others have swallowed uninflated balloons or pieces of balloon they were sucking on. If a balloon breaks and is not discarded, for example, some children may continue to play with it, chewing on pieces of the balloon or attempting to stretch it across their mouths and suck or blow bubbles with it. These balloon pieces are easily sucked into the throat.

WARNING: *The CPSC recommends that parents not allow children under the age of six to play with uninflated balloons unsupervised. The Commission feels that a completely inflated balloon does not present a hazard to young children. If the balloon breaks, however,*

CPSC recommends that parents immediately collect the pieces of the balloon and dispose of them.

Electric Toys

Electrically-operated toys, though intended for use by children, can be extremely hazardous for their young users. Possible dangers include: electric shock; burns (especially if the product has a heating element); and a wide variety of mechanical hazards common to toys in general, like sharp edges and points and dangerous moving parts.

★ REMEMBER: When Buying an Electrically Operated Toy

☐ Check the label—every electric toy must contain certain precautionary information on the label. This information can help you choose the right toy for the right age and warn of potential hazards. *No item with a heating element may be recommended for children under 8 years of age, for example.*

☐ Certain areas of the product itself must also be labeled:

—All hot surface *temperatures* must be clearly labeled;

—Toys with replaceable electric lights must carry a warning of the maximum safe wattage for a replacement bulb and a notice to disconnect the plug before changing the bulb;

—Nonreplaceable lights must be marked; and

—Products not designed to be immersed in water must say so.

☐ *Do not buy an electric toy—or any toy—for a child too young to use it safely.* Always check the age recommendation on the shelf package. Remember that this is a *minimum* age recommendation. If a toy is labeled "Not Recommended for Children Under Four Years of Age," it does not mean that every child who is four years old is mature enough to operate it. Take into account your child's capabilities.

☐ All potentially hazardous moving parts should be enclosed or guarded to minimize the chance of accidental contact. You should not be able to open the enclosure with ordinary household tools.

☐ Products requiring cleaning with a wet cloth must be designed to prevent seepage of water into electrically active areas that might produce a hazardous condition.

☐ Electric plugs must have a finger/thumb grasping area and safety shield to protect small fingers from accidentally contacting energized prongs when the toy is being plugged into a wall outlet.

Tips for Safe, Efficient Use:

1. Read the instructions accompanying the product carefully and then read them with any child who will be using the product. Be sure the child knows how to use the item safely, understands all the instructions and is aware of the hazards of misusing the toy. The instructions should be kept with the toy or in a safe place where they can be found easily.

2. Supervise the use of any electric product. Just how much supervision is necessary is, again, a matter of judgement. Consider both the maturity of the child and the nature of the toy.

3. Be sure that the plug of an electric product fits snugly into wall outlets or (if they must be used) extension cord receptacles. No prongs should be exposed. Do not allow young children to disconnect electric appliances themselves.

4. Keep infants and toddlers out of the area where an electric toy is being used.

5. All electric toys should be put away immediately after use in a dry storage area, out of the reach of younger children.

6. Deterioration of electrically operated toys can cause many hazards. Check their condition periodically. Be alert for broken parts, frayed cords, and damage to wiring enclosures and other protected parts. Protective maintenance is particularly recommended for those products known to have been manufactured before the CPSC requirements went into effect in September 1973.

7. Never let your child replace a light bulb on an electric toy as it is extremely important that the replacement bulb be of the proper wattage and the plug be disconnected when the change is made.

Party Favors

The party favors that are purchased as inexpensive gifts to be given to children at birthday parties are usually quite hazardous. The Toy Committee of the Americans for Democratic Action (ADA) found numerous examples of party favors composed of tiny parts that could easily be ingested by a child.

The manufacturers of most of these party favors protect themselves legally by putting a tiny caution on the package: "small parts, not recommended for children under three years old."

These party favors also pose a serious hazard to children over three who may not only ingest them, but stuff them in their ears and noses. Further, if children under three, perhaps younger siblings, get hold of these favors—as they inevitably will—the potential for danger is even more intense.

Toys that Last

The most popular toys in today's toy boxes have probably been around for quite some time. Here is the era when the toys your children are playing with today were introduced:

1920s & 30s	Erector sets, Lionel trains, Lincoln Logs, Duncan yo-yos, teddy bears, Yahtzee, and Raggedy Ann
1940s	View Master, Tonka trucks, Slinky, Chutes & Ladders, and Candy Land
1950s	Scrabble, Mr. Potato Head, Cutie Bug, Silly Putty, Play Dough, and Colorforms
1960s	Frisbees, Hula-hoops, Etch-A-Sketch, Hot Wheels, Barbie, Twister, Operation, Life, and Mousetrap
1970s	Uno, Nerf balls, Simon, Battleship

Source: Toy Manufacturers of America

Top Selling Toys

Toy marketing is one of the more controversial components of the American marketplace. Are children and their parents manipulated by TV ads into buying products they don't need or that don't live up to their expectations? Consumer advocates say misrepresentation is rampant in the marketing of children's toys. The industry claims that children are bright enough to discern fact from fiction intuitively. Who is right?

Whatever the answer, children's toys and games represent a multi-billion dollar marketplace. In fact, in 1988 we spent nearly $13 billion buying over 2 billion toys and games. Like most industries, records are kept on the best selling items. The following list presents *Toy and Hobby World's* top sellers for January, 1990—although, best selling toys don't necessarily mean the best toys.

Best Selling Toys

1. Nintendo Ent. System - Nintendo
2. Barbie - Mattel
3. Game Boy - Nintendo
4. Teenage Ninja Turtles - Playmates
5. Teenage Mutant Turtles - Ultra
6. Li'l Miss Dress Up - Mattel
7. Micro Machines - Galoob
8. P.J. Sparkles - Mattel
9. Oopsie Daisy - Tyco
10. Real Ghostbusters - Kenner
11. Super Mario Brothers II - Nintendo
12. G.I. Joe - Hasbro
13. Bouncin' Babies - Galoob
14. Party Kitchen - Little Tikes
15. Baby Bubbles - Ideal
16. Zelda II - Nintendo
17. Robocop - Kenner
18. Little Tikes Place - Little Tikes
19. Scattergories - Milton Bradley
20. Batman figures - Toy Biz

Toys — the Best and the Worst

Each year the Washington office of the Americans for Democratic Action (ADA) surveys and analyzes popular new toys. In addition to rating the toys on safety, good play, realistic packaging and advertising, sturdiness and durability, they also test the toys with children. Upon completion of their study they announce their annual "Toy Box" and "Trash Box" lists, revealing the best and the worst of the new toys.

Each year they publish their results in an excellent guide called the *ADA Toy Report*. For the latest copy send $10 to ADA Toy Committee, 1511 K Street, N.W., Washington, DC 20005.

Following are some toys that have appeared in the ADA's Toy and Trash boxes during the past few years. The descriptions are based on the published comments of the actual testers (children) and the ADA researchers. We have also listed the year the toy was rated. For the complete story and lots of additional information on the best and worst of toys, contact the ADA at the address above and request their latest *Toy Box/Trash Box* Report.

The ADA's Toy Box

AM-FM Radio Fisher-Price (3 yrs & up)
"This sturdy, durable child's radio has big control knobs, a clear AM-FM dial, and a sing-along microphone that works! Despite all the times it dropped, the mike didn't become detached, and the radio still worked. The battery cover has a special plastic attachment that makes it difficult to lose, it's small, easy to carry, has a one-year warranty, and sounds good too!" ADA Rating: 1985

Baby Talk Lewis Galoob Toys (4 yrs & up)
"Not only are her mouth and eye movements synchronized with her voice— this doll doesn't need a tape to talk. She tells you when she's hungry; when she wants to play, when she wants to be turned over, etc. And after a few moments, if you don't respond to her, Baby Talk tells you she's sleepy, then closes her eyes—and the battery automatically shuts off. (It's a good thing, too—because it takes eight of them to keep Baby Talk talking!)...[T]his doll is beautiful and cuddly...our kid testers loved her!" ADA Rating: 1986

Barbie 30th Anniversary Edition Mattel (3 yrs. & up)
"Barbie has become a socially aware young woman. This special-edition Barbie, whose sale benefits UNICEF...is among the Barbies are several with beautifully detailed dresses from around the world...The new line of Barbie dolls features an easily stylable, settable hair..." ADA Rating: 1989

Cabbage Patch Kids Hasbro (3 yrs & up)
With bodies that look like a stuffed nylon stocking...each of the dolls manufactured is different in some way...When a "parent" decides to "adopt" a Cabbage Patch Kid, there are papers to be signed and an oath of adoption to be taken. When the proper papers are sent in, he or she will receive a validated adoption form...A year later, a birthday card for the Cabbage Patch Kid will arrive! The clothes are the highest quality we have ever seen on a mass produced doll. This doll doesn't DO anything tricky—so it's up to the child to...[play] with it in imaginative ways." ADA Rating: 1983

Color Champs Road Champs (4 yrs. & up)

This new item is a series of cars treated with thermally-sensitive paint, which causes dramatic changes in color and decor when the cars are dipped in cold or warm water. Unlike some of the other color-changing items reviewed this year, COLOR CHAMPS really works!...We don't know whether or not they may eventually rust from being repeatedly dipped in water...The children were impressed with the color changes, however, and warm (not hot) water was sufficient to produce the changes, so safety was no problem." ADA Rating: 1988

Dirty Dunk Charlico, Inc. (No age requirement)

"This is a realistic basketball backboard, hoop and long mesh laundry bag, attractive enough to display in a kid's bedroom. It encourages neatness and improves your shooting at the same time! It is sturdy enough to accommodate a "nerf"-type indoor ball, and large enough to hold a load of dirty clothes. It unzips at the bottom for emptying out the dirties. It must be anchored securely to wall or door surface. It is decorative and fun, and it's hard to resist shooting things into it, which is the whole point, after all." ADA Rating: 1988

Discovery Map Fisher Price (5 yrs & up)

"The map...of the United States...contains a revolving display of facts about each state...A plastic magnifying lens is provided...The map is sturdily constructed, framed, and provided with recessed space in the back so you can hang it on a wall. It also has an easel stand for use on floor or table top. The facts selected for the map and its companion booklet are good, interesting ones. This is one of those toys that can be a fixture throughout childhood." ADA Rating: 1988

Fun with Food: Kitchen Fisher-Price (3 yrs. - 7 yrs.)

"The Fisher-Price Kitchen is the best new toy of the year!...All the major appliances of a kitchen...are included in the one unit. Other appliances include a pop-up toaster, telephone message center, radio, and clock with turning hands. There are dish towels and pot holders, chalk for the message center, even a fold-down counter and lots of storage space. [I]f your kitchen has it, this one probably does too! There are only two drawbacks as we see it. One is the high price tag of roughly $65 to $90...The second drawback is, it is in short supply." ADA Rating: 1987

Giant Pre-School Loc Blocs 100 pc. Set Entex (3 yrs & up)

"This toy has realistic packaging and advertising, it is sturdy, safe, and has good play value. The Loc Blocs are very much like the Lego system in style, and they come in a heavy-duty plastic bucket with handle and lid for easy storage. The blocs are brightly colored and easy to manipulate. Some pieces have wheels and people. Even children who were beyond pre-school age enjoyed playing with this toy."

Glo Worm Hasbro (2 yrs & up)

"Glo Worm is a cozy, bright green stuffed animal with a night light that lights up the face when the body is pressed. Glo Worm is a good security blanket for young children, and a friendly companion to snuggle up with in bed. One note to parents: The battery assembly is a bit difficult, but once done it lasts for a long time, and the child-proof battery box can be removed completely to machine wash and then dry the toy." ADA Rating: 1984

Hot Wheels Inside Track Mattel (5 yrs & up)

"Hot Wheels Inside Track is a portable, self-contained raceway that comes with two Hot Wheels race cars. The set opens like a book, the child pulls out seven feet of dual lane track, and is ready to race the cars. When play is finished, the child winds up the track, closes the case and can then carry everything away. There are no batteries, no electricity, it works, and the kids loved it. In two months of testing, our set didn't break, and the cars didn't get misplaced, because they store inside." ADA Rating: 1982

Hot Wheels Service Center Mattel (4 yrs & up)

"The Hot Wheels Service Center is a garage for little cars. It is made of hard plastic, folds up instantly into a sturdy carrying case, and there is no assembly required or batteries needed. There are lots of little action gimmicks for children to try...One car is included. Here is a well-made toy of good quality plastic that does what it promises. Its play value is outstanding—none of our testers tired of playing with it." ADA Rating: 1980

Kitchen Set Fisher-Price (3 yrs & up)

This is a collection of colorful, heavy-duty, plastic utensils and a stove that has "coils" that turn red, and a timer with a bell. On the bag that the parts are wrapped in, there is a safety note *in four languages* about the possible danger of suffocation from plastic bags. It also comes with a tablecloth (machine washable and dryer safe!) that turns out to be a storage bag for the equipment! Fisher-Price also urges parents to teach their children about the difference between a toy stove and the dangers of heat from a real stove." ADA Rating: 1979

Lights Alive Tomy (3 yrs & up)

"A cross between Etch-a-Sketch and *Lite-Brite*, this sturdy, lap-sized toy has a "magic" screen filled with rows of tiny holes. Using any one of six different shaped tools, which store handily in the sides of the unit, you can make all kinds of designs and pictures by pressing into the screen, allowing the colored lights to shine through. Our three year olds, our thirteen year olds, and their parents all fought for a turn." ADA Rating: 1983

Little Brown Pony Playskool (3 yrs & up)

"Little Brown Pony is an attractive riding toy for toddlers. Covering the sturdy plastic body is a soft brown plush coat that can be unsnapped for machine washing. The vinyl saddle can also be removed and wiped clean. The pony is on sturdy bright yellow wheels and makes a nice clippity-clop sound when the child rides him. This is a sweet toy that our toddlers enjoyed." ADA Rating: 1980

Little Tikes Place Little Tikes Company (3 yrs & up)
"This new dollhouse will strike a familiar chord in young children, for it is furnished with mini-versions of Little Tikes' greatest hits (full-size real toys). The dollhouse family of five, plus dog, enjoy a roomy home with a backyard...you can't help but be impressed by the clean design and durability of the products highlighted in the dollhouse. These toys were designed with safety in mind. The people in the dollhouse family have well-built, jointed bodies. Unlike other "little people" toys, the Little Tikes family are designed to be too big to get stuck in a child's mouth. A black and an Asian family will be joining the dollhouse line-up in the near future. ...Preschoolers up through 10-year olds flat-out loved the toy. Group or single play is made easy by the open-sided design of the house...For its charm, quality and high play value, we recommend Little Tikes Place." ADA Rating: 1989

Garden Tractor and Cart Little Tikes (3 yrs. - 6 yrs.)
"This is a trike with a nice steady wheel-base. It's a riding tractor, and it pulls a wagon. The wagon is emphatically NOT for towing children, but almost anything else is okay...For a child too mature for a trike but not yet ready for a two-wheeler, or for an interesting substitute for a trike, this is a good choice. It is made of heavy-gauge plastic and it looks extremely durable...We were quite impressed by this toy." ADA Rating: 1988

Magic Show Fisher-Price (4 yrs & up)
"The Magic Show is great fun, and holds the attention of both the "magician" and his audience. The instructions are color-coded, have step-by-step illustrations, and have different levels of tricks for the beginner, intermediate, and advanced-level child. The self-contained trunk, made of durable plastic, has sliding panels, false doors, and all of the accessories store inside!" ADA Rating: 1982

Marching Band Fisher-Price (3 yrs & up)
"Fisher Price's Marching Bank is a colorful pre-school set of musical instruments. It has two cymbals, two colorful maracas, one tambourine, an 8-note harmonica and a drum...all the equipment stores. This is not the only good pre-school instrument set on the market, but it is attractive, well made, and provides easy storage. More than one child can play at a time or a child can creatively combine musical instruments." ADA Rating: 1980

Micro Machines Secret Auto Supplies Lewis Galoob Toys (5 yrs & up)
"Boys and girls both love these tiny topscale cars, with lots of details...The add-on accessories this year are inarguably neat, and not horribly expensive...(Each set...costs under $10.) The "Secret Auto Supplies" series includes a total of six transformables. A can of "gas additive," for instance,

unfolds to reveal a gas station...Each set affords some storage place for Micro Machines. The worst thing about Micro Machines is that they are not safe for children who still put things in their mouths, and you have to think not only about the kid for whom the toy is intended, but about whether there are toddlers or babies in the family who may get hold of them...They are highly collectible, conveniently portable—all in all, a winner." ADA Rating: 1989

Mini Push 'N' Go Preschool Tomy (3 yrs & up)

"These mini-versions of the classic friction toys are new from Tomy. Because they do contain some small parts,...the manufacturer has raised the recommended minimum age for this toy to three years, to minimize the risk of a part such as a wheel coming off and being eaten. These toys can be propelled across a smooth floor easily, and children are quick to master them...A simple and colorful action toy for preschoolers." ADA Rating: 1985

Mini Wizard V-Tech (4 yrs & up)

"Remember Simon—the electronic game of imitating a pattern of light and sounds by pressing brightly colored buttons? It is still around, but now there is Mini Wizard, which gives you four games for about half the price. The four games: Match Me (which is like Simon), Break Out, Music Maker, and Hot Corners. Each game requires memory, logic and concentration. Three of the games...can be played by just one player." ADA Rating: 1988

My Buddy Hasbro (2 yrs & up)

"A tall (22″) and heavy (2 ½ pounds) boy doll dressed in overalls and sneakers that can wear infants clothing. Dressed in high quality clothing, and attractive. We like him." ADA Rating: 1985

Pipeworks Playskool (3 yrs. & up to play; 5 yrs. & up to build)

"Pipeworks is a colorful, oversized construction set that makes it easy for kids to build things they can actually use—like desks, slides, wagons, etc...All of Pipeworks' parts snap together easily without tools, and can be unlocked only by using the Pipeworks Pipewrench...The instruction manual was a pleasure to use, with colorful, clear drawings, and a listing, with illustrations, of every part needed to build each structure." ADA Rating: 1987

Pocket Simon Milton Bradley (4 yrs & up)

"Pocket Simon, new this year, is the hand-held version of the now classic and extremely popular Simon. The game tests your concentration by asking you to repeat, in order, his randomly generated sequences of sound and colored lights." ADA Rating: 1980

Power Workshop Fisher-Price (3 yrs. - 7 yrs.)

"The Power Workshop is a cleverly designed and colorful toolkit filled with all the necessary equipment for a young builder. There is a motorized handle, onto which you can attach a drill bit, a power saw attachment, a buffer, a saw, a screwdriver and wrench...Best of all, when the work is done, all the equipment stores in the portable took caddy, and the workbench acts as a lid!" ADA Rating: 1986

Roller Skates Fisher-Price (4 yrs & up)
"These brightly colored, sturdy roller skates...include an optional wheel control mechanism...slide the switch underneath the skate to "on," and only the forward wheels move—No more backward slides! As the child becomes more comfortable on the skates, just switch the wheel control to "off," and all four wheels move forward and back...The roller skates also have big, fat heel and top "stops" to help prevent falls, adjustable Velcro fasteners on the ankle straps, and a switch to adjust for shoe size (no key or screws necessary)." ADA Rating: 1984

Sky Talkers Fisher-Price (4 yrs & up)
"At last—walkie talkies that work! Fisher-Price's new Sky Talkers are expensive, but they should last. Made with flexible antenna that don't break off, the units also have large, easy to use volume knobs, a hinged battery cover so it can't get lost, talk switches, and a button to use the Morse code, which is clearly printed on the front. When our kids tested them, they were delighted to learn that their voices could be heard through the microphone almost a block away." ADA Rating: 1983

Tap-A-Tune Little Tikes (2 yrs. - 6 yrs.)
"At last—someone has made a preschool instrument that sounds like music...It is a sturdy, well-made, colorful xylophone with keys—no hammer to hit kids over the head with. The different colored notes are coordinated with a song book that is easy to follow. A built-in handle makes it easy to carry, and the strong casing is designed to protect the keys when it falls over. This is a real winner." ADA Rating: 1985

Questron Price/Stern/Sloan-Random House (3 yrs & up)
"Questron is a small pen-like wand with a microchip which senses correct or incorrect answers to questions in the accompanying question books...The Questron Wand is powered by a 9 volt battery which is activated only when an answer is given—no on-off switch to be left on accidentally to wear down the battery. The accompanying workbooks are printed on high quality paper with very colorful graphics. Thirteen early childhood books are available; seven...for grades 1-5; four...aimed at the whole family. With Questron you get big value for a relatively small price—and an "educational toy" that is really fun." ADA Rating: 1985

ADA's Trash Box

D. Compose, An Inhumanoid Hasbro (No age on box)
"These creatures...are the "bad guys" in this "good vs. evil" storyline that is a Saturday morning cartoon. A 14-inch figure with a skeleton rib cage that opens, exposing lumpy red plastic that is probably supposed to be the lungs,

D. Compose "turns anything he touches into a rotting skeleton mutation." That's what to box says, anyway. He really doesn't do anything. He costs alot, though. Would you believe $25 for a pock-marked piece of plastic that doesn't do anything?" ADA Rating: 1986

DoubleDooz ABC's Mattel (3 yrs & up)

"DoubleDooz ABC's is a really cute idea: these are changeable toys for preschoolers that "do double duty" as two toys in one... Transform the toy from letter to object, and learn your ABC's at the same time... Some of the letters don't even "work" that well as objects. Each letter costs about $3, so if you bought all 26 individually... it would cost about $75—a pretty steep price for the alphabet." ADA Rating: 1986

Duncan Hines Tastybake Oven H G Toys H.K., Ltd.

"This electric oven must be used with a 100 watt bulb that makes the oven too hot to touch—a burn waiting to happen... The baking trays that come with the oven... are metal. The top surface of the oven warns "WARNING: HOT to surface. DO NOT TOUCH." Faulty construction, however, makes it impossible to push the baking pans into the oven without touching the top. Fumes from a toy electric oven can also present a hazard." ADA Rating: 1988

Hot Wheels Dinosaur "Mud" Pit Mattel (3 yrs & up)

"Hot Wheels Dinosaur "Mud" Pit is a 12"x15" hunk of molded plastic that comes with a package of squishy brown "mud"... a bunch of tiny pieces of plastic dinosaur "bones," a collapsible bridge, a crane, plastic cactus, and a Hot Wheels car... The mud is cold and clammy; when it's wet, you can roll it in a ball, throw it at your friends and watch it stick to their hair. If you leave it out by mistake, when it dries, it will have stained the furniture... Basically, this toy is a piece (or several pieces) of junk. It's a mess, it has very little play value, and has no purpose. This Mud Pit is the pits." ADA Rating: 1987

Modern Miss Hair Curling Set Blue Box Toys (3 yrs & up)

"The set contains a cute set of empty cosmetic containers and applicators. A wide-tooth comb, a mirror, and a battery-operated play curling iron with several attachments complete the set... Unfortunately, the wand and attachments kept falling apart during play. But the round styling brush is the biggest problem. Once a child has this thing enmeshed in her hair, it is difficult to untangle without pain, unless you choose to take a scissors and just cut the thing loose." ADA Rating: 1989

Modern Play Iron Hingham Ent., Ltd. (4 yrs. & up)

"This realistic iron comes with an extendable cord and a play plug. The realistic looking plug will send a kid directly to the nearest electric socket to try to plug in the iron. That spells DANGER! Extendable electric cords have been involved in many strangling accidents, according to CPSC statistics. They are an obvious hazard... The warning should read "Keep this Modern Play Iron away from kids."" ADA Rating: 1988

Molly and Her Magic Make-Up Well-Made Toy Mfg. Corp. (3 yrs & up)

"Molly is a rag doll. Her "make-up" is already printed on her face...Thermal ink on the face is supposed to change shades from no more than the touch of a child's "warm" fingertips...While we got the colors to change ever so slightly, the changes lasted no more than a few seconds each time. Children got tired of this toy quickly. Molly is no more than a cheap stuffed doll whose manufacturers are trying to capitalize on the hot "color changing" trend with a minimal amount of ink. Not a good buy." ADA Rating: 1989

Paint, Peel & Stick Adica Pongo, Inc. (3 yrs & up)

"Paint, Peel & Stick is advertised as a "reusable" paint. The instructions for this new product clearly state that all the child needs to do is to paint the product on any clean, smooth surface, let the paint dry, peel the dry paint off, and stick it on another surface—reusable stickers to apply to notebooks, doors, and other surfaces...It doesn't work, it makes a mess. And although the label says "non-toxic," the toy gives off a distinct odor of solvent." ADA Rating: 1989

Shark Attack Milton Bradley (5 yrs & up)

"Shark Attack is a violent, motorized board game. The losers meet "death" in the jaws of a fierce-looking motorized shark who devours playing pieces shaped like cute little fish...It requires absolutely no skill, no thinking and entails no learning of any sort. Nothing the players do alters the course of play. Nothing is learned...Shark Attack may be too scary for 5 and 6 year olds." ADA Rating: 1989

Skateboard Smack-Ups Playtime (4 yrs & up)

"Skateboard Smack-ups is a...4" long skateboard with a different figure on top illustrating all the disasters that can happen to a child who has an accident on a skateboard. There is, for example, "Rich Stitched," a figure that is covered with bandages, and what looks like blood and an incision scar...What do the Skateboard Smack-Ups do? Absolutely nothing." ADA Rating: 1987

Sweetie Pops Playskool (2 yrs. - 5 yrs.)

"Sweetie Pops are, to quote the manufacturer, "lovable dolls with easy to dress outfits and long flowing hair that is fun to comb and style."...Sweetie Pops' clothes have the arms and legs attached so that when you take her dress off her limbs are off too. There is a grotesque quality about this toy...The doll is supposed to be easy to dress and undress. That simply is not true...Even older children with better developed small motor coordination found it hard to manipulate the dress on and off. But what did come off easily was the head." ADA Rating: 1987

Tuffies Tyco (3 yrs & up)

"Can you imagine a toy that specifically teaches your child to squeeze a dog's neck *hard* enough for you to take something out of its mouth? That is exactly what Tyco's Tuffies asks you to do...The instructions on top of the picture say: "Give Tuffie a squeeze and he opens wide." The box goes on to state: "the action jaw can grip onto a newspaper, catch a ball, or hold your slippers!" This is a bizarre toy which gives a message that is potentially harmful beyond belief...Imagine the consequences if a young child repeated that behavior with a real animal." ADA Rating: 1987

RECALLED PRODUCTS: Toys

If more than 18 months have elapsed since the recall date, the manufacturer may no longer honor the recall. If the company refuses to comply, you should discard the product to ensure the safety of your child.

Aerosol String Streamers
WHICH ONES: Approximately 1,135,000 cans of five different brands of string streamers sold nationwide during 1989 and February 1990. The products are used like confetti at birthday parties and packaged in aerosol cans. Recalled products include: Streamer Spray, Northeast Imports, Inc., 3.5 oz. cans; MASQUERADE CRAZY STRINGS, Masquerade, Inc., 150 gram cans; Tricky Fun String, Topstone Industries, Inc., 3.5 oz. cans; GOOFY FLYING STRING, Franco-American Novelty Co., Inc., 3.5 oz. cans; and ITS FUN TYME! STRING CONFETTI, Fund World Inc., 3.5 oz. and 7 oz. cans. PROBLEM: The product is flammable, and using it around flames such as birthday candles could cause a serious burn. WHAT TO DO: Return to store where bought for a refund. RECALL DATE: 2/90

Big Mouth Water Toys
WHICH ONES: Big Mouth Fish, Big Mouth Hippo, and Big Mouth Frog plastic wind-up toys sold separately between May 1987 and July 1988. PROBLEM: The small parts may present a choking hazard for small children. WHAT TO DO: Return to point of purchase for refund. RECALL DATE: 7/88

Cap'n Mickey's Motorboat
WHICH ONES: Six-inch long red, white and blue toy motorboat with seated figures of Goofy, Donald Duck, and Cap'n Mickey Mouse, model 8230, sold from 1982 to spring 1988. PROBLEM: The propeller of the boat can come off and pose a choking hazard. WHAT TO DO: Return to point of purchase for a full refund or exchange. RECALL DATE: 11/88

Cheerios Powerball
WHICH ONES: All powerballs contained in 10 million 15- and 20-ounce Cheerio boxes sold from May 1987 to September 1987. The ball

is sealed in a heavy plastic wrapper and has "Powerball" printed on it. PROBLEM: Although the ball meets current federal regulations for minimum size requirements for toys intended for children under three, it has been involved in the choking death of a one-year-old child; there have been four other incidents of toddlers putting the ball in their mouths. WHAT TO DO: Take the ball away from children under three or those who still put toys in their mouths. If you have questions call General Mills at 800-328-1144. RECALL DATE: 9/87

Cook Cuffs Hi-C Promotional Toy

WHICH ONES: Toys distributed in packs of Hi-C fruit drink boxes between February and April 1989. The toy was also available through a mail-in offer. "Cook Cuffs" are brightly colored wrist bands resembling those used in hospitals, with a plastic locking device that holds the bracelet in place. PROBLEM: The plastic locking device can be removed and poses a choking hazard for small children. WHAT TO DO: Return the bracelet to Hi-C Stick-On Cook Cuff, P.O. Box 1133, Maple Plains, MN 55348. A replacement premium will be sent. RECALL DATE: 5/89

Creative Years Magnetic Building Blocks

WHICH ONES: Magnetic building blocks, model 9516 (16-piece set) and model 9521 (21-piece set), sold between 1987 and 1988. The model number is only found on the package—a blue box with the Creative Years logo. PROBLEM: Magnets and pieces of plastic may come off and choke a child. WHAT TO DO: Return to the point of purchase for a full refund or call AMC collect at 212-536-4338. RECALL DATE: 6/89

Creative Years Magnetic Toy Train

WHICH ONES: Mini-magnet auto transport trains sold between 1987 and 1988 with a wooden locomotive and five wooden freight cars. The product was packaged in a blue box with the Creative Years logo and style number 505 printed on it. PROBLEM: The smokestack of the locomotive may detach and present a choking hazard. WHAT TO DO: Take the toy train to the store where bought for a full refund or call AMC collect at 212-536-4338. RECALL DATE: 6/89

Cutie Pie Dolls

WHICH ONES: Dolls sold in retail stores in 1988 singly and with doll clothing and nursery equipment. "Largo Toys, New York 20222" is printed on the back of the head. The following model numbers appeared only on the packaging: 86996, 86201, 86203, 86205, 86207, 86209,

86210, 96211, 96214, and 87791. The 5 ¼-inch dolls have either brown or white soft plastic bodies and blond, black, or brown hair. PROBLEM: The doll's arms, which can be pulled off, and the small parts of the bathtubs and high chairs can pose a choking hazard. WHAT TO DO: Return the doll and accessories to store where purchased for a refund. RECALL DATE: 3/89

Delux and Miniature Voltron Lion Robots
WHICH ONES: Made in Taiwan for Bandai and distributed by Matchbox Toys in 1985 and 1986. PROBLEM: Toy has high levels of lead in paint. WHAT TO DO: Discontinue use. RECALL DATE: 11/86

Disney World on Ice Plastic Toy Figures
WHICH ONES: Five-inch plastic toy figures of Donald Duck, Mickey Mouse and Minnie Mouse sold at Walt Disney's "World on Ice" shows in 1988. PROBLEM: The arms of the toys and Donald Duck's legs can be pulled off and present a choking hazard. WHAT TO DO: For a full refund send the toy to Sells Floto, Inc., 3201 New Mexico Avenue, Washington, DC 20016. RECALL DATE: 10/88

Fisher-Price Pop-up Playhouse
WHICH ONES: Model 2306 Pop-up Playhouses sold between 1987 and 1988. Model number is located on a tag sewn into the seam. PROBLEM: If any of the support tubes break or the tension is released, the playhouse parts can come apart with enough force to break glass, stick into drywall or seriously injure a person nearby. WHAT TO DO: Call Fisher-Price at 800-334-5439 for a free modification kit. RECALL DATE: 7/88

Hardee's Ghostblaster Toys
WHICH ONES: Ghostblasters noisemaking toys distributed nationwide at Hardee's between June 26 and July 23, 1989. PROBLEM: The small batteries may be swallowed by children if dislodged from the unit. WHAT TO DO: Return to Hardee's for a full refund or call Hardee's Food Systems, Inc., at 800-346-2243. RECALL DATE: 7/89

Ice Cream Doll
WHICH ONES: Twelve-inch-tall doll with a plastic ice cream cone sold March 1985 through November 1987 by the Wisconsin Toy Company. PROBLEM: The small ice cream cone presents a choking hazard to children. WHAT TO DO: Return to point of purchase for a full refund or call Wisconsin Toy at 201-279-9518. RECALL DATE: 5/88

Kellogg's Cook Flute and Binoculars

WHICH ONES: Toys packaged in Kellogg's products and sold nationwide in 1988. PROBLEM: Both toys fail the federal small parts regulations and pose a potential choking hazard. WHAT TO DO: To get a free product coupon as reimbursement, send either toy to Kellogg's, P.O. Box 3599, Battle Creek, MI 39016 or call Kellogg's collect at 616-961-2277 or 616-961-2278. RECALL DATE: 12/88

Lawn Darts

WHICH ONES: All Franklin Sports Industries Lawn Darts sold separately as Model 3210 Yard Dart Set, as Model 3283 and 3284 Three Game Combination Set, and as Model 3287 Five Game Combination Set. PROBLEM: The sale of lawn darts has been banned by the CPSC because of the risk of injury the blunt metal tips pose, especially to children. WHAT TO DO: Send the darts to Yard Dart Recall, Franklin Sports Industries, Inc., 17 Campanelli Parkway, Stoughton, MA 02072. RECALL DATE: 12/88

Lively Squeaking Snake

WHICH ONES: Coiled Cobra in striking position sold between May 1987 and July 1988. PROBLEM: The toy contains lead, which can be hazardous to young children who may chew it. WHAT TO DO: Return to store where bought for a refund. RECALL DATE: 7/88

Moving Toy Panda

WHICH ONES: Wind up and battery powered pandas pushing another panda in a cart sold between November 1987 and January 1988. PROBLEM: The balls on the umbrellas and other small parts can come off and present a choking hazard. WHAT TO DO: Discontinue use and return to store where purchased for a full refund. RECALL DATE: 7/88

Peek-A-Boo Clown

WHICH ONES: Style 29/81, made in Taiwan, sold in 1984. PROBLEM: Small parts choking hazard. WHAT TO DO: Return to point of purchase for refund or send to F.J. Strauss Co., 3900 West Side Avenue, North Bergen, NJ 07047; 201-864-0100. RECALL DATE: 10/86

Play Brooms

WHICH ONES: Red toy brooms with "Hungary" written in gold. PROBLEM: Red paint contains excess lead, a chronic poisoning hazard. WHAT TO DO: Return to point of purchase for refund. RECALL DATE: 8/89

Pull Along Bears

WHICH ONES: Pull Along Bear Brother and Pull Along Bear pull toys sold between September and October 1987. PROBLEM: Both toys have small parts which pose a choking hazard. WHAT TO DO: Return to point of purchase for a full refund. RECALL DATE: 8/88

Romper Room Animal Train

WHICH ONES: Number H732R, sold primarily by Pathmark and Rite-Aid stores in Eastern U.S. in 1985. PROBLEM: The toy fails the federal small parts standard and may cause choking. WHAT TO DO: Return to point of purchase for refund or call Electro Plastics at 201-589-2525. RECALL DATE: 11/86

School Days Scissors Desk Sets

WHICH ONES: Scissors Desk Sets sold in July 1988. PROBLEM: The razor blade cutting knife poses a serious laceration hazard to young children. WHAT TO DO: Return set to K Mart for a full refund. RECALL DATE: 9/88

See-Thru Loco Toy Train

WHICH ONES: Clear plastic train sold in 1987 in New York, Maryland, North Carolina, and Pennsylvania; has No. 7980 on the bottom. PROBLEM: Small parts may break off and present a choking hazard for young children. Even though the toy package is labeled "Ages 3 and up," the CPSC has determined that the toy is intended for children under three and must not have small parts. WHAT TO DO: Return to the store where purchased for a full refund or exchange. RECALL DATE: 7/88

Snoopy Wind-Up Train

WHICH ONES: Twelve-inch-long red and white plastic train with Snoopy Figures, sold between October 1988 and November 22, 1988. PROBLEM: The toy breaks apart on impact creating small parts which could choke a child. WHAT TO DO: Return to point of purchase for a refund or exchange or call Lionel Leisure collect at 215-671-3800. Tell the operator that you are calling concerning CPSC. RECALL DATE: 5/89

Spinning Bee Toy Top

WHICH ONES: Toy tops model number 64063, sold between July 1 and December 20, 1988. PROBLEM: The rubber feet on the bottom can be removed and pose a choking, aspiration or ingestion hazard to children. WHAT TO DO: Remove all four rubber feet and send them to Chicco at Artsana of America/Chicco, 200 Fifth Avenue - Room 910, New York, NY 10010. Chicco will issue a $3.00 gift certificate toward the purchase of another Chicco toy. RECALL DATE: 5/89

Submarine Stationery Set

WHICH ONES: Toy stationery sets sold between October and December 1987 shaped like a submarine. PROBLEM: The razor blade cutting knife is inappropriate for young children and could easily cut them. WHAT TO DO: Return to nearest Toys "R" Us for a full refund. RECALL DATE: 7/88

Sweet Home Shoe House

WHICH ONES: Plastic house in the shape of a workboot sold June 1985 through October 1987 by the Wisconsin Toy Company, Inc. PROBLEM: The small parts present a choking hazard to children. WHAT TO DO: Return to point of purchase for a full refund or call Wisconsin Toy at 201-279-9518. RECALL DATE: 5/88

Sweetheart Rainbow Kids Doll

WHICH ONES: Five-and-a-half-inch dolls sold between February 1986 and March 1988. PROBLEM: The arms and shoes can come off and present a choking hazard. WHAT TO DO: Return doll to point of purchase for a refund or call the Oriental Trading Company at 800-228-0475. RECALL DATE: 5/88

Tonka Love Me Tender Dolls

WHICH ONES: Model numbers 8900 or 8901 sold from July 1987 to December 1988. The number is on a tag on the back of the doll. PROBLEM: The eyes could come off and pose a choking hazard. WHAT TO DO: Return doll to point of purchase or to Tonka Products, Attention: Department K, 2950 Robertson Avenue, Cincinnati, OH 45209 for a full refund. For a prepaid mailing label, call the company at 800-458-7262. RECALL DATE: 11/88

Toot Toot Tug Boats

WHICH ONES: Pull toys sold from August to December 1988 at Toys "R" Us stores. Model number 4768 is on the bottom of the toy. PROBLEM: The toy's wheels may come off easily allowing a small metal rod to fall out which could present a choking hazard. WHAT TO DO: Return tug boat to the nearest Toys "R" Us for a full refund or call Toys "R" Us at 800-548-0364. RECALL DATE: 6/89

Great Gifts (2 Years to 5 Years)

Here are just some of the great products available for children ages three to five. We have noted where the product contains small figures. Such toys may be age-labeled for children three and up; however they may pose a choking hazard to younger children. Remember that between ages three and four, children are generally ready to start playing games.

Binoculars
By Fisher-Price—they really work! We especially like the break-away neck strap. (3 yrs. & up)

Boggle Junior
A simplified version of the popular Boggle game, this edition provides the words and matching pictures on cards. Contestants search for the letters on cubes to spell the word. A timer and cover are included for older spellers. (4 yrs. & up)

Cassette Tape Recorder
By Fisher Price—high quality, durability and simple operation. (4 yrs. & up)

Child-size backpack
Look for padded shoulders, reinforced seams; great for storage and travel, and lets kids carry their own stuff! (3 yrs. & up)

Count A Color
Game by Ravensburger. No reading necessary. (3 yrs. & up)

Crackers in My Bed
Game by Parker Brothers. No reading necessary. (3 yrs. & up)

Creeper Keeper
By Today's Kids. Most children love to collect insects. Here's a creative alternative to breakable jars and plastic containers which no one can see through. With a built in flashlight and magnifying glass, this toy makes bug collecting lots of fun. (4 yrs. & up)

Disney Videos
Any of their classics, such as Mary Poppins, Lady & the Tramp, or Cinderella, are sure to please. (3 yrs. & up)

Duplo Train Set by Lego
Includes track, trains and figures; contains small figures, and track is easily manipulated. (3 yrs. & up)

Etch-a-Sketch
By Ohio Art, a classic! (4 yrs. & up)

Flashlight
By Playskool. One of the better designed products for children, this flashlight gradually turns off when your child releases the handle, saving battery power for future use. We recommend this flashlight as an antidote for "night frights."

Globe
We perfer the no-frills model on a stand for first geography lessons.

I-80 Expressway by Little Tikes
This first car track is easy for children to set up and can be used with all kinds of cars. The two curved ramps combine with straight and curved track to form a great roadway. (3 yrs. & up)

Large wood blocks
Consistently mentioned by parents as the product their children return to again and again. (3 yrs. & up)

Magna Doodle
A magnetic drawing board using attached pen. A flick of a knob clears the slate for another drawing. This toy contains small parts. (3 yrs. & up)

Movers and Rakers
By Discovery Toys. A large shovel and rake that make sand castle construction and kids' gardening a breeze. These are two of the strongest products of this type and their large handle makes them easy to use. Well worth the price!

Play figures and sets by Playmobil
An incredible variety of playsets, from school room to hospital and castle to pirate ship, all to spark the imagination of youngsters, but it does contain small parts. (4 yrs & up)

Play Kitchens

Good versions are made by Little Tikes and Fisher-Price. Pretend play in the kitchen is a favorite of boys and girls, and both kitchen sets provide the tools to prepare imaginary meals. (2 yrs. & up)

Reverse Puzzles

By Ravensburger, these puzzles are really two in one, plus their pieces interchange so the puzzles can be solved lots of different ways to make many different pictures. (5 yrs. & up)

Scooter

By Little Tikes or Playskool. Both brands are appropriate and fun for young riders.

Tapes by Joe Scruggs

"Late Last Night," "Traffic Jams," and "Oh By the Way" are three funs musical tapes with good lyrics and catchy tunes. (3 yrs. & up). Children this age still enjoy Raffi tapes, see *Great Gifts* in Chapter Two.

One of the most difficult purchase decisions that most parents will make is selecting child care. While we don't have the perfect formula for finding the perfect person or facility, we do have the key steps that you'll need to take to make the best possible choices.

The demand for child care is at an all-time high, which can make it difficult for you to find the type of child care services you want, so it's essential that you start looking early. Just how early depends on the number of child care facilities and providers in your area and the demand. In many places, there are waiting lists, so it's important to check with other parents to see what their experience has been.

Preschool and babysitting choices can also be difficult—we'll guide you along these decisions and give you some advice on what to do after you've made your selection to keep things on track.

Services You Purchase for Your Child
Child Care, Preschool, and Babysitting

Child Care

This section outlines the different types of child care, some of the tax ramifications and offers pointers on hiring and using babysitters.

The cost of child care is generally a function of what type you choose. If you have just one child, day care outside of the home is generally less expensive than in-home care. However there are types of in-home care, such as hiring an au pair (see below) that can make the cost of in-home care competitive with many day care centers.

Day Care

Choosing a safe and loving day care environment for your child may be one of the most important, and difficult, decisions you will make. The options range from nationally franchised day care centers to local churches to family day care homes, and quality varies widely. It really pays to ask a lot of questions.

In developing your list of day care possibilities, licensing is one factor to consider. Family run day care *homes* may be licensed or certified, depending on individual state laws. All day care *centers* however, must be licensed. The day care licensing agency in your state will tell you what regulations must be followed and provide a list of licensed centers in your area. Always visit your options and check references before making a final decision.

In choosing day care, make sure there are a sufficient number of care givers. For children under age two, there should be one care giver for every three children. For children under ages two and three, there should be at least one care giver for every four to five children. For children three to five, there should be at least one care giver for every seven to nine children.

On your visit you should observe how the care givers deal with the children. Look for common sense, setting reasonable limits, and patience with the children. If the care givers appear frazzled, then something's amiss.

Is the environment friendly and comfortable? Does each baby have his own crib and is there a quiet room for napping? Is the environment generally safe? You should look for the same safety considerations as you have in your own home.

Are the children taken outdoors each day and is there separation of small babies from older children? Find out how the facility deals with sick children. Is there a sick room where children can be watched? What is it like? Do the care givers appear healthy? Does the center require care givers to have annual physical checkups and TB tests? Look for smoke detectors, first aid kits, fire extinguisher, and well secured windows above the first floor. Has the facility been childproofed, as you would your house? Make sure the facility has a safety plan for emergencies and adequate fire exits.

Find out what arrangements are made if you are late picking up your child. Some facilities charge extra and regular arrangements can be made if the day care schedule doesn't match your work schedule.

On your visit, check out how well organized (not necessarily neatness) the place is and look at the play equipment. Is it in good condition? Are outdoor play areas clean and well protected? Are toys, games and furniture suitable for the children being cared for?

Watch how the care givers position themselves when relating to the children—they should be on the child's level and speak with them eye to eye. Also observe how the staff handles transitions—they should be relatively smooth and free from chaos.

When considering day care costs, remember that some centers offer sliding fees based on your income. In addition, some parents offer alternative service to help cover costs such as office help, repairing toys, or other professional services. Be sure to ask about any additional and optional expenses and find out the payment policy for days your child is absent.

An increasingly popular day care option is called family day care. Typically, this is a home in your neighborhood in which a mother takes care of three to five neighborhood children. While many areas require family day care facilities to meet basic safety standards such as have a fire extinguisher and basic childproofing, there may be limited or no licensing or screening of the facility.

Sick-child Care

There are a growing number of centers around the country which accept children who are moderately ill—colds, the flu, eye and ear infections. Unlike regular day care centers, which have lots of organized activities, sick-child care centers stress naps and quiet time.

Hospital-based facilities made up about half of the sick- child care centers. Soon, most hospitals will probably have some form of child care.

Typically, the centers are open weekdays from 6:30 a.m. to 6:30 p.m. at a cost of $10 to $25 a day, depending on a variety of factors, including age, medications needed and severity of illness. Most centers do not accept children with chicken pox, lice, measles, mumps, or other communicable diseases.

In-Home Care

Full time in-home child care is considerably more expensive than day care if you have just one child. In addition to the basic salary and taxes there are the hidden costs of in-home care—increases in your food, utility and maintenance budget. Some parents have attributed increases in home operating costs of $50 to $100 dollars per month with the addition of in-home care.

The actual cost of in-home child care will be determined by what kind you choose. These following are four popular choices arranged in order of their relative costs.

✔ **TIP:** *Consider sharing in-home care with a friend or neighbor, especially if you each have only one child. Not only are your expenses halved, but your children get an instant companion!*

Au Pair

One of the least expensive forms of in-home child care is an "au pair." An au pair is usually a young (18-25) European woman who is willing to live in and take care of children in order to have the opportunity to live in the U.S. While wages are traditionally very low, there are potential problems. You are essentially hiring someone to live with you sight-unseen. If the arrangement doesn't work out—whether you don't like the au pair or she decides to leave—not only do you lose the cost of their transportation to the U.S., but you will find yourself frantically scurrying around for a replacement. Many parents have found that because the average age of au pairs is only 18-25 they are faced with the responsibilities of an instant teenage daughter. The success of using an au pair also depends upon your living situation. Although not necessary, parents have told us it worked best for everyone if the au pair has her own room and bath on a different level from the rest of the family.

Despite the potential problems, the au pair concept has been used by parents for years and the potential exists for an excellent situation. Many au pairs are from large families and have lots of experience with children. You also get the added benefit of exposing your child to another language and culture. And of course there is the cost. The typical wage for an au pair is 100 dollars per week in addition to her room and board. Generally, you will also have to pay a $2500 to $3000 program fee up front that covers airfare, insurance, counseling and social programs for you au pair. Using an au pair simplifies your tax life because you are not required to withhold any tax from the $100-a-week stipend.

While au pairs are traditionally European, many East Coast parents are discovering that young women from the Central and Southwest U.S. are willing to work as au pairs.

Numerous agencies have opened to help find American au pairs. Check your local newspaper or yellow pages under child care.

Using an American au pair removes the advantages and disadvantages of the cultural differences that you'll experience using a European au pair.

Full Time Babysitter

The next step up in expense is finding a full time in-home, (but not live-in) child care provider. Because many parents pay full time sitters less than minimum wage, good ones are hard to find. (If you decide to pay less than minimum wage, don't forget that you could be subject to certain penalties if discovered).

Check with church and community groups, senior citizen groups and friends for possible suggestions. A creative search could land just the right person and save you money. Many other parents are turning to family members for child care and compensating them. While careful consideration should be made before mixing business and family, in most cases, hiring a relative is the best of both worlds - your child gets to develop a close relationship with a member of your extended family and you may be helping them meet financial needs.

Housekeeper

A housekeeper is one of the more expensive forms of in-home care. A housekeeper cares for the baby, does basic housekeeping, and often cooks. Many busy parents turn over the complete management of the home to a competent housekeeper. Housekeepers can live in or out of the home. Surprisingly enough, there is little difference in what you pay. Live-in housekeepers receive about the same amount as live-out because, while they get room and board, they are usually on call for longer hours. A live-in housekeeper can be an imposition on your privacy, but this is a price many working parents are willing to pay for flexibility in the time they have to be home. A live-in or live-out housekeeper will cost more in large cities than smaller towns. The range is around $1000 to $1500 per month in large cities and $500 to $1000 per month in smaller towns.

Nanny

A professional nanny is generally the most expensive child care option. There are a growing number of schools being established solely to train people to care for children. Professional nannies not only receive training in the basic physical care of a child, but also in child development. You can expect that someone who has made the commitment to educate themselves in this area is likely to show a special interest in your child's development. Nannies graduating from schools in this country command salaries of $1300 to $2000 per month. The best way to find one of these professionals is to contact nanny schools in your area and interview some recent graduates. Also, check the child care placement agencies.

Legal Obligations

If you decide to hire someone to help you take care of your children, keep in mind the legal requirements regarding wages and taxes. These extra expenses can add from 15 to 25 percent to the amount you pay your child care person. Some of your responsibilities include:

☐ Child care providers are entitled to the highest minimum wage set by state or local law. In most cases, the local minimum is the same as the federal minimum.

☐ If your child care person does not live with you, she is also entitled to overtime at one and one-half times her hourly rate for work over 40 hours. The National Urban League has a Code of Standards that says live-in housekeepers should be paid regular overtime for more than 44 hours per week and double time for over 52 hours per week.

☐ Federal unemployment tax must be paid for anyone who has earned more than $1000 from you during a three month period. *Contact the IRS and ask for form 940 for the complete details.* In addition, your state probably has special requirements regarding unemployment and worker's compensation taxes.

☐ If you pay anyone over $50 over a three month period, you must pay Social Security tax. Usually, you and your employee each pay one-half of the tax. *Contact the IRS and ask for form 942 for the complete details.* Many parents pay the entire tax for their child care person. Paying Social Security tax is important, not only to keep the system functioning, but because if the IRS finds out you have not been paying, you can suffer severe penalties, no matter how long ago the incident occurred.

☐ At the end of the year, (no later than January 31), you must give your employee a W-2 form indicating how much you have paid her and how much (if any) taxes you have withheld. You also have to send a copy of the W-2 to the Social Security Administration by the end of February.

Tax Credits

You will receive a tax credit for expenses associated with child care if both parents work. While a tax credit is better than a tax deduction (a tax credit directly reduces the amount of tax you owe, a tax deduction reduces the income on which you are taxed), it is not the great windfall that you might expect. First a little about the tax credit:

☐ You are eligible if you are paying for child care and both parents are working (or looking for work) either full or part-time or one is a full time student while the other is working. In addition to the traditional forms of child care, day and overnight camps are also included if your intention is for child care and not the educational or fun experience for the child. If questioned, you must be able to demonstrate this to the IRS.

☐ To get the credit, you must file the IRS long (1040) form and form 2441. Remember to keep all of your receipts indicating that you have, in fact, paid for child care.

Your tax credit is based on your actual child care expenses and your adjusted gross income. For parents who meet the child care criteria, the maximum child care tax credit, if your combined adjusted income is over $28,000, is $480 for one child and $960 for two. While this will hardly offset your expenses, it is certainly worth applying for.

Babysitting

Even if you have a full time child care arrangements, you will probably need to use a babysitter. Generally, the best babysitters are youngsters from the neighborhood whom you know and trust. If you are new to the area, check bulletin boards at stores and schools near your home. Many schools, civic associations, hospitals, and community groups sponsor baby sitting workshops for teenagers. Find out if the sitter you are considering has participated in one of these programs.

Another source of babysitters, (often popular at resorts) is babysitter agencies. Agencies are less desirable because you cannot screen your sitter and they are usually very expensive.

✔ **TIP:** *Check with senior citizens in your neighborhood or a local senior centers. If you live near a college or university, place ads on student bulletin boards.*

Babysitter pay rates depend on a number of factors including the going rate in your region, (suburban teenager average $3.00 an hour), the number of children being watched, the time of day and length of care (some sitters have a minimum charge and some charge more if you are out past midnight), age and experience of sitter, and their duties.

Establish ahead of time what the babysitter charges. If your babysitter is a teenager and does not specify a rate, discuss this before leaving to avoid misunderstandings.

Have the correct amount of money when you return home. Don't ask the babysitter to make change or take a check unless this has been agreed upon ahead of time.

Discuss with your babysitter what you expect of her or him. For example, if you don't want them to go in certain rooms of the house, eat certain foods or have friends over while you are gone, say so. Make sure you tell the babysitter about pet habits.

Invite a sitter who is babysitting for you for the very first time to come to your house at least a half-hour before you intend to leave. Use this time to acquaint the sitter with your child. Also take the sitter on a complete tour of your home. Show her or him what is off limits for children; where every exit to your house is; how to lock and unlock windows; products or areas in your home that you believe are hazardous and that you want your child kept away from; where bandages, washcloths, tissues and paper towels are; where you keep your children's books and toys and which ones you allow them to use while you are gone.

Don't expect your babysitter to do more than she or he is being hired to do—that is, watch your child. Don't ask your sitter to do laundry, bake cookies, or clean house. Don't expect your sitter to fix more than very simple meals and do a minimal amount of clean-up. Watching children is a full-time job. Discuss with your sitter ahead of time whether you expect them to tidy up *after* the children are asleep.

We don't recommend asking your babysitter to bathe a baby or toddler. Bathing children requires utmost care and supervision and is a difficult procedure for those who haven't done it a number of times. The risks of hot water scalds, drowning and falls demand careful attention and experience.

Babysitter Checklist

☐ Prepare a list of important names and telephone numbers, including:
   — where you will be;
   — a nearby friend, relative or neighbor;
   — the child's doctor;
   — fire department;
   — police department;
   — poison control center and hospital.

☐ Advise the sitter never to tell a phone caller she is alone, but to take messages.

☐ Discuss with your babysitter specific instructions for your child's care, including:
   — what your child may and may not eat or drink;
   — bed or nap time;
   — warning not to open doors to strangers;
   — when certain lights should be turned on or off;
   — what play activities your child enjoys;
   — what activities are not allowed while you are gone;
   — how certain baby equipment works (be aware that your sitter may not realize hazards associated with some children's products);
   — what to do in case of an emergency;
   — whether or not the child can play outside, and if so where;
   — and whether the child needs a coat.

Selecting a Preschool

The enrollment rate of three and four year-olds in preschools has doubled since 1970 and continues to increase. As a result, there is often tremendous competition for spaces in good schools. We believe that, although difficult, it is important not to become disheartened by the preschool competition. Getting your child into the "right" preschool is *not* a precursor to their future success. The key to finding a good school is to start looking early. We recommend checking out the schools at least a year before you will need to enroll or apply. Here are some other tips on finding a preschool.

General Considerations

The preschool is often the child's first experience beyond the home, and the philosophy and values practiced there should coincide with and reinforce those practiced at home.

When considering different preschool programs, give some thought to your own needs, expectations and goals as well:

☐ Discipline: is the school's philosophy of discipline compatible with that used at home? This is probably the single most important criterion to consider.

☐ Location: do you want a neighborhood school that enables your child to play with his or her schoolmates after school? Do you want a school near your work? Will you be able to car pool?

☐ Hours: do you want your child in a half day or full day program? A two-day, three-day or five-day program?

☐ Curriculum: do you want your child guided through the activities of the day by the teacher or left free to pick and choose? (Your own style of guiding the child at home will help determine this.) Do you want your child exposed to certain subjects such as music, dance, art or reading? Do you want indoor or outdoor activities emphasized?

☐ Environment: how important is the school's facility to you? Do you want a large, well-equipped school that has available elaborate equipment for sports, science, art, music, etc.?

☐ Price: what are you willing to pay? Price may reflect the extent of the physical facilities and/or the quality of the staff.

☐ Feeder School: is your purpose to enable your child to enter a specific elementary school? If it is, find out what preschools feed into the desired elementary school.

Many parents choose a preschool based on a certain teacher. The teacher is a very important element because he or she sets the tone of the class. But remember that the teacher may easily be changed at the last minute, so it is also very important to look at the school's overall philosophy. The chances are good that any new teacher would conform to it. Asking about staff turnover would be worthwhile because an unusually high turnover of teachers indicates dissatisfaction with the administration and can be stressful for the children.

Another thing to remember is that preschools can change very rapidly. If there is a significant change in staff at one time, the school can take on a totally new character. Also, for schools limited to three- and four-year-olds, the school population changes completely every two years. A school that had a certain reputation a few years ago may have an entirely new one at present.

You may also want to ask about the criteria the school uses for accepting children. Many do it on a first come, first served basis. Other possible criteria include church membership and preference to siblings of current students. Some schools also try to balance their classes by age, sex, temperament, race or culture.

Check Out the School

After you have determined your needs and those of your child, look at what programs are available. Ask to observe the programs in which you are interested. Most schools plan group tours on certain days. If you feel the need, ask to come again another day when a group is not planned. On your visit, see if the children are happy and comfortable. Try to picture your own child in this environment.

To help you evaluate the schools you are considering, the National Association for Nursery Education (NANE) offers the following checklist:

☐ Are there at least two teachers for every group of 20 children or fewer? On occasion can one teacher devote individual attention to a child while the other teacher takes over the group? In a good nursery school, the number of children is small. When groups are too large, children become overstimulated, strained and tense, and tend to feel insecure.

As a result, behavior problems may cancel out the benefits of the group experience.

☐ Are the teachers qualified by education and training in nursery school work? Good nursery school teachers are involved with the children rather than simply monitoring the group or organizing activities. These teachers are gentle yet firm as they encourage youngsters to learn and share.

☐ Do the children seem cheerful and spontaneous in their activities? Bored, aimless children are as much a warning signal about the atmosphere of a nursery school as squabbling ones.

☐ Are the children involved with one another, talking and playing freely? You can always expect to find a few children playing alone, but anything approaching universal isolation is not a good sign.

☐ Is there enough space—indoors and out—for both active and quiet play? Is there a place to temporarily isolate a child who becomes ill?

☐ Is there large equipment for active play, such as carts, shovels, climbing apparatus and balancing boards? Is the equipment sturdy and in good condition?

☐ Are there lots of materials to stimulate creativity—paints, large crayons, clay, building blocks, dolls and action figures, simple musical instruments? Are there storybooks, picture books and phonograph records? Stay away from schools that lack abundant playthings and equipment, or that stringently ration these and activities for fear of "overstimulating" the children.

☐ Are the rooms well heated and lighted, well ventilated and clean? Are sinks and toilets clean? Are safety standards high —is there protection against fires, falls and other accidents?

☐ Have the teachers had first-aid training? Are first-aid supplies readily available? Is a medical checkup required for admission to the school?

☐ Is there a school policy to notify all parents if a child has come down with a contagious disease?

☐ Is there a good balance of quiet and rigorous activity? Do the children get enough rest? In the case of a full-day nursery school program, is a long nap included?

☐ Is the program planned so that the children feel the security of a routine, yet flexible enough to include short trips, special events and new experiences?

☐ Do the children have ample opportunity to experiment, question and investigate?

☐ If the school provides transportation, does the bus or station wagon meet safety standards? Does the driver insist that the children stay seated en route?

☐ Are parents welcome to visit, make suggestions, ask questions and discuss their children? Take the time to go to the school and observe it in operation;-go several different times if you can, and visit the school by yourself. Do not tell the school ahead of time that you will be visiting so that you can get an unrehearsed look at the kind of teaching and atmosphere that the school provides.

Keep in mind that a good nursery school atmosphere reflects both relaxation and a high level of focused activity. While you are observing, try to remain unobtrusive, so that you aren't disruptive to the children's activities.

Interview

Decide on which schools you really like and apply. Most schools require a non-refundable application fee. Many also require a parent interview. This is a chance for you to ask some in-depth questions about the program and the staff. Make a list of questions you have about the program. Some questions you might ask include:

☐ What is done with a child who's lagging or speeding?

☐ What are your strategies for handling different kinds of behavior? What would you do if one child bit another? If a child wet his pants?

☐ How do you help a child adjust to school?

☐ When do you call in a parent for a conference?

Some schools also have a play period for prospective students which enables them to see how your child interacts with others and to see if he or she is ready for a school experience. These play periods will give you the opportunity to get a feel for the general atmosphere from the teacher and administrator. Other things to look for when observing a class include:

☐ Is the room well organized and clean?

☐ Do the children respect and care for the materials?

☐ Do the children take initiative or wait to be told What to do?

☐ How does the teacher treat the children?

☐ Does the teacher speak to individual children with her full attention?

☐ Does the teacher respect the children?

☐ Is the teacher warm and friendly?

☐ Is the teacher aware of what is going on in all areas of the classroom?

☐ How does the teacher discipline a child?

☐ Does the teacher encourage independence by having the children solve their own problems?

☐ Does the teacher plan the day so there are many different kinds of activities?

☐ Does the teacher intersperse quiet activities with noisy, active ones?

For a list of accredited nursery schools in your community, check with your local Chamber of Commerce, as well as with the Department of Health. And, by all means, make inquiries through the parents' network in your area. The advice and recommendations of parents whose children have attended, or are presently attending nursery schools in your community can be invaluable.

The statisticians tell us that children under five suffer an average of 3.6 minor illnesses each year. What the statistics don't reveal is the impact that childhood illnesses have on your own psyche. To see a little one suffering with a cold or fever can be as difficult for the parent as the child. As a result of these inevitable illnesses, purchasing medical services and products can become a significant expenditure. And making the right choice isn't always easy.

In this chapter we will look at many of the medical services and products you will be using, including a pediatrician. We also will provide some tips on handling medical emergencies and offer some suggestions on dealing with the "hidden hazards" in your child's life. Our intent is not to be exhaustive or give medical advice, but rather to review health questions you are likely to have. You should *always* consult your child's doctor or dentist on health matters affecting your child.

Services You Purchase for Your Child: Health Matters

Pediatric Care

Most of us don't really shop around for medical services. One reason is that the profession is shrouded in such mystery. It's ironic, but we will probably spend more time and effort shopping for a car than for our child's pediatrician. This section will give you the information you'll need to ask the right questions and make the best possible choice for your child.

We recognize that many families may choose to use a doctor who specializes in family practice for their child's medical needs. While referring to pediatricians in this chapter and throughout this book, we believe that the information provided is still useful whichever of the two medical specialties your family opts for.

Selecting and Working with Your Pediatrician

One of the first sources you should use when looking for a pediatrician is other parents. Your obstetrician can often also recommend a doctor for your child, or you might inquire at a teaching hospital or medical school for the names of pediatricians. A county medical society, if there is one in your area, can also provide you with names.

Your pediatrician should be certified by the American Board of Pediatrics. But this is only one criterion you should use in selecting your baby's doctor. Equally important is the doctor's concern, the ability to listen and willingness to answer your questions fully and patiently.

A phone conversation with the doctor, nurse, or even receptionist can yield important information about the doctor's medical training, hospital affiliations, and fees for services. It is always good to meet your pediatrician in person before you make a final commitment. While you may have to pay a fee for the visit, it can be well worth the investment; not only will it help selecting the right pediatrician, but you will have the chance to ask some questions about your upcoming birth. Find out during the visit what system is used for answering routine questions, how the doctor can be reached in an emergency, and if house calls are made.

It is very important that you and your pediatrician are compatible. Are the doctor's views in line with yours on breast-feeding versus bottle-feeding? Working outside the home? "Spoiling" a baby? The doctor's reactions to your questions are just as important as his or her answers. *Remember, this is someone whose judgment you've got to trust—occasionally in an emergency— and it must be someone you feel comfortable talking to.*

✔ **TIP:** *One question many parents ask is whether the pediatrician has children of her own. Chances are she will have much more empathy and understanding for your concern about sleepless nights or uncontrollable fussy periods.*

Many pediatricians now offer a morning call-in service during which they are available to answer your routine questions. This is especially reassuring for first-time parents. Offering such a service is one indication that a doctor cares about helping you through the little crises as well as the big ones. Another nice, although not essential, practice is having different waiting rooms for well-child and sick-child patients.

The cost of pediatric care will vary widely from one area of the country to another. If you cannot comfortably afford a private pediatrician's fees, you might consider a well-baby clinic for routine care. Many are run by hospitals or health departments, and are staffed by pediatricians. For more information, call your local hospitals and the city, county, or state health department.

If you are considering a health maintenance organization (HMO), you'll need to ask specific questions about its pediatric services, including:

☐ Are the pediatricians board certified?

☐ Does the HMO facility have a separate waiting room for children?

☐ How long have the parents you encounter when you visit been waiting to see the doctor?

☐ What arrangements are available for after-hours care?

☐ What exactly is the HMO's policy on pediatric specialists, should your child need one?

Going to the Doctor

During the first year, most family practitioners or pediatricians will want to see the baby every one or two months. During these visits, the doctor not only checks on your infant's weight and growth but also examines heart, lungs, liver, spleen, eyes and ears; looks for the closing of the soft spots on your baby's head; checks for the emergence of teeth; and looks for possible signs of anemia.

He or she will also check on development—including the baby's responses and vocal sounds, and when the baby rolls over, crawls, sits up, stands, and starts to walk. Many pediatricians include a test for hypertension (high blood pressure) in the checkup. At about two months, the first immunizations are begun to prevent childhood diseases—polio, measles, mumps, rubella, diphtheria, tetanus, whooping cough.

During the second year, many physicians want to check the child's health and development three or four times. Then, they check once or twice a year from ages two to six and before your child enters school for the first time.

What to Ask the Doctor

The following are some typical questions asked by parents during their child's first year:

☐ What should I do if the baby cries a lot?

☐ When should I phone and what should I do if my child gets sick?

☐ What is considered a high fever? How and when should I bring it down?

☐ What about diarrhea? . . . Spitting up a lot?

☐ What should I do and whom should I call in an emergency when the doctor is out?

☐ In general, what's "normal" for a child of this age?

You can expect advice on such matters as proper nutrition and accident prevention, as well as what to expect in child development. If you have questions about your child's health or behavior between appointments, you should feel comfortable calling the doctor or nurse or the health center.

Preparing Your Child for a Doctor's Visit

Children differ in their reactions to doctors and checkups. Many are curious and enjoy the visits. Others resist no matter how reassuring the doctor, nurses, and parents are. A parent's positive attitude together with a doctor's friendly manner can help a child learn to accept checkups and treatment more easily.

Even very young children can be told why they go to the doctor, and what to expect:

☐ "The doctor will listen with a stethoscope to your heart and lungs."

☐ "This (shot) will hurt at first."

☐ "Mommy (or Daddy) will give you the medicine from the doctor to make you better."

Here's some more advice on making a visit to the doctor easier on your child:

☐ Avoid scheduling appointments during nap and meal times. Appointments first thing in the morning may be great for both of you—especially if you're working.

☐ Select clothes that are easy to take on and off.

☐ If possible, leave siblings at home and bring the child's favorite toy, book, or blanket.

☐ If the doctor asks that the child lie down and he is restless, try not to let him sit up; pushing him down again will only increase his anxiety.

☐ Let your child watch while being given a shot. If you tell her to look away, you'll contribute to her fear that something horrible is about to happen.

Generally, it is good for children to participate in decisions concerning their health care and treatment. Encourage your child to ask questions and try to provide simple but accurate answers to them. Encourage your child to ask the pediatrician about the questions you don't have answers to.

To help your children appreciate and learn more about their health, don't hesitate to discuss the importance of eating certain foods, brushing teeth, washing hands before meals, and the need for sleep.

After-Hours Pediatric Clinics

An alternative to hospital emergency rooms, gaining in popularity as a way of treating minor injuries that occur after your pediatrician closes her door, is the after-hours pediatric clinic. Staffed by pediatricians and nurses, they are generally open from 5 p.m. to midnight on weekdays and from noon to midnight on weekends and holidays.

After-hours clinics typically handle health problems such as earaches, sore throats, fevers, cuts, and rashes. They are usually less traumatic for your child than an emergency room, and they are also less expensive.

✔ **TIP:** *When you use one of these clinics, make sure they send your child's records to your pediatrician so she can follow up on the problem.*

Going to the Hospital

If your child requires hospitalization for tests, treatment, or surgery, you will want to discuss the following with your child's doctor:

☐ Kinds of treatment to be administered and why.

☐ How to prepare the child for the hospital.

☐ Length of the hospital stay.

☐ Benefits to be expected from the treatment.

☐ Rooming-in facilities, if any.

☐ Risks and/or side effects.

☐ Convalescence and home care.

Using clear, reassuring terms, explain to the child exactly why he or she is going to the hospital and what to expect. You do not have to burden him with every detail, but tell him enough so he can express his feelings and concerns. Then, you can correct misconceptions or distortions. Don't hesitate to enlist the doctor's or nurse's help.

It's best to visit the hospital before admission. Most children's hospitals have a special program (often on Saturdays or Sundays) to introduce your child to the hospital.

Ask whether you can stay overnight. If you can't, visit as often as possible so that you can be there during most of the child's waking hours.

Dental Care

Dental hygiene is as important for babies and young children as it is for adults. This section touches on some of the dental issues important during your child's first five years. Many future dental problems can be averted by establishing a regular routine of dental care for your child. Almost total prevention of tooth decay can be achieved through proper care of teeth, dental visits, fluoridated water and other sources of fluoride. Start early and establish good dental habits; your children will thank you when they reach their 20s and 30s.

Bottle Mouth

Nursing bottle mouth or bottle mouth syndrome is a serious form of tooth decay that can occur when an infant drinks from a bottle of milk, formula, sugar water, or fruit juice during naps or at night. While the child is asleep, these liquids pool around the teeth; acid then attacks the teeth and decay begins. Decay also results from daytime pacifying; since the child is awake, however, saliva does help rinse some of the liquid out of the mouth.

To prevent nursing bottle mouth, the American Dental Association recommends that you avoid feeding an infant sugar water, sweetened gelatin, soft drinks, and other sweetened liquids. In particular, it warns against allowing infants to fall asleep with a bottle containing these liquids. Pacifiers dipped in honey or sugar can also have damaging effects. If your baby needs a bottle for comfort, fill it with water or use a clean pacifier.

It's best to clean a baby's teeth if she has had a bottle of any liquid other than water.

Brushing and Flossing

The American Dental Association recommends that parents use a damp washcloth or gauze pad to wipe off their infant's teeth after every feeding. Later, when all of your child's primary teeth have erupted (about age two to two-and-a-half; see Dental Development Chart above) you should begin brushing and flossing them. At age four or five, teach your child to brush his teeth thoroughly but continue to supervise each brushing and to floss your child's teeth for him.

Children generally need brushes that are smaller in design than the typical adult brush. Brushes should be replaced every three or four months or when bent or frayed. Preschool children often need new brushes faster because they tend to chew on the brush or to brush with uneven or imperfect strokes.

Dental Development Chart for Primary Teeth

	Eruption Date	Shedding Date
Upper Teeth		
Central incisor	8 - 12 months	6 - 7 years
Lateral incisor	9 - 13 months	7 - 8 years
Canine (cuspid)	16 - 22 months	10 - 12 years
First molar	13 - 19 months	9 - 11 years
Second molar	25 - 33 months	10 - 12 years
Lower Teeth		
Second molar	23 - 31 months	10 - 12 years
First molar	14 - 18 months	9 - 11 years
Canine (cuspid)	17 - 23 months	9 - 12 years
Lateral incisor	10 - 16 months	7 - 8 years
Central incisor	6 - 10 months	6 - 7 years

This chart is only a guideline: months and years given are approximate dates.

Source: American Dental Association

Dental Visits

Some experts recommend that the child's first dental visit occur before age two. During that first visit, the dentist will ensure that the first few teeth are in good shape, and provide you with advice on healthy dental hygiene practices. It's a good idea for the child to visit the dentist without getting a filling, in order to foster a positive attitude about going to the dentist.

Regardless of the age you and your dentist decide to start routine check ups, remember that primary teeth (or baby teeth, as they are often called) can get cavities too, and that these teeth play an important role in chewing, speech habits, and preserving space for the child's permanent teeth.

In selecting a dentist, we recommend choosing one with a pediatric practice or who has a considerable number of child patients.

Diet

Teeth, like other parts of the body, need a well-balanced diet to remain healthy. The American Dental Association recommends that parents daily give their children food from the four basic food groups (fruits and vegetables; bread and cereals; milk and dairy products; and meat, fish and eggs). Other diet factors affecting your child's dental health include the frequency of eating foods containing carbohydrates, the length of time these foods stay in the mouth, and the physical characteristics of these foods (such as stickiness).

Fluoride

It is well documented that fluoride is a very effective factor in preventing tooth decay. Fluoride can have a beneficial impact on teeth in two ways: through ingestion of small quantities of fluoride, such as is found in fluoridated water or fluoride drops or tablets; or through the topical application of fluoride to the tooth surface, such as treatments in the dentist's office or from fluoride toothpastes and rinses.

Studies have shown that children who drink water containing the right amount of fluoride have up to 65 percent fewer cavities. It's important to realize that not all water is fluoridated; only just over 50 percent of the U.S. population drinks fluoridated water.

In addition to showing the effectiveness of fluoride, numerous studies have proved it safe. Statistics also show that fluoridation is inexpensive. It costs, on average, only 35 cents per person per year. Some estimate that for every dollar spent on fluoridation, up to 50 dollars may be saved in dental bills.

If the water in your area is not fluoridated, ask your city or county officials how this issue can be brought before the community for a vote. Citizen initiatives in this regard can be very effective, and the long-term benefits of fluoridated water are substantial. Topical fluoride treatments also help reduce the potential for tooth decay, but are not as effective as fluoride ingested through water or tablets and passing into the bloodstream. Consult your dentist for advice concerning fluoride treatments and rinses.

For a free brochure on flouride and dental health, send a self-addressed, stamped business-sized envelope, with 25 cents postage, to the American Academy of Pediatrics, P.O. Box 927, Elk Grove Village, IL 60009.

Swimming Pools

Unfortunately, a growing dental concern centers around one of the healthiest of children's activities—swimming. Pools with high chlorine levels will also have high levels of acidity, and acid causes the erosion of tooth enamel. In a recent study, 18 percent of the swimmers in a high-acid pool showed increased levels of tooth decay. Those who used the pools most often—including 59 percent of the swim team—were most likely to have problems. The American Public Health Association recommends that pool acidity levels be kept at a pH of 7.2 or above.

Sealants

Sealants are a method of fighting cavities in which a thin covering of plastic material is painted over the deep grooves and pits of the tooth's chewing surfaces to keep food and plaque out and thus reduce the risk of decay.

Sealants are meant to ease a child through his or her cavity-prone years. They may eventually wear off, but can be reapplied. The process is painless (there is no drilling involved) and relatively inexpensive. A sealant is not the same as a filling, however. It is important to seal a tooth when it first erupts, before any decay sets in. If you are considering sealing your child's teeth, be on the lookout for the first permanent molars, which come in around age six or seven. These do not replace any teeth but erupt behind the last baby teeth, and parents are often unaware that they have appeared.

Thumb Sucking, Orthodontic Nipples and Pacifiers

Thumb sucking is a natural habit for many children and generally decreases after the age of two. Some children, however, continue thumb sucking past the age of four. And this can cause problems with normal dental development. Consult your dentist if you are concerned that your child's thumb sucking may interfere with good dental health.

Look for orthodontic pacifiers and nipples designed to prevent incorrect sucking, which can later lead to tooth problems. These products are usually marked "orthodontic" or are shaped to resemble the human nipple.

Drugs

Antibiotics

At one time or another, your doctor will probably prescribe an antibiotic to help your child get rid of a persistent cold or infection. Antibiotics can work wonders in getting rid of the illness, but combined with each other or with certain foods, they can lose their effectiveness or even become poisons. Here are some general guidelines to consider if your child is taking antibiotics. Of course, your physician should be consulted immediately if you suspect any problems.

☐ Oral penicillins, with a few exceptions, should be taken with water on an empty stomach. And some penicillins may not work as well if citrus juice is drunk within one hour of taking the medicine.

☐ Food and dairy products often interfere with tetracyclines. The best time to take tetracyclines orally is usually one or two hours after meals, with water. Take care not to give this medicine to your baby with milk formulas, and remember that if you're taking it, it may be present in your milk if you're breast-feeding. Tetracyclines could cause permanent discoloration of your infant's teeth.

☐ Tetracyclines and penicillins should not be taken together.

☐ Erythromycins, too, are best taken on an empty stomach with a full glass of water. If, however, this causes stomach distress, taking them with a cracker or toast will not significantly impair their effectiveness. Erythromycins can also be passed into the breast milk, and although no clear effects on the child have been shown, many doctors advise against taking erythromycins if you're breast-feeding. Like tetracyclines, erythromycins should not be taken with penicillins.

Later on in the chapter we have some important information on food and drug interactions.

Aspirin and Reye's Syndrome

Aspirin is one of the leading causes of drug poisoning of young children in the United States. A tablet of adult aspirin or acetaminophen (Tylenol) is too high a dosage for a child weighing less than 50 pounds. Children's tablets contain about one fourth the amount of aspirin or acetaminophen found in an adult dose. When giving a child chewable medication, however, be sure to stress that it is medicine, not candy; flavored, chewable aspirin is responsible for many poisonings of children under five.

Past U.S. Surgeon General C. Everett Koop, M.D., has said that most childhood illnesses are self-limiting and usually don't require any medication at all. Doctors often suggest that a child with fever simply be made comfortable with cool compresses. Then, consult with your physician should the fever be persistent or high. Of course, physicians continue to find aspirin useful and safe for adult, teen, and childhood arthritis and other conditions.

Always check with your pediatrician before administering aspirin to your child. When given to children with chicken pox or flu, aspirin has been linked to the development of Reye's syndrome—a rare, sometimes fatal condition. Important new information has become available about the development—in children and teens with flu—of this *rare* but serious condition. It is described as a swelling of the brain, combined with liver malfunction and blood disorders. Reye's syndrome kills 20 to 30 percent of its young victims and leaves many survivors brain damaged. The U.S. Public Health Service acknowledges a possible link between the use of aspirin in treating flu or chicken pox and an increased risk of Reye's syndrome. The National Academy of Sciences, after reviewing the pilot studies, has also found "strong support" for the link.

As a result, the Secretary of Health and Human Services has asked manufacturers not to recommend aspirin for use in treating the flu and chicken pox in children, and to add a warning to all aspirin-containing products against using aspirin for treating flu and chicken pox in children and teens.

While only a few cases of Reye's syndrome occur each year, it is important to familiarize yourself with its symptoms. The first sign generally is persistent vomiting. The child may be sleepy and lethargic, but still responsive. Within half a day, he or she can become disoriented, combative, and delirious. Untreated, the result could be fatal.

Even though the initial symptoms certainly don't confirm its presence, Reye's syndrome is a medical emergency. A child with Reye's syndrome symptoms must be taken *immediately* to a hospital, where blood and body fluids can be monitored and a respirator used if breathing fails. Surgery may be needed, in some cases, to relieve pressure on the swollen brain.

Cold and Cough Remedies

Many children's cold and cough remedies contain alcohol as a significant ingredient. The American Academy of Pediatrics recommends against giving children medicine containing more than 5 percent alcohol. Check the percentage of alcohol before you buy. It will always be listed in the ingredients. Even products specifically labeled for children can contain significant amounts of alcohol. Contac Jr., for example, contains 10 percent alchohol. Vick's Children's Cough Syrup and Dorcol both contain 5 percent alcohol, as do some types of Triaminic and Robitussin. Children's CoTylenol and Cogespirin contain no alcohol.

Generic Drugs

One of the ways you can cut 50 to 70 percent off of your child's medicine bills is to buy generic drugs. Generic drugs are identical to their name brand counterparts, so you need not fear that you are buying inferior drugs. In fact, many of the generic equivalents are made by the same manufacturer that makes the name brand drug.

Ipecac

Ipecac is a must for the medicine chest. Ipecac is used to induce vomiting in the event of accidental poisoning. It will safely last for two or three years. When buying ipecac, make sure you ask the pharmacist when it expires, and mark the expiration date clearly on the bottle if it is not already there.

Ointments

Many topically applied skin products that are perfectly safe for adult use can be hazardous if used on infants or young children. They sometimes contain hormones, mercury, or insecticides that are not absorbed by adult skin. Infant skin can absorb these toxic ingredients easily because it is very thin and contains more blood. Even some cosmetic products may contain ingredients harmful to children and infants. To be safe, never use a skin treatment on infants or children unless it is specifically recommended for pediatric use or by your pediatrician.

Dispensing Medicines

When giving a child medicine it is very important to use a medicine dispenser because most teaspoons are not true measures. Because your child weighs so little, even small discrepancies between the correct dosage and what you actually give her can be dangerous.

In a study of 13 million American children who need and use prescription medicine, the National Council on Patient Information and Education found that almost half received too much, too little, or none of the medicine. Common problems included parents using any available spoon or forgetting to give the medicine, the child refusing to take it, and stopping a medication too early because the child *looked* well.

It's also very important to wash the dispenser each time you use it. If you put a dropper back into the medicine or vitamin bottle, bacteria picked up from the child's saliva can multiply in the solution. Most children's medicines and vitamins have a sugar base, which is an ideal environment for bacterial growth.

Eye droppers can also become contaminated if the applicator touches an infected eye. If bacteria are introduced into the solution, the drops should be discarded. Some doctors recommend disposing of eye drops after treating conjunctivitis to keep from infecting others who may use the medicine.

Drugs and Foods That Interact

Thousands of people lose the full benefit of the drugs they take because they consume food or drink that inactivates the medication or slows its absorption. There are so many drugs that physicians sometimes have difficulty keeping up with the safety rules for taking them. Ask your doctor and/or pharmacist how each drug prescribed should be taken and what food, if any, should be avoided. While your child is on medication, be sure to inform your doctor of any unusual symptoms that occur after eating a particular food.

Drugs and Foods That Do Not Mix

Fruit juices, citrus fruits, tomatoes, vinegar, cola, pickles
INCOMPATIBLE DRUGS: Antibiotics (such as penicillin, ampicillin, and erythromycin) and aspirin. WHAT COULD HAPPEN: Decreased antibiotic action, increased irritation of stomach (aspirin), ulcers, or gastric bleeding.

Dairy products, sardines
INCOMPATIBLE DRUGS: Tetracycline. WHAT COULD HAPPEN: Reduced effectiveness of drug.

Monosodium glutamate (MSG)
INCOMPATIBLE DRUGS: Diuretics. WHAT COULD HAPPEN: Elimination of too much sodium from body.

Drugs and Foods That Do Not Mix (cont'd.)

Brussels sprouts, cabbage, cauliflower, kale, rutabaga, mustard greens, soybeans, turnips
INCOMPATIBLE DRUGS: Thyroid hormones. WHAT COULD HAPPEN: Interference with hormones; goiter.

Green leafy vegetables, asparagus, bacon, broccoli, brussels sprouts, beef liver
INCOMPATIBLE DRUGS: Anticoagulants. WHAT COULD HAPPEN: Neutralization of blood-thinning effects.

Excessive licorice (artificial does not produce harmful effects)
INCOMPATIBLE DRUGS: Any drug that affects heart or blood pressure. WHAT COULD HAPPEN: Excessive potassium loss, which can result in fatigue; high blood pressure; heart failure.

Foods containing sugar
INCOMPATIBLE DRUGS: Antidiabetics. WHAT COULD HAPPEN: Drug action blocked.

Immunization

Surprisingly, millions of American youngsters remain unprotected from the seven childhood diseases (polio, measles, rubella, mumps, diphtheria, pertussis, and tetanus). There are a variety of reasons for this lack of immunization, including economics and lack of local health-care facilities. In addition, however, many parents are simply not aware of or not impressed with the dangers of the diseases. Unlike our parents, we did not grow up with these childhood diseases. Surprisingly few of us have ever seen or even known of someone who had polio, tetanus, or diphtheria. As a consequence, we don't always take the trouble to protect our children, and we remember immunization, perhaps, only when school-entrance requirements force us to.

Public health officials have become worried that cases of measles, mumps, and whopping cough (pertssis), have risen steadily over the last several years because the percentage of young children receiving vaccines has dropped. If the trend continues, childhood diseases that are now considered minor problems in the United States could return in force.

Because immunization is a major component of your child's early medical care, we thought we would briefly review exactly what immunization is. The use of vaccinations to create immunity takes advantage of complex natural defensive machinery. When the human body is invaded by germs—bacteria or viruses—the body protects itself by creating antibodies against them. The invading germs also cause the white blood corpuscles to increase in sensitivity, and thus in germ-fighting effectiveness. Some germs produce a toxin (poison), and the body acts to counter it with an antitoxin.

If, however, you survive a particular invasion of germs and get well, your body retains the ability to recognize the germs and to manufacture antibodies to fight them. If a second invasion takes place, the antibodies will fight the germs off. You are now "immune" to that particular disease and will not become ill. Anyone who has had measles, for example, will not get them again.

In the past, when the diseases were more prevalent, many people went through mild—sometimes symptomless—episodes of infection that left them unharmed yet protected. This is why today's children are in special danger: with prevalence of the germs in the environment much reduced after years of immunization programs, many youngsters have never encountered the invaders, as previous generations did, and have therefore not built up resistance. If not immunized, they remain highly vulnerable to the germs they do meet.

With more vaccines being developed every year, vaccination can now protect against about 25 common diseases. But most important are the Seven immunizations that should be used routinely to protect children.

Immunization Schedule

According to the schedules suggested by the American Academy of Pediatrics (AAP) and the U.S. Public Health Service (PHS), some shots can be started at two months of age and can be given in combinations of two or three vaccines at a time. Most require a series of shots over the child's early years in order to build up the full level of immunity. Some, such as tetanus and diphtheria shots, should be renewed every ten years—for life.

Following, then, is the schedule suggested by the AAP for the immunization. Along with immunization, the AAP calls for a skin test at 12 months to detect tuberculosis infection.

Any suggested schedule of immunization is only a guideline, which may be modified by the physician to fit a child's state of health, relative risk of exposure, and, with certain limits, seasonal considerations or parental convenience. The important point is to consult your physician or child health clinic just after your child's birth so that arrangements can be made for a complete series of immunizations. Keep a careful record of the type and date of each injection or vaccination.

Be sure to get your child's immunization record from your doctor or health department. Take it with you each time you take your child to the doctor and keep it up to date. That way you will know whether the series is complete and when booster doses are due. You will need to present the record when your child enters school or a preschool program, goes to camp, and if you move or get a new physician.

Recommended Immunization Schedule

Age	Preparation
2 months	DPT (diphtheria-pertussis-tetanus), OPV (triple-type oral polio vaccine, given earlier if in danger)
4 months	DPT, OPV
76 months	DPT (OPV optional, given if polio is around)
12 months	Tuberculin skin test
15 months	MMR (measles, mumps, rubella in combination)
18 months	DPT, OPV
4 to 6 years	DPT, OPV
14 to 16 years	Td (tetanus-diphtheria toxoid, adult type)
thereafter	Td every 10 years

[NOTE: 4-6 years DPT and OPV boosters between child's 4th and 7th birthdays]

*Adapted from the 1982 Report of the Committee on Infectious Diseases of the American Academy of Pediatrics.

DPT

Because of the publicity surrounding cases of children who suffered serious side effects or even died after a whooping cough vaccination, many parents have nagging doubts about whether the prevention is worse than the diease.

Whooping cough, or pertussis, is the "P" in the DPT vaccine. Children generally get the three-pronged vaccine, which also protects against diphtheria and tetanus, at 2, 4, 6, and 18 months, with a final booster between the ages of four and six years.

The vaccine used today is essentially the same as the one introduced in the mid-1940s. Because it contains the whole bacterium, weakened by heat or chemicals so it won't grow in the body, it can cause some of the same neurological problems associated with a whooping cough infection itself. Ideal vaccines contain only components of the bacterium or virus, lessening the chance of side effects.

The American Academy of Pediatrics estimates that a "serious, permanent neurological disorder" will follow 1 of every 310,000 DPT vaccinations. About 15 million doses are given in the United States each year. Because physicians are not required to report side effects of the vaccine, exact figures on side effects are not available.

The side effects identified by the Food and Drug Administration include swelling and pain at the injection site, fever, and, less commonly, seizures. In rare cases there may be brain disease or death.

Dissatisfied Parents Together, a national group started by parents whose children became severely ill or died after a DPT shot, notes that the scientific literature reports episodes of diarrhea, rashes, abscesses, coughing, vomiting, unconsolable crying, shocklike collapse, and sudden infant death syndrome (SIDS).

But the American Academy of Pediatrics has concluded that "pertussis the disease produces 10 times the rate of brain damage as pertussis the vaccine. And if large numbers of children are left unprotected, it could become a disaster."

Dissatisfied Parents Together advises that parents make sure the person administering the shot takes a complete family history, including information about neurological disease and siblings' experience with the vaccine. The group also says the child should be healthy when the shot is given, and administration of the vaccine should be delayed for premature babies or babies with neurological problems. Following the shot, they recommend that parents watch their children carefully for three days.

Their advice differs little from that of the American Academy of Pediatrics, which suggests that children who have histories of convulsions or certain neurological conditions not be given the pertussis vaccine. The Academy also recommends that children who suffer serious side effects not be given further pertussis vaccinations. That advice is echoed by federal agencies.

Children who do have these problems can still be protected from diphtheria and tetanus with a DT shot.

Poisons

According to the Poison Prevention Council, "About one out of every three childhood poisonings occurs at the home of a child's grandparents." A contributing factor is that older people often request their prescription drugs (plus over-the-counter medicines and household products) without child-resistant caps. While this is a convenience to grandparents, they should be aware that it could pose dangers for their grandchildren.

Poisoning is a medical emergency. Thousands of people are poisoned every year; unfortunately most of these are children under the age of five.

It is amazing how many common household products are poisonous when swallowed or inhaled by children. Most people know that rat poison and medicines can be dangerous, but how many suspect that bath oil or cigarette butts can be harmful?

In many cases, children are poisoned because they are curious. Youngsters can't resist putting things into their mouths. Medicine looks like candy, motor oil looks like cola, poisonous bright red berries are attractive and tempting. Anything within reach can wind up in a child's mouth.

Sometimes, children are poisoned when they try to imitate their parents. Children see their parents using perfume, furniture polish, fertilizers, and paint thinners. Both parents may take vitamins in the morning or have a drink in the evening.

Once parents are aware of the many poison hazards in the home, it is easier for them to protect their children. Keeping dangerous products out of reach, using locked cabinets, and making sure that safety caps are secure are ways of preventing children from being poisoned. (See Chapter Nine for more childproofing tips.)

In order to reduce the risk of your child ingesting medicines accidentally, always buy prescription and nonprescription drugs in child-resistant packaging. Keep the product in its safety packaging and resecure the safety cap after each use. Be sure to read all labels and follow the directions. If the medicine is not already dated when you purchase it, record your purchase date. Check the expiration date before administering.

Never give or take medicine from an unlabeled bottle. Never give medicine in the dark. *Never tell children that medicine is candy.* Because children love to imitate adults, never take medicine in front of your child.

When your child's illness is over or the prescribed amount of the medicine has been taken, pour the leftover medicine into the sink or flush it down the toilet, rinse and reseal the container, and put it in the trash. Remind grandparents and other friends who may be visiting not to leave medicines out where children can get into them.

If your child should accidentally ingest a medicine or other poison, call your Poison Control Center immediately. Keep syrup of ipecac on hand, since the Poison Control Center may direct you to use it; however, because some poisonings require dilution rather than vomiting, be sure to get the poison expert's advice before administering anything.

We strongly recommend calling the nearest *certified* poison control center. Only a small percentage of poison centers are accredited. Most of the non-accredited centers consist of a phone in a local hospital emergency room, answered by people not necessarily trained in clinical toxicology. In addition, they may not be answered 24 hours a day.

Each of the American Association of Poison Control Centers (AAPCC) members is affiliated with a hospital and is staffed by a physician with a background in family medicine, pediatrics, or emergency medicine. The people who answer the phone are trained in toxic substances and their effects. They all have computerized information on hundreds of thousands of commercial products, plants, poisonous snakes and insects, and street drugs.

If a child has ingested a potentially toxic substance, have the following information available when you call the poison control center:

☐ your name and telephone number

☐ age of child

☐ weight of child

☐ name of product and ingredients

☐ the container itself

☐ amount ingested

☐ time poisoning occurred

☐ symptoms

☐ any first aid provided.

Be certain to have syrup of ipecac in your house, but do not administer this inexpensive emetic unless advised to do so by a professional.

Accredited Poison Control Centers

For an up-to-date list of the Certified Regional Poison Control Centers, write to Dr. Theodore Tong, Secretary, AAPCC, College of Pharmacy, University of Arizona, Tucson, AZ 85721.

The following is an outline of emergency procedures to follow if you think your child may have ingested a poison *and you are unable to reach a poison control center or doctor.* Note that the poisons have been divided into two basic types—noncaustics, and caustic/petroleum products. *The two types require radically different first aid procedures.*

First Aid for Noncaustic Poisons

Look for these signs of poisoning: an empty container nearby; nausea; dizziness; drowsiness; slurred speech; clammy or very dry skin; thirst; odor of poison on breath; convulsions; coma.

Take these steps only if you cannot reach a poison control center or doctor:

1. Give the child one or two glasses of milk (use water if no milk is available).

2. Induce vomiting by giving one tablespoon of syrup of ipecac or by wiggling your finger or a spoon handle at the back of the tongue.

3. When the child is through vomiting, give five or six teaspoons of activated charcoal mixed in a glass of water.

4. To avoid choking in case of additional vomiting, do not allow the child to sleep unattended for at least an hour.

5. Treat for shock: Lay child down. Elevate the legs 8 to 12 inches. Cover with a light blanket.

6. If the child becomes unconscious, maintain an open airway. Administer artificial respiration if breathing stops.

7. Get medical help as soon as possible.

★ REMEMBER:

☐ Do not try to give liquids if the child is unconscious.

☐ Do not force liquids, as this may cause vomiting.

☐ Do not give syrup of ipecac or induce vomiting in any other way for caustic poisons or petroleum products.

☐ Save the poison container.

Noncaustic Poisons

Acetone
Aftershave lotion
Antifreeze
Arsenic
Barbiturates
Boric acid
Chlordane
Cologne
Deodorant
Fireworks
Hair dye
Ink
Insecticide
Laxatives
Liniment
Mistletoe berries
Mushrooms (any wild kind)
Naphthalene
Paint (lead)
Perfume
Prescription drugs
Sedatives & sleeping pills
Tobacco
Varnish
Weed killer

Acetaminophen
Alcohol
Antihistamines
Aspirin
Benzene
Carbon tetrachloride
Cigarettes & cigars
DDT
Diet pills
Fluoride
Holly berries
Insect repellent
Iron tablets
Leather dye
Indelible markers
Mothballs, flakes & cakes
Nail polish remover
Oil of wintergreen
Paregoric
Pesticides
Rat poison
Suntan products
Tranquilizers
Vitamins (more than a few tablets)

First Aid for Caustic Poisons and Petroleum Products

Look for these signs of poisoning: An empty container nearby; burns around the mouth; burning sensation in mouth, throat, and stomach; odor of poison on breath; cramps, bloody diarrhea, coughing, gagging, difficulty swallowing, or drooling.

Take these steps only if you cannot reach poison control center or doctor:

1. Give one or two glasses of milk (use water if no milk is available).

2. Treat for shock: Lay child down. Elevate legs eight to twelve inches. Cover lightly with a blanket.

3. If child becomes unconscious, maintain an open airway. Administer artificial respiration if breathing stops.

4. Get medical help as soon as possible.

★ REMEMBER:

☐ Do not give liquids if child is unconscious.

☐ Do not force liquids, as this may cause vomiting.

☐ *Do not* give syrup of ipecac or induce vomiting in any other way for caustic poisons or petroleum products.

☐ Save poison container.

Caustic Poisons and Petroleum Products

Ammonia	Battery acid
Benzine (not Benzene)	Brush cleaner
Charcoal-lighter fluid	Bleach
Corn remover	Crude oil
Depilatories	Diesel oil
Drain cleaners	Electric dishwashing detergent
Fabric softener	Floor polish
Furniture polish	Gasoline
Gun cleaner	Hair permanent-wave solution
Hydrochloric acid	Lighter fluid
Liquid disinfectant	Lye
Metal polish & cleaner	Mineral seal oil
Naphtha	Nitric acid
Oven cleaner	Pine oil
Quicklime	Rust remover
Scouring powder	Spindle oil
Sulfuric acid	Toilet-bowl cleaner
Wart remover	Washing soda
Wax (furniture, floor)	

We do not intend this section to be a substitute for medical advice. Regular communication with a trusted pediatrician is one of the most important ways to safeguard your child's health. But since more and more Americans are concerned about personal health and helping their children avoid many of their own bad habits, we have tried to touch on those areas that you might want to explore further with your doctor or medical provider. As with anything else that is important to your child, ask questions and don't be afraid to shop around.

Most of us remember the family trips of our childhood—and what a production they were! These infrequent forays into other lands were preceded by weeks of planning and packing, culminating in a marathon car ride to the mountains, lake or seashore. Car seats were unheard of and the family station wagon was set up so that the "way-back" became a wrestling ring, art room and bed.

Services You Purchase for Your Child: Traveling Together

Times have changed and while most of us can still remember our first plane ride, our children are likely to have that experience at a time well before memories begin. We've become an extraordinarily mobile society and family trips are more frequent and for longer distances than ever before. With this greater mobility, we need faster and safer ways to travel. And that's what this chapter is all about—getting ready and getting there. We've complied numerous tips that have helped experienced traveling parents, not only survive the family trip, but actually enjoy it. The key is being prepared and being flexible.

Air and car travel are the most popular forms of transportation, so that's where we focussed most of our attention. But don't forget about the train—intercity rail travel can be a thrill that your child (and you!) will never forget. Because you may not know the safety seat requirements in the states you plan to visit, we've included a list of laws that apply in each of the fifty states. Finally, check out our travel tips and have a great trip!

Air Travel

A veteran traveling parent we know likes to tell the story of the young flight attendant working her way down the aisle during her pre-flight check who gasped in amazement when she discovered our friend busily applying stick-on stars all over her child's clothing! As she continued applying the remaining stickers on socks, shoes, legs, arms, tummy and just about everywhere— she looked up and calmly explained that rearranging the stars would occupy her 2 ½ year old for a major portion of the 2 hour flight. And she was right!

If this sounds like a crazy travel tip, then you haven't been airborne with a toddler who wants to do everything but what you and the passengers seated around you want him to do. Unfortunately it doesn't take a youngster long to learn that your ability to discipline at 30,000 feet in the air—with no "time out" chair—virtually evaporates. Before divulging some more of our best time-occupying and kid-pleasing travel tips, we'll start with the basics. Here is a checklist to use when planning your family's next plane trip.

Fares

Most airlines do not charge for lap children (under 2 and not occupy their own seat) and many parents have been known to stretch this rule. While many airlines offer discount fares for children over 2 (some up to 50% off; see chart), these are discounts from the full adult coach fares. Most of the time, you'll do better with adult "Super Saver" tickets than the child's fare.

Routes

Another important factor in choosing an airline for travel with a child is the route. It may be worth it to your family to pay more or adjust your travel schedule to take a non-stop flight.

Seating and Boarding

When booking your flight ask for a bulk head seat, the first row in the coach section. There is generally more room—a real bonus when changing diapers or letting a toddler stretch his legs. Also, window seats often give toddlers and pre-schoolers the chance to watch the activity outside before takeoff and after landing. When making your reservation, be sure to tell the clerk that you are traveling with a child; many airlines will try to note this and keep the seats next you empty for as long as possible.

✔ **TIP:** *When traveling with a non-paying infant, reserve your seats around a middle seat. They're always the last to go and if the plane's not full, you'll get a seat for your child.*

Most airlines pre-board families with young children. Some parents take advantage of this opportunity to get everybody and their family gear on before the rush begins. We like to board at the last possible moment—to minimize the time our kids are confined to the cabin.

Northwest Airlines offers a bassinet service on half of their domestic flights. If you request this service, you'll get the first row bulk head with a bassinet that fastens to the wall of the bulk head. The bassinet can be used during the entire flight, except landing and take-off. It gives everyone in the family more room to move and gives baby a comfortable place to sleep on long flights. This service is also offered on most international flights. But sign up early—it's first come, first serve.

Child Safety Seats on Airlines

All major U.S. airlines now allow passengers to use automobile safety seats if the seat has been approved by the Federal Aviation Administration (FAA) for use on aircraft. Seats manufactured after February 26, 1985 are approved but must have *two* stickers on the seat: one signifying FAA approval and the other compliance with Federal Motor Vehicle Safety Standards. Seats manufactured between January 1, 1981 and February 25, 1985 must have a sticker indicating compliance with the Federal Motor Vehicle Safety Standards. Seats without these labels and seats manufactured before January 1, 1981 may not be used on aircraft.

Physician groups, including the American Academy of Pediatrics and the American Medical Association, strongly recommend that children under 2 use a safety seat on all flights. In a crash, the parent's weight can crush a child sitting on the parent's lap or the parent may not be able to hold onto the child.

If you purchase a ticket for your child, you are assured of being able to use your FAA-approved child safety seat. If you have not purchased a seat for a child under 2, many airlines will let you use a safety seat in an adjacent vacant seat. However, if the flight is fully booked you will not be allowed to bring the seat on. (It can be checked as luggage). Check with the airline when making reservations regarding their policy on child safety seats and the use of seats.

For a free copy of the FAA publication *Child/Infant Safety Seats Acceptable For Use in Aircraft*, write to the Office of Public Affairs, AA-200, Federal Aviation Administration, Washington, D.C. 20591.

Keeping Kids Comfortable

Give children gum or something to chew on during takeoff and landing and give a baby a bottle to help reduce the pressure that can build up in their ears. Try to do this as soon as the plane starts its descent or when you feel the first early changes in pressure in your ears. To help avoid motion sickness, don't let a child who is prone to stomach upsets read while in the air. Before and during the trip, avoid strong odors and spicy or greasy foods that may upset the stomach. Consult your pediatrician for advice before travel if you believe motion sickness will be a problem for your child.

Food

All the major airlines will warm bottles and are usually well stocked with apple juice! On meal flights they all offer special lunches and dinners for children—but you must pre-order them. We strongly recommend pre-ordering a child's meal, especially for younger kids. Airline meals are definitely adult oriented!

Luggage and Baby Equipment

Pack a carry-on bag for use during the flight and as a backup for lost luggage. Include extra clothes, food, and diapers—anything that you may need during the first 12-24 hours after your flight (See below for more tips on what to pack). If traveling for more than a few days, you can save yourself a lot of hassle at your destination by buying a carton of diapers before leaving and just checking them with your luggage. If your stroller will fit in the overhead storage compartment (a few will), keep it with you for use in the airport and during layovers.

Children Traveling Alone

Special forms must be completed when a child is traveling alone, including the name, address and telephone number of the person delivering the child, the person picking up the child and the child's destination. Only the person named on the form will be allowed to pick up the child.

Unaccompanied children do not qualify for children's discounted fares, but will, of course be able to purchase "Super Saver" fares. Some airlines charge an extra fee ($20-$25) for assisting a child with a flight connection. All of the nine major domestic airlines we surveyed allow children 5 or older to travel alone. With the exception of Eastern Airlines, children traveling alone must be at least 8 years old to change planes. Eastern allows children 5 and older to change.

Mileage Programs

Even if your child doesn't travel frequently, enroll her in the mileage award programs offered by most of the major airlines. These programs keep track of passenger miles and award free or reduced air travel, seating upgrades, and hotel and rental car prizes. After a few years of even infrequent flying, you may qualify for a free trip. Our children have been enrolled since they were two and have almost earned enough miles for a free trip.

All of the programs allow children to participate if a ticket has been purchased in the name of the child.

Airline Clubs and Airport Amenities for Kids

Recognizing that little children grow up to be adult flyers *and* that they influence their parents' purchase decisions, some airlines have developed special clubs for their young air passengers. Delta Airlines has the Fantastic Flyer program for children ages 2-12. The program is free and members are sent a poster, membership certificate, I.D. card, the Fantastic Flyer Magazine, and a Mickey Mouse or Donald Duck cardboard visor. Continental Airlines' Young Travelers Club hosts special children's club rooms in Houston, Denver, Newark and Dulles (Washington, D.C.). British Airways' Skyflyers Club, for children 15 and younger, offers in-flight toys and games for children and a magazine for teens, in addition to their children's lounge in London's Heathrow Airport. When making your travel arrangements, inquire with the airline about any special clubs or other features for children.

Like the airlines, airports have jumped into the children's market too as more and more young travelers frequent their facilities. If you have a long layover or delay at the airport, inquire whether the airport has a playroom for kids. The Kids' Port play area in Terminal C at Boston's Logan Airport has amused many a young traveler. Airports are also increasingly adding such parent pleasing features as diaper changing areas in both women's *and* men's restrooms.

Activities in the Air

We have found that the secret to happy family flying is keeping our children busy, busy, busy! Here are some suggestions to make your flight a smooth one:

Toys—Avoid toys that have small parts that can be pulled apart. Instead, a favorite small car, doll, stuffed animal, puppet, or action figure are all great choices. Older children enjoy hand-held electronic games. Children of all ages enjoy a toy they've never used before—so save a new one to unwrap on the plane.

In-flight Art—Coloring books, crayons, markers, Etch-A-Sketch, magic slates, blank paper, activity books (connect dots; crosswords), lacing cards, and tracing paper are all great activities. Suggest that your children prepare art work for grandparents or whoever is at your destination. Color with your child (they'll stay at it longer) or make up projects together; 3-5 year olds like to play school and be given assignments like draw a triangle, a house, a person—this will kill at least 10 minutes, if not more! Don't forget the stickers and stars, even if you don't put them all over your child!

Books—Pack several and include one or two favorites and some new books your child has never heard before. Help older children who can read select a new paperback or two for the trip.

Music—but headsets only! We have found that, if carefully supervised, a 2-year old can use a Walkman with a song or story tape (with accompanying book) and stay amused for a good while.

Blanket or other beloved object—For the very young traveler, it helps to have that special something, be it a "blankie" or whatever, to cuddle (and maybe even nap) with.

Thinking Games—With children 3 years and up you can play simple thinking games where you take turns asking each other questions. With your youngest players start off with questions like "name a fruit that is red" or "who is Ernie's friend on Sesame Street." This is a favorite game of our kids and its a fun way to stretch their minds and shorten their travel time. Older children enjoy the old favorite "20 Questions," taking particular delight in stumping Mom or Dad with their own questions.

Plan in time segments—When planning activities for the flight, think of the total travel time in 10 minute segments and plan more activities than needed to account for delays and ground time. Chances are a 3-year old will not color for *all* of a two-hour flight. Also, don't count on the meal taking up too much time either.

Your Carry-On Bag—In addition to toys, books and other fun stuff, be sure to include:

- ☐ moistened towelettes or wipes for quick clean-ups;
- ☐ extra food—select individually wrapped items you know your child will eat;
- ☐ a bottle, sugar free gum, or candy to chew for take-off and landing (pack bottles and other food for warming in containers that can be heated by flight attendants);
- ☐ change of clothes (at a minimum, extra underpants or diapers);
- ☐ Ziplock bags for soiled clothing or diapers;
- ☐ a changing mat for diapered children.

Back Packing—If your child is big enough to carry her own backpack, have her pack and carry her own flight amusements.

Dinnertime—If traveling with a spouse, take turns eating, to cope with bumps and splashes. If traveling alone ask for assistance from a flight attendant after he or she has completed other duties.

Flightwalking—On a smooth flight, take your child to the restroom or for a walk down the aisle. Wait till the beverage and meal service is over and beware of hot surfaces in the kitchen.

Hidden Hazard—Watch out for the ashtrays. Children under 2 are fascinated by the peek-a-boo action of the cover and by dipping their little fingers into the often grimy insides. In addition, Micro Minis and other small objects stuffed inside are very tricky to extricate.

Finally, you might as well forget about your own amusements—while it might be nice to catch up on office paperwork or finish several rows of needlepoint during the flight, these items will more likely take up space than get done. Instead of frustrating yourself, just bring a small paperback or magazine in your carry-on bag. Concentrate on keeping your child happy and if you're really lucky, your youngster will take a snooze and you'll get a few moments to read or rest.

Domestic Airline Policies on Children

Airline	Discount with parents[1]	Children's Menu (pre-order)	Infants Menu (pre-order)	Bottle Warming	Changing Tables	Children's Audio Program	Children's Activities
American	20%	Yes	No	Yes	Yes[2]	Yes	No
Continental	Yes	Yes	Yes[2]	Yes	No	No	Yes[3,4]
Delta	Yes	Yes	Yes	Yes	No	No	Yes[4]
Northwest	20%	Yes	Yes	Yes	Yes[5]	No	No
Pan Am	Yes	Yes	Yes	Yes	No	Yes	Yes
TWA	20%	Yes	Yes	Yes	No	No	Yes
United	Yes	Yes	No	Yes	No	No	Yes
US Air	20%	Yes	No	Yes	Yes[6]	No	Yes[7]
Eastern	Yes	Yes	Yes	Yes	Yes[8]	No	No

1 Ages 2-11; 2 On international flights; 3 On some flights; 4 Children's Club; 5 On A320 aircraft; 6 On 767 aircraft; 7 With meal; 8 On A-300 and L 1011 aircraft.

Automobile Travel

Children under 40 pounds should always be in a child-safety seat when traveling in a car. When your child outgrows the safety seat, he or she should always use the car's safety belt. The belt should be snug and as low on the hips as possible. If the shoulder part of the belt crosses the face or neck, place it behind the child's back after the buckle is fastened. You should never use pillows or cushions to boost your child. In an accident, they may allow a child to slide under the lap belt or allow a child's head to strike the car's interior.

Never put a belt around you and a child in your lap. In an accident or sudden stop, both your weight and the child's would be forced into the belt, with the child absorbing a much greater share of the crash. Most likely, the pressure would push the belt deeply into the child's body, causing severe injury or death. Strapping two children into one belt also can be very dangerous. This makes the proper fit impossible.

WARNING: *Don't be tempted to let your child sleep lying down on the seat during long trips. Instead, bring along some large pillows so that she can lean against the locked door. A child must be sitting upright in order to be protected by a safety belt.*

Safety Seat Laws

Every state has passed laws requiring that children be in child safety seats or buckled up when riding in automobiles. The following table provides an overview of the requirements in each state. You will note that most states use the child's age to define the law. In most states the laws are not limited to children riding with their parents. They require that any driver with child passengers ensure that those children are buckled up.

Child Restraint Laws

Alabama
LAW APPLIES TO: All drivers. CHILDREN COVERED: 0-6 years. VEHICLES COVERED: Vehicles registered in state except trucks or buses over one ton. FINE: $10. COMMENTS: Violation does not affect insurance rates.

Alaska
LAW APPLIES TO: All drivers. CHILDREN COVERED: 0-5 years. VEHICLES COVERED: All vehicles except for school buses & emergency vehicles. FINE: Two points and up to $300. (Fine waivable on first offense or proof of safety seat ownership.) COMMENTS: Safety belts OK for 4 & 5 year-olds.

Arizona
LAW APPLIES TO: Resident parent/guardian. CHILDREN COVERED: 0-4 years or under 40 lbs. VEHICLES COVERED: Non-commercial vehicles registered by parent in state. FINE: $50. (Fine waivable on first offense or proof of safety seat ownership.) COMMENTS: Fine may be waived with proof of purchase.

Child Restraint Laws (cont'd.)

Arkansas
LAW APPLIES TO: Driver who regularly transports children. CHILDREN COVERED: 0-4 years. VEHICLES COVERED: All vehicles, including pickups & vans. FINE: $10-$25. (Fine waivable on first offense or proof of safety seat ownership.) COMMENTS: Safety belt OK for 3 & 4 year-olds.

California
LAW APPLIES TO: All drivers. CHILDREN COVERED: 0-3 years or under 40 lbs. VEHICLES COVERED: Vehicles under 6000 lbs. registered in state. FINE: $50-200. (Fine waivable on first offense or proof of safety seat ownership.) COMMENTS: If parent is not driving, safety belt may be substituted for child seat. Driver subject to fine if parent not in car.

Colorado
LAW APPLIES TO: All drivers. CHILDREN COVERED: 0-3 years and under 40 lbs. VEHICLES COVERED: All passenger vehicles. FINE: $25. (Fine waivable on first offense or proof of safety seat ownership.) COMMENTS: Safety belt is ok if not in parent's car.

Connecticut
LAW APPLIES TO: All drivers. CHILDREN COVERED: 0-3 years. VEHICLES COVERED: All passenger vehicles operating in state. FINE: $25-$100. (Fine waivable on first offense or proof of safety seat ownership.) COMMENTS: RVs and trucks over one ton exempted. Safety belt OK for 1-3 year-olds in back seat.

Delaware
LAW APPLIES TO: All drivers. CHILDREN COVERED: 0-3 years. VEHICLES COVERED: All passenger vehicles. FINE: $25. (Fine waivable on first offense or proof of safety seat ownership.) COMMENTS: State-wide loaner program available.

District of Columbia
LAW APPLIES TO: Resident drivers or persons driving vehicles registered in D.C. CHILDREN COVERED: 0-5 years. VEHICLES COVERED: Vehicles registered in D.C. FINE: $25. (Fine waivable on first offense or proof of safety seat ownership.) COMMENTS: Safety belt OK for 3-5 year-olds. Exemption if number in family exceeds number of seating positions.

Florida
LAW APPLIES TO: All drivers. CHILDREN COVERED: 0-5 years. VEHICLES COVERED: Passenger cars, vans or pickups registered in state. FINE: $15. (Fine waivable on first offense or proof of safety seat ownership.) COMMENTS: Safety belt OK for 4 year-olds.

Georgia
LAW APPLIES TO: All drivers. CHILDREN COVERED: 0-3 years. VEHICLES COVERED: Passenger cars, vans or pickups registered in

Child Restraint Laws (cont'd.)

state. FINE: $25. (Fine waivable on first offense or proof of safety seat ownership.) COMMENTS: Safety belt OK for 3 year-olds. Exemption for attending to personal needs of child.

Hawaii
LAW APPLIES TO: All drivers. CHILDREN COVERED: 0-3 years. VEHICLES COVERED: All vehicles. FINE: $100 maximum. COMMENTS: Safety belt OK for 3 year-olds. $25 income tax credit for purchase of seat.

Idaho
LAW APPLIES TO: Resident parent/guardian. CHILDREN COVERED: 0-3 years or under 40 lbs. VEHICLES COVERED: All non-commercial vehicles. FINE: $100 maximum. COMMENTS: Exemption if more passengers than belts and for attending to personal needs of child.

Illinois
LAW APPLIES TO: Resident parent/guardian. CHILDREN COVERED: 0-5 years. VEHICLES COVERED: All vehicles owned and operated by parent/guardian. FINE: $25-$50 (Fine waivable on first offense or proof of safety seat ownership.) first offense, $50 thereafter. COMMENTS: Safety belt OK for 4 & 5 year-olds.

Indiana
LAW APPLIES TO: All drivers. CHILDREN COVERED: 0-4 years. VEHICLES COVERED: All vehicles registered in state except taxis & rental vehicles. FINE: $50-$500. (Fine waivable on first offense or proof of safety seat ownership.) COMMENTS: Safety belt OK for 3 & 4 years olds.

Iowa
LAW APPLIES TO: All drivers. CHILDREN COVERED: 0-5 years. VEHICLES COVERED: All vehicles weighing less than 10,000 lbs. FINE: $10. (Fine waivable on first offense or proof of safety seat ownership.) COMMENTS: Safety belt OK for 3-5 year-olds. Emergency vehicles exempt.

Kansas
LAW APPLIES TO: All drivers. CHILDREN COVERED: 0-3 years in front seat. VEHICLES COVERED: All vehicles registered in state. FINE: $10. (Fine waivable on first offense or proof of safety seat ownership.)

Kentucky
LAW APPLIES TO: All drivers. CHILDREN COVERED: Under 40" tall. VEHICLES COVERED: All passenger vehicles. FINE: None.

Child Restraint Laws (cont'd.)

Louisiana
LAW APPLIES TO: Resident driver. CHILDREN COVERED: 0-4 years. VEHICLES COVERED: All vehicles. FINE: $25-$50. (Fine waivable on first offense or proof of safety seat ownership.) COMMENTS: Tax credit for full purchase price. Safety belt OK for 3-4 year-olds in back seat. If more children than belts, unrestrained children to be in back seat. Stronger legislation is being considered.

Maine
LAW APPLIES TO: All drivers. CHILDREN COVERED: 0-12 years. VEHICLES COVERED: All vehicles. FINE: $25 first offense, $50 thereafter. COMMENTS: If driven by non-parent, safety belt OK for 1-3 year-olds. Parent/guardian required to use child seat under 4 years of age.

Maryland
LAW APPLIES TO: All drivers. CHILDREN COVERED: 0-4 years. VEHICLES COVERED: Passenger or multi-purpose vehicles registered in state. FINE: $25. (Fine waivable on first offense or proof of safety seat ownership.) COMMENTS: Safety belt OK for 3-4 year-olds.

Massachusetts
LAW APPLIES TO: All drivers. CHILDREN COVERED: 0-11 years. VEHICLES COVERED: All vehicles. FINE: $25. (Fine waivable on first offense or proof of safety seat ownership.) COMMENTS: Safety belts OK for 0-11 year-olds. Exemption if all seating positions are filled or occupant is physically unable to use restraints.

Michigan
LAW APPLIES TO: Resident driver. CHILDREN COVERED: 0-4 years. VEHICLES COVERED: All vehicles. FINE: $10. (Fine waivable on first offense or proof of safety seat ownership.) COMMENTS: Safety belt OK for 1-4 year-olds if in back seat. Exemption while baby is being nursed.

Minnesota
LAW APPLIES TO: All drivers. CHILDREN COVERED: 0-3 years. VEHICLES COVERED: All vehicles. FINE: $25.

Mississippi
LAW APPLIES TO: Resident parent/guardian. CHILDREN COVERED: 0-1 years. VEHICLES COVERED: All vehicles registered in state. FINE: $10 Maximum. (Fine waivable on first offense or proof of safety seat ownership.)

Missouri
LAW APPLIES TO: Resident driver. CHILDREN COVERED: 0-3 years. VEHICLES COVERED: All vehicles registered in state. FINE: $25. (Fine

Child Restraint Laws (cont'd.)

waivable on first offense or proof of safety seat ownership.) COMMENTS: Safety belt may be substituted if in rear seat.

Montana
LAW APPLIES TO: Resident parent/guardian. CHILDREN COVERED: 0-3 years or under 40 lbs. VEHICLES COVERED: All vehicles owned/operated by parent. FINE: $10-$25. (Fine waivable on first offense or proof of safety seat ownership.) COMMENTS: Safety belt OK for 2 & 3 year-olds.

Nebraska
LAW APPLIES TO: Resident driver. CHILDREN COVERED: 0-3 years. VEHICLES COVERED: All vehicles since 1963, except taxis. FINE: $25. (Fine waivable on first offense or proof of safety seat ownership.) COMMENTS: Exemption for medical waiver from doctor. Safety belt OK for 1-3 year-olds.

Nevada
LAW APPLIES TO: All drivers. CHILDREN COVERED: 0-4 years. VEHICLES COVERED: All vehicles registered in state, except taxis & rental cars. FINE: $35-$100. (Fine waivable on first offense or proof of safety seat ownership.) COMMENTS: If more children than seating positions, preference must be given to children under 3 years old.

New Hampshire
LAW APPLIES TO: All drivers. CHILDREN COVERED: 0-12 years. VEHICLES COVERED: All passenger vehicles. FINE: $500. COMMENTS: Safety belt is OK for children over 1 year old. Exemption for children with physical problems.

New Jersey
LAW APPLIES TO: All drivers. CHILDREN COVERED: 0-4 years. VEHICLES COVERED: All vehicles. FINE: $10-$25. (Fine waivable on first offense or proof of safety seat ownership.) COMMENTS: Safety belt OK for children 18 months to 4 years old in rear seat.

New Mexico
LAW APPLIES TO: All drivers. CHILDREN COVERED: 0-10 years. VEHICLES COVERED: All vehicles registered in state. FINE: $50. (Fine waivable on first offense or proof of safety seat ownership.) COMMENTS: Safety belt OK for 1-4 year-olds in rear seat. Exemption if all seating positions equipped with belts are occupied.

New York
LAW APPLIES TO: All drivers. CHILDREN COVERED: 0-10 years. VEHICLES COVERED: All vehicles registered in state. FINE: $25. (Fine waivable on first offense or proof of safety seat ownership.) COMMENTS: Safety belts mandatory for 4-9 year-olds.

Child Restraint Laws (cont'd.)

North Carolina
LAW APPLIES TO: All drivers. CHILDREN COVERED: 0-5 years. VEHICLES COVERED: State registered vehicles owned/operated by parent. FINE: $25. COMMENTS: Safety belts OK for 3-5 year-olds. Exemption for attending to personal needs of child or if all other seating positions are filled.

North Dakota
LAW APPLIES TO: All drivers. CHILDREN COVERED: 0-5 years. VEHICLES COVERED: All passenger vehicles. FINE: $20 maximum. (Fine waivable on first offense or proof of safety seat ownership.) COMMENTS: Safety belt OK for children over 2 years old.

Ohio
LAW APPLIES TO: All drivers. CHILDREN COVERED: 0-3 years or under 40 lbs. VEHICLES COVERED: All vehicles registered in state except taxis. FINE: $10. (Fine waivable on first offense or proof of safety seat ownership.) COMMENTS: Safety belt OK for children over 1 year old only when driven by non-parent.

Oklahoma
LAW APPLIES TO: Resident drivers. CHILDREN COVERED: 0-4 years. VEHICLES COVERED: All vehicles. FINE: $50. COMMENTS: If in rear seat, safety belt can be substituted for all children. If in front seat, safety belt can be substituted for 4 year-olds only.

Oregon
LAW APPLIES TO: All drivers. CHILDREN COVERED: 0-15 years. VEHICLES COVERED: All vehicles under 8,000 lbs. FINE: $50 maximum. (Fine waivable on first offense or proof of safety seat ownership.) COMMENTS: Safety belt OK for children over 1 year old. Exemption if all seating positions are occupied or for medical reasons and emergencies.

Pennsylvania
LAW APPLIES TO: All drivers. CHILDREN COVERED: 0-3 years. VEHICLES COVERED: All vehicles registered in state. FINE: $25 maximum. (Fine waivable on first offense or proof of safety seat ownership.) COMMENTS: Safety belt OK in rear seat for children over 1 year old. Exemption for physical or medical reasons.

Rhode Island
LAW APPLIES TO: All drivers. CHILDREN COVERED: 0-12 years. VEHICLES COVERED: All vehicles. FINE: $10. (Fine waivable on first offense or proof of safety seat ownership.)

South Carolina
LAW APPLIES TO: All drivers. CHILDREN COVERED: 0-6 years. VEHICLES COVERED: All vehicles registered in state. FINE: $25. (Fine

Child Restraint Laws (cont'd.)

waivable on first offense or proof of safety seat ownership.) COMMENTS: Safety belt OK in rear seat for children over 1 year old. Exemption if child is being fed or has medical problems.

South Dakota
LAW APPLIES TO: All drivers. CHILDREN COVERED: 0-4 years. VEHICLES COVERED: All vehicles. FINE: $20. COMMENTS: Safety belt OK for children over 2 years old. Exemption for attending to personal needs of child or if all seating positions are occupied.

Tennessee
LAW APPLIES TO: All drivers. CHILDREN COVERED: 0-3 years. VEHICLES COVERED: All vehicles registered in state except RVs & one ton trucks. FINE: $2-$10. COMMENTS: Exemption while attending to needs of child.

Texas
LAW APPLIES TO: Resident driver. CHILDREN COVERED: 0-3 years. VEHICLES COVERED: All vehicles registered in state, except those for hire. FINE: $25-$50. (Fine waivable on first offense or proof of safety seat ownership.) COMMENTS: Seat belt OK for children over 2 years old. Exemption if all seating positions are occupied.

Utah
LAW APPLIES TO: Resident parent/guardian. CHILDREN COVERED: 0-4 years. VEHICLES COVERED: All vehicles. FINE: $20. (Fine waivable on first offense or proof of safety seat ownership.) COMMENTS: Safety belt OK for children over 2 years old. Exemption if all seating positions are occupied.

Vermont
LAW APPLIES TO: All drivers. CHILDREN COVERED: 0-4 years. VEHICLES COVERED: All vehicles registered in state. FINE: $25. (Fine waivable on first offense or proof of safety seat ownership.) COMMENTS: Safety belt OK for children over 1 year old in rear seat. Exemption if number of children exceeds number of belts.

Virginia
LAW APPLIES TO: All drivers. CHILDREN COVERED: 0-3 years. VEHICLES COVERED: All vehicles registered in state. FINE: $25. (Fine waivable on first offense or proof of safety seat ownership.) COMMENTS: Safety belt OK for children over 3 years old or over 40 lbs. Exemption for medical reasons. Driver must carry physician statement.

Washington
LAW APPLIES TO: Resident parent/guardian. CHILDREN COVERED: 0-4 years. VEHICLES COVERED: All vehicles registered in state & owned & operated by parent/guardian. FINE: $30. (Fine waivable on

Child Restraint Laws (cont'd.)

first offense or proof of safety seat ownership.) COMMENTS: Safety belt OK for children over 1 year old. Primary safety belt law now makes all drivers responsible for restraining children under 16.

West Virginia
LAW APPLIES TO: All drivers. CHILDREN COVERED: 0-8 years. VEHICLES COVERED: All vehicles. FINE: $10-$20. (Fine waivable on first offense or proof of safety seat ownership.) COMMENTS: Safety belt OK for children over 3 years old.

Wisconsin
LAW APPLIES TO: Resident driver. CHILDREN COVERED: 0-3 years. VEHICLES COVERED: All vehicles except taxis. FINE: $10-$200. (Fine waivable on first offense or proof of safety seat ownership.) COMMENTS: Safety belt OK for children over 2 years old. FINE increases for younger children and second offense.

Wyoming
LAW APPLIES TO: All drivers. CHILDREN COVERED: 0-2 years old or under 40 lbs. VEHICLES COVERED: All cars excluding small cars, pickups and vans. FINE: $25.

SOURCE: *The Car Book* (Harper & Row)

Bus Travel

Children traveling on Greyhound who are under five years of age must travel with a companion who is at least twelve years old. Children five years to eleven years may travel alone but only on trips less than five hours long. Unaccompanied children have to pay full fare.

Children between the ages of five through eleven pay a child's fare which is half price. One child under five traveling with a full fare companion is free. Additional children under five traveling with one adult, will be charged half fare.

Child safety seats are allowed on board but for infants and toddlers you'll have to pay a child's fare. Most buses do not have safety belts, so securing a child safety seat will be impossible.

School Bus Safety

A growing number of parents, aware of the safety advantages of wearing seat belts in passenger cars and trucks, are questioning why most school buses are not equipped with safety belts for their children's protection. There is a grassroots movement to require lap belts when new school buses are purchased. Currently, only a few school districts require school buses to have safety belts.

Both the American Medical Association and the American College of Preventive Medicine support safety belts on large school buses. But, the issue is not without controversy. Surprisingly, some studies indicate that children buckled up would be more seriously injured in a crash than those not buckled up. The reason is that the head seems to absorb more of the crash impact. For more information contact the Insurance Institute for Highway Safety, 1005 North Glebe Road, Arlington, VA 22201 and ask for their Status Report on School Buses and Safety Belts.

Train Travel

A child between the ages of two and eleven traveling with an adult on Amtrak pays one-half of the adult fare if traveling on the excursion fare and one-fourth of the adult fare if traveling on the family plan. Only one child under the age of two per adult can travel for free.

A child between the ages of eight and eleven may travel alone on Amtrak but only under certain provisions. The child can only travel during daylight hours and no overnight trips are permitted. The child must have an interview with the station manager for manager's approval for the child traveling alone. Forms must also be filled out with the child's name, destination, who will bring him to the train and who will pick him up. All unaccompanied children pay an adult fare.

Child restraints are allowed if you reserve a seat. But there are no safety belts to secure the seat.

Amtrak offers children's meals and will heat a bottle or baby food. They will also refrigerate baby formulas or foods for you during the trip.

Travel Tips

Here are some ideas for amusing children on long trips:

☐ Hand puppets—older children can put on their own puppet shows and parents can use them to amuse infants.

☐ Cassette recorder—provide some blank tapes so the kids can record their own stories after they tire of prepackaged songs and stories. (Fisher Price makes an excellent recorder that is easy for children to use.)

☐ Coloring books, magic slates, Etch-A-Sketch, books—all old standbuys. You may want to reserve special books only for the car, making the car seat someplace special.

☐ Electronic games—these hand held arcade-style games can be expensive ($10.00 - $50.00) but provide hours of enjoyment on long trips.

☐ On car trips, it's a good idea to take a rest break every two to three hours.

☐ Check the library for "Games to Play in the Car" by Michael Harwood and "Steven Caney's Play Book".

☐ Check with hotels and motels in advance, to make certain they have cribs, high chairs and other essentials.

☐ Carry baby's food in containers that can be heated in restaurants and in the plane's microwave oven.

☐ When traveling in a car, never put luggage on the back window shelf because it might hit passengers in the event of a sudden stop.

☐ Pack some clothes pins, they're great for fastening napkins or towels to children's clothing during meal time.

A First Aid Kit for the Road

Here are a few things you should make room for in your suitcase:

☐ Bandages
☐ Tweezers
☐ Thermometer
☐ Aspirin or acetaminophen
☐ Sunscreen
☐ Insect repellent
☐ Ipecac

In addition, be sure you have any prescription medications that the family uses and an extra prescription from your doctor. If you're traveling abroad, make a note of your child's eyeglass prescription (and yours!) and be sure you have a record or you child's immunizations just in case.

CHAPTER SEVEN

A typical house contains a seemingly endless number of products that can pose hazards to infants and toddlers. Many of these items, which you probably take for granted, provide unusual and challenging climbing obstacles or have lights and knobs that are absolutely fascinating to little ones. Your child's first avenue of protection from these seemingly innocent items is your efforts to childproof your home. We recommend childproofing when your child is four months or younger—*before* he starts crawling. Many of the items we suggest you use to get the job done are described in detail in Chapter Two.

You'll also want to make sure that the environment that your child experiences *outside* the home is also safe. We've included what to look for, and look out for, on the playground, sidewalk and neighborhood. Finally, there are the *hidden hazards*, including indoor air pollution, that you'll want to know about in order to protect your little one.

Safety Inside and Outside the Home

Childproofing Your Home

Don't be fooled into thinking that childproofing is a one time job; rather, it should be a continuing effort. Just when you think you got everything battened down and locked away, your young explorer is bound to discover a new challenge. We recently asked parents what areas of their home they overlooked when childproofing. Their responses included: a home office; an older child's room; furniture, picture frames, and fireplace tools in the living room; telephone wires and electrical cords; family's game and jigsaw-puzzle cupboard; garage; basement; refrigerator water dispenser; dining room china closet; TV remote control; and the sharp points at the base of a staircase bannister. Like these parents, there are probably areas of your house which you discover need childproofing once your child is mobile.

To begin your childproofing task, read this chapter, and then walk *and* crawl around your home to assess your problem areas. We have organized this chapter by room or area of the home, so as you tackle each room you can consult the appropriate section. The second half of this chapter addresses hazards outside your house and includes safety tips regarding places and events, such as amusement parks and Halloween. Below, we have set out most of the major things to look out for, but remember that each house and family is unique.

Finally, keep in mind the reasons for childproofing: Home accidents are responsible for hundreds of deaths and thousands of injuries to children under age five annually. Resist the temptation to think "it won't happen to my child" or "I'll always keep an eye on my child, so all this childproofing advice doesn't apply to me." If anything, childproofing will allow your family to relax at home and avoid the tragic, painful and costly consequences that can easily result from your child's natural inquisitiveness.

Kitchen

Appliances—Many kitchen appliances, such as electric coffee pots, grills, broilers, corn poppers, toasters, toaster ovens, frying pans, griddles, waffle irons, blenders, mixers and food processors, can cause serious injuries to children. Never permit young children to use these products by themselves. Long cords on electrical appliances can be easily pulled or tripped on by young children. Therefore, never let the cords dangle; look for appliances with shorter cords; if possible, plug in the appliance above the counter or table level; and place your child's high chair away from counters and tables that have these appliances on them.

Cabinets and Drawers—Invest in safety latches for all kitchen cabinets and drawers within your child's reach. In addition to providing a measure of safety to your kitchen, they also help prevent some messy clean-up jobs.

Foil and Plastic Wrap—Store these items out of your child's reach since the serrated edge on the boxes can easily cut your child. Plastic wrap and grocery vegetable bags pose a suffocation hazard to the small child who is tempted to place them over his head.

Household Cleaners—A closed cabinet under the kitchen sink is not a deterrent to an inquisitive child. Consider moving drain cleaners, oven cleaners, lighter fluids, caustics, lye, ammonia, bug sprays, furniture polish and other cleaners to another, safer, location or locking the cabinet containing these items until your child is older. Always store these items in their original containers. (Any liquid in a juice carton looks like juice to your child.) Also, the label on the original container often lists the ingredients, which is important information should your child ingest these products. (See Chapter Five for more information on what to do in the event of an accidental poisoning.)

Knives and Other Utensils—Keep knives and other sharp kitchen utensils out of your child's reach. Remember that many childhood knife accidents occur when the parent using the knife is hurried or distracted. If something diverts your attention while you are using a knife or other sharp instrument, make sure to put it in a safe place, before turning elsewhere. Move toothpicks out of reach too, since their small size is particularly intriguing to young children.

Microwave Ovens—Your toddler or preschooler may like to push buttons and hear the beeping sound made by some microwave ovens. Try to position your microwave out of reach and teach your child that the microwave, like other electrical appliances, is off limits. As your child gets older, teach your child that although a container heated in a microwave may be cool, food heated in microwave ovens is hot enough to cause scald burns.

Pet Food and Supplies—Pet food bowls and supplies should be moved out of reach of your crawling child who may be tempted to share a meal with the family pet. Place aquariums on sturdy structures that can not be pulled over and re-route their electrical cords out of your child's reach.

Range/Stove—Although it may be considered common sense to keep your child away from a hot kitchen stove, it can be just as dangerous when it's *not* in use. An electric burner coil can reach over 1,000 degrees F and can ignite fabric on contact, *even after the stove has been turned off.* Gas stove surfaces also can retain heat. When purchasing a stove look for one with knobs that are difficult for children to turn on. When cooking on the stove top, turn cook ware to the inside or back of the stove to keep the handles out of reach. Do not store cookies or other "favorites" in or above the stove where children might be tempted to climb onto the stove to reach them.

Refrigerators and Freezers—Old refrigerators and freezers are favorite hiding places, since they make great "forts" or "secret rooms" for youngsters. Between 1980-1988, 59 children died when they became entrapped in old style latch-type refrigerators and freezers. Because of this danger, federal law requires that all household refrigerators manufactured after October 1958 have a door that opens easily from the inside. However, regardless of the age of the refrigerator, remove the door and the latch, or chain and padlock the door shut when discarding it. Picnic coolers have also been associated with suffocation deaths, so keep these stored away when not in use. In addition to the asphyxiation hazard, refrigerators and freezers can cause lacerations, contusions or sprains when a child's hand gets caught in the door or bumps his or her head on the door or handle.

Bathroom

The general rule for the bathroom is to keep young children out of it unless they are supervised closely. The bathroom is a haven for a variety of injuries, including falls, burns, poisonings, and drownings.

Bathroom Appliances

Be sure to unplug electric hair rollers, hair dryers, curling irons and other electrical appliances found in the bathroom when they are not in use. Children have been electrocuted when plugged in hair dryers fell into bathroom sinks or tubs. *Remember, even if the appliance is off, it still can cause an electrocution.* If an electrical appliance is accidentally dropped into water while plugged in, be sure to *unplug it* before touching the appliance. Also, because of the electrocution hazard, never use a portable electric space heater in the bathroom.

Bathtubs and Basins—Since children can be scalded or drown in very small amounts of water, bathroom supervision is important. The CPSC reports that hundreds of children have drowned in bathtubs, basins, hot tubs, showers, and whirlpool baths in as little as six inches of water.

To avoid falls and bumped heads, apply nonskid appliques to your bathtub surface or use a rubber bath mat; attach a cushioned spout guard over the faucet.

To avoid burns, check the water temperature of the water with your elbow before placing your child in the tub. Run your elbow through the water from one end of the tub to the other. Young children's skin is tender, so the water should feel warm, not hot. Since some scalds are the result of children turning on the hot water while playing, bathe your child facing away from the faucet and handles. To further guard against tap water scalds, we recommend, as does the American Academy of Pediatrics, lowering your water temperature to 120 degrees F.; many water heaters come preset at a dangerous 140-150 degrees F.—temperatures that could fatally burn a young child. To test your water temperature: Turn on the hot water at the tub faucet, let the water run for three to five minutes, and measure temperature with a bath thermometer.

Cosmetics, Bathroom Cleaners, and Other Hazards—In addition to medicines, there are many other substances found in the bathroom which your child may be tempted to taste. Cosmetics, aerosol sprays, vitamins and bathroom cleaners all pose hazards. For the last few years, cosmetics have represented the leading cause for calls to poison centers. Be aware that too much mouthwash, if swallowed by a child, can be fatal. Like mouthwash, artificial-fingernail glue remover is also not required to be sold in child resistant packaging; yet this product contains the chemical acetonitrile, which can be deadly if swallowed. Keep all of these products out of reach. Place only nonpoisonous items under the sink, or use safety latches on these cabinet doors. Dispose of bathroom waste, such as used razor blades and pills, in a covered trash receptacle in your home.

Toilet—Keep the lid of your toilet down at all times when not in use or install a toilet lock. The CPSC has received numerous reports of deaths to young children playing in toilet-bowl water. Of those victims, most died as a result of their heads becoming entrapped between the toilet seat and bowl.

Medicines—Keep both prescription and nonprescription medicines out of children's reach. The best way to achieve this is to keep medicines locked away out of sight. Consider using a medicine cabinet insert. Always purchase prescriptions and other hazardous products in child resistant containers, and resecure these containers after each use. Child- resistant packages can become loose or clogged with liquid medicine, such as cough syrup, and lose their effectiveness, so replace worn or ineffective child-resistant tops.

Living, Dining, and Bedroom

These rooms share common hazards that are easy to overlook. We do not specifically address your child's bedroom here; however, the furniture descriptions contained in chapters 1, 2, and 3 contain many tips for safe use of these products. In older siblings' bedrooms, watch out for small parts from toys and games, room decorations, sports equipment, jewelry, and cosmetics that could tempt a younger brother or sister.

Beds and Waterbeds—Both regular innerspring mattresses and waterbed mattresses have been associated with infant suffocation. The majority of these deaths resulted when the baby became entrapped between the bed or mattress and a wall or other product. Deaths also occurred when the child suffocated in the face-down position, or in pillows or linens, or when an adult lay over them.

CPSC has received reports of 190 deaths, between 1985 and 1989, to infants 12 months of age and younger who suffocated while on *regular mattresses*. Between 1982 and 1989, 32 infants and two children ages 9 and 12 with cerebral palsy died of asphyxiation when left unattended on adult-size waterbeds. With both regular mattresses and waterbed mattresses, there are two typical suffocation scenarios: (1) the infant rolls or moves to the edge of the mattress, where his or her head or entire body becomes wedged between the mattress and the bed frame or the mattress and the wall, and cannot breathe; and (2) the infant or child, asleep in the face-down position, has his nose and mouth trapped in the depression caused by the weight of his head and body. Infants sleeping in both regular beds and waterbeds have also died when an adult accidentally laid over them during the night and suffocated the child.

Beds, regardless of their construction, are not safe sleeping or napping areas for infants. When away from home and your child cannot sleep in a crib, place a mattress on the floor away from the walls, or use a bed with added guardrails on both sides (including the wall side).

Fireplaces—Teach young children to avoid fireplaces even when no fire is burning in them. Keep in mind that a fire is an interesting event for a young child. Sometimes, the fact that it is hot and can burn is not understood or is quickly forgotten. *Never leave your child unattended in a room in which there is a fire burning in the fireplace.* An *unlit* fireplace may contain soot, which can be ingested, and fireplace irons usually contain sharp points and surfaces that could injure a young child. Make sure that your fireplace is covered by a secure safety screen that cannot be opened or pulled over by a young child.

Furniture—Each year a variety of furniture pieces are associated with a staggering number of injuries to young children. For example, in 1987, CPSC estimated that children ages four and under were involved in, and required a trip to the emergency room for over 32,900 sofa and couch injuries and over 57,700 chair injuries. These injuries typically result falling off furniture against sharp corners.

To decrease the chance of your child being involved in a furniture-related accident, consider the following precautions:

☐ Apply cushioned corner covers to coffee tables and other sharp corners of furniture.

☐ Never allow jumping or standing on any piece of furniture.

☐ Make sure bookshelves and other tall furniture pieces are secured to the wall so that they cannot be pulled over.

☐ Make it a habit to push kitchen and dining room chairs in under the table to take away an attractive climbing gym.

☐ Keep drawers fully closed to prevent them from being climbed on or pulled out entirely.

☐ Discourage your child from hiding in or under furniture.

☐ If you think a particular piece of furniture poses a real hazard or you are worried about it being broken or damaged, consider moving it to the attic or basement until your child is older.

☐ Watch out for reclining chairs; children have died and received severe brain damage when their head became caught between the chair seat and leg rest. Toddlers, as young as one and two years old are capable of pushing a reclining chair closed. Store away a recliner until your child is older or never leave her in a room alone with such chairs. Also watch out for rocking chairs, which may pinch or cut small fingers.

☐ Place furniture against wall outlets to prevent easy access by your child. Do not place furniture directly in front of windows on the second story or above.

For more information on baby furniture and equipment, see Index.

Heaters and Stoves—All accessible heat sources, including coal and wood burning stoves, kerosene heaters, electric, gas and oil space heaters, electric baseboard heaters, and open radiators, expose your child to potentially serious burns. When using any of these products, it is critical to keep your child away from the heat source. In addition to flames or hot coils, all may have very hot exterior surfaces, and these should not be regarded as protective coverings. It may be possible to place some type of barrier at a safe distance from the heat that will keep your child from getting burned, yet allow the heat to circulate.

With respect to portable heaters, you might consider heating a room before you plan to spend time with your child there and then moving the heater to another room to avoid burns. If you use the heater in the room you are in do *not* close the room off entirely, since heaters that rely on combustion (such as kerosene heaters, gas and oil space heaters) give off noxious emissions that can severely contaminate your indoor air and affect your child's breathing. Always maintain some ventilation in a room being warmed by these kinds of heaters.

Finally, if you are using an electric space heater, position the cord out of pathways to reduce tripping and remember to never use it in the bathroom or in other wet places.

Rugs and Floors—Take a *crawl* around your home sometime. Even the most scrupulous housekeeper will be amazed at the variety of things imbedded in rugs and hidden under furniture. Try, as best you can, to keep your rugs and floors free from small and sharp objects while your child is in the crawling and "everything-goes-in-the-mouth" stage (up to one year of age). Watch for pieces of toys and other small objects left behind by older siblings. Also keep in mind that children can easily slip on scatter rugs. Look for rugs that have rubber backing, or apply double-faced adhesive tape to the rug's underside to prevent tumbles.

Tablecloths—If your child has crawling access to a dining-room or kitchen table, discontinue use of tablecloths for a while because the temptation to give a persistent tug or play-peek-a-boo could mean the toppling of dishes and hot liquids onto your child.

Video Cassette Recorders—To guard against injury to little fingers and hands, move front-loading videocassette recorders out of reach of children or use a device to prevent access by exploring fingers. Also watch out for little ones who want to feed the VCR their favorite snack!

Garage and Workshop

Antifreeze—Because it is sweet tasting, antifreeze is an attractive yet deadly drink for young children. Make sure you keep antifreeze in a child-resistant container and out of your child's reach. Contact your Poison Control Center immediately if antifreeze is ingested.

Garage Doors—Both automatic and manual garage doors pose significant hazards to children. Manual garage doors using a counterbalance system are safer than those using a long coil spring on each side of the door that is attached by a hook-shaped bend in the spring end. Sectional nonautomatic doors can easily crush fingers. Automatic garage door accidents have resulted in the deaths of fifty-four children in the last 15 years. In the typical automatic garage door accident, the child activates the open garage door and then tries to race out of the garage to beat the door before it closes. Even doors equipped with an automatic reverse feature have been involved in fatal accidents. To avoid automatic garage door accidents, never let your child play in the garage alone, place a wall-mounted switch for an automatic garage door high on the wall out of children's reach, and lock remote control devices that open and close the garage door in the glove compartment of your car to prevent use by children. Since automatic garage door openers manufactured after 1982 offer more protection, check to see that your opener incorporates the more recent technology. If you live in a housing complex that has a motorized parking gate to secure the parking area, never let your child engage in a similar type of "race-the-gate" game. These gates have injured and killed children and do not reverse upon impact.

Garbage Cans—Whether you keep your garbage cans in a garage or outside the house or apartment, make sure that your child does not have easy access to its contents. If the trash can lids do not fit snugly or snap on, purchase special straps to make them difficult for a young child to open. Remember, many young children associate trash cans with the Sesame Street character Oscar the Grouch (who lives in a trash can) and may be tempted to explore a place which most adults find disgusting. Since most trash cans contain sharp objects, spoiled foods, and other harmful items, take the time to make sure lids are tightly secured.

Gasoline and Gasoline Containers—Keep gasoline in a container specifically designed to store it. Check to see that the container has a flame arrester, a fine mesh in the spout which prevents flames from racing up the stream of fuel as it is being poured and possible causing an explosion. Store your gas container out of the reach of children. If your child ingests gasoline, call your Poison Control Center immediately.

Insecticides and Pesticides—All insecticides and pesticides (including herbicides, rodenticides, fungicides, and others) are poisonous, so take particular care when using them around children. Always use these products according to directions, and refrain from using them if someone in your family has allergies or asthma. Remember that aerosol insecticide sprays are extremely flammable and should not be used near an open flame. Avoid using insecticides that contain diazinon (an extremely toxic substance) and dichlorvos or DDVP (under study for adverse effects). Because of toxic effects, consider using non-toxic alternatives to pesticides. Store all insecticides and pesticides in child-resistant containers and keep out of reach of children. Call your Poison Control Center immediately if an insecticide is ingested. For more information on the safe use of pesticides, clean-up and disposal procedures, and health and environmental effects, call the National Pesticide Telecommunications Network at their 24-hour toll-free number: (800) 858-7378. (See Chapter 9 for additional information sources on pesticides.)

Paint—Securely hammer down all paint can lids. If you suspect your child has ingested paint, call your Poison Control Center immediately.

Lead-based paint is the most common source of lead for children found to have lead poisoning. In 1973, CPSC banned paints containing more than 0.5% lead for household use. In 1978, the commission extended these regulations, requiring consumer-product paint, as well as toys, children's articles and furniture, to contain no more than 0.06% lead content. Despite these laws, the walls of many older homes are still covered with highly-leaded paint. (See our discussion below on lead to learn of the deadly consequences of lead exposure.)

Laundry Room

Detergent—Detergents are a leading cause of household product poisonings each year. Store all detergents, fabric softeners, and other laundry room cleaning supplies out of your crawler or toddler's reach. (See kitchen cleaning supplies.) If your child should ingest a detergent or other cleaner, call your Poison Control Center immediately. In addition to being poisonous, detergents are strong irritants. Keep in mind that children may be more attracted to detergents with candy or fruit, such as lemon or orange scents.

Irons & Ironing Boards—Always place your ironing board out of your child's play path. Avoid letting the iron's cord dangle over the ironing board; your child could pull over the iron *and* the board. Remember that an iron stays hot for a good while after it has been turned off. Store iron in cupboard or storage space away from children's grasp. Do not lean the ironing board against a wall where it could fall or be pulled over on your child.

Washers & Dryers—Place your washing machine and dryer away from other equipment or furniture that a young child could climb to gain access to them. Old-fashioned wringer washers are particularly hazardous since children are often incapable of pulling their fingers, hair or clothing out of the power-driven rollers. Newer models have safety features to help prevent this from occurring. Most newer-model clothes dryers have safety devices that require buttons on the control panel be pushed after the door is shut, rather than starting automatically after the door is closed as older models did. Regardless of the age of the dryer, children can get trapped inside because they panic or are unable to push open the door. Between 1980-1988, eight children died when they became entrapped inside clothes dryers or combination washer/dryer units. Avoid purchasing a dryer with a door that can be opened only by means of a latch from the outside. Teach your child never to climb on, hide or play inside a washer or dryer.

Other Hazards

Batteries—Batteries come in a variety of shapes and sizes, all of which pose hazards to children. Button batteries, used to power watches, calculators, cameras, hearing aids and games, are easily ingested and can cause choking. It is estimated that 500 to 800 button batteries are swallowed annually by consumers. While the majority of these will pass through the body without any difficulty, severe complications and fatalities have been reported. Button batteries may get lodged in the esophagus or intestine and slowly leak alkaline electrolytes, causing internal chemical burns.

Dry-cell batteries (carbon-zinc, alkaline, or mercury) are used in flashlights, radios, battery-operated toys, and a variety of other consumer products. These batteries present chemical-burn or skin-irritation hazards, which result from swallowing or chewing on the battery.

Wet-cell batteries, most often found in cars, pose hazards when being jumped or charged, and when battery acid or corrosion gets into the eyes.

Keep all batteries out of children's reach. Keep children away from cars while working under the hood.

Buckets—Large buckets, filled with water or other liquids, particularly five-gallon plastic or metal containers used for commercial-size quantities of construction materials, paint or food, have been involved in 67 drowning deaths to children from 1985 through 1987. Most of the victims were between the ages of eight and 12 months old. When leaning forward to play in the water, they toppled into the bucket, were unable to free themselves, and drowned. Never leave any bucket of water or other liquid unattended when young children are around; even a partially filled bucket can be a drowning hazard. When doing household chores, immediately empty out buckets when finished, or move them to a safe place before taking a break.

Christmas Decorations—The novelty of new colorful objects around the house make Christmas decorations a ready target for the exploring child. Therefore, avoid placing breakable ornaments or ornaments with small detachable parts on the lower branches of a Christmas tree. Mistletoe and holly berries may be poisonous if more than a few are swallowed, so keep these plants out of the reach of children. Likewise, keep poinsettias out of reach since they produce a milky juice which may cause a severe irritation to susceptible children. While your child is still too young to understand the difference between real candy and glass ornaments, avoid putting candy canes and other edible, or edible-looking, decorations on your tree. To a small child, if one decoration can be eaten, they all can. Avoid bubbling lights since they contain toxic chemicals and can break. Do not use tinsel that contains lead—if in doubt, throw it out. Be careful to keep decorative candles up high and away from children. Fire salts, which produce a multicolored effect when thrown on a wood fire, contain heavy metals and also should be kept away from children. If you use artificial snow sprays to decorate, remember that they can irritate lungs if inhaled. Lastly, do your best to keep the Christmas tree lights' electrical cords, as well as the base of the Christmas tree, out of the direct crawling path of your child. Secure your tree with a wide-based stand to prevent toppling. Since tree needles can severely injure the eye, trim lower branches that protrude at your child's eye level and below.

Artificial Snow—At least two brands of artificial snow contain the chemical methylene chloride which has been found to cause cancer in animals. If you decorate with artificial snow, neither you or your children should breath the vapors. The two brands are BLIZ Snow and Frosty Simulated Snow Flock from Rauch Industries in Gastonia, NC. Other brands have chlorinated solvents which may be methylene chloride.

Cigarette Lighters and Matches—Despite the age-old adage that "children shouldn't play with matches," many children are treated each year for injuries associated with matches, lighters, and lighter fluid. Studies show that children as young as 18 months are capable of igniting a lighter. In 1986 alone, 170 people died as a result of fires started by children playing with cigarette lighters. Property damage from lighter fires is estimated at an annual cost of $300 to $375 million. So don't forget to keep lighters, matches, and lighter fluid out of the reach of children.

Coins, Pencils, Scissors, Paper Clips—All those objects that you empty from your pocket or often use are attractive hazards to the curious child who is always ready to poke around with sharp points and taste anything that fits in his mouth. Get in the habit of putting these everyday items out of reach.

Guns & Ammunition—*Everyday*, one child under the age of 14 is killed with a handgun. If you must keep a gun in your house, never let your child see it, never keep it loaded, never store the gun and ammunition in the same place, and never keep the gun in an unlocked place. Additionally, place a padlock around the top strap of a revolver or secure it with a trigger lock. Remove the magazine, disassemble the frame from the slide and magazine, or lock the trigger of a semi-automatic handgun.

Plants—Many common indoor and outdoor plants are poisonous when chewed, swallowed, or rubbed on the skin. Because of the increase in popularity of house plants, poisonings from plants have risen dramatically over the past few years. Some plants can also be toxic if touched or inhaled. A child's reaction to a poisonous plant can range from an upset stomach or skin rash to depression of the circulatory and central nervous systems, violent vomiting, heart failure, and even death. Following is list of common plants and potential reactions.

The two plants responsible for the most calls to poison control centers are philodendron and dieffenbachia. In fact, just by touching the dieffenbachia, a child can pick up toxic sap which, if transferred to the mouth, can cause severe burning and choking. Chewing on a leaf can cause intense pain, swelling, and sometimes blisters in the mouth. If a child swallows the plant, he or she can have breathing problems that can last for several days. Elephant ear and jack-in-the-pulpit can have similar, though less toxic, effects.

English ivy, daffodils, poinsettias, and the leaves of tomato and rhubarb plants are also poisonous. Children are often attracted to colorful berries and flowers, and sometimes confuse toxic leaves, stored bulbs, and seeds with safe foods.

Other plants frequently mentioned in poison control cases include holly berries, pyracantha, pokeweed, black elder, woody nightshade, jerusalem cherry, begonia, oleander, acorns, mimosa seeds, jimsonweed, and even marijuana.

Here are some tips on protecting children from plant related accidents:

☐ Know both the common and the botanical names of your house plants, and label them. If necessary, take a piece of each plant with you to a plant store or nursery for positive identification. When buying a new plant, keep the name tag.

☐ If you have any poisonous plants, supervise children closely when they are playing near them.

☐ If possible, keep plants that are colorful or have berries out of reach.

☐ Call the Poison Control Center immediately if you suspect that your child has put any part of a poisonous plant into his or her mouth.

☐ Don't put plants in young childrens' bedrooms.

☐ Never use plants as "pretend" food.

Here are some tips if you suspect that your child has *eaten* a plant:

☐ Determine what plant was eaten and how much. Note your child's reaction.

☐ If any part of the plant is still in the child's mouth, remove it, and save it.

☐ Call your local Poison Control Center or get in touch with your child's pediatrician. If you bring your child in for an examination, take a fresh sample of the suspected plant with enough leaves and fruit to allow positive identification.

☐ Do not induce vomiting without checking first with your doctor or the Poison Control Center. (See Chapter Nine for a compete list.) Some plants contain juices that, if vomited, could cause damage to the digestive tissue or asphyxiation.

☐ Keep syrup of Ipecac on hand in case you are instructed to induce vomiting.

Common Harmful Plants

Arisaema triphyllum
NICKNAME: Jack-in-the-pulpit, Indian-turnip TOXIC PARTS: Leaves (toxic substance: calcium oxalate acid) SYMPTOMS PRODUCED: Corrosive action to gastrointestinal tract, producing swelling of tongue, lips and palate.

Atropa belladonna
NICKNAME: Deadly nightshade TOXIC PARTS: All parts (toxic substances: tropane alkaloids, atropine, and hyoscyamine) SYMPTOMS PRODUCED: Fever, visual disturbances, burning of mouth, thirst, dry skin, headache and confusion.

Caladium
NICKNAME: Fancy-leaf caladium TOXIC PARTS: All parts (toxic substance: calcium oxalate crystals) SYMPTOMS PRODUCED: Intense irritation to mucous membranes, producing swelling of tongue, lips and palate.

Cicuta maculata
NICKNAME: Water-hemlock, Spotted cowbane, Poison Parsnip TOXIC PARTS: Root and rootstalk (toxic substance: cicutoxin) SYMPTOMS PRODUCED: Increased salivation, abdominal pain, nausea, vomiting, tremors, muscle spasms and convulsions.

Colocasia
NICKNAME: Elephant ear, Dasheen TOXIC PARTS: All parts (toxic substance: calcium oxalate crystals) SYMPTOMS PRODUCED: Intense irritation to mucous membranes, producing swelling of tongue, lips and palate.

Conium maculatum
NICKNAME: Poison hemlock, Fool's parsley, False parsley TOXIC PARTS: All parts (toxic substances: lambdaconiceine, coniine, n-methyl coniine) SYMPTOMS PRODUCED: Gastrointestinal distress, muscular weakness and respiratory distress.

Daphne mezereum
NICKNAME: Daphne TOXIC PARTS: All parts, especially berries, bark and leaves (toxic substance: daphnin) SYMPTOMS PRODUCED: Local irritation to mouth and stomach, nausea, vomiting and diarrhea.

Datura meteloides
NICKNAME: Moonflower, Angel's trumpet, Locoweed TOXIC PARTS: Leaves, flowers, nectar, seeds (toxic substances: belladonna alkaloids) SYMPTOMS PRODUCED: Dilated pupils, dry mouth, increased body temperature, intense thirst, confusion, delirium, hallucinations and pulse disturbances.

Common Harmful Plants (cont'd.)

Datura stramonium
NICKNAME: Jimsonweed, Jamestown weed, Thorn apple, Angel's trumpet TOXIC PARTS: All parts (toxic substance: belladonna alkaloids) SYMPTOMS PRODUCED: Intense irritation to mucous membranes, producing swelling of tongue, lips and palate.

Dieffenbachia
NICKNAME: Dumb cane, Elephant ear TOXIC PARTS: All parts (toxic substance: calcium oxalate crystals) SYMPTOMS PRODUCED: Intense irritation to mucous membranes, producing swelling of tongue, lips and palate.

Digitalis
NICKNAME: Foxglove TOXIC PARTS: Leaves, seeds, flowers (toxic substances: cardioactive glycosides-digitoxin, digoxin, gitoxin and others) SYMPTOMS PRODUCED: Local irritation of mouth and stomach, vomiting, abdominal pain, diarrhea and cardiac disturbances.

Gelsemium sempervirens
NICKNAME: Yellow jessamine, Carolina jessamine TOXIC PARTS: All parts (toxic substances: alkaloids-gelsemine, gelsemicine) SYMPTOMS PRODUCED: Heart arrest, visual disturbances, dizziness, headache and dryness of mouth.

Hedera helix
NICKNAME: English ivy TOXIC PARTS: All parts (toxic substance: hederagenin, or steroidal saponin) SYMPTOMS PRODUCED: Local irritation, excess salivation, nausea, vomiting, thirst, severe diarrhea and abdominal pain.

Ilex
NICKNAME: Holly TOXIC PARTS: Bright red berries (toxic substance unidentified) SYMPTOMS PRODUCED: Nausea, vomiting, abdominal pain and diarrhea.

Iris
NICKNAME: None TOXIC PARTS: Rootstalk or rhizome (toxic substance unidentified) SYMPTOMS PRODUCED: Nausea, vomiting, abdominal pain and diarrhea.

Lantana
NICKNAME: Bunchberry TOXIC PARTS: All parts, especially the green berries (toxic substance: lantadena A) SYMPTOMS PRODUCED: Vomiting, diarrhea, weakness, ataxia visual disturbances and lethargy.

Ligustrum
NICKNAME: Common privet, Waxed-leaf ligustrum TOXIC PARTS: Leaves and berries (toxic substance unidentified) SYMPTOMS PRODUCED: Nausea, vomiting, abdominal pain and diarrhea.

Common Harmful Plants (cont'd.)

Monstera
NICKNAME: Swiss-cheese plant, Ceriman TOXIC PARTS: All parts (toxic substance: calcium oxalate crystals) SYMPTOMS PRODUCED: Intense irritation to mucous membranes, producing swelling of tongue, lips and palate.

Narcissus
NICKNAME: Daffodil, Jonquil TOXIC PARTS: Bulb (toxic substance unidentified) SYMPTOMS PRODUCED: Nausea, vomiting, abdominal pain and diarrhea.

Nerum Oleander
NICKNAME: Oleander TOXIC PART: Leaves, stems and flowers (toxic substances: cardioactive glycosides-oleandroside, oleandrin and nerioside) SYMPTOMS PRODUCED: Local irritation to mouth and stomach, vomiting, abdominal pain, diarrhea and cardiac disturbances.

Philodendron
NICKNAME: Elephant ear TOXIC PARTS: All parts, (toxic substance: calcium oxalate crystals) SYMPTOMS PRODUCED: Intense irritation to mucous membranes, producing swelling of tongue, lips and palate.

Phytolacca americana
NICKNAME: Pokeweed, Pokeroot, Poke salad, Inkberry TOXIC PARTS: All parts, especially the root, leaves and green berries (toxic substance: spanonin, resin) SYMPTOMS PRODUCED: Oral burning sensation, sore throat, nausea, vomiting and blurred vision.

Podophyllum peltatum
NICKNAME: Mayapple, Mandrake, Ground lemon TOXIC PARTS: Rootstalk, leaves, stems and green fruit (toxic substance: podophylloresin) SYMPTOMS PRODUCED: Abdominal pain, vomiting, diarrhea and pulse irregularities.

Poinciana gillieii
NICKNAME: Poinciana, Bird-of-Paradise TOXIC PARTS: Green seek pods (toxic substance unidentified) SYMPTOMS PRODUCED: Nausea, vomiting, abdominal pain and diarrhea.

Prunus
NICKNAME: Apricot, Cherry, Nectarine, Peach, Plum TOXIC PARTS: Leaves, stems, bark and seed pits (toxic substances: cyanogenic glycosides) SYMPTOMS PRODUCED: Nausea, vomiting, abdominal pain, diarrhea, difficulty in breathing, muscular weakness, dizziness, stupor, and convulsions.

Common Harmful Plants (cont'd.)

Prunus virginiana
NICKNAME: Choke cherry TOXIC PARTS: Leaves, stems, bark and seed pits (toxic substances: cyanogenic glycosides) SYMPTOMS PRODUCED: Nausea, vomiting, abdominal pain, diarrhea, difficulty in breathing, muscular weakness, stupor and convulsions.

Quinquafolia parthenocissus
NICKNAME: Virginia creeper, American ivy TOXIC PARTS: Berries and leaves (toxic substance: oxalic acid) SYMPTOMS PRODUCED: Corrosive action to gastrointestinal tract, nausea, vomiting, abdominal pain, diarrhea and headache.

Rheum rhabarbarum
NICKNAME: Rhubarb TOXIC PARTS: Berries and leaves (toxic substance: oxalic acid). SYMPTOMS PRODUCED: Corrosive action to gastrointestinal tract, nausea, vomiting, abdominal pain, diarrhea and headache.

Ricinus communis
NICKNAME: Castor bean, Castor oil plant, Palma Christi TOXIC PARTS: Seed, if chewed (toxic substance: ricin) SYMPTOMS PRODUCED: Burning sensation in the mouth, nausea, vomiting, abdominal pain, thirst, blurred vision, dizziness and convulsions.

Robinia pseudoacacia
NICKNAME: Black locust, White locust TOXIC PARTS: Young leaves, inner bark, seeds, (toxic substances: aphytotoxin and aglycoside) SYMPTOMS PRODUCED: Nausea, vomiting and abdominal pain.

Solanum dulcamara
NICKNAME: European bittersweet, Climbing night-shade, Deadly nightshade TOXIC PARTS: Leaves and berries, (toxic substance: salanine) SYMPTOMS PRODUCED: Vomiting, diarrhea, abdominal pain, drowsiness, tremors, weakness and difficulty in breathing.

Solanum pseudocapsicum
NICKNAME: Jerusalem cherry, Natal cherry TOXIC PARTS: All parts, (toxic substances: leaves contain cardioactive substance solanocapsine; berries contain glycoalkaloid solanine and related glycoalkaloids) SYMPTOMS PRODUCED: Nausea, vomiting, abdominal pain, diarrhea and hemolysis.

Taxus
NICKNAME: Japanese yew TOXIC PARTS: Seeds and leaves (toxic substances: alkaloid toxine) SYMPTOMS PRODUCED: Stomach problems and cardiac disturbances.

Common Harmful Plants (cont'd.)

Wisteria
  NICKNAME: none TOXIC PARTS: Whole pods or seeds (toxic substances: resin and glycoside wisterin) SYMPTOMS PRODUCED: Nausea, vomiting, abdominal pain and diarrhea.
Source: Natural Poison Center Network

Common Non-Poisonous Plants

The following are some non-poisonous plants. While these plants are not known to cause specific, harmful reactions, it makes good sense to teach your child to avoid eating any plant.

Common name	Botanical name
African violet	Saintpaulia ionantha
Begonia	Begonia
Christmas cactus	Schlumbergera bridgesii, Zygocactus truncatus
Coleus	Coleus blumei
Dandelion	Taraxacum officinale
Dracaena	Dracaena
Impatiens	Impatiens
Jade	Crassula argentea
Marigold	Tagetes
Peperomia	Peperomia caperata
Prayer plant	Maranta
Purple passion	Cynura aurantiaca
Rose	Rosa
Schefflera	Brassaia actinophylla
Snake plant	Sanservieria trifasciata
Spider plant	Chlorophytum comosum
Swedish ivy	Plectranthus australia
Wandering Jew	Tradescantia fluminensis
Wax plant	Hoya carnosa
Wild strawberry	Fragaria
Zebra plant	Aphelandra squarrosa

Plastic Bags—Keep *all* plastic bags away from children. This includes dry cleaning, trash, produce, and shopping bags, as well as thin plastic wrapping found in packaging materials. Young children often find these fun to hide in or try on, but they can easily smother in them. Make it a practice to tie the plastic up in knots and throw it away as soon as you are through using it.

Purse and Briefcase—It almost seems as if your child knows that you keep important items in your purse or briefcase which makes them all the more attractive. A purse or briefcase's hooks, latches, and buttons can be unsafe, as can their contents. Find a regular, safe, out-of-the-way spot in which to store your purse, attache case or book bag.

Stairs—The staircase provides an irresistible climbing apparatus, full of places to explore, for the young crawler or walker, besides being the path to rooms upstairs. Make the stairs "off limits" unless you plan to be within inches of your climber. Expandable gates will prevent stair use by children (see Chapter Two). As your child gets older, teach him or her to descend stairs on his stomach, feet first, and later the importance of using the handrail. If your stairs do not have a handrail, install one.

Trash Cans—Until your child is older, consider limiting trash cans to the kitchen and bathroom instead of placing one in every room. No matter how many you have, remember that each wastebasket presents its own hazard. Place trash cans, if possible, out of the reach of children, or at least out of direct view. Under-the-sink kitchen and bathroom cabinets are good possibilities. Try to take safety precautions when you throw your trash away, like putting sharp cans inside something else and tying up plastic bags in knots.

Wall Outlets and Extension Cords—Electrical wall outlets, typically found close to the floor, present a real hazard to young children. Fatal shocks and severe burns can result from a child inserting a metal object into an empty outlet. To avoid this danger, insert plastic safety caps into any unused outlet in your home. Buy some extra caps to use when you travel.

An electrical burn to the mouth is the most common extension cord injury to young children. Children also are injured when they tug on or trip over an extension cord, pulling a lamp, coffeepot or other appliance over on themselves. To avoid these injuries, use extension cords only when absolutely necessary; never let a cord dangle from a counter top or tabletop where it can be pulled or tripped over; never leave unused extension cords plugged into outlets; discard worn, frayed, or damaged extension cords; insert plugs fully so no part of the plug is exposed while the extension cord is in use. Obviously, many of these same precautions apply to all types of electrical cords.

Windows—Each year windows are associated with many injuries to young children. For example, in 1987 CPSC estimated that 39% of all window-screen injuries and 39% of all window sill or window frame injuries occurred to children four years of age and younger. Windowpane and jalousie glass windows were also associated with injuries.

Many window accidents result when children climb up on furniture to see what is going on outside. Try to avoid placing furniture right underneath a window. A window screen is not strong enough to withstand a child's weight being pressed against it. Special locks are available that allow for ventilation but only allow the window to be opened to a certain height. When not in use, be sure to store storm windows and screens out of the reach of children. Children can also get entangled in window blind or drapery cords and possibly be strangled. To secure such cords: Clip the cord to itself or to the window covering with a clamping device, such as a clothes pin; wrap or tie the cord to itself; wrap the cord around a cleat mounted near the top of the window covering; or install a tie-down device.

Safety Outside the Home

Starting at a very young age, children are fascinated with the out of doors. Included in this section are a number of outdoor products, places, and activities that are childhood favorites. In addition to highlighting their hazards, we have set out safety tips to help ensure that these remain favorites, rather than sources of injury.

All Terrain Vehicles

All-terrain vehicles (ATVs), intended for off-road use and more difficult to maneuver than motorcycles or cars, have been the subject of intense scrutiny by CPSC. In December 1987, the agency entered into an agreement with the industry to halt the sale of the three-wheel ATV models; however, four-wheel models continue to be sold, and injuries and deaths associated with these vehicles continue to mount. Of the over 1,300 ATV deaths reported to CPSC, over 40% of the victims have been children ages 15 and younger; almost 20% of these were children ages 11 and younger. The American Academy of Pediatrics strongly recommends against the use of an ATV by any child, regardless of age or size. It is also dangerous for an adult to ride with a child.

Amusement Parks

Amusement park accidents are not limited to older children and adults. According to CPSC, amusement rides each year cause over 1,000 injuries requiring hospital emergency treatment to children ages four years and younger. The following tips will help to keep your family's trip to the amusement park or neighborhood carnival from becoming a disaster:

- ☐ No matter how much your child insists, always follow height and age requirements for rides.

- ☐ Harness children securely into seats. If no harness or restraining strap is available and you think there is a possibility that your child may fall out, don't let him or her on that ride.

- ☐ Never allow your child to run in an amusement park or at a carnival.

- ☐ If you plan to use the amusement park's stroller, take a harness or restraining strap with you. Many parks do not put straps on their strollers for sanitary purposes. The amusement park contains many distractions for both parents and children, so use the restraining strap at all times when your child is in the stroller.

- ☐ Designate an easily recognizable place to meet your child in the event that you get separated.

- ☐ Because it is difficult to handle children in such an excited environment, try to have one adult supervise every two children for your outing.

- ☐ As the popularity of water slides has increased, so have injuries. Water-slide injuries include lacerations, concussions, fractures, bruises, sprains and broken teeth. Make sure your child understands and obeys safety rules. Never allow children to ride tandem as this increases the risk of spinal-cord injury.

No matter what parents do to prevent accidents, the responsibility for safe and well-maintained equipment rests with those who run the park or carnival. Amusement ride laws vary from state to state. Most states differentiate between two types of rides: fixed-site rides are those generally found in theme parks; mobile rides move from site to site, such as those found at a shopping center or church carnival.

If you believe that a particular amusement ride is unsafe, or if you or your child have been injured, report this to CPSC and to your state consumer protection office. Reports of such incidents are important in preventing further incidents and provide support for improved amusement-ride legislation. The following list, compiled by CPSC, indicates which states have amusement park inspections and which do not.

States that Inspect or Regulate Amusement Rides: Alaska, Arkansas, California, Colorado (Insurance companies also inspect.), Connecticut, Delaware (Insurance companies also inspect.), District of Columbia (Mobile units only; permanent parks *not* inspected.), Florida (Mobile units only.), Hawaii, Idaho, Illinois, Indiana, Iowa, Kentucky, Maine, Maryland, Massachusetts (Insurance companies also inspect.), Michigan, Minnesota (Mobile units *not* inspected.), Nebraska (Insurance companies also inspect.), New Hampshire, New Jersey (Insurance companies also inspect.), New Mexico (Mobile units *not* inspected.), New York, North Carolina, Ohio, Oklahoma, Oregon, Pennsylvania (Insurance companies also inspect.), Rhode Island (Mobile units only; permanent parks *not* inspected.), South Carolina, Texas (Insurance companies also inspect.), Virginia (Insurance companies also inspect.), Washington, West Virginia, Wisconsin.

States that *do not* inspect or regulate amusement rides: Alabama, Arizona, Kansas, Louisiana, Mississippi, Missouri, Montana, Nevada, North Dakota, South Dakota, Tennessee, Utah, Vermont, Wyoming

Deck, Balcony, and Stair Railings

To avoid falls and prevent entrapment of your child's head or other body parts, make sure that vertical posts or pickets in your deck, balcony or stair railings are no more than 3-½ inches apart if a young baby will have access to this area. If your deck has horizontal railings, the space between horizontal rails or bars, and between the floor and the first horizontal rail or bar, should be no more than 3-½ inches. This amount of space will prevent the child's feet from sliding out first and trapping the child at the head and neck.

Fireworks

Fireworks can cause blindness, amputation, severe burns, and even death. They present a serious safety hazard, especially to young children who are unable to perceive the dangers. Each year, several hundred children four years of age and younger are injured seriously enough by fireworks to require emergency-room treatment.

Many states and local governments *prohibit* or limit the sale and use of Class C (ordinary) fireworks. These include: fountains, California candles, spike and candle cylindrical fountains, Roman candles, rockets with sticks, wheels, snakes, illuminating torches, sparklers, mines and shells, whistles without report, toy smoke devices and flitter devices, helicopter-type rockets, party poppers, missile-type rockets, and firecrackers with no more than 50 milligrams of powder.

Under federal law it is *illegal* to make, distribute or sell M-80 salutes, M-100s, and M-100 firecrackers (powder-filled silver or red-colored cardboard tubes, three to six inches long, one inch in diameter), aerial bombs, and cherry bombs. CPSC also enforces regulations requiring that the permissible charge in fireworks be no more than 50 milligrams of powder and that a fuse burn at least three seconds, but no longer than six seconds.

We recommend leaving firework displays up to the experts, or at least experienced adults. If you do plan to purchase them, it is wise to first check your state or local municipality's policy regarding what is allowed.

When using fireworks, it is particularly important for parents and other adults to exhibit extreme caution near children. *Never allow young children to use fireworks.* Even sparklers, which are often considered safe, burn at very high temperatures and can easily ignite clothing. While children are fascinated by the bright lights and sparklers, they cannot appreciate the dangers of fireworks. They are also not able to react effectively to an emergency situation.

If you should decide to buy fireworks, read and follow all warnings and instructions before using them. Always ignite fireworks outdoors and away from houses and flammable products. Keep a bucket of water nearby for emergencies. Never re-light or handle malfunctioning fireworks. When not using fireworks, store them in a cool, dry place that is inaccessible to children.

Fences

Having a fenced-in yard where your children can play often eases the tensions of allowing them to play outside. The fence *usually* prevents small children from wandering away or into the street and keeps uninvited people and pets out of the play area. But don't let a fence give you a false sense of security. Fences, as everyone knows, can be climbed. For a fence to be effective and safe some thought must go into planning its placement and maintenance.

Accidents involving fences occur frequently. Children may try to climb on or over fences and get hurt by getting caught on the fence or falling off. Falling against fences, coming into contact with their sharp edges and even accidentally running into fences while playing or riding bikes, scooters, or skates are all common causes of injuries. If the fence is rusty, a scratch can easily get infected. If it is wooden and not well-sanded, your child could get splinters. Even old, peeling paint presents a danger to children. In short, don't be fooled into thinking that having a fence—any fence—will guarantee a safe place for your child to play.

When buying a chain-link fence look for one with knuckle-to-knuckle barbs on top and bottom. This type of barb is hooked rather than twisted, so the sharp edge is turned downward or into the fence, rather than left facing outward where it can easily catch a child.

If you decide on a wooden fence, it is best to choose boards that are cut straight across or rounded on the top. This will lessen the likelihood of a child getting caught on sharp edges. Sand the wood well to avoid splinters. Openings in the pickets or bars should be no more than 2-⅜ inches to protect against a baby's head becoming entrapped.

No matter which type of fence you choose, discuss the specific requirements with a reputable dealer, and consider the dealer's recommendations for height and type. There are specific fence requirements in many areas, so check the municipal codes/ordinances of your locality—especially requirements for fences used around a swimming pool. Fences intended to keep toddlers in or out should have self-closing, self-latching gates. In order to prevent small children from reaching the latch, place it at least three feet above ground, and preferably at the top of the gate, rather than part-way down the post. Keep in mind that the fence should be installed as close to the ground as possible to keep your child from trying to crawl under it.

Once the fence is installed, educate your children about the dangers of fence climbing. Remember to keep fence gates locked or securely fastened, especially if the fence surrounds a swimming pool. Inspect the fence regularly for damage and repair promptly, especially if rusty. Replace loose hinges or other parts that may fall off or cause the gate or fence to come apart.

Halloween Safety

Halloween is an exciting time for children, but costumes, candy, and trick-or-treating can pose hazards. These guidelines will help ensure a safe and happy Halloween:

☐ Allow your child to trick-or-treat only at homes of friends or neighbors you know personally.

☐ Small children should always be accompanied by an adult. Do not allow them to walk in the street or otherwise ignore pedestrian safety rules.

☐ Make sure your child's costume (including the wig and mask) is flame resistant, easily visible at night (consider using reflective tape), and allows for safe walking. Avoid masks, scarves, and hats that obscure vision or restrict breathing. Costume accessories, such as swords and knives, should be of a soft, flexible material.

☐ Teach your child not to sample any of the treats until he or she gets home. Provide a good nutritious meal before your child goes out to trick-or-treat.

☐ Inspect all of your child's treats before allowing him or her to sample any. Discard anything not in its original and undamaged wrapper. Keep homemade food only if you are certain who prepared it.

☐ Cut open all fruit and inspect for foreign objects, like razor blades.

☐ Call the Poison Control Center if you suspect your child has ingested something harmful.

☐ Notify the police of any suspicious treats.

☐ If you decide to give out non-edible treats, make sure they are not small enough to pose a choking hazard to young children who may put them in their mouths.

☐ Consider throwing a Halloween party for your child and his or her friends in lieu of extended trick-or-treating.

Hot Tubs and Spas

Today, hot tubs and spas have become popular for both health and relaxation. While for most adults these products offer few hazards, for children under five, there are dangers of hypothermia, drowning, or becoming trapped. Drownings often occur when a child is left unattended or wanders alone to the site of the tub or spa. If your child can swim, he obviously has a reduced chance of drowning, but, the jetted action or other circumstance may cause him or her to panic and lose control. In addition, the suction from outlet grates and drains can trap body parts or hair. Young children are generally not strong enough to withstand the force of the suction and can be trapped under water long enough to drown.

Other hazards of hot tubs and spas include: burns and fires resulting from the chemicals used to clean the water; electrocution or electrical shock when an electrical current comes into contact with the tub or spa water; and cuts, abrasions, and contusions from slips and falls related to the hot tub or spa use.

If you own a hot tub or spa, or plan to use one, consider the following safety recommendations:

☐ Children's lighter body weights and developing organs make them much more sensitive to stress caused by higher water temperatures. For this reason, pediatricians warn that *children under the age of five should not use a hot tub or spa.* If an older child is taking medication or has heart disease, diabetes, high or low blood pressure, or any illness, do not allow him or her to use a hot tub or spa without prior approval from your doctor.

☐ Keep all water chemicals safely locked out of the reach of children. Have a complete first-aid kit nearby, as well as a telephone and a list of emergency phone numbers. Consider getting training in artificial respiration and/or cardiopulmonary resuscitation (CPR), including special procedures for administering CPR to children.

☐ If your hot tub or spa has a cover, always remove it completely before use. Do not allow your child to play on top of the cover. When purchasing a new cover, look for one that complies with the ASTM Safety Standard for Safety Covers. Some covers, such as solar covers, are *not* safety covers and do not protect against drowning.

☐ Place a fence around an outdoor hot tub or spa—but do not allow access from the house directly to the hot tub or spa. Make sure the fence is equipped with a self-closing and self-latching gate to keep out small children and intruders.

The latch should be above the reach of children; consider a permanent lock for more security. Check local, municipal or county codes/ordinances to determine if there are any specific fence requirements. If your hot tub or spa is indoors, keep the door to that room locked when the tub is not in use.

☐ Inspect your spa or hot tub's inlet and outlet fittings, grates, skimmer, and main drain often to see if they are missing, loose, cracked, or broken. Prohibit use until any needed repairs are made.

☐ Make sure handrails, steps, and ladders are securely in place. Check regularly to see that nuts and bolts are tight and that there are no broken treads or sharp edges.

☐ If you have not already done so, have a licensed electrician install ground fault circuit interrupters (GFCIs) to protect all nearby electrical outlets. This device helps prevent electrical shock by quickly cutting off the flow of electrical current.

Lawn Darts

Lawn darts are an outdoor game in which pointed darts are thrown through the air and then stick in the ground near a target. At least three children have been killed and many others blinded, brain damaged, or otherwise injured by lawn darts when the heavy metal tip punctured their skull. Although CPSC banned lawn darts in December 1988, millions of sets are still found in consumer homes. Lawn darts should never be used but should be discarded in a manner that will prevent others from using them.

Playgrounds

While playground equipment provides a wonderful outlet for children to release their energy and develop muscle coordination, there are several potential hazards to be avoided. CPSC estimates that 200,000 children annually suffer injuries requiring hospital emergency-room treatment as a result of playground equipment mishaps; 40% of these occur to children under age six. This estimate is based on injury data on sliding boards, seesaws, teeter boards, monkey bars, climbing equipment, swings, swing sets, and other playground equipment.

The majority of playground-related injuries are, not surprisingly, due to falls. Almost half of the reported injuries are to the head. These range in severity from minor bruises to skull fractures, concussions, brain damage, and even death.

Consider working with other neighborhood parents and community officials to make your neighborhood playground safer. *Existing* playground structures can be made safer by making the following changes:

☐ Remove equipment from asphalt or concrete surfaces. Install more resilient surface materials—such as mulch, wood chips, shredded tires, outdoor rubber mats, or synthetic turf—as these provide the best cushion for falls. Grass, soil, and sand become worn and hard-packed too quickly to serve as an adequate surface. Increase the resiliency of these surfaces by adding an organic material, such as mulch, over them. Remember that the resiliency of the surface can be the difference between a bruise and brain damage.

☐ Whenever possible, equipment should, however, be firmly *anchored* in the ground by concrete at the base of the supports. Make sure no one can trip over the anchoring devices. All concrete patches should be covered by cushioning material like the ones mentioned above.

☐ Install non-swinging equipment at least eight feet from fences, walls, or other equipment, since injuries from falling off a swing, slide, or jungle gym can be compounded by striking a nearby fence. Swings should be 20 feet (measure from the point underneath the top crossbar) from fences, walls, and other equipment, since the arc of a swing moves your child much closer to these objects.

☐ Remove obstacles to your vision that can impair adult supervision. Arrange equipment in a manner that allows a supervising adult to keep an eye on children at the playground.

☐ Surround the play area with a fence or dense shrubbery to prevent children from wandering off into street or other off-limit areas.

☐ Replace heavy swing seats with lightweight seats. Canvas, plastic, or tire swings are good alternatives to heavy metal ones. Make sure to drill holes in tire swings to insure water drainage.

☐ Consider color-coding equipment for different age groups in public playgrounds. Explanatory signs should be easy to read and prominently posted. Brightly colored tape or paint can also make a potentially hazardous edge easier to avoid.

☐ If a particular piece of equipment has been associated with a high number of injuries, replace or remove it.

☐ Set up a regular inspection and maintenance schedule. Make sure that all nuts, bolts, and clamps are tight; replace those that have rusted. Sand and repaint all rusted and sharp edges on metal tubing. Check swings and swing chains for rust and replace if necessary. Replace missing, damaged, or broken seats, steps, and rungs. Equipment made of logs, railroad ties, or landscape timber, especially if it is community-built or homemade, should be inspected regularly for rough edges, splinters, and sharp corners. Check for protrusions which can catch children's clothing.

☐ Consider applying slip-resistant surfaces to gripping and climbing surfaces.

☐ When replacing equipment look for: metal parts that have been galvanized or painted to prevent rust; wood components that have been treated to withstand moisture. Rungs on climbing equipment should be cylindrical and not more than 1-⅝ inches in diameter so children can grasp them safely. Openings in the equipment should be less than 3-½ inches, or greater than nine inches so a child's head or other body parts do not get trapped. (See our discussion in Chapter 3 on purchasing *home* playground equipment.)

☐ For more information on playground equipment and safety, write to CPSC for a copy of: "A Handbook for Public Playground Safety," CPSC, 5401 Westbard Ave., Washington, D.C. 20207.

Playground Safety Tips—No matter how much time and effort has gone into planning a safe playground, children often use playground equipment improperly. For this reason, it is important that young children be supervised while in the playground area and taught proper playground behavior. Teach your child the following playground safety rules:

☐ Don't run, push, shove, or fight, especially while on the equipment.

☐ Don't twist the swing chains, swing empty seats, or walk in front of moving swings.

☐ Sit properly on the swings and other equipment. If a piece of equipment is meant to hold a specific number of children, don't try to get more children on it.

☐ Don't get off a seesaw suddenly while someone is still on it, up in the air.

☐ Be careful when walking near seesaws, merry-go-rounds and other moving equipment.

☐ Don't climb up the slide on the wrong side—use the ladder.

☐ If you see a problem in the playground-for example, if someone is hurt or there is a fight-ask an adult for help.

☐ Don't abuse the equipment. Use it as it was meant to be used, and you and your friends will be less likely to fall or get hurt.

☐ Take turns in using the most popular equipment.

Play Sand—News reports have alleged that certain types of children's play sand contains asbestos, a cancer-causing agent. After a review of scientific studies, CPSC has concluded that there is no evidence of an asbestos hazard. The CPSC staff did find low amounts of a non-asbestos form of tremolite in two types of play sand; however, to their knowledge, there is no data to suggest that this type of tremolite poses a risk. However, Public Citizen, a consumer advocacy group, disagrees with this conclusion and recommends that parents purchase natural sand. It is coarser than the controversial sand containing tremolite, which is made from crushed rock and is white and powdery.

Shopping with Children

Shopping with a young child can be one of the most frustrating experiences for a parent. The following tips might help things go more smoothly and prevent tears, accidents, and abductions.

☐ If your outing is more than a quick trip to one store, plan ahead. Try to avoid going at nap or eating times. As your child gets older, explain where you plan to go and what will be purchased. Let him or her know your shopping limits; if you don't plan to buy the child anything during the trip, say so ahead of time. Remember that some stores are very boring for children, so a "time-out" in a toy store might help things along. If shopping for long periods, let your child out of the stroller once or twice for a stretch. Keep an eye out for little hands reaching for attractive objects on nearby shelves and racks.

☐ Watch out for shopping carts. According to CPSC, each year approximately 15,000 children age four and under are injured seriously enough from shopping carts to require hospital emergency-room treatment. Children can suffer lacerations, contusions, fractures, and concussions when they jump or fall from the shopping carts, the cart overturns, they get pinched in the folding mechanism of the seat, or they fall against the cart. Consider carrying a harness or safety belt with you, to keep your child from climbing out.

☐ Be careful with your child on escalators. Getting on and off takes motor coordination that is somewhat difficult for a young child. Tennis shoes, long shoelaces, and baby strollers don't mix well with moving stairs. Teach your child how to properly ride an escalator: standing upright (never sitting!) and holding onto the rail.

☐ Never leave your child alone in the car. A parking lot is an easy place to abduct a child. Additionally, the temperature inside the car may be uncomfortable, if not hazardous; on a sunny day, the temperature inside a car parked in the shade can reach as high as 130 degrees F., a lethal temperature for young children. A child who can climb out of a car seat may also be tempted to try to drive.

☐ If shopping with a child who is not in a stroller, try, whenever possible, to hold him or her by the hand. In any case, don't let the child out of your sight. Never drop your youngster off in a toy, television, or other department while you run errands elsewhere in a store. This can subject your child to a possible abduction. Teach your child that if he or she becomes separated from you, not to look for you but to go to the nearest checkout counter. The child should only ask for assistance after asking if the clerk actually works there. Instruct your child to never go to the parking lot in search of you.

Swimming Pools

Not only is swimming an activity enjoyed by most young children, but it can be one of the most healthy forms of recreation. Unfortunately, as most parents know, the swimming pool and surrounding area can pose very real hazards. For the children five years of age and under, the most serious of these is drowning. CPSC estimates that each year more than 300 children under age five drown in backyard swimming pools, spas, and hot tubs. An additional 3,000 are treated in hospital emergency rooms for conditions resulting from potential drownings. In one study, CPSC found that: 75% of the backyard pool drowning victims were between 12 and 35 months of age; 65% were male; and 46% of the victims were last seen inside the house prior to being found in the pool.

Another very serious, though infrequent, hazard to young children occurs when pool drain holes have broken or are missing drain grates. Children are attracted to the sucking action of the drain and like to explore the drain hole itself. But, the suction in an uncovered pool drain can be powerful enough to pull a child's intestines from his body and can result in permanent disability or death. CPSC investigations show that these accidents generally occur in in-ground wading pools in which a pump draws water from the base of the pool, through the drain hole to the filtering system, and then returns the water to the pool.

Other pool hazards include poisonings and burns from chemicals used to clean the pool and electrical shock from contacting the pool water with electrical appliances. Still the most common injuries—cuts, contusions, and abrasions—are from falls, horseplay, or the improper use of pool equipment. While horseplay and improper dives can cause paralysis, this injury is more likely to happen to teenagers and adults, rather than young children.

In order to reduce the risk of accidents in and around the pool, follow these precautions:

☐ Maintain constant and close supervision of your child around a pool, even if he or she has had swimming lessons. A child can drown in less time than it takes to answer the telephone. Prohibit use of the pool when you are not there.

☐ Require that children wear a life jacket if they are unable to swim on their own. Bear in mind, however, that this never takes the place of a responsible adult in constant attendance.

☐ Teach your child to swim or enroll him or her in an American Red Cross, YMCA, YWCA, community pool, or other organization's swimming lessons. Note, however, that the American Academy of Pediatrics advises against swimming lessons for children under age three because they swallow too much water, and some parents rely too much on swimming lessons as a means of preventing child drownings. Proper diving instructions are also very important for older children and should include techniques for steering up with the arms to avoid hitting the bottom of the pool.

☐ Teach children that fittings, drains, and grates are not toys and that they should *never* stick their fingers or toes into them, or sit on them. Be sure to keep children with shoulder-length or longer hair away from a pool outlet so their hair doesn't get caught in the suction.

☐ Prohibit running, horseplay, pushing, or throwing others in the pool area. Never allow diving through an inner tube since very serious spinal cord injuries can occur, regardless of the pool depth. Prohibit diving in water depths of less than five feet; 95% of all diving accidents occur in five feet of water or less. There should also be a clear dive path of 25 feet.

☐ Remember that inflatable toys and rafts can deflate, so non-swimmers should not use them in water over their heads.

☐ Do not use, or allow your child to use, any electrical appliances near the pool.

☐ Do not allow your child to stay in the pool during lightning or rainstorms because of the electrocution hazard.

If you have your own pool in the backyard, follow these extra precautions, in addition to those listed above:

☐ Place a five-foot-high fence around all four sides of your pool area to keep out small children and intruders. However, the house should not form part of the fence since access to the pool from the house is a major factor in child drowning incidents. The fence should have no vertical opening more than four inches wide. Don't defeat the fence's purpose by leaving it unlocked or by propping the gate open. Check the municipal or county codes/ordinances for your locality to determine the requirements for pool fences.

☐ The fence gate should be self-closing and have a self-latching mechanism above a toddlers' reach. In addition, there should be hardware that allows the fence to be permanently locked.

☐ Be wary of pool alarm devices which purportedly sound an alarm to alert you when someone enters an unattended pool. A CPSC study on these devices found that they did not always sound when they should have or gave a false alarm. We do not advise relying solely on these devices, since a child could easily drown in the time it takes you to get pool side after the alarm has sounded.

☐ As the pool owner you have the right to prohibit all of the following and should to so: any jumping, diving, head-first entries from pool slides; horseplay or other activity that may cause an injury; diving into an above-ground pool; diving into an in-ground pool where the water depth is less than five feet. To reinforce your pool rules, consider posting them, and instruct young children individually. In addition, properly placed warnings at pool side will serve as a reminder that, for example, diving is only permitted in certain depths of water. Safety lines placed across the width of the pool also alert users to variations in pool depth.

☐ All doors from the house to the pool should be locked whenever possible.

☐ Do not allow the use of any glassware in the pool area. If food is served near the pool, use plastic drinking glasses and plates.

☐ Keep all pool chemicals safely locked out of the reach of children.

☐ Have a complete first-aid kit at pool side, as well as lifesaving equipment, such as a life ring, rope, or solid pole. Training in artificial respiration and/or cardiopulmonary resuscitation (CPR) is strongly advised, including special procedures for administering CPR to children. Also keep a telephone at pool side, with a list of emergency numbers posted on or beside it.

☐ Inspect drain grates daily to be certain that they are in good condition and cannot be removed without tools. Immediately replace or repair missing or broken drain covers and prohibit use of the pool until the work is finished.

☐ If you own a pool cover, always remove it completely before using the pool. Remove any standing water in the cover, since even very small amounts are a drowning hazard. If you plan to purchase a cover, look for one that complies with the ASTM Safety Standard for Safety Covers. Some pool covers, such as solar pool covers, May not be able to hold children who may wander out on to the pool cover.

☐ Make sure that handrails, steps, and ladders are securely mounted. Periodically inspect them for broken treads, sharp edges, and loose nuts and bolts. If you have an above-ground pool, buy a removable ladder, or one that can be swung out of reach, to prevent anyone from using your pool without permission.

☐ If you have not already done so, have a licensed electrician install ground fault circuit interrupters (GFCIs) in all electrical outlets near the pool. This device helps prevent electrical shock by quickly cutting off the flow of electrical current.

Traffic Safety

Young children need adult supervision when crossing streets. According to the SAFE KIDS Campaign, children ages 7 and younger are at risk when it comes to traffic because of their age and size. Young children mistakenly believe if they can see a driver, a driver can see them, and that cars can stop instantly. Children can't tell where sounds come from and few can judge how fast traffic is moving. And their field of vision is one-third that of adults, and they don't recognize danger and react to it. Because of these limitations, children should be supervised and taught about traffic safety.

Teach your children the following traffic-safety rules before they begin to play outdoors without constant supervision:

☐ Never to run into the street, even to chase a ball or toy. Reinforce this rule by explaining the consequences.

☐ Forbid them from crossing the street by themselves until you are confident that your child can do so safely.

☐ Explain the use of traffic lights, and make sure that *you* always follow the same rules you set, since safety advice is often discounted by children when their parents do not adhere to it themselves.

☐ If you're raising a child in the city or in an area near heavy traffic, give instructions regarding *"walk/do not walk"* signals, and crossing at the light or corner, rather than jaywalking.

Waste Dumpsters

Many older refuse bins have an improper design which allows them to tip over easily. These unstable bins have been banned by CPSC; however, some are still in use. Besides being unstable and holding a lot of smelly unsanitary trash, waste dumpsters contain dangerous materials, sharp, and sometimes rusty edges and surfaces, and are tall enough to cause serious consequences should a child fall from the top of one. Explain these hazards to your child and make these containers strictly off-limits. If children play on or can easily get to a dumpster in your neighborhood, report this to the property owner.

Hidden Hazards

There are plenty of well-known hazards in your child's life: swings can pinch little fingers; baby walkers can catapult a child down steps, a cord on a pacifier can cut off air and cause strangulation. With these hazards, you can easily learn what steps to take to avert injury. But what about *hidden* hazards? What, if anything, should you, as a parent, do to uncover and diminish them?

By *hidden hazards* we are referring to the quality of air in your home, exposure to harmful chemicals, possible sources of radiation in your environment.

You may have heard someone (perhaps yourself) say, at one time or another, "Everything causes cancer, so why bother getting upset about another scare?" As safety advocates, we, too, often feel this way, but the fact is there are things that we can do to protect our children.

There are several reasons why it is important that, as parents, we get concerned. First, these hazards are more potent to our children than they are to us as adults. A child's body weight is substantially less than an adult's, and children's vital organs are still in their developing stages. Since the respiratory rate of children is ten times faster than adults', they inhale more frequently. And since they are indiscriminate "tasters", often putting objects in their mouth, their exposure to harmful substances is increased. Some of these hazards are the result of technology, formulations, and inventions that have come about in the last 10 or 15 years. Thus, our children will be exposed to them from birth (or even prenatally), whereas today's adults, over their lifetimes, will have been exposed considerably fewer years.

We should also be concerned about the possible cumulative effects of all of these intangible hazards. Exposure to a harmful element of one product may not be enough to alarm even the most fearful parent. But the list of toxic substances in our environment grows daily, and our children are receiving, and will continue to receive, a barrage of exposure to these during their lifetimes. While the risk of one chemical may be known, questions regarding their cumulative interaction and effect remain unanswered.

Indoor Air Pollution

It is very possible that the air inside your home is unhealthy. Recent studies show levels of indoor pollutants up to ten times higher than those found outdoors. While polluted air can affect all family members, many researchers are particularly concerned about the health consequences for young children. Because their respiratory systems and vital organs are still developing, and because they typically spend more time indoors, young children may be much more affected by unhealthy indoor pollutants than the average adult.

Indoor air quality is a complex problem. Unfortunately, indoor air pollutants cannot be linked to just one source. There are a variety of contaminants emanating from many sources in the home. What's worse is that some of these pollutants cannot be seen, smelled, tasted, or touched. Their health consequences may be as simple as headache or itchy eyes, or as serious as emphysema or heart, liver, or kidney disease. Consult the chart below for pollutant sources found in the home and for the corresponding health effects. Consider the suggestions listed in order to begin to remove some sources of indoor pollutants from your family's living quarters.

Your state health department may be able to provide more information; ask if they will test your home for contaminants. In combating indoor pollutants, beware of quick fixes: A tabletop air filter, for example, will do nothing to remove the majority of pollutants from the air.

Indoor Air Pollution

Radon

Odorless, colorless, radioactive gas; a decay product of radium, which occurs naturally in the earth's crust. HEALTH EFFECTS: Believed responsible for about five percent of all lung cancers. SOURCES: Earth and rock beneath home. TO REDUCE EXPOSURE: Increase ventilation, open windows, add crawlspace vents, avoid home-insulating measures like weather stripping, or install air-to-air heat exchanger, seal cracks, and other openings in the floor.

Formaldehyde

Strong-smelling, colorless, water soluble gas; a component of some insulation and of glues used in making plywood, particle board and textiles. HEALTH EFFECTS: Nose, throat, and eye irritation; possibly nasal cancer. SOURCES: Various materials including urea-formaldehyde foam insulation (UFFI), particle board, plywood, furniture, drapes and carpet. TO REDUCE EXPOSURE: Use materials that are relatively low in formaldehyde. Examples are low-formaldehyde particle board and exterior grade plywood, which release less formaldehyde than interior grades.

Carbon Monoxide

Colorless, odorless, tasteless gas from fuel burning. HEALTH EFFECTS: Lung ailments, impaired vision and brain functioning; fatal in high concentrations. SOURCES: Kerosene heaters, wood stoves, unvented gas stoves, attached garages. TO REDUCE EXPOSURE: Be sure stoves are properly vented, install exhaust fan above gas stoves, keep gas appliances properly adjusted, clean chimneys, do not let fires smolder, and do not leave car idling in garage.

Nitrogen Oxide

Colorless, tasteless gas formed during combustion. HEALTH EFFECTS: Lung damage, lung disease after long exposure. SOURCES: Kerosene heaters, unvented gas stoves. TO REDUCE EXPOSURE: Install exhaust fans above gas stove, keep gas appliances properly adjusted, and increase ventilation.

Indoor Air Pollution (cont'd.)

Respirable Particles

Particles in the air small enough to be inhaled. HEALTH EFFECTS: Nose, throat, and eye irritation, lung cancer, emphysema, heart disease, bronchitis, and respiratory infections. SOURCES: Tobacco smoke, wood smoke, unvented gas appliances, kerosene heaters, asbestos construction materials, and house dust. TO REDUCE EXPOSURE: Avoid smoking tobacco inside or smoke near open window, be sure pipe from wood stove does not leak, vent combustion appliances outdoors, change air filters regularly, and increase ventilation.

Benzo-A-Pyrene

A tarry organic particle from incomplete combustion. HEALTH EFFECTS: Nose, throat, and eye irritation, lung cancer, emphysema, heart disease, bronchitis, and respiratory infections. SOURCES: Wood smoke, tobacco smoke. TO REDUCE EXPOSURE: Avoid smoking inside or smoke near open window, be sure pipe from wood stove does not leak, vent combustion appliances outdoors, change air filters regularly, and increase ventilation.

Household Chemicals

Organic compounds found in household products. HEALTH: Irritation of skin, eyes, nose, and throat, effects on central nervous system and metabolic process. SOURCES: Synthetic materials, pesticides, aerosol sprays, cleaning agents, paints. TO REDUCE EXPOSURE: Follow directions on labels for use, use chemicals only in well-ventilated areas, store chemicals in a garage or outdoor shed, and substitute less hazardous products.

In addition to those listed in the chart above, asbestos and lead are other indoor air contaminants which pose a health risk to your family. Asbestos is a proven carcinogen which was used in ceilings, in insulation for heating systems, and in some consumer products because of it's fire resistant properties. When asbestos deteriorates, it forms a powder which can be inhaled and only a very small amount can cause disease. To determine whether to remove or repair and seal off asbestos, consult your state health or environmental protection department. (See our discussion about lead contamination below.)

Finally, if you or someone in your family is a smoker, consider quitting for your child's sake, if not for your own. A report by the National Research Council Committee on Passive Smoking concluded that children of smoking parents have bronchitis, pneumonia, and other lower-respiratory tract illnesses up to twice as often during the first year of life as the children of nonsmokers. They are also hospitalized more frequently during their first year as a result of these illnesses. Former U.S. Surgeon General C. Everett Koop, M.D. concluded in his report on involuntary smoking that the children of parents who smoke get more respiratory infections, increased respiratory symptoms, and have slightly smaller rates of increase in lung function as the lung matures. In addition, the Surgeon General's report cites studies which determined that chronic middle ear effusions are more common in children of smokers than in children of non-smoking parents. Involuntary smoking is a cause of disease, including lung cancer, in healthy nonsmokers, warns Koop, so parents should eliminate tobacco smoke from their own and their child's environment.

Lead

The evidence is clear: too much lead in the body can cause serious damage to the brain, kidneys, nervous system, and red blood cells. Children who have lead poisoning may exhibit the following symptoms: unusual irritability, poor appetite, stomach pains and vomiting, persistent constipation, and sluggishness or drowsiness. But some victims may not show any symptoms until it is too late. Lead poisoning can result in permanent neurological damage, or even death. Children may be exposed to lead *paint* poisoning by chewing or tasting objects covered with lead paint (children's furniture, toys, window sills, etc.), eating chipped pieces of paint, or by inhaling lead dust during restoration or repair of lead-painted homes. If you plan to renovate an older home, keep your child away from the area until the work and clean-up is complete.

Children may also be exposed to lead through household *drinking water*. Lead levels in your drinking water are likely to be highest if your home or water system has lead pipes or has copper pipes with lead solder. Since you cannot see, taste, or smell lead dissolved in water, testing is the only sure way to tell if your water supply is affected. To obtain information about testing for lead in your home's water supply, contact your local water utility or state health department.

Although less prevalent, children can also be exposed to lead in *ceramic ware* treated with a *lead glaze*. If the glaze is incorrectly formulated, applied, or misfired, lead can leach from the pottery and be ingested when it is used for food and drink. FDA recommends that consumers not store acidic food and beverages, including fruit juice, in ceramic ware and, the agency warns that the "safe" glaze applied in art class may actually leach lead if not applied properly.

If you believe your child has been exposed to lead, regardless of the source of exposure, it is extremely important to take him or her to your doctor for testing; lead poisoning must be treated early to be cured. Pregnant women should also follow the above precautions regarding limiting lead exposure since its adverse effects can harm the fetus.

Because lead is a significant hazard to children, the American Academy of Pediatrics (AAP) is asking for widespread screening of high-risk children, a national program to screen for and remove lead hazards from housing, and restoration of federal funding to rid the U.S. of lead hazards.

The Academy says that exposure to lead is widespread and causes serious, largely irreversible, impairments to children at relatively low levels of exposure. The AAP recommends that all preschool children be screened for lead absorption, especially those who live in older or dilapidated housing.

Children and Lead

Source	# of Children	Where Frequently Found
Leaded paint	12.0 million	Old or run-down housing
Drinking water	10.4 million	Lead pipes or leachable solder
Dust, soil	5.9-11.0 million	Airborne particles from leaded paint, gasoline, and industrial pollution
Leaded gasoline	5.6 million	Airborne particles in areas with heavy traffic
Food	1.0 million	Lead-soldered food cans
Stationary sources	200,000	Airborne particles from industrial incinerators, smelters, and foundries

Nitrosamines

Nitrosamines are known cancer-causing substances. They are found in a variety of products, including baby nipples and pacifiers. Nitrosamines are also present in many foods in which nitrites, a chemical used as a preservative, have combined with naturally occurring amines (hence the word nitrosamine). Cured meats, such as hot dogs, bacon, bologna, ham and corned beef, have been identified as containing nitrosamines.

The level of nitrosamines in baby nipples and pacifiers have been under scrutiny by two federal government agencies. CPSC is responsible for the regulating the level of nitrosamines in pacifiers, and the Food and Drug Administration sets nitrosamine levels for baby nipples. Both agencies have taken regulatory steps to reduce the nitrosamine levels in these products. While several years ago it was not uncommon to find nitrosamine levels in pacifiers at 300 to 1400 parts per billion (ppb), the average pacifier level now is well below government requirements. Therefore, boiling nipples and pacifiers, which was once recommended, is no longer necessary.

CPSC and FDA continue to scrutinize these products' nitrosamine levels, so you may want to keep an eye out for any recalls of such products. Also, to be on the safe side, you may want to limit your child's intake of cured meats.

Ozone

There are two types of ozone, both of which we hear about through the media. *Ozone gas* trapped in our atmosphere results in poor air quality; the *ozone layer*, in what scientists call the ozonosphere, protects the earth from harmful ultraviolet radiation.

Ozone gas is formed by the action of sunlight on mixtures of nitrogen oxides and volatile organic chemicals released into our air supply. Ozone is a respiratory irritant that can cause inflammation of the airways, coughing, tightness in the chest, pain, and difficulty breathing; it can provoke asthma attacks in some people, too. According to some experts, as with other pollutants, children are more susceptible to the adverse effects of ozone than adults. Studies show that children exposed to ozone levels even below the current standard, show acute changes in breathing function. The American Academy of Pediatrics has urged Congress to demand that strict measures be implemented to decrease concentration of harmful air pollutants contributing to adverse ozone levels.

The ozone layer is eroding and, hence the news reports on "holes in the ozone." Chlorofluorocarbons (CFCs) are one of the major contributors to the depletion of the ozone layer—eroding it three times faster than previously estimated. By avoiding or reducing the use of products that produce chlorofluorocarbons as a by-product, such as, Styrofoam and air conditioning, your family can contribute to the fight to save the protective ozone layer. And in doing so, your children will be sensitive to environmental concerns that will so affect the world they live in tomorrow.

Radiation

As you are probably aware, there are a variety of sources of radiation in our everyday environment. Again, because of your child's size and developing organs, you should be aware of potential radiation sources to which he or she may be exposed.

Television sets, particularly those manufactured before 1970, may give off radiation. Television radiation exposure increases with the amount of time a child watches, and a child's proximity to the set. Often old TV sets are used for video games, and this increases radiation exposure even more. The National Council for Radiation Protection and Measurement estimates that a child who sits 16 inches from the set, and uses it two hours a day, receives 890 millirems of radiation in the eyes each year. A chest X-ray, by comparison, produces only 20 to 30 millirems. Newer televisions are not thought to pose a risk; FDA testing found that televisions made after 1980 emit no measurable radiation.

An improperly maintained microwave oven can also expose your child to radiation. To avoid possible low-level exposure from microwave ovens, make sure that the door hinges, latches, and seal are all intact. Check to see that the oven will not operate with the door open, and consider investing in a microwave detector to determine if your oven is leaking. Finally, do not let your child lean against the oven while it is operating.

Choking

Most of us have been in the presence of a child who chokes on something. Luckily, most of those incidents have a happy ending. That's no reason not to be prepared with the latest information of what to do if your child really starts to choke.

The American Heart Association, the American Red Cross, the

American Academy of Pediatrics (AAP) all recommend abdominal thrusts (the Heimlich maneuver) as treatment for a choking child, except in infants younger than one year old. The good news is that there has been a dramatic decline in deaths from choking among infants and children younger than four years old. In 1983, 170 choking deaths were reported, compared with 600 in 1974.

These recommendations on first aid for a choking small child are as follows:

1. The child should be placed on his or her back with the rescuer kneeling next to him and placing the heel of one hand on the child's abdomen in the midline between the umbilicus (belly button) and rib cage. Apply a series of six to ten abdominal thrusts until the choking object is expelled. The maneuver should consist of rapid inward and upward thrusts. Older, larger children can be sitting, standing or lying down.

2. If the obstruction is not relieved using the Heimlich maneuver, open the victim's mouth using the tongue-jaw lift; this draws the tongue away from the back of the throat and may help relieve the obstruction. If the foreign body can be seen, it may be manually extracted by a finger sweep. However, blind sweeps may cause further obstruction and should be avoided.

3. If the child does not begin to breathe spontaneously, attempt to ventilate him with mouth-to-mouth, or mouth-to-mouth and nose, technique. If unsuccessful, repeat a series of six to ten abdominal thrusts.

4. Repeat steps 1 to 3. Make sure to call emergency medical services.

If the choking victim is an infant:

1. The infant should be placed face-down on the rescuer's forearm in a 60-degree head-down position with the head and neck stabilized. Brace your forearm against your body, for additional support.

2. Administer four back blows rapidly with the heel of the hand, high between the shoulder blades.

3. If the obstruction is not relieved, turn the infant over. Place him on his back on a firm surface and deliver four rapid chest thrusts (similar to external cardiac compressions) over the sternum, using two fingers.

4. If breathing does not resume, open the airway using the tongue-jaw lift technique and see if you can see the foreign body. *No* blind finger sweeps should be used.

5. If the infant does not begin to breathe spontaneously, attempt ventilation with four breaths by mouth-to-mouth or mouth-to-mouth and nose technique.

6. Repeat steps 1 to 5 while seeking aid from emergency medical services.

Teaching Your Child Safety and Simple Emergency Procedures

Many of us, as we raise our children, find ourselves repeating many of the old adages that our parents said to us as we were growing up. Lines like *look both ways before you cross the street* seem to be stock phrases in every parent's vocabulary. Other well-worn pieces of advice are conveyed in different ways but contain the same message no matter where you live.

In this section we'd like to review some of these, as well as adding a few that are appropriate for children of the '80s and '90s. As you probably know, these messages are best taken to heart if they are reinforced by repetition, as well as accompanied by an explanation your child can understand. When the consequences are discussed, children are better able to appreciate why these are rules to live by.

☐ If you burn yourself, *immediately* put the burn under cool water. Keep it there as long as it feels comfortable.

☐ If you or your clothing catch fire, *stop* where you are, immediately *drop* to the ground and *roll* over and over until the fire is out. [Parents: Practice this stop, drop, and roll technique with your child so that it becomes an automatic reaction.]

☐ If you start to bleed or are stung by a bee or other insect, stop playing and get first aid from Mom, Dad or another adult you trust.

☐ Never drink anything or take any kind of medicine without your parents' permission. Teach your child what "Mr. Yuk," (see diagram below), Mr. Ugg, the skull and cross bones, or other poison symbols mean. Your local poison center may be able to supply you with stickers that show the poison symbol used in your area.

Mr. Yuk!

Mr. Yuk, the most frequently used poison symbol, was developed at the Children's Hospital of Pittsburgh. Other poison centers have developed their own symbols. What ever symbol you use, poison warning symbols play a very important part in preventing child poisonings. (Permission to reprint Mr. Yuk has been granted by Children's Hospital of Pittsburgh. For more information about Mr. Yuk, write to the Poison Center, Children's Hospital, 125 DeSoto St. Pittsburgh, PA 15213.)

☐ If you ever drink anything that burns your mouth or that you know you should not have swallowed, immediately tell your mom, dad or another adult.

☐ Do not play with electrical outlets, microwave ovens, power tools or other machinery and equipment around the house your mom or dad have deemed "off limits."

☐ Always tell your mom or dad where you'll be playing, and never play in parking lots, empty buildings, or alleys.

☐ Look left, right, and then left again, before crossing the street.

☐ Never tell anyone over the phone that you are home alone, and never open the door to strangers when you are home alone.

☐ Never talk to strangers, and beware of anyone trying to give you candy, gifts, or money, or asking you to help them find a lost dog or cat.

☐ If someone touches you and you don't feel comfortable about it, tell your mom, dad or an adult friend; keep telling people until you are sure someone believes you.

☐ Always buckle your seat belt and lock your car door.

In addition to the above rules, teach your child the following basic skills:

☐ His or her name, address (including city and state), and phone number, as well as your work phone numbers.

☐ How to use both a push button and rotary-dial telephone.

☐ Emergency telephone number 911 (if you are in a 911 service area) or dialing "0" to reach the operator; and when to use these numbers.

☐ How to lock and unlock all your doors and windows.

☐ What the smoke detector buzzer means and what to do when it goes off. Plan an escape route and practice a family fire drill with preschoolers.

Books, magazines and videotapes are additional means to teach your child safe behavior, foster additional discussion, and reinforce the messages you try to convey over and over again. For example, "Play Safe," a Golden Learn About Living Activity Book, contains puzzles, stickers, pictures to color, and a poster all geared to teaching children about common dangers indoors and out, at home and away. Although intended for children ages five to seven, some of the activities are easier than others, and it can be read and discussed with three- and four-year-old children.

Courses that teach children safety measures may also be available in your area. For example, the Kid Safe program, aimed at children ages four to 14, is sponsored by over 100 organizations in 30 states and Canada. Depending upon the sponsor, program topics might include: Water, Traffic, Gun, Electrical, Fire and Personal Safety; Responsible Baby sitting; Emergency Telephone Training; CPR; First Aid; Alcohol and Drug Abuse; and This is Me (photo ID and fingerprinting). To find out if there is a Kid Safe program in your area, call: 1-800-KID-SAFE. Your local YMCA, Red Cross, or community group may offer similar instruction for children.

We do not intend this section to be a substitute for medical advice. Regular communication with a trusted pediatrician is one of the most important ways to safeguard your children's health.

However, as more and more Americans become concerned about personal health and helping their children avoid many of their bad habits, we have tried to touch on those areas that you might want to explore further with your doctor or medical provider. As with anything else that is important for your child, ask questions, and don't be afraid to shop around.

In this chapter we discuss a different kind of safety: protecting your child from being abducted or abused. This is probably the chapter you will be least inclined to read and for us, it was our least favorite to prepare. Abduction, parental snatching, physical, sexual, and emotional abuse, are practices that *all* parents, sadly, need to understand and prevent. While we may want to believe that "it could never happen to us," it is important to know the facts and take precautions to ensure that it will not. This section will help you educate your children about these problems in the same way you teach them to buckle their seat belts or to use playground equipment safely. We have included information aimed at preventing these events as well as steps to take if, unfortunately, they occur.

Protecting
Your
Child

Missing Children

Each year in the United States, between 1.3 and 1.8 million children are reported missing. These children may be kidnapped, lost, runaways; some are taken by a noncustodial parent. Still others disappear with few clues as to the reason.

The National Center for Missing & Exploited Children (NCMEC) points out that, in many cases, an abductor is not a stranger to the child. So, while the warning to "stay away from strangers" is good advice, it provides very limited protection. Children are more often abducted or exploited by people who have some type of familiarity with them, but who may not be known to the parents. NCMEC explains that the term "stranger" misleads children into believing that they should only be aware of individuals who have an unusual or slovenly appearance. Instead, it is more appropriate to teach children to watch out for certain situations or actions, rather than certain kinds of individuals.

There are steps you can take to minimize the chances of your child being abducted. Experts recommend that you teach your child the following:

☐ Her full name, address, and phone number, and parents' names, work addresses, and phone numbers.

☐ How to make a long distance call (both directly to you using the area code, and by dialing "0" for the operator).

☐ Never to go into anyone's home without your permission. Children should learn whose homes they are allowed to enter.

☐ Never to look for you if he becomes separated from you while shopping or in a public place. Instead, to go to the nearest checkout counter, security office, or lost and found, and tell the person in charge that he has lost his mom or dad and needs help in finding them. And he should never go to a parking lot without you.

☐ To walk and play with others and to use the buddy system. If your child walks to school, have her walk with other children. A child is most vulnerable when alone.

☐ That adults do not usually ask children for directions or help, but should be asking other adults. If someone in a car should stop to ask for directions, they should not go near the car.

☐ That if someone is following him on foot or in a car, to go to a place where there are other people—to a neighbor's home or into a store, for instance—and ask for help. He should not go near the car to talk to anyone inside and should not try to hide behind bushes.

☐ That no one should ask her to look for a "lost puppy" or tell her that either of her parents is in trouble and that he will take her to mom or dad.

☐ To never go near a car with someone in it or to get into a car without your permission. Your child should learn in whose car he is allowed to ride. Warn your child that someone might try to lure him into a car by claiming you said to pick him up; tell him to never obey such instructions. Instead, he should go back to the school for help.

☐ Never to tell anyone over the phone that she is home alone.

☐ Never to answer the door when home alone. Remind your child to talk through a door or window to anyone delivering a package, and to tell the person to leave the package at the door. Teach your child how to call your community's emergency assistance number (often 911). Make sure he knows a neighbor to call if someone tries to get into the house or if there is any kind of emergency.

☐ To tell you if any adult asks her to keep a "secret."

☐ To tell you if someone offers him gifts or money or wants to take his picture.

☐ That no one should touch her in any part of her body covered by a bathing suit. She should not touch anyone in those areas either. Explain to her that the body is special and private.

☐ To yell "HELP" if someone tries to take her away.

☐ To ask your permission to leave the yard or to go to a neighbor's house. Older children should phone home to tell you where they are, especially if they change locations.

☐ To never hitch hike or get a ride with anyone, unless you have told him it is okay to accept the ride.

☐ To come home before dark.

- ☐ To avoid dark or abandoned places.
- ☐ To avoid adults who are waiting around a playground—particularly an adult who wants to play with them and their friends.
- ☐ To ask anyone who drives him anywhere, not to leave him alone in the car—but if he *is* alone in a car, to put up the windows, leaving a "finger" space between the window glass and the rim, and to lock the doors and stay near the car horn. If a stranger approaches the car, he should blow the horn until help arrives.
- ☐ That she has the right to say NO to anyone who tries to take her somewhere, touches her, or makes her feel uncomfortable in any way.

What You Should Know As a Parent

Parents can also take other steps to prevent abductions and to assist the police and others in locating a missing child:

- ☐ Never leave a child unattended; never leave a child alone in a car.
- ☐ Know your child's friends. Be involved in your child's activities.
- ☐ Listen when your child tells you he or she does not want to be with someone; there may be a reason you should know about.
- ☐ Notice when someone shows your child a great deal of attention and find out why.
- ☐ Be sensitive to changes in your child's behavior or attitudes. Encourage open communication. Never belittle any fear or concern your child may express to you.
- ☐ Keep a complete description of your child, including hair and eye color, height, weight, date of birth, and other identifying characteristics (such as glasses, braces, pierced ears, birth marks).
- ☐ Take a photograph of your child every six months (four times a year for children under age two). Head-and-shoulder portraits taken from different angles (like school pictures) are preferable.

☐ Know where your child's medical records are located (and learn how to access them should the need arise). These records could contain valuable information to help identify your child.

☐ Make sure your dentist keeps up-to-date dental records of your child. (If you move, get a copy of your child's dental records.)

☐ Have your child's fingerprints taken by your local police department. Do not attempt to make these prints yourself; police are *trained* to do this. They will give you the fingerprint card but will not keep a record of it. Keep in mind that fingerprinting is *not* a primary tool when searching for and identifying missing children. However, if the child is too young or can't identify him or herself, prints can confirm identity.

☐ Have a set plan outlining what your child should do if you become separated while away from home.

☐ Do not buy items that have your child's name on them such as a hat, jackets, and T-shirts. It is an easy way for an abductor to learn your child's name and start up a friendly conversation.

☐ Make a game of reading license plate numbers. By learning the various numbers and state colors your children will be able to recognize any license plate.

☐ Be sure their day care center or school will not release children to anyone but their parents or someone designated by their parents. Instruct the school to call you if your child is absent.

☐ NCMEC recommends that children should not take self-defense training (such as the martial arts) for the sole purpose of thwarting an abduction. (Young children, in particular, should not attempt to defend themselves in this manner.) However, the martial arts, or other methods of self-defense, can help a child develop self-confidence and athletic ability.

☐ Be leery of gadgets and gimmicks that purport to protect your child. (See Chapter Three for a discussion of the pros and cons of such products.)

What to Do If Your Child is Missing

Below are recommendations from The National Center for Missing & Exploited Children and the National Crime Prevention Council on steps to take in the event a child is missing.

☐ Act *immediately*. Search your house thoroughly, including closets, piles of laundry, in and under beds, old, stored, refrigerators, or wherever a child might hide, fall asleep, or get trapped.

☐ If you still haven't found your child, think where he or she could have gone. Check with your neighbors, your child's friends and school; if you are divorced, call your ex-spouse.

☐ If you still haven't found your child, call the police and start procedures *immediately*. Provide as much precise information as possible, including the clothing your child was wearing when he or she disappeared. If your child is under 13 years of age, or is mentally incapacitated, or drug dependent, police response may be expedited.

☐ Make sure the police put information about your child into the National Crime Information Center (NCIC) Missing Persons File to ensure that any law enforcement agency in the country will be able to identify your child. If your local police refuse to do this, the FBI will enter your child's name into the NCIC computer. There is no waiting period for entering a child's information and this entry will not give your child a police record.

☐ After you have notified your local police, also call The National Center for Missing & Exploited Children's toll-free hotline to report your child missing. One of their technical advisors may be able to follow up with you and the police department during the investigation. Call 800-843-5678; in Washington, D.C., call 235-3900; TDD Hotline (for the hearing impaired), 800-826-7653. These numbers are also for use by any person who has information on a missing child.

☐ Now look for clues at home that may help you to find your child. Check your child's room for notes, letters, missing clothing. Check your telephone bill: Are there any unfamiliar long-distance calls that may indicate where your child might have gone? Request duplicate bills if necessary.

☐ Look for clues in your neighborhood. Ask the postal carrier, local storekeepers, building employees, and anyone who might have been on the street and seen your child; check arcades and "hangouts;" inform area hospitals, drug-treatment centers and children's shelters that you are looking for a missing child.

☐ Look for clues at your child's school. Speak to teachers, the principal, the guidance counselor; talk to your child's friends and enlist their help.

☐ Check out all areas of your child's life: adults, peers, clubs, your church or synagogue. Talk to any adult your child might have looked up to. Explore any interests or activities that your child pursued that would introduce him or her to new people. Tell everyone and anyone that your child is missing, and ask for their help.

☐ Canvass distant friends and relatives to whom your child might have gone.

☐ In urban areas, have searches made of locked or generally inaccessible areas, such as roofs, basements, and garages.

☐ Alert the police of any bus and train terminals, airports, any parkways, and national parks near your home, particularly if your child might try to reach a divorced parent, camp friend, or favorite vacation area.

☐ If there had been tension between you and your child, tell friends, neighbors, relatives, and authorities who may speak to him, to convey a message of love, and that you only want him to return home safely.

☐ If your child calls, communicate love and concern for her safety—not fear, and not anger about the past.

☐ Publicize your child's disappearance: make flyers with the child's recent, clear photograph attached, along with a description that includes sex, age, height, weight, eye and hair color, any identifying marks or scars, and details of clothing and jewelry when last seen. At the top of the flyers should be the heading "Missing" or "Have You Seen This Child?" in bold letters. Give the name and phone number of a law enforcement office that can receive calls around the clock. Post these flyers in store windows, at shopping malls—anywhere you can. Enlist the support of local newspapers and television stations, and drop off or mail flyers to all area hospitals and other treatment centers.

☐ If you employ a private investigator, get references and check them carefully. Call your state's licensing bureau, the Better Business Bureau, and your Consumer Protection Office regarding the investigator's standing.

☐ One video tape on preventing child abuse which you may want to rent or buy is "Strong Kids, Safe Kids." The tape retails for $29.95, but some stores are selling or renting it at a discount, and some even let people borrow it for free. For those who buy the tape, there are 15 blank minutes at the end of it for parents to make a video reproduction of their children in case of abduction.

Many businesses and organizations print pictures of missing children along with pertinent descriptive information on product packages and public signs. Milk cartons, shopping bags, billboards, subway and truck posters, and newsletters are all used to alert the public to missing children. The National Center for Missing and Exploited Children coordinates these efforts and supplies the pictures and information to interested companies and organizations.

Preventing Parental Child Snatching

Each year, hundreds of thousands of children are abducted by noncustodial parents, many of whom are motivated by revenge. If you suspect that a former spouse would consider abducting your child, there are steps you can take. The National Crime Prevention Council and The National Center for Missing & Exploited Children recommends the following:

☐ Maintain a friendly—or at least civil—relationship with your former spouse. In this way, you can help reduce the anger and frustration that often lead to a child's abduction. Don't withhold or unfairly manipulate legally determined visitation times.

☐ Talk openly and often with your child. Keep reinforcing the fact that you love and always want her, no matter what anyone else might tell her. Make sure your child knows that she *always* has the right to try to reach you. Again, be sure your child knows her home phone number and area code, and how to place a long-distance call.

☐ Have certified copies of your legal custody order readily available, and make sure it gives explicit authority to the police to recover your child.

☐ If you are concerned that your child may be abducted by the noncustodial parent, speak to your attorney immediately. There are legal steps that can be taken to minimize the risk of abduction.

☐ Keep a list of information about your former spouse: his or her social security number, driver's license number, car registration number, and checking and savings account numbers. Be discreet in collecting this information so as to not set off an abduction.

☐ Keep information about your child and semi-annual photographs.

☐ Do not ignore abduction threats. Obtain professional advice from the police, a family counselor, and your attorney.

☐ Notify authorities at school or day care facilities that the child is not to be released to anyone (including the noncustodial parent) without your permission.

☐ If you are not married, get a custody order anyway. State laws vary and unmarried mothers are not always automatically given custody.

☐ In the event of an abduction, call the police immediately. Tell them your former spouse's possible whereabouts and the names of his or her friends and relatives. Tell the police you want this to be handled immediately, as a kidnapping.

☐ For information on what protection you can achieve through your custody decree, and other valuable information, request a copy of "Parental Kidnapping—How to Prevent an Abduction and What to Do If Your Child Is Abucted" from the National Center for Missing & Exploited Children, 2101 Wilson Blvd., Suite 550, Arlington, VA 22201; (703) 235-3900. Single copies are free.

Abuse

All parents worry that their child may be subjected to physical, sexual, or emotional abuse. While in some cases parents themselves are responsible for abuse, investigations in recent years have uncovered many examples of nonparental abuse. Physical, sexual, and emotional abuse transcend all economic, ethnic, religious and racial boundaries. Many abusers lack emotional support from family and friends or are isolated from those who once gave them support. Sadly, studies show that abused children very often grow up to be abusive adults.

Physical Abuse

Physical abuse—any intentional act leading to possible injury—is the most prevalent type of child abuse. Like other types of abuse, physical abuse is defined as a recurrent problem and is usually committed by relatives, neighbors, and other close acquaintances. A common opinion is that abusers are "sick," but statistics show that *chronic* mental illness is rarely the cause for child maltreatment.

The many forms of physical abuse include violent assault with an implement, such as a strap or knife, human bites, immersion in scalding water, and strangulation. While spanking generally is not considered child abuse, it can be associated with other acts that are abusive or it can deteriorate into an abusive situation.

Prevention

If you have physically abused your child or feel you may physically hurt them or are frightened of what you might do to them, *seek immediate help.* A variety of programs are available, including child abuse hotlines and crisis nurseries, where you can drop off your child for a short period until a crisis passes. For advice on where to get help contact a local health clinic or mental health center, family service's agency or your family doctor. Parents Anonymous can also provide assistance. For a group close to you, call: (800) 421-0353. In California call (800) 352-0386.

If you want to help others in preventing child abuse, there are many avenues to take. A simple but very helpful service is to offer to care for a friend or relative's children for a while to help alleviate that parent's stress. Also, community organizations and support groups often need help with hotlines, foster-grandparent programs, and community parent-education courses.

Detection

If you are concerned that your child or another child has been physically abused, look for the following signs: unusual bruises; welts; burns; fractures; bite marks. These signs, in themselves, may not necessarily indicate abuse, but if injuries appear repeatedly and are consistently explained as being accidental, if possible, look for the additional signs, below.

A child may have been abused if he or she:

☐ reports injury by parents or others.

☐ gives an explanation of how an injury occurred that is not believable, given the type or seriousness of the injury.

☐ is afraid of one or both parents and is not reluctant to be separated from them.

☐ avoids physical contact with others.

☐ wears concealing clothes (long sleeves, high collars) to hide injuries.

☐ is hard to get along with, is demanding and disobedient, frequently damages things and causes trouble or interferes with others; *or* is unusually shy, avoids other people, including children, is overly anxious to please, and seems ready to let others say or do things without protest.

Taking Action

If you suspect that a child has been abused, report this suspicion to your local child protection services (you can do so anonymously). While the child abuse laws vary in different states, at least one state agency in every state is required to receive and investigate reports of child abuse, whether physical, sexual, or emotional abuse. (See Chapter Nine for where to report physical abuse in your state.) Remember, it is not necessary to wait until you can *prove* abuse. Early reporting may save a life or prevent much pain and suffering. In most states, persons who report in good faith are granted immunity from civil and criminal action even if the report proves to be wrong.

Sexual Abuse

Sexual abuse of children takes many forms, including fondling, rape, incest, exhibitionism, and prostitution, and pornography. Each year an estimated 100,000 children suffer from some type of sexual abuse. In the majority of cases the sexual molester is a person known and trusted by the child and family. Because of this close association, the child may feel pressured to give in to an adult or older adolescent's sexual advances out of fear of losing their love or friendship or of being punished.

Prevention
Children often instinctively know what distance should be kept between themselves and other people, but they may not recognize sexual abuse when it happens or they may not know it is wrong. Teach children to say NO if someone wants to touch them in a way that makes them uncomfortable, especially in their genital areas. Explain to them what is inappropriate touching and the proper names of sexual organs.

While talking about sexual abuse is never easy, communication is a key tool in prevention. Make time to talk to your child every day about his or her activities and feelings. Encourage your child to share problems and concerns with you.

Discuss with your child the possibility of an adult trying to entice him into doing things that may hurt him or make him uneasy. Mention that these adults often persuade children of the necessity to keep a secret, sometimes by threatening to harm them or their parents. Emphasize that the adult's behavior is wrong and that it is important that the child tell you about it.

Let your child know that, although many adults are good people and would never do anything to harm her, there is the possibility that someone trustworthy and loving, or in a position of authority, might try. This discussion is not meant to scare your child, but it is important to set the scene for effective communication on such a sensitive subject.

Detection
Signs that your child has been sexually abused may be physical or behavioral. Physical signs include: irritation; pain or injury of the genital or rectal areas; vaginal or rectal bleeding; swollen genitals; vaginal discharge; vaginal infections or venereal disease; and torn or stained underclothing.

A child who has been sexually abused may exhibit a wide range of changes in behavior, such as:

☐ difficulty sleeping.

☐ bed-wetting.

☐ fear of the dark.

☐ nightmares.

☐ loss of appetite.

☐ regression to infantile behavior (for example, thumb sucking, excessive crying, withdrawal into a self-induced fantasy world).

☐ refusal to go to school or fear of a particular place, person, or activities.

☐ fear of being alone or being left alone with certain people.

☐ uncharacteristically aggressive or disruptive behavior or other behavior changes, such as extreme mood swings, withdrawal, fearfulness, and excessive crying.

☐ unusual interest in, or knowledge of, sexual matters.

☐ expressing affection in inappropriate ways to other children.

If your child tells you of an abusive experience, express your support, commend him for telling you about it, and let him know that you will protect him from future harm. Remember that although children often tell stories, they rarely lie about sexual abuse. No matter how vivid a young child's imagination may be, they usually do not have the facility to imagine the sexual events they are able to recount.

It is important to believe your child. Your response as a parent is crucial, as it will greatly influence the child's reaction to— and recovery from—the assault. Take care not to convey your own horror or fears about the abuse to your child. Explain to your child that he or she has done no wrong. Remember that sexually abused children often fear that they are to blame, and alleviating this self-blame is extremely important.

Taking Action

Sexual abuse of children is a community concern and taking action is critical to protecting your child and others from future occurrences. Report a suspected molestation to the police and to the child protection service agency in your state. (See Chapter 9 for a complete listing.)

The child may need a medical examination: A child who has been sexually exploited may also be physically injured. Your family pediatrician may want your child to see a doctor with expertise and training in detecting and recognizing sexual abuse.

Consider the need for counseling. Look for an agency or professional that specializes in evaluating sexual abuse victims; again, your pediatrician may be able to make such a recommendation.

You might also want to contact other parents of children who may have been abused by or had contact with the same person to see if their children have exhibited any unusual behavior or physical symptoms.

The social service agency in your area can give you information on the laws in your state regarding sexual crimes and additional advice.

Emotional Abuse

Although our society has made advances in recognizing and treating children and families who suffer from physical and sexual abuse, it is only fairly recent that the potential effects of emotional or psychological abuse of children have been recognized. Emotional abuse is difficult to define but may include: verbal or emotional assault; constant teasing or belittling; threatening, excessive, aggressive or unreasonable demands that place expectations on a child beyond his capabilities; lack of care, affection, support or guidance; close confinement, such as tying up or locking in a closet; inadequate nurturing such as infant neglect; knowingly allowing antisocial behavior, such as delinquency or serious alcohol or drug abuse; refusal to allow medical care for a diagnosed emotional problem.

The emotional abuser is generally someone with whom the child has frequent contact: a teacher, sibling, babysitter, friend of the family, parent, or grandparent. Often this type of abuse occurs in conjunction with physical or sexual abuse. While there may be no physical marks on a child who has been emotionally abused, the psychological wounds left by this kind of abuse can scar a child for life.

Emotional abuse is often verbal. Many times adults say things to children, sometimes out of a lack of patience, which they would not say to other adults. And often adults tease children in such a way that the child feels ridiculed. Repetition of these kinds of assaults is frequently a factor in emotional abuse. Unfortunately, some adults forget that they hold the key to helping a child develop self-esteem and healthy social attitudes and that they can easily undermine the child's emotional development.

Prevention

Be aware of the psychological effects adult attitudes and actions can have on young children. If you feel comfortable doing so, discuss this issue, in a calm and nonthreatening manner, with those you feel may be abusive. They may not realize the impact their actions have on the child. Often such abusers were abused themselves as children and do not recognize the destructiveness of their own behavior. Lastly, be kind to children and encourage other adults to do the same. Every child needs to feel valuable, and even limited contact can have a profound effect on a child's self-esteem.

Detection

To detect this type of abuse, observe the child's behavior for any of the following signals. While most normal children exhibit some of these symptoms at some time, a pattern or combination may suggest further investigation.

- [ ] self-destructiveness, apathy, depression, withdrawal, passive behavior.

- [ ] lacks a positive self-image.

- [ ] experiences problems in school (for example: academic failure, developmental delays, hyperactivity).

- [ ] seems overly anxious when faced with new people or situations or displays a pseudo-maturity inconsistent with age.

- [ ] takes on adult or parental role and responsibilities.

- [ ] becomes either disorganized or rigidly compulsive.

- [ ] throws tantrums, seems impulsive, defiant, antisocial, aggressive; constantly tests limits.

- [ ] creativity and exploration decrease; child becomes anxious, fearful, or hyperalert.

- [ ] has difficulty making friends and dealing with others; shows a lack of familial attachment.

- [ ] is prone to nightmares; is oblivious to hazards and risks.

- [ ] exhibits indiscriminate friendliness; seeks affection and gratification from any adult, even strangers, but in a superficial manner.

☐ engages in excessive fantasizing, appears autistic, delusional or paranoid.

Taking Action
Many of the suggestions given for physical abuse apply for emotional abuse. Again, you can report the abuse to the social service agency in your state listed in Chapter Nine.

Preventing Day Care Abuse

You've probably read or heard stories about child abuse in day care settings. For parents, particularly those anxious about placing their child in day care, these stories bring to mind the worst possible scenarios. However, The National Center for Missing & Exploited Children (NCMEC) reports that a 1988 nationwide study on sexual abuse in day care confirms that children are generally safe; more abuse occurs in the home than in day care facilities.

But because day care abuse can happen, you'll want to take some precautions when selecting a program and teach your child about unsafe situations. NCMEC recommends:

☐ Look for day care centers with mature, responsible staff members. Observe their interaction with children.

☐ Arrange to meet other individuals who may have contact with your child, such as bus drivers, janitors, and relatives of day care personnel. In 36% of the cases examined in a national study on day care abuse, the children were molested by family members related to the day care provider—mainly husbands and sons.

☐ Check the day care center's references carefully. Contact the police and social service agencies to find out if any reports have been made on the center.

☐ Make certain parents of enrolled children are allowed to visit the center without having to make an appointment first and that there are no areas that are off limits to parents. Day care abuse and exploitation are far more likely to occur in centers that have limited parental access.

☐ Determine if the center is licensed and whether they make a criminal history background check on employees, including a history of sexual or physical assault against children.

☐ Make sure the bathrooms do not contain areas where a child can be isolated. Ask about the bathroom schedule and who handles it. Two-thirds of all day care sexual abuse and exploitation occurs during toileting.

☐ Stay involved in your child's day care center. If you can, volunteer a few hours or chaperone field trips. This will give you a chance to observe day care center personnel in action.

☐ Teach your child the protections discussed above under missing children and sexually exploited children, such as not keeping a secret, telling you if anyone takes their picture, or not letting anyone touch their private parts. Caution your child against remaining alone with an adult in an isolated place—such as the office, bathroom, bedroom, or closet. Advise your child that nap time is for sleeping and resting and should not be spent interacting with an adult.

☐ If your child is abused, or you suspect abuse, do not return the child to the day care center until you are convinced that it is safe. Immediately report abuse to the police and child protective services agency. See recommendations for spotting signs of abuse under sexual, physical, and emotional abuse above.

We have included an extensive list of *Corporations Producing Children's Products* because we often hear parents complain about a product or service but fail to take action because they don't know the address of the problem company. As consumer activists we believe strongly that you should make your concerns known to the companies who profit from your purchases. We also think that it pays to compliment a company for providing a particularly good or safe product.

If you're a busy parent, check out the catalog section. We included companies that we believe provide good values. You also find *Health Organizations,* a list of special interest groups that deal with children's health. Most of these groups offer free or low cost information about their issues and we have found them to be valuable resources.

Everything Else You Wanted to Know: Resources for Parents

Abuse

National Organizations

National Center on Child Abuse and Neglect
Children's Bureau/Administration for Children, Youth, and Families
U.S. Dept. of Health and Human Services
P.O. Box 1182
Washington, DC 20013
(703) 821-2086

National Committee for the Prevention of Child Abuse
332 S. Michigan Ave., Suite 1250
Chicago, IL 60604
(312) 663-3520

National Organization for Victim Assistance
National Headquarters
717 D Street, N.W.
Washington, DC 20004
(202) 393-6682

National Center for Missing and Exploited Children
1835 K St., N.W., Suite 700
Washington, DC 20006
(202) 634-9821

National Crime Prevention Council
The Woodward Building
733 15th St., N.W.
Washington, DC 20005
(202) 393-7141

Where to Report Abuse: State Agencies

The responsibility for investigating child maltreatment lies at the state level. Below are the names and addresses of the child protective services agency in each state, followed by the procedures for reporting suspected child maltreatment.

Alabama:
Alabama Department of Pensions and Security
64 North Union St.
Montgomery, AL 36130
Reports made to county 24-hour emergency telephone service

Alaska:
Department of Health and Social Services
Division of Family and Youth Services
Pouch H-05
Juneau, AL 99811
Reports made to Division of Social Services field offices.

American Samoa:
Government of American Samoa
Office of the Attorney General
Pago Pago, American Samoa 96799
Reports made to the Department of Medical Services

Arizona:
Department of Economic Security
P.O. Box 6123
Phoenix, AZ 85005
Reports made to Department of Economic Security local offices.

Arkansas:
Arkansas Department of Human Services
Social Services Division
P.O. Box 1437
Little Rock, AR 72203
Reports made to the statewide toll-free hotline 800-482-5964

California:
Department of Social Services
714-744 P St.
Sacramento, CA 95814
Reports made to County
Departments of Welfare and the
Central Registry of Child Abuse
(916)445-7546 maintained by the
Department of Justice

Colorado:
Department of Social Services
1575 Sherman St.
Denver, CO 80203
Reports made to County
Departments of Social Services

Connecticut:
Connecticut Department of
Children and Youth Services
Division of Children and
Youth Services
170 Sigourney St.
Hartford, CT 06105
Reports made to 800-842-2288

Delaware:
Delaware Department of Health
and Social Services
Division of Social Services
P.O. Box 309
Wilmington, DE 19899
Reports made to statewide toll-free
reporting hotline 800-292-9582

District of Columbia:
District of Columbia Department of

Human Services
Commission on Social Services
Family Services Administration
Child Protective Services Division
First and I Sts., S.W.
Washington, DC 20024
Reports made to (202)727-0995

Florida:
Florida Department of Health and
Rehabilitative Services
1317 Winewood Blvd.
Tallahassee, FL 32301
Reports made to 800-342-9152

Georgia:
Georgia Department of Human
Resources
47 Trinity Ave., S.W.
Atlanta, GA 30334
Reports made to County
Departments of Family and
Children Services.

Guam:
Child Welfare Services
Child Protective Services
P.O.Box 2816
Agana, Guam 96910
Reports made to the State Child
Protective Services Agency at 646-
8417

Hawaii:
Department of Social Services
Public Welfare Division
Family and Children's Services
P.O. Box 339
Honolulu, HI 96809
Reports made to the hotline
operated by KapiolaniChildren's
Medical Center on Oahu, and to
branch offices of the Division of
Hawaii, Jaui, Kauai, Mokalai.

Idaho:
Department of Health and Welfare
Child Protection Division of
Welfare
Statehouse
Boise, ID 83702
Reports made to Department of
Health and Welfare Regional
Offices

Illinois:
Illinois Department of Children and
Family Services
State Administrative Offices
One North Old State Capital Plaza
Springfield, IL 62706
Reports made to 800-25-ABUSE

Indiana:
Indiana Department of Public
Welfare
Division of Child Welfare -
Social Services
141 S. Meridian St., 6th Floor
Indianapolis, IN 46225
Reports made to County
Departments of Public Welfare.

Iowa:
Iowa Department of Social Services
Division of Community Programs
Hoover State Office Bldg.
5th Floor
Des Moines, IA 50319
Reports made to the legally
mandate toll-free reporting hotline
800-362-2178

Kansas:
Kansas Department of Social and
Rehabilitation Services
Division of Social Services
Child Protection and Family
Services Section
Smith-Wilson Bldg.
2700 W. 6th St.
Topeka, KS 66606
Reports made to Department of
Social and Rehabilitation Services
Area Offices

Kentucky:
Kentucky Department for Human
Resources
275 E. Main St.
Frankfort, KY 40621
Reports made to County Offices
within 4 regions of the state.

Louisiana:
Louisiana Department of Health
and Human Resources
Office of Human Development
Baton Rouge, LA 70804
Reports made to the parish
protective service units.

Maine:
Maine Department of Human
Services
Human Services Bldg.
Augusta, ME 04333
Reports made to Regional Office or
to State Agency at 800-452-1999.

Maryland:
Maryland Department of Human
Resources
Social Services Administration
300 W. Preston St.
Baltimore, MD 21201
Reports made to County
Departments of Social Services or
to local law enforcement agencies

Massachusetts:
Department of Social Services
Protective Services
150 Causeway St.
Boston, MA 02114
Reports made to Regional Offices.

Michigan:
Department of Social Services
300 S. Capitol Ave.
Lansing, MI 48926
Reports made to County
Departments of Social Welfare.

Minnesota:
Department of Public Welfare
Centennial Office Bldg.
St. Paul, MN 55155
Reports made to the County
Departments of Public Welfare.

Mississippi:
Department of Public Welfare
Division of Social Services
P.O. Box 352
Jackson, MS 39216
Reports made to (800) 222-8000.

Missouri:
Department of Social Services
Division of Family Services
Broadway Bldg.
Jefferson City, MO 65101
Reports made to (800) 392-3738.

Montana:
Department of Social and
Rehabilitative Services
Social Services Bureau
P.O. Box 4210
Helena, MT 59601
Reports made to County
Departments of Social and
Rehabilitation Services.

Nebraska:
Department of Public Welfare
301 Centennial Mall South
5th Floor
Lincoln, NE 68509
Reports made to local law
enforcement agencies or to County
Divisions of Public Welfare.

Nevada:
Dept. of Human Resources
Division of Welfare
251 Jeanell Dr.
Carson City, NV 89710
Reports made to Division of
Welfare local offices

New Hampshire:
New Hampshire Dept. of Health
& Welfare
Division of Welfare
Bureau of Child and Family
Services
Hazen Dr.
Concord, NH 03301
Reports made to Division of
Welfare District Offices

New Jersey:
New Jersey Division of Youth and
Family Services
P.O. Box 510
One South Montgomery St.
Trenton, NJ 08625
Reports made to 800-792-8610.
District Offices also provide 24-
hour telephone service.

New Mexico:
New Mexico Department of
Human Services
P.O. Box 2348
Santa Fe, NM 87503
Reports made to County Social
Services Offices or to 800-432-6217

New York:
New York Department of Social
Services
Child Protetive Services
40 North Pearl St.
Albany, NY 12207
Reports made to 800-342-3720 or to
District Offices

North Carolina:
North Carolina Department of
Human Resources
Division of Social Services
325 North Salisbury St.
Raleigh, NC 27611
Reports made to County
Departments of Social services

North Dakota:
North Dakota Department of
Human Services
Social Services Division
Children and Family Services Unit
Russel Bldg., Hwy. 83 North
Bismarck, ND 58505
Reports made to Board of Social
Services Area Offices and to 24-
hour reporting services provided
by Human Serivce Centers

Ohio:
Ohio Department of Public Welfare
Bureau of Children Services
30 E. Broad St.
Columbus, OH 43215
Reports made to County
Departments of Public Welfare

Oklahoma:
Oklahoma Dept. of Institutions,
Social and Rehabilitative Services
Division of Social Services
P.O. Box 25352
Oklahoma City, OK 73125
Reports made to 800-522-3511

Oregon:
Dept. of Human Resources
Children's Services Division
Protective Services
509 Public Services Bldg.
Salem, OR 97310
Reports made to local Children's
Services Division Offices and to
(503)378-3016

Pennsylvania:
Pennsylvania Dept. of Public
Welfare
Office of Children, Youth and
Families
Bureau of Family and Community
Programs
1514 N. 2nd St.
Harrisburg, PA 17102
Reports made to the toll-free
CHILDLINE 800-932-0313

Puerto Rico:
Puerto Rice Dept. of Social Services
Services to Families with Children
P.O. Box 11398
Fernandez Juncos Station
Santurce, Puerto Rico 00910
Reports made to local offices or to
the Dept.

Rhode Island:
Rhode Island Dept. for Children
and their Families
610 Mt. Pleasant Ave.
Providence, RI 02908
Reports made to State agency child
protective services unit at 800-662-
5100 or to District Offices

South Carolina:
S. Carolina Dept. of Social Services
P.O. Box 1520
Columbia, SC 29202
Reports made to county Depts. of
Social Services

South Dakota:
Dept. of Social Services
Office of Children, Youth and
Family Services
Richard F. Kneip Bldg.
Pierre, SD 57501
Reports made to local offices

Tennessee:
Tennessee Dept. of Human Services
State Office Bldg.
Room 410
Nashville, TN 37219
Reports made to county Depts. of
Human Services

Texas:
Texas Dept. of Human Resources
Protective Services for Children
P.O. Box 2960
Austin, TX 78701
Reports made to 800-252-5400

Utah:
Department of Social Services
Division of Family Services
150 W. North Temple, Rm. 370
P.O. Box 2500
Salt Lake City, UT 84103
Reports made to Divison of Family
Services District Offices

Vermont:
Vermont Dept. of Social and
Rehabilitative Services
Social Services Division
103 S. Main St.
Waterbury, VT 05676
Reports made to State agency at
(802)828-3422 or to District Offices
(24-hour services)

Virgin Island:
Virgin Islands Department of Social
Welfare
Division of Social Services
P.O. Box 500
Charlotte Amalie
St. Thomas, Virgin Island 00801
Reports made to the Division of
Social Services

Virginia:
Virginia Dept. of Welfare
Bureau of Family and Community
Programs
Blair Bldg.
8007 Discovery Dr.
Richmond, VA 23288
Reports made to 800-552-7096 in
Virginia, and (804)281-9081 outside
the States.

Washington:
Dept. of Social and Health Services
Community Services Division
Child Protection Services
Mail Stop OB 41-D
Olympia, WA 98504
Reports made to local Social and
Health Services Offices

West Virginia:
Dept. of Welfare
Division of Social Services
Child Protective Services
State Office Bldg.
1900 Wshington St., E.
Charleston, WV 25305
Reports made to 800-352-6513

Wisconsin:
Wisconsin Dept. of Health and
Social Services
Division of Community Services
1 W. Wilson St.
Madison, WI 53702
Reports made to County Social
Services Offices

Wyoming:
Dept. of Health and Social Services
Division of Public Assistance
and Social Svcs.
Hathaway Bldg.
Cheyenne, WY 82002
Reports made to County Depts. of
Public Assistance and Social
Services

Adoption

Adoptive Parents' Education Program
P.O. Box 32114
Phoenix, AZ 85064
(602) 957-2896

This organization provides pre-adoption classes as well as a brochure and a bimonthly newsletter which contains adoption information and referrals.

Auto Safety

Auto Safety Hotline
(202) 426-0123 (DC)
800-424-9393 (toll free elsewhere)

National Highway Traffic Safety Administration
Washington, DC 20590
(202) 426-0670

Center for Auto Safety
2001 S Street, NW, #410
Washington, DC 20009

Non-profit consumer group which offers a child safety seat product guide. Send a stamped, self-addressed business size envelope to "Childwise" in care of the Center.

Breast-Feeding

LaLeche League
9616 Minneapolis Avenue
P.O. Box 1209
Franklin Park, IL 60131
(312) 455-7730

LeLeche offers encouragement and information for breastfeeding mothers or those considering this option. They also do referrals to their local groups that are located in all 50 states and 44 countries. LaLeche has produced many books and reprints and offers a monthly newsletter for $20/year. Also available is a free catalog dealing with breastfeeding, nutrition, childbirth and parenting products.

Catalogs

Books

A Child's Collection
611 Broadway
Suite 708
New York, NY 10012
(215) 492-9628

Books for babies and children of all ages in hardback and softcover. Also sell some tapes, records and videos. Their offerings include many classics, such as Goodnight Moon and Curious George, Children's Book, Newberry and Caldecott award winners, and boxed sets, such as The Chronicles of Narnia.

Chinaberry Book Service
2830 Via Orange Way
Suite B
Spring Valley, CA 92078
800-776-2242

Books for kids of all ages and their parents. Wide selection of books in soft and hardcover, video and audio cassettes, story tapes, sticker books, rubber stamps and crafts. This catalog offers extensive descriptions of books and provides useful reading tips for parents. Collection includes classics, award winners and even a collection of Soviet books for children.

Children's Products & Equipment (includes Childproofing products)

Heir Affair
625 Russell Drive
Meridian, MS 39301
800-332-4347

This catalogue contains a wonderful collection of clothes, toys, gifts, and equipment for children. While some of the items that first catch your eye are on the expensive side (like the $279 Gloucester Rocker boat), many others are competitively priced. Products include: christening gown, silverplated baby gifts, kites, all kinds of toys, holiday decorations, puppets, clothes, nursery monitor, and baby bathtub.

Perfectly Safe Catalog
7245 Whipple Ave., N.W.
N. Canton, OH 44720
(216) 494-4366

This is a great catalog of safety-related products at very reasonable prices! All the hard-to-find childproofing products are included, as well as bicycle helmets, elbow and knee pads for skaters, and a safety tricycle. There are a few products (like the pool alarm) which we do not recommend, but all in all this catalog serves a terrific market and we suggest you check it out.

Right Start Catalog, The
Right Start Plaza
5334 Sterling Center Drive
Westlake Village, CA 91361
800-LITTLE-1 or 800-707-7132

This comprehensive catalogue contains all kinds of products for children—from back packs, swings, highchairs and bedding to toys, child proofing products and nursing products. Some of their products are very good and quite innovative; others we dislike— such as the stroller packs which can cause a stroller to tip backwards. This catalogue is worth reviewing for hard-to-find kids products such as their juice box covers and stair rail nets, but keep safety in mind as you shop.

Safe-Strap
180 Old Tappan Road
Suite 4A1
Old Tappan, NJ 07675
800-356-7796

This company sells an adjustable restraining strap with an easy to use plastic buckle that can be affixed to high chairs, strollers, chairs, and shopping carts. Parents can purchase these colorfast belts directly from the company. To order send a check or money order for $2.98 (includes postage & handling) with your name and address and specify red or blue.

Clothes

Biobottoms
P.O. Box 1060
Petaluma, CA 94953
(707) 778-7945

Features biobottoms diaper covers (used instead of rubber pants) and biobottoms terry diapers. Also includes: coveralls, buntings, long johns, jogging suits, blankets, diaper bags, hats, slippers, cardigans, no-skid socks, bibs, diaper shirts, and layette combination packages. Sizes: infant through 4T. Free catalog.

Garnet Hill
262 Main Street
Franconia, NH 03580
800-622-6216

This natural fibers catalog includes a small section of children's clothes. Playclothes, rubber boots and crib sheets and quilts are featured.

Kids Catalog, The
4020 Nine-McFarland Dr.
Alpharetta, GA 30201
(404) 475-8851

Offering clothing for girls and boys sized 3 months to size 14, The Kids Catalog carries both playwear and clothes for party occasions. Their collection includes: Jack Tar, Cole for Kids, Jockey, Her Majesty, O'Neal, Simi, Camp Beverly Hills, and Joggles.

Brights Creek
Bay Point Place
Hampton, VA 23653-3116
800-622-9202; (804) 827-1850

A collection of children's clothes and shoes for newborns through size 14 for girls and size 16 for boys. They also carry baby bottles, diaper bags, receiving blankets, crib sheets, boots, rain coats, and jewelry. If you're looking for character or superhero costume flame-resistant pajamas, Brights Creek has a great selection. Infant stretchies and coveralls are discounted 20% if you buy three or more.

Company Store, The
500 Company Store Road
La Crosse, WI 54601
800-356-9367

This catalog features a limited assortment of children's clothes and linens. Included are down snowsuits, mittens, booties and bonnets for infants, jackets, trenchcoats, snowsuits, and bib pants for children, and crib sheets, shams, playpens and stroller throws.

Children's Wear Digest
2515 E. 43rd St.
P.O. Box 22728
Chattanooga, TN 337422
800-433-1895

Attractive clothing for children size 6 months through girls size 14 and boys size 16. Brands include Oshkosh, Imp, Hartstrings, Weather Tamer, Head tennis wear, Eagles Eye, Guess, and Izod shirts.

Lands' End
1 Lands' End Lane
Dodgeville, WI 53595
800-356-4444

This popular catalogue now includes children clothing in all sizes. Their new line of infant clothes (sizes 12, 18, and 24 months) joins their growing collection of children's clothes, sized: toddlers 2T-4T, little girls 4-6X, girls 7-14, little boys 4-7, and boys 8-16, as well as their line of children's bedding products. Parents we spoke with like Lands' End children's wear because it is attractive, easy to care for and extremely durable!

Les Petits
6510 Eastwick Ave.
Box 33901
Philadelphia, PA 19142-0961
800-33333-2002

All clothes in this catalog are made in France; sizes will fit newborns through age 16. In addition to clothes the catalog includes shoes, hats, belts and other accessories. These clothes are attractive and original and most are reasonably priced.

Maggie Moore
P.O. Box 1564
New York, NY 10023
(212) 543-33964

A large portion of this catalog's collection is 100% cotton playwear for children size 6 month to 14. On the expensive side, this cute collection also includes party dresses, hats, shoes, socks, hair bows, jewelry, toys, dolls and costumes.

Seventh Generation
Products for a Healthy Planet
10 Farrell St.
South Burlington, VT 05403
800-456-1177

As its name implied, this catalog features household items that are less damaging to our environment. In addition to selling cloth diapers and diaper pants, this catalog markets biodegradable diapers— for sale by the package or case or through their home delivery service. Organic baby food, baby shampoo, talc and wipes, and science kits with an environmental angle are also included.

Special Clothes
P.O. Box 4220
Alexandria, VA 22303
(703) 683-7343

Special Clothes is a unique collection of adaptive clothing for children with disabilities. The catalog includes pants, shirts, underwear, shoes, hats, coats, gloves, swimwear, and bibs in sizes XXS (3-4) through XL (16-18). These garments meet a variety of special needs; adaptations, such as velcro closures, full snap crotches, and gastrostomy-tube access, are designed to be inconspicuous. Special Clothes will work with parents to adapt clothing to solve a special problem.

Starr Enterprises
Children's Outdoor Specialty Catalog
P.O. Box 82
Long Creek, SC 29658
800-67-STARR; (803) 638-3180

This catalog specializes in hard-to-find children's outdoor specialty items, including: rain gear, children's outdoor sleeping bags, hats, mittens, bootliners, back child carrier, frame packs sized for children, children's lifejackets, and child size skis.

Talbots Kids
175 Neal Street
Hingham, MA 02043-1586
800-KIDS-123 or 800-543-7123

Top quality clothes for kids: girls sizes 4-14 and boys sizes 4-12. In addition to selling their own house brand, they also carry brands such as Eagle's Eye, Izod, Sahara Club, J.G. Hook, Gant, Levis, and E-I-E-I-O. Although on the expensive side, this catalog has great clothes for school and best dress occasions, and also includes belts, ties, bow

ties, socks, barrettes and head-
bands, purses and backpacks.

The Wooden Soldier
North Hampshire Common
N. Conway, NH 03860-0800
(603) 356-7041

This catalog contains a wide selection of dress clothing for children,
infants through size 14. It also
includes playwear, sleepwear,
matching outfits for parents, costumes, gifts and decorations. This
catalogue is expensivebut it may
be the place to look if you need a
beautiful outfit for a special
occasion.

Special Needs

Communication Aids for Children
and Adults
Crestwood Company
6625 N. Sidney Place
Milwaukee, WI 53209
(414) 352-5678

This is a catalog for adults and children with special needs. Adapted
toys for children with special needs
as are educational toys and language development sets. This catalogue also carries an extensive line
of Uniset Moveable Sticker scenes
that all children play with and
enjoy.

Toys

Childcraft
20 Kilmer Rd.
P.O. Box 3143
Edison, NJ 08818-3143
800-631-5657

Toys for kids of all ages: art supplies, building toys, dolls, musical
instruments, magnetic toys, electronic toys, sports games, costumes, children-size furniture and
room organizers, dress-up clothes,
and some children's clothing. Par-

ents we know recommend their
wood unit building blocks set and
their vinyl-coated animal bath
stickers!

Constructive Playthings
1277 East 119th Street
Grandview, MO 64030
800-255-6124

All kinds of toys for newborns to
teens, including: first playthings,
blocks and building sets, toy for
pretend play, books, musical
insturments and records, arts and
crafts materials and kits, learning
games, active play equipment, and
family games. They say that their
prices are the lowest and will
refund the difference if given proof
that the identical item is advertised
for less. Constructive Playthings
has supplied schools and day care
center for the past 30 years; you
can get a copy of their school edition catalog too.

Hearth Song
P.O. Box B
Sebastopol, CA 95473-0601
800-325-2502

This is a very different kind of
children's toy catalog—featuring
hard-to-find playthings and books.
The majority of their items are for
children 3 and up. Toys include
pick-up sticks, chinese checkers,
Ravensburger games, blocks, and
Matreshkas. This catalog also features an extensive collection of
crafts kits and art supplies.

Just for Kids!
75 Paterson St.
P.O. Box 15006
New Brunswick, NJ 08906-5006
800-654-6963

This catalog features toys for children of all ages; including: games,

dools, building toys, baby toys, pretend materials, bath toys, sports equipment,art, science, room decorations and party supplies, and a small collection of books and videos.

Lego Shop At Home Service
P.O. Box 640
Enfield, CT 06082-0640
(203) 749-2291

If you have a LEGO-aholic in your family, this is the catalog for you. A complete line of LEGO toys and systems are offered, including: Duplo toys and building sets, Fabuland playsets, Legoland Town, Castles and Space sets, and LEGO Technic sets. The catalog contains many hard-to-find accessories, baseplates (an essential for DUPLO builders), extra bricks, storage cabinets and cases, and motors.

My Child's Destiny
Post Office Box 7349
San Francisco, CA 94120

Toys; art supplies, dolls; furniture; books; clothes; safety equipment; educational software; quilts. Newborn-Preteen. Free catalog.

Pleasant Company
P.O. Box 190
Middleton, WI 53562-0190
800-845-0005

The American Girls Collection of dolls by Pleasant Company is in a class by itself! The dolls (Kirsten, Samantha, and Molly) each have their own clothes, books, and accessories that relate to the era in American history that the doll represents. Matching clothes and shoes for the little girl owner can also be purchased. One doll (with complete outfit) and accompanying book costs $74.

Sesame Street Catalog
2515 East 433rd Street
P.O. Box 182228
Chattanooga, TN 337422-7228
800-446-9415

This catalog contains virtually every type of Sesame Street product available—clothes, toys, puzzles, books, stuffed animals and figures, bedroom and bath products, tableware, computer software, playpens and strollers—-all featuring Big Bird, Bert, Ernie, or one of the Sesame Street gang.

Toys To Grow On
P.O. Box 17
Long Beach, CA 90801
(213) 537-8600

All kinds of toys, including: toys for travel; books; records; tapes; first playthings, musical instruments; dolls; playground equipment; blocks; sports equipment; sand and water play toys; art supplies; crafts materials; puzzles; games; safety products; and more. Newborns to Teens.

Learn & Play for Kids
Troll Associates
100 Corporate Drive
Mahwah, NJ 07498-1053
800-247-6106

This catalog is jammed full of toys and books for newborns on up. Collection includes: super blocks, American history library, the Super Safety Tricycle, arts and crafts materials, Playmobile sets, finger puppets, dinosaurs and much more.

Video and Audio

Blackhawk Catalog, The
800-826-2295

Specializes in older theatrical films.

Children's Radio Theatre
P.O. Box 53057
Washington, DC 20009
   To obtain information about the
   organization and a list of tapes,
   write for the Complete Cassette
   Catalog.

Listening Library
800-243-4504
   Specializes in videos based on
   books.

Music for Little People
800-346-4445
   Specializes in music videos from
   around the world.

Parent Care
800-334-3889
   Stocks 1,200 videos for children
   and teenagers.

Special-Interest Video
800-522-0502
   Sells nonfiction titles exclusively.

Child Identification

Kid's IDs
P.O. Box 2241
Coeur D'Alene, ID 83814
   Kid's IDs manufacturers lightweight aluminum tage embossed
   with the child's name, address, and
   two phone numbers. The tags sell
   for $4 each, with an optional $1
   neck chain.

Lifesaver™ Charities
6950 Aragon Circle #4
Buena Park, CA 90620
   This organization provides tear-
   proof, waterproof ID tags upon
   which parents write pertinent
   information with indelible ink. The
   tags are worn on shoelaces and are
   free if you send a self-addressed,
   stamped envelope with your
   request. Iron-on shoulder patch
   IDs are available for $1.

Medic Alert Foundation International
P.O. Box 1009
Turlock, CA 95381
   These metal tags immediately alert
   rescue workers to a hidden chronic
   medical problem. The non-profit
   organization includes a wallet-
   sized card and instant access to
   computer records in its one time
   fee of $20.00.

Wee Kare ID
2739 Sugarmaple Drive
Cedar, MI 49621
   These IDs are made of light-weight
   reflective plastic and attach to the
   child's shoelace. Parents decide
   what information should be
   embossed on the tag. ID comes
   with a booklet on safety for kids,
   written by a child therapist. The
   price is $4.99 or $9 for two.

Children's Issues

Association for Childhood Education
International
3615 Wisconsin Avenue, N.W.
Washington, DC 20016
ACEI focuses on children and their
needs as it helps members grow in
their roles as teachers, teacher edu-
cators, teachers-in-training, super-
visors, administrators, librarians,
parents and other care-givers. The
organization publishes an educational journal on childhood education as well as numerous materials
for parents and teachers.

Public Information/Education Office
Administration for Children, Youth
and Families
P.O. Box 1182
Washington, DC 20013

Child Trends, Inc.
1990 M St., N.W.
Washington, DC 20036
(202) 223-6288
Child Trends is a research organization that has looked at issues
such as: the needs in maternal and
child health; national surveys and
observations of child development;
television viewing and children's
development; trends in the behavior and emotional well-being of
U.S. children; the condition of
American children; and children's
mental health.

Children's Defense Fund
122 C Street, N.W.
Washington, DC 20001
(202) 628-8787
The Children's Defense Fund is a
national children's advocacy organization that examines issues such
as adult jobs and children's care,
children and the president's bud-

get, children without homes, children in adult jails, children out of
school, health care for poor children, handicapped children and
education, paying children's health
bills, and a parent's guide to child
advocacy.

Children's Legal Rights Journal
Publisher: William S. Hein & Co., Inc.
1285 Main Street
Buffalo, NY 14209
800-828-7571
This periodical examines legal
issues in the field of children's
rights, including: child abuse and
neglect, foster care, child custody
and adoption, juvenile delinquency
and status offenses, medical care,
mental health and mental retarda-
tion, education for the handicapped and student's rights. Subscription price: $27.00

The National Center for Clinical
Infant Programs
733 15th Street, N.W.
Suite 912
Washington, DC 20005
A non-profit organization established to improve and support professional initiatives in infant mental
health and development. Publications include: "Infancy in the
Eighties: Social Policy in the Earli-
est Years of Life" and "Who Will
Mind the Babies?"

Public Affairs Pamphlets
381 Park Avenue South
New York, NY 10016
(212) 683-4331
Publishers of pamphlets on parenting, marriage, and family problems.
The pamphlets answer questions
about child development, family

crisis, marriage, alcohol and drug abuse, child and adult health, sex education, the teenage years, growing older and more.

Corporate Publications on Children's Issues

Aetna Life & Casualty
Film Librarian, Public Relations and Advertising Dept.
151 Farmington Avenue
Hartford, CT 06115
Free publications: *Keeping Danger Out of Reach*

Gerber Products Company
445 State Street
Fremont, MI 49412
Attn: Medical Marketing Service
Free Publications: *A Handbook of Child Safety, So You've Decided to Breast Feed Your Baby, Baby's Book, Feeding Baby, Questions and Answers About Feeding Your Baby Meat Base Formula, Ingredients-Gerber Baby Foods, Nutrient Values-Gerber Baby Foods, Guidelines-Child Safety*

Johnson & Johnson
Baby Products Company
Consumer & Professional Services
Grandview Road
Skillman, NJ 08558
Free Publications: *Guide for the First Time Baby Sitter, Parenting Insights, Baby Care Basics, Getting To Know Your Newborn, Common Sense Care for Baby's Tender Skin, How Your Baby Grows*

Metropolitan Life Insurance Co.
One Madison Avenue
New York, NY 10010
Free Publications—But must include first-class stamped, self-addressed envelope: *Personal Health Record, Your Child's Health Care, Immunization: When & Why, Fire Safety, First Aid for the Family, Planning for Safety, Emergency Medical Card, Dental Care: Questions and Answers, Child Safety, Health & Safety Educational Materials Catalog, You can See Tomorrow (film brochure).*

Ross Laboratories
625 Cleveland Avenue
Columbus, OH 43216
Publications: Some are free; others for a fee: *Nutrition, Growth & Development During Your Baby's First Year, Breast Feeding Your Baby, Your Child's Appetite, Feeding Your Baby a Soy Protein Formula, Your Child and Discipline, Ross Educational Services Department-Publications Booklet*

Twins

National Organization of Mothers of Twins Club
5402 Amaberwood Lane
Rockville, Maryland 20853
(301) 460-8180

Corportations Producing Children's Products

A-Plus Products, Inc.
P.O. Box 2975
Beverly Hills, CA 90213
(213) 475-6914

A. Lock & Co. Div. of Brodart Co.
1609 Memorial Avenue
Williamsport, PA 17705
800-233-8467

A.D.I. Lamps
Div. Phoenix Art Corporation
P.O. Box 6357
Phoenix, AZ 85005
(602) 253-4548

A-Plus Products, Inc.
2601 Ocean Park Blvd., #304
Santa Monica, CA 90405
213-399-1177

ABC Television Network
1330 Avenue of the Americas
New York, NY 10019
212-456-7777

Accessory Sales, Inc./Royal Haeger
   Lamp Co.
3878 Sheridan Street
Hollywood, FL 33021
305-966-7330

Ace Novelty Company
1855 Industrial Street
Los Angeles, CA 90021
213-626-0500

Adorable Baby Company
5036 W. 63rd Street
Chicago, IL 60638
319-581-5956

Aetna
330 5th Avenue
New York, NY 10001
212-736-5657

Ainsley Lamps - Gear Kids
1099 Flushing Avenue
Brooklyn, NY 11237
718-366-5400

Alison's Design, Inc.
117 35th Street
Manhattan Beach, CA 90266
213-546-4227

Alnor Trading International Ltd.
811 Sinclair Avenue
State Island, NY 10309
(718) 317-6587

Ambassador Corporation
500 Library Street
San Fernando, CA 91340
800-824-8147

American Baby Imports, Ltd. Inc.
8815 Shirley Avenue
Northridge, CA 91324
(213) 349-6050

American Baby Books
P.O. Box 26189
Wauwatosa, WI 53226
(414) 771-0226

American Baby Concepts
108 E. Jefferson Street
Wheatland, IA 52777
319-374-1231

American Business Center, Inc.
2507 Creek Meadow
Houston, TX 77084
(713) 578-8710

American Family Scale Company,
   Inc.
3718 S. Ashland Avenue
Chiacgo, IL 60609
(312) 376-6811

American Toy & Furniture Co., Inc.
5933 N. Lincoln Avenue
Chicago, IL 60659
(312) 271-2600

AMF/Head
P.O. Box CN 5227
Princeton, NJ 08540
(609) 797-9000

Amisco Industries, Ltd.
35 5th Street
L'islet, Quebec, Canada G0R 2C0
(418) 247-5025

Animal Fair, Inc.
7780 Bush Lake Road
Edina, MN 55435
(612) 831-7200

Ansa Bottle Company, Inc.
425 W. Broadway
Muskogee, OK 74401
918-687-1664

Antics
Div. Bellstone Trading & Co. Ltd.
49 W. 23 Street
NY, NY 10010
(212) 989-9285

Applause Inc.
6101 Variel Avenue
Woodland Hills, CA 91365-4183
818-992-6000

Apple Computer Inc.
20525 Mariani Avenue
Cupertino, CA 95014
408-974-2244

Aprica Kassai, U.S.A., Inc.
Div. Merchants Corp. of America
1200 Howell Avenue
Anaheim, CA 92805
(714) 634-0402

Aqua Learn
932 Parker Street
Berkley, CA 94710
(415) 841-9188

Armstrong World Industries
Liberty Street
Lancaster, PA 17604
717-397-0611

Artistic Reed & Willow Mfg. Co.
4401 W. Ogden Avenue
Chicago, IL 60623
(312) 277-7636

Artsana of America, Inc.
200 Fifth Avenue, #910
New York, NY 10010
212-255-6977

Atari
1312 Crossman Road
Sunnyvale, CA 94086
800-678-1404 (inside CA)
800-538-8543 (outside CA)

B J Toy Company, Inc.
04 Applegate Avenue
P.O. Box 58
Pen Argyl, PA 18072
(215) 863-9191
(215) 863-9084

Babi Bags by Romar International
  Corp.
112 W. 34th Street
New York, NY 10001
212-736-9555

Babies By Storm
101 Aniston
White Sands Msl. Range, NM 88002
(505) 678-4121

Babies' Alley - Div. of La Rue
Distributors, Inc.
339 Fifth Avenue
New York, NY 10016
212-679-4700

Baby & Child
7 Shadow Court
Owings Mills, MD 21117
(301) 252-1611

Baby Bag Company
P.O. Box 566
Cumberland Center, ME 04021

Baby Bjorn of North America Inc.
P.O. Box 1322
Shaker Heights, OH 44120
(216) 662-2922

Baby Care, Inc.
5427 S. 99th E. Avenue
Tulsa, OK 74146
800-346-2680

Baby Chair Corp.
2515 Cumming
Superior, WI 54880
(715) 392-5800

Baby Connections, Ltd.
3743 Mermaid Ave.
Brooklyn, NY 11224
(718) 372-3604

Baby Doll Infants Wear
300 Monroe Street
Passaic, NJ 07055

Baby Dreams by Bibb
P.O. Box 4207
Macon, GA 31208
912-752-6700

Baby Furniture Outlet
P.O. Box 1400
Marathon, FL 33050
(305) 743-7177

Baby Lamb Products Inc.
31 Drakewood La.
P.O. Box 1424, Dept. SW
Novato, CA 94948
(415) 897-2578

Baby League
1 Argonaut
Laguna Hills, CA 92656
714-588-8595

Baby Seat-er Corp.
P.O. Box 19535
Seattle, WA 98109
(206) 364-0707

Baby Tenda Corp.
123 S. Belmont Blvd.
Kansas City, MO 64123

Baby Things by Dakin
7000 Marina Boulevard
Brisbane, CA 94005
800-227-6598
(415) 952-1777

Baby Trend, Inc.
17970 E. Ajax Circle
City of Industry, CA 91748
800-328-7363

Baby World Co. Inc.
Pike Street
Grafton, WV 26354
(304) 265-2123

Badger Basket Company
Div. Standard Container of
Edgar, Inc.
616 N. Court
Palatine, IL
(312) 991-3800

Bantam Collections, Inc.
131 W. 33rd Street, #1703
New York, NY 10001
212-564-6750

Bantam Doubleday Dell
666 Fifth Avenue, 21st Floor
New York, NY 10103
212-492-9640

BAP Distributing Co. Inc.
200 Fifth Ave.
NY, NY 10010
(212) 691-6242

Barclay Co.
P.O. Box 37
Teaneck, NJ 07666
(201) 836-9686

Baron Manufacturing Corporation
7250-A Fulton Avenue
North Hollywood, CA 91605
818-764-8024

Bassett Furniture Industries, Inc.
P.O. Box 262
Main Street
Bassett, VA 24055

Battat Incorporated
2 Industrial Blvd. W Circle,
   P.O. Box 1264
Plattsburgh, NY 12091
518-562-2200

BBI Corp.
508 S. Airport Blvd.
South San Francisco, CA 94080
(415) 583-1023

Beatrice Companies Inc.
2 North LaSalle Street
Chicago, IL 60602
312-558-3755

Bedtime Originals
5978 Bowcroft Street
Los Angeles, CA 90016
213-839-5155 or 800-345-2627

Benbio Group America, Inc.
9211 Alberene
Houston, TX 77074
713-981-5656

Berg Furniture
90 Dayton Street
Passaic, NJ 07055
201-471-2099

Bilt Rite Juvenile Products
Div. Gerber Products
71 Blaisdell Rd.
Orangebury, NY 10962
(914) 359-4500

Binky Griptight, Inc.
519-523 Paterson Avenue
Wallington, NJ 07057
800-526-6320

Blazon-Flexible Flyer, Inc.
100 Tubb Ave.
West Point, MS 39773
(601) 494-4732

Bonny Bunting Co.
2869 Towerview Rd.
Herndon, VA 22070
Mailing Address:
P.O. Box 17345
Washington, DC 20041
(703) 435-3915

Boobear Products, Inc.
21 Auerbach Lane
Lawrence, NY 11559
516-569-0742

Borden Inc.
180 East Broad Street
Columbus, OH 43215
614-225-4411

Bowland-Jacobs International, Inc.
Fox Industrial Pk.
Yorkville, IL 60560
(312) 553-9559

Boynton for Babies Division of
  Perfect Fit
303 Fifth Avenue
New York, NY 10016
212-679-6656

Brandee Danielle, Inc.
3042 South Orange Avenue
Santa Ana, CA 92707
714-540-2331

Bright Ideas
12442 SW 117th Court
Miami, FL 33186
305-252-0777 or 800-842-7555

Brights Creek
5000 City Lane Road
Hampton, VA 23661
804-827-1850

Brio Scanditoy Corp.
6555 West Mill Road
Milwaukee, WI 53218
800-558-6863
(414) 352-5760

Brown Group, Inc.
P.O. Box 354
St. Louis, MO 63166
314-854-2797

Bundles of Joy
117 E. Main Street, #307
Milford, MA 01757
508-478-5554

C'est Jolie
420 Austin Place
Bronx, NY 10455
212-292-8533

C.R. Gibson Company
32 Knight Street
Norwalk, CT 06856
203-847-4543

C&T International, Inc.
12 Caesar Pl.
Moonachie, NJ 07074
(201) 896-2555

Cabbage Patch Mfg.
125 Newton
Westminster, CO 80030
(303) 428-5565

Cabbage Patch, Inc., The
5653 Chenango Ave.
Aurora, CO 80015
(303) 693-8566

Calco-Hawaiian Mfg. Inc.
2002 W. 139th Street
Gardena, CA 90240
800-858-6534
(213) 538-5782

Calico Cottage, Inc.
12974 SW 132nd Avenue
Miami, FL 33186
305-233-1404

California Concepts
2206 Gladwick
Compton, CA 90220
(213) 537-0161

California Kids
621 Old Country Road
San Carlos, CA 94070
(415) 637-9054

Calstate International
539 E. Carlin St.
Compton, CA 90220
(213) 268-2061

Cambium Design Co.
P.O. Box 2304
Leucadia, CA 92024
(619) 753-7310

Campbell Soup Company
Campbell Place
Camden, NJ 08101
609-342-3714

Canvas Uncommon, Ltd.
1219 Greenwood Road
Baltimore, MD 21208
(301) 653-9787

Carnation Company
5045 Wilshire Boulevard
Los Angeles, CA 90036
(213) 932-6000

Carriage Craft, Inc.
1133 Broadway, Rm. 1226
NY, NY 10010
(212) 807-6007

Carry Covers, Inc.
Div. Wee Concepts
6520 S. 300 West
Murray, UT 84107
(801) 262-0989

Carry Me, Inc.
737 South Vinewood Street
Escondido, CA 92025
619-739-8911

Carvel Coroporation
201 Saw Mill River Road
Yonkers, NY 10701

Casser Infant Products
P.O. Box 414
Manhasset, NY 11030
(516) 759-2020

CBS Broadcast Group
524 West 57th Street
New York, NY 10019
212-975-3166

Century Mattress and Padded
  Goods Div.
Div. Gerber Products
5170 B Naiman Parkway
Solon, OH 44139
(216) 349-2640

Century Products, Inc.
Div. Gerber Products
9600 Valley View Road
Macedonia, OH 44056
(216) 468-2000

Certified Home Products
420 Chestnut, Box 4187
Wallejo, CA 94590
(707) 557-5515

Chang Hsing Hanidcraft Co. Ltd.
1-1 Nan Wan Tsuen
Yung Kang, Tainan Hsien, Taiwan
R.O.C.
(062) 352-2069

Charles D. Owen Manufacturing Co.
875 Warren Wilson Road
Swannanoa, NC 28778
704-298-6802

Chatham Mfg. Co.
P.O. Box 620
Elkin, NC 28621
(919) 835-2211

Cherry Kay Products Inc.
32 Highland Ave.
Barrington, RI 02806
(401) 247-0864

Cherubs Collection
700 Fairfield Avenue, P.O. Box 11064
Stamford, CT 06904
203-356-8000

Chesebrough-Pond's, Inc.
33 Benedict Place
Greenwich, CT 06830
(203) 661-2000

Child Craft/Child Line
East Market St.
P.O. Box 444
Salem, IN 47167
(812) 883-3111

Child Guidance
Div. CBS Toys
500 Harmon Meadow Blvd.
Seacaucus, NJ 07094
(201) 330-3000

Children on the Go
1670 S. Wolf Road
Wheeling, IL 60090
800-537-2684

Christopher Winkle Products
22503 Meyler Street, #27
Torrance, CA 90502
213-320-0569 or 213-326-5281

Chuck E. Cheese/Show Biz Pizza
4441 West Airport Freeway
Irving, TX 75062
214-258-8500

Clothworks Inc.
1750 N. Wolcott
Chicago, IL 60622
312-276-2283

Coca-Cola Company
Drawer 1734
Atlanta, GA 30301
1-800-438-2653 (toll free)

Coleco Industries Inc.
80 Darling Drive
Avon, CT 06001
203-676-7000

Coleco Industries, Inc.
999 Quaker Lane S.
West Hartford, CT 06110
(203) 725-6000

Colgate Mattress Co. Inc./Colgate
International
1339 Garrison Avenue
Bronx, NY 10474
(212) 991-0750

Collier-Keyworth Co.
P.O. Drawer 528, 1 Tuttle Pl.
Gardner, MA 01440
(617) 632-0120

Combi Industries Inc.
1698 Post Road East
Westport, CT 06880
203-255-1166

Comfortcare Company, Inc.
740 N. Plankinton Avenue #336
Milwaukee, WI 53203
414-276-6580

Comfort Lines, Inc.
4500 Kolin Ave.
Chicago, IL 60632
(312) 254-0700

Comfort Products
1421 Champion Drive, #311
Carrollton, TX 75006
214-241-4340

Connor Forest Ind., Inc.
330 Fourth St., P.O. Box 847
Wausau, WI 55401
(715) 842-0511

Continental Banking Company
Checkerboard Square
St. Louis, MO 63164
314-982-4953

Continental Quilting Co., Inc.
6201-15th Ave.
Brooklyn, NY 11219
(718) 259-3131

Corrado Nursery Furniture Mfg. Co., Inc.
140 West 22 St.
NY, NY 10011
(212) 929-8575

Cosco Juvenile Furniture
(formerly Nockonwood)
2525 State St.
Columbus, IN 47201
(812) 372-0141

Cosco Juvenile Products
2525 State St.
Columbus, IN 47201
(812) 372-0141

Cosmos Trading, Inc.
12 Edgeboro Rd.
East Brunswick, NJ 08816
(201) 238-3377

Cothran & Co., Inc.
P.O. Box 912
Selma, AL 36701
800-253-1785

Cougar Books
6448 Oakridge Way
Sacramento, CA 95822
303-778-8383

Country Bumpkin
3354 Hillside Ln.
Fallbrook, CA 92028
(619) 723-8101

Country Pleasure Mfg. Inc.
825-D Kenneth
Nixa, MO 65714
417-725-2894

Cozy Baby Products Inc.
360 Hayward Avenue
Mt. Vernon, NY 10552
914-668-1686

Cozy by J.E. Morgan Knitting Mills
5010 Empire State Building
New York, NY 10118
212-947-2710

Cozy Carrier Co., Inc.
1709 Western Ave.
Eau Claire, WI 54703
(715) 835-4777

Crawl Space Inc.
1900 Section Rd.
Cincinnati, OH 45237
(513) 531-3300
(800) 543-8616

Creative Learning Products, Inc.
3567 Kennedy Road
South Plainfield, NJ 07080
201-755-3666

Creative Lifestyle Inc.
100 Wayland Ave.
Providence, RI 02906
(401) 272-5136

Crib Mates (Gudi Enterprises)
650 Fountain Avenue
Brooklyn, NY 11208
718-257-7800

Cudlie Diaper Bags
1 E. 33rd Street
New York, NY 10016
212-686-7550

Dan Dee Belt and Bag Co. Inc.
115-131 Grand St., P.O. Box M-461
Hoboken, NJ 07030
(201) 659-5951

Danara International, Ltd.
14 Central Boulevard
So. Hackensack, NJ 07606
201-641-4350

Dannon Company, Inc.
1111 Westchester Avenue
White Plains, NY 10604
914-697-9700

Danskin
P.O. Box M 16
York, PA 17405
717-846-4874 or 800-87-DANSKIN

Daust Juvenile Products, Inc.
401 Marcy Avenue
Brooklyn, NY 11206
718-384-3200

Decorate It!, Inc.
6320 Canoga Avenue, #1600
Woodland Hills, CA 91367
818-595-1013

Degree Baby Products
23457 Haynes Street
West Hills, CA 91307-3319
818-713-0485 or 800-234-9777

Del Monte Corporation
P.O. Box 3575
San Francisco, CA 94119
415-942-4803

Delby System
119 W. 57 St.
NY, NY 10019
(212) 586-4921

Delta Enterprise Corp.
175 Liberty Avenue
Brooklyn, NY 11212
(718) 385-1000

Denbi Products
192 10 St.
Oakland, CA 94607
(415) 839-8711

Dimensions West
1928 W. 135th Street
Gardena, CA 90249
213-538-9614

Diplomat Juvenile Corp.
118 Railroad Avenue
W. Haverstraw, NY 10993
(914) 786-5552

Discovery Music
4130 Greenbush Avenue
Sherman Oaks, CA 91423
818-905-9794

Doll Watcher Inc., The
275 Shady Gr. Rd.
Hot Springs, AK 71901
(501) 623-9995

Dolly, Inc.
320 N., 4 St.
Tipp City, OH 45371
(513) 667-5711

Domodidovo Ltd.
365 West End Ave.
NY, NY 10024
(212) 362-0648

Douglas Co., Inc.
Krif Rd., Drawer D
Keene, NH 03431
(603) 352-3414

Dragons Are Too Seldom, Inc.
604 Mt. Rushmore Road
Rapid City, SD 57701
(605) 343-8200

Dream Machine
7192 Patterson
Garden Grove, CA 92641
714-895-4943

Dundee Mills Inc.
111 W. 40 St.
NY, NY 10018
(212) 840-7200

Dutailier, Inc.
298 Chaput
St-Pie, Quebec, Canada J0H 1W0
514-772-2403

E-Z Enterprises, Inc.
901 N. Broadway
Wichita, KS 67214
(316) 262-7305

Eden Toys, Inc.
112 West 34 St.
Suite 2208
NY, NY 10120
(212) 947-4400

Encyclopedia Brittannica, Inc.
310 South Michigan Avenue
Chicago, IL 60604
(312) 347-7232

Encylcopedia Britannica
310 South Michigan Avenue
Chicago, IL 60604
312-347-7230

ETC (Environmental Teen Concepts)
P.O. Box 444, East Market Street
Salem, IN 47167
812-883-3111

Evenflo Juvenile Furniture
   Company
1801 Commerce Dr.
Piqua, OH 45356
(513) 773-3971

Evenflo Products Company
771 N. Freedom Street
Ravenna, OH 44266
216-296-3465

Evergreen Equipage Co.
dba Turtle Corp.
7421 S. Brook Forest Dr.
Evergreen, CO 80439
(303) 674-9618

Everything Personalized, Inc.
P.O. Box 650610
Vero Beach, FL 32965
407-778-8045

Expo Industrial Co., Ltd.
P.O. Box 13-334
Taipei, Taiwan

Fairland Products Inc. (USA)
16737 S. Parkside Avenue
Cerritos, CA 90701
(213) 926-3837

Fairyland Collection
1908 Cowart Street
Chattanooga, TN 37408
615-821-3804

Family Home Products
P.O. Box 243
Blythebourne Station
Brooklyn, NY 11219
(718) 851-2700

Family Life Products
Box 541 - 12 Lunette Ln.
Dennis, MA 02638

Family Tree, Inc.
P.O. Box 1467
Jasper, AL 35501
(205) 387-0548

Fashioncraft-Excello, Inc.
100 Rose Ave.
Hempstead, NY 11550
(516) 489-4000
800-645-4040

Federated Department Stores, Inc.
Seven West Seventh Street
Cincinnati, OH 45202
(513) 579-7000

Fine Art Pillow & Specialties Corp.
601 W. 26 St.
New York, NY 10001
(212) 929-0229

First Years/Kiddie Products, Inc.
1 Kiddie Drive
Avon, MA 02322
508-588-1220

Fischer America, Inc.
175 Rt. 46 W.
Fairfield, NJ 07006
(201) 227-9283

Fisher Price
636 Girard Avenue
East Aurora, NY 14052
716-652-8402

Fisher-Price Infant Bedding and
  Accessories
295 Fifth Avenue, #612
New York, NY 10016
212-545-4033

Floppie Originals, Inc.
Rt. 2, Box 161G
Indian Head, MD 20640
301-283-CUTE

Food Products, Inc.
P.O. Box 1667
Richmond, CA 94802
(415) 234-2078

Forever Children
13641 John Glenn Road, #A
Apple Valley, CA 92307
619-247-1123

Fruit of the Loom, Inc.
One Fruit of the Loom Drive
Bowling Green, KY 42101
(502) 781-6400

Fulton Baby Products
979 Rupley Dr.
Atlanta, GA 30306
(404) 875-4455

Fun Fair Hi-Ho Products
1600 Mary
Sharpsburg, PA 15215
(412) 782-2552

G.W. DMKA Inc.
168 East Main Street
Prospect Park, NJ 07501
(201) 595-5599

Galvis Foam Corp.
890 E. 62 St.
Los Angeles, CA 90001
(213) 232-3511

Gendron
501 Alliance Avenue
Toronto, Ont., Canada M6N 3J3
416-763-3801

General Foods Corporation
250 North Street
White Plains, NY 10625
800-431-1001

General Foods Corporation
250 North Street
White Plains, NY 10625

General Mills, Inc.
P.O. Box 1113
Minneapolis, MN 55440
612-540-4295 or 800-231-0308

Gerber Baby Products Company
12520 Grant Drive
Denver, CO 80233
303-457-0926

Gerber Products Company
445 State Street
Fremont, MI 49412
616-928-2000 or 800-4-GERBER

Gerry Childrenswear, Inc.
One Financial Center
Boston, MA 02111
617-330-1800

Glenna Jean Manufacturing Co.
230 N. Sycamore Street,
   P.O. Box 2187
Petersburg, VA 23803
804-861-0687

Gold Bug
4999 Oakland Street
Denver, CO 80239
303-371-2535

Graco Children's Products, Inc.
Route 23, Main Street
Elverson, PA 19520
(215) 286-5951

Gramco Mfg., Inc.
22600 Lambert St., Bldg. B/805
El Toro, CA 92630
800-854-8035
800-432-3676 (in CA)

Great Kid Company, The
P.O. Box 654
Lexington, MA 02173
617-862-0717

Gu-Di Enterprises, Inc.
112 W. 34 St.
NY, NY 10001
(212) 736-9120

Gund Inc.
44 National Rd.
Edison, NJ 08818
(201) 287-0880

H G Arms Company
1449 37 St.
Brooklyn, NY 11218
(718) 436-2711

H P Books
1019 W. Prince Rd.
P.O. Box 5367
Tuscon, AZ 85703
(602) 888-2150

H.J. Heinz Company
1062 Progress Street
Pittsburgh, PA 15212
(412) 237-5740

H.W. Originals, Inc.
P.O. Box 1211
Clearwater, FL 33517
(813) 446-1787

Hamco
4306 Rhoda Drive
Baton Rouge, LA 70816
504-291-0424

Handy Chair Remond For Babies
6105 Portal Way
Ferndale, WA 98248
(206) 384-0446
(800) 426-9244

Hanson Scale Co.
P.O. Box 30 Highway 45 N
Shubuta, MS 39360
(601) 687-1531

Happi Faces
P.O. Box 2087
Peabody, MA 01960
(617) 535-5277

Happy Family Products, Inc.
12300 Venice Blvd.
Los Angeles, CA 90066
(213) 390-9649

Happy Times
P.O. Box 6037, 921 Windflower
San Diego, CA 92106
619-226-7661

Harber Inc.
7216 Washington Avenue
Eden Prairie, MN 55344
612-944-6880

Hasbro, Inc.
1027 Newport Avenue
Pawtucket, RI 02861
401-431-8097 or 800-237-0063

Health-Tex by Triboro
172 S. Broadway
White Plains, NY 10605
914-428-7551

Healthmed Inc.
P.O. Box 413
Fords, NJ 08863
(201) 225-5016

Healthteam/Gentle Expressions
625 Montrose Avenue
South Plainfield, NJ 07080
201-561-4100

Hedstrom Co.
P.O. Box 432
Bedford, PA 15522
(814) 623-9041

Heinz U.S.A.
P.O. Box 57
Pittsburgh, PA 15230
412-237-5740

Herko Inc,.
283 Liberty Ave.
Brooklyn, NY 11207
(718) 498-1110

Hershey Foods Corporation
P.O. Box 815
Hershey, PA 17033
800-468-1714

Hokus Pokus America, Inc.
P.O. Box 376
Southampton, PA 18966
(215) 947-6175

Hopkins Mfg., Co.
10015 Railroad St.
Lake City, PA 16423
(814) 774-3171

Hot Tots, Inc.
13325 S.W. 108 Pl.
Miami, FL 33176
(305) 238-7230)

House of Hatten, Inc.
9516 Neils Thompson
Austin, TX 78759
(512) 837-4467

Huffy Corporation
7701 Byers Road
Miamisburg, OH 45342
513-866-6251

Ideal Toy Company
184-10 Jamaica Avenue
Hollis, NY 12423
(212) 481-6400

Illco Toy
2266 Davie, #110
Los Angeles, CA 90040
213-727-7232

Infinity Corporation
5812 E. Burnside street
Portland, OR 97215
503-231-9243

Inglesina Baby
1190 Stirling Road
Dania, FL 33004
305-922-6991

Innovative Distributing Ltd.
1853 Welch Street
N. Vancouver, B.C., Canada V7P 1B7
604-987-0455

Intelligent Playtime Corp.
43 Thaxter St.
Hingham, MA 02043
(617) 749-6452

International Dairy Queen, Inc.
5701 Green Valley Drive
Minneapolis, MN 55435
612-830-0200

International Mfg. Co.
2500 Washington St., P.O. Box 541
Boston, MA 02119
(617) 442-9700

International Playthings, Inc.
116 Washington St.
Bloomfield, NJ 07003
(201) 429-2700

International Products Trading Inc.
380 Franklin Turnpike
Mahwah, NJ 07430
(201) 529-4500

It's a Corker, Inc.
1083 Manor Lane
Bay Shore, NY 11706
516-666-4774

J.C. Penney Company
1301 Avenue of the Americas
New York, NY 10019
(212) 957-6612

Jagco Enterprises
8406 Sedan Ave.
Canoga Park, CA 91304
(213) 888-1967

James David Home Office
4025 Lakefront Court
St. Louis, MO 63045
314-291-0400

Janco
P.O. Box 1374
Aptos, CA 95003
408-684-1894

JED Products Corp.
101 Cedar Ln.
Teaneck, NJ 07666
(201) 692-9090

Johnson & Johnson Personal Products
    Company
Van Liew Avenue
Milltown, NJ 08850
800-631-5294

Johnson & Johnson Consumer
    Products, Inc.
199 Grandview Road
Skillman, NJ 08558
800-526-2433

Jolly Jumper Inc.
144 Water St. S
Cambridge, Ontario, Canada N1R 3E2
(519) 623-5830

Joy Baby Inc.
300 Harris Avenue, #E
Sacramento, CA 95838
916-927-8800

Joy of CA
831 S. Fifth St.
San Jose, CA 95112
(919) 643-6322

Judi's Originals
15035 N. 75th Street
Scottsdale, AZ 85260
602-991-5885

Juvenile Heirlooms
1051 Sousa Drive
Walnut Creek, CA 94596
707-745-8439

K Mart Corporation
3100 West Big Beaver Road
Troy, Michigan 48084
(313) 643-1643

Kaleidoscope Design, Inc.
1755 North Oak Road, P.O. Box 699
Plymouth, IN 46563-0699
219-936-7950

Kalencom Corporation
740 Clouet Street
New Orleans, LA 70117
504-943-0123

Kamar International Inc.
25550 Hawthorne Blvd.
Torrance, CA 90505
(213) 378-5216
Produts: Dolls, Toys(Crib),
Toys(Stuffed)

Karyn B. Toys
P.O. Box 538
Lebanon, NJ 08833

Kaz, Incorporated
10 Columbus Circle, #1620
New York, NY 10019
212-586-1630

Keebler Company, Inc.
1 Hollow Tree Lane
Elmhurst, IL 60126
(312) 833-2900

Kel-Gar, Inc.
P.O. Box 796934
Dallas, TX 75379-6934
214-250-3838

Kellogg Company
P.O. Box CAMB
Battle Creek, MI 49016
616-961-2277

Kewaunee Equipment Co.
401 Park Street
P.O. Box 224
Kewaunee, WI 54216
(414) 388-3232

Kico Inc.
21 W. 280 Coronet Road
Lombard, IL 60148
(312) 620-0661

Kid Kraft, Inc.
7175 Newton
Westminster, CO 80403
(303) 427-0066

Kiddie Kingdom
Div. CA Stuffed Toy
611 S. Anderson Street
Los Angeles, CA 90023
(213) 268-0141

Kiddie Lites
P.O. Box 202
Roxbury, NY 12474
607-326-4923

Kiddie Products
1 Kiddie Drive
Avon, MA 02322
(617) 588-1220

Kidentials
7101 E. Slauson Avenue
Commerce, CA 90040
800-762-6872

Kids Basics
Box 3202 R.S.
Stamford, CT 06905
203-325-1117

Kids Corp. International
11500 SW 150 Street
Miami, FL 33176
(305) 255-0014

Kids Line Inc.
6800 Avalon Boulevard
Los Angeles, CA 90003
213-758-6096

Kidsprints/Petco Prints
12 I Linscott Road
Woburn, MA 01801
617-938-7966

Kidstar, Division of Monogram
Models
6123 Monroe Court, P.O. Box 317
Morton Grove, IL 60053
312-966-1050

Kidstuff Pals, Inc.
5101 Rio Vista Avenue
Tampa, FL 33634
813-888-7408

Kimberly-Clark Corporation
P.O. Box 2020
Neenah, WI 54956
(414) 721-5308

Kindercraft Juvenile Furniture Co.
901 South Neeley, P.O. Box 704
Benton, AR 72015
501-778-8210

Kindergard Corp.
14822 Venture Drive
Dallas, TX 75234
(214) 243-7101
800-527-2338

Kindergund
P.O. Box H, 1 Runyons Lane
Edison, NJ 08818
201-248-1500

Kinderworks Corporation
P.O. Box 1441
Portsmouth, NH 03801
603-692-2777

Kiwi Products International
P.O. Box 5009
Woodland Hills, CA 91365
(818) 888-7494

KLM Woodworks
103 S. White Oak Road
White Oak, TX 75693
214-759-5305

Koalakins Inc.
P.O. Box 2701
Eugene, OR 97402
(503) 683-BABY

Kolcraft Enterprises, Inc.
3455 W. 31st Place
Chicago, IL 60623
312-247-4494

Kolcraft Products of CA, Inc.
5430 E. Union Pacific Avenue
Los Angeles, CA 90040
(213) 724-9403

Kraft Consumer Service
Retail Food Group Kraft, Inc.
Glenview, IL 60025
(312) 998-2000

KTR Inc.
13040 SW 120 Street
Miami, FL 33186
305-235-0396

L.L. Bean, Inc.
Casco Street
Freeport, ME 04033
800-341-4341

Lady Margaret Inc.
323 Brown Street
Petersburg, VA 23803
804-862-2731 or 800-553-0495

Lambs & Ivy
5978 Bowcroft Street
Los Angeles, CA 90016
213-839-5155 or 800-345-2627

Lamby
3820 Bodega Avenue
Petaluma, CA 94952
707-763-4222

Lands' End
One Lands' End Lane
Dodgeville, WI 53595
800-356-4444

Laurie Love Creates
357 Scotland Street
Dunedin, FL 33528
(813) 733-2405

Lea Industried, A Ladd Furniture,
    Inc. Company
P.O. Box HP-3
High Point, NC 27261
919-889-0333

Lear Siegler Seymour Corp.
885 North Chestnut Street
Seymour, IN 47274
812-522-5130

Lee Hy Mfg. Co. Inc.
P.O. Box 5
Lehighton, PA 18235
(717) 386-4144

Lemon Bear
406 E. Lake Street
Minneapolis, MN 55408
(612) 823-8231

Lewis of London
25 Power Drive
Hauppauge, NY 11788
516-582-8300

Life Mfg. Co. Inc.
20 Meridian Street
East Boston, MA 02128
(617) 569-1200

Lil Lamb's Keeper, Inc.
P.O. Box 36189
Birmingham, AL 35236
800-472-3736

Lillian Vernon Corporation
510 South Fulton Avenue
Mount Vernon, NY 10550
914-633-6400

Lipper International, Inc.
235 Washington Street
Wallingford, CT 06437
203-269-8588

Little Bedding (Div. of Red Calliope)
13003 S. Figueroa Street
Los Angeles, CA 90061
213-516-6100

Little Fox Designs
7786 SW Nimbus Avenue
Beaverton, OR 97005
(503) 626-3019

Little Kids, Inc.
Wayland Square, P.O. Box 3192
Providence, RI 02906
401-751-8669

Little Tikes Inc.
2180 Barlow Road
Hudson, OH 44236
(216) 650-3000

Little Vikings, Ltd.
252 Norman Avenue
Brooklyn, NY 11222
(718) 889-0966

Lullabye Garden
1717 E. 28th Street
Signal Hill, CA 90806
213-426-7519

Luv N' Care
112 West 34th Street, #920
New York, NY 10120
212-594-4780

Luv Stuff
10254 Miller Road
Dallas, TX 75238
214-343-0794

Maclaren-Marshall Products, Inc.,
   Juvenile Div.
600 Barclay Boulevard
Lincolnshire, IL 60069
312-634-6300

Major Lab Mfg. Co.
4408 N. Sewell
Oklahoma City, OK 73118
(405) 524-2281

Mapes Industries, Inc.
6 Grace Avenue
Great Neck, NY 11021
(516) 487-7995

Marcus Bros. Crib Prod. Inc./Rosebud
1755 McDonald Avenue
Brooklyn, NY 11230
718-645-4565

Marriott Concepts, Inc.
200W 900 N
Springville, UT 84663
801-489-8691

Marshall Products, Inc.-Juvenile
   Division
Div. Marshall Electronics
600 Barclay Boulevard
Lincolnshire, IL 60069
(312) 634-6300

Marston Inc.
P.O. Box 29006
Richmond, VA 23229
(804) 270-4187

Mary Meyer Mfg. Co., Inc.
Mary Meyer Station
Townshend, VT 05353
(802) 365-7793

Matt 'N Alli, Inc.
2 Lawson Avenue
East Rockaway, NY 11518
516-593-5466 or 800-736-4571

Mattel Toys, Inc.
5150 Rosecrans
Hawthorne, CA 90250
213-978-6127 or 800-421-2887

McDonald's Corporation
McDonald's Plaza
Oak Brook, IL 60521
312-575-6198

McNeil Consumer Products Company
Johnson & Johnson
Camp Hill Road
Fort Washington, PA 19034
215-233-7000

Meadowbrook Press
18318 Minnetonka Boulevard
Deephaven, MN 55391
612-473-5400 or 800-338-2232

Media General, Inc.
333 East Grace Street
Richmond, VA 23219
804-649-6000

Mericom Corporation
24355 Capitol Avenue
Redford, MI 48239
313-255-6700

Miles Kimball
41 West 8
Oshkosh, WI 54906

Million Dollar Baby
16326 Bloomfield Avenue
Cerritos, CA 90701
213-921-0353

Mini Togs Inc./Panda Knits
112 West 34th Street, #920
New York, NY 10120
212-594-4780

MM's Designs
7450 Harwin Drive
Houston, TX 77036
713-952-5656

Moonbeam Baby Products, Inc.
461 West Broadway
Gardner, MA 01440
508-630-1493

Morigeau Furniture USA
48 Sunnyhill Drive
Pittsburgh, PA 15228
800-326-2121

Mustela De Paris
6611 Heidi Court
McLean, VA 22101
703-893-7128

N.D. Cass Co.
00 Fifth Ave.
NY, NY 10010
(212) 675-2644

N.K.R. Precision Mfg. Corp.
Rt. 17M, Box 333
Harriman, NY 10926
(914) 782-8562

Nabisco Brands, Inc.
Parsippany, NJ 07054
(201) 898-7460

Nanci Industries
P.O. Box 241
Germantown, MD 20874
(301) 948-0008

Nancy C. McNealy Designs
59 S. Clay Street
Morresville, IN 46158
(317) 831-6506

National Woodworks
6270 N.W. 37 Avenue
Miami, FL 33147
305-696-1720

NBC
30 Rockefeller Plaza
New York, NY 10112
212-664-4444

Nelson Juvenile Products Inc.
301-1111 W. Georgia Street
Vancouver, B.C. Canada V6E 3G7
604-689-0223

Nestle Company, Inc.
100 Bloomingdale Road
White Plains, NY 10605
(914) 682-6585

Newborne Co.
River Road
Worthington, MA 01098
(413) 238-5551
(800) 237-1712

Newport Exchange, Inc.
4902 N. 18th Street
Sheboygan, WI 53083
414-452-9894

Nike, Inc.
9300 Nimbus Road
Beaverton, OR 97005
503-644-9000 or 800-344-6453

Nimble Thimble Inc.
260 Starling Road
Englewood, NJ 07631
(201) 567-4717

Noel Joanna Inc.
15091 Bake Parkway
Suite A
Irvine, CA 92718
(714) 770-6303

Nogatco International Inc.
86 Lackawanna Avenue, P.O. Box 2007
W. Paterson, NJ 07424
201-785-4907

North States Industries Inc.
1200 Mendelssohn Avenue, #210
Minneapolis, MN 55427
612-541-9101

Northland Children's Furniture
70 Oswald Drive, P.O. Box 3382
Spruce Grove, Alberta, Canada,
   T7X 3A7
403-962-4622

Nu-Line Industries
214 Nu-Line Street
Suring, WI 54174
414-842-2141

Nurse-Dri Breast Shield Co.
105 Belvedere Dr. #2
Mill Valley, CA 94941
(415) 381-1758

Nursery Craft
6270 N.W. 37th Avenue
Miami, FL 33147
305-696-1720

Nursery Originals
Div. Century Products
1366 Commerce Dr.
Stow, OH 44224

Nurserytyme Products
649 39th Street
Brooklyn, NY 11232
(718) 853-7000

Nurturing Technologies Corporation
Milton Rd. #163
Litchfield, CT 06759
(203) 567-8123

Nutrasweet Company
1751 Lake Cook Road
Deerfield, IL 60015
800-321-7254

Oaklawn Press, Inc.
1318 Fair Oaks Ave.
S. Pasadena, CA 91030
(213) 799-0880

Ocean Spray Cranberries Inc.
One Ocean Spray Drive
Lakeville/Middleboro, MA 02349
508-946-1000

Okla Homer Smith Furn. Mfg. Co.
Div. Gerber Products
416 S. 5th Street
Ft. Smith, AR 72901
(501) 783-6191

Once Upon A Whimsy - Division of
   The Nursery Collection, Inc.
110 Ridge Drive
Naples, FL 33963
813-597-1744 or 800-338-1184

One-of-a-Kind Workshop
24 Pine Mountain Road
Ridgefield, CT 06877
(203) 743-0247

Oscar Mayer and Company
P.O. Box 7188
Madison, WI 53707
(608) 241-6822

Osgood Trading Inc.
3740 Palos Verdes Way
S. San Francisco, CA 94080
(415) 878-0569

Our Baby's First Seven Years
5841 S. Maryland Ave.
Chicago, IL 60637
(312) 667-5184

Our Way Studios
95 Madison Ave.
New York, NY 10016
(212) 685-0505

Pansy Ellen Products, Inc.
1245 Old Alpharetta
Alpharetta, GA 30201
(404) 751-0442

Paris Mfg. Corp.
P.O. Box 250
South Paris, ME 04281
(207) 743-5111

Pat Higdon Industries, Inc.
Lake Talquin Rd
Quincy, FL 32351
(904) 627-9524

Patchkraft Mfg. Co.
89-B Glen Avenue
Lodi, NJ 07644
(201) 340-3300

Pecoware DBA Peco
1313 John Reed Court
City of Industry, CA 91745
818-330-4646

Pee Wee Perch, Inc.
517 Glade Rd.
Loveland, CO 80537
(303) 669-0050

Peg-Perego U.S.A., Inc.
3625 Independence Drive
Fort Wayne, IN 46818
219-482-8191

Perego Products, Inc.
55 Barell Ave.
Carlstadt, NJ 07072
(201) 935-5055

Perfect Fit Industries
303 Fifth Avenue
New York, NY 10016
212-679-6656

Pet, Inc.
400 South Fourth Street
St. Louis, Mo 63102
800-325-7130 (toll free)

Peter Pan Products
49 39th St.
Brooklyn, NY 11232
(718) 853-7000

Petrus Imports, Inc.
161 Worcester Road, 4th Floor
Framingham, MA 01701
508-875-8338

Pfizer Consumer Products
35 East 42nd Street
New York, NY 10017
(212) 573-2323

Pilgrim Infants Products Co.
P.O. Box 836
Fitchburg, MA 01420
508-345-6901

Pillsbury Company
200 South Sixth Street
Minneapolis, Mn 55402
(612) 330-4966

Pinky Baby Products
8450 Westpark
Suite 104
Houston, TX 7706377257
(713) 781-9200

Plakie, Inc.
105 Simon Rd., P.O. Box 3386
*Youngstown, Oh 44512
(216) 788-4021

Playskool
see Hasbro, Inc.

Playtex Family Products Corporation
700 Fairfield Avenue
Stamford, CT 06904
203-356-8000

Pockets of Learning
31G Union Avenue
Sudbury, MA 01776
508-443-5808 or 800-635-2994

Posture Support
P.O. Box 39515
Solon, OH 44139
(800) 321-6870

Premarq, Inc.
2069 Highway 101
Warrenton, OR 97146
503-861-0386

Pride-Trimble
15132 S. Vermont Avenue
Gardena, CA 90247
213-532-3570

Prince Lionheart
3070 Skyway Drive, Bldg. #502
Santa Maria, CA 93455
805-922-2250

Prism Leisure Corporation U.S.A.
10475 Perry Highway, #G-103
Wexford, PA 15090
412-935-5066

Priss Prints, Inc.
3002 Jeremes Landing
Garland, TX 75043
214-278-5600

Procter & Gamble Company
P.O. Box 599
Cincinnati, OH 45201
513-983-2200

Prodigy Corp.
916 Main Street
Acton, MA 01720
508-263-9041

Puck Children's Furniture, Inc.
3675 N.W. 37th Street
Miami, FL 33147
305-693-9363

Quaker Oats Company
P.O. Box 9003
Chicago, IL 60604-9003
312-222-7843

Quiltex Company
112 W. 34th Street
New York, NY 10001
212-594-2205

Racing Strollers, Inc.
516 N. 20th Avenue
Yakima, WA 98902
509-457-0925 or 800-548-7230

Radio Shack
see Tandy Corporation

Railnet Corporation
604 E. 45th Street, #18
Garden City, ID 83714
208-377-2844

Red Calliope
13003 S. Figueroa Street
Los Angeles, CA 90061
213-516-6100

Redmon
P.O. Box 7
Peru, IN 46970
317-473-6683

Reebok International, Ltd.
150 Royall Street
Canton, MA 02021
617-821-2800 or 800-843-4444

Regent Baby Products Corp.
43-21 52nd Street, P.O. Box 473
Woodside, NY 11377
718-458-5855

Relative Industries
500 Library Street
San Fernando, CA 91340
800-824-8147

Remco Baby, Inc.
1107 Broadway
New York, NY 10010
212-675-3427

Renolux
9 Sunbelt Park
Greer, SC 29650
803-244-5273

Riegel Consumer Products Division,
    Mt. Vernon Mills, Inc.
P.O. Box E, 1 Riegel Road
Johnston, SC 29832
800-845-3251

Rochelle Furniture
P.O. Box 8
Duncannon, PA 17020
717-834-3031

Rock-A-Bye-Baby, Inc.
P.O. Box 24160
Ft. Lauderdale, FL 33307
305-561-5111

Royal Heritage Collection From Poly
    Commodity Corp.
175 Great Neck Road
Great Neck Plaza, NY 11021
516-829-3606

Safety 1st, Inc.
210 Boylston Street
Chestnut Hill, MA 02167
617-964-7744

Sandbox Industries
P.O. Box 477
Tenafly, NJ 07670
201-567-5696

Sanitoy Nursery Needs
P.O. Box 2167
Fitchburg, MA 01420
508-345-7571

Sara's Ride, Inc.
2448 Blake Street
Denver, CO 80205
303-292-2224

Sassy, Inc.
1534 College S.E.
Grand Rapids, MI 49507
616-243-0767

Schwinn Bicycle Company
217 North Jefferson Street
Chicago, IL 60606
312-454-7400 or 800-633-0231

Sears, Roebuck and Co.
Sears Tower
Chicago, IL 60684
312-875-5188

Sherkit Div. Sheres Industries, Inc.
10280 Ray Lawson Blvd.
Montreal, Quebec, Canada H1J 1L9
514-351-7910

Silgo International
650 Arizona Street
Chula Vista, CA 92011
619-420-9920

Silver Cross America Inc.
P.O. Box 4377
Highland Park, NJ 08904
800-387-5115

Simmons Company
P.O. Box 95465
Atlanta, GA 30347
404-321-3030

Simmons Juvenile Products
   Company, Inc.
613 East Beacon Avenue
New London, WI 54961
414-982-2140

SJL Products
6130 E. Slauson Avenue
Commerce, CA 90040
213-721-4333

Snap Ups Kids
131 W. 33rd Street, #1106
New York, NY 10001
212-244-6440

Snugli Inc.
12520 Grant Drive
Denver, CO 80233
303-457-0926

Soundesign Corporation
Harborside Financial Ctr.,
   400 Plaza Two
Jersey City, NJ 07311
201-434-1050

Spalding & Evenflo, Inc.
425 Meadow Street
Chicopee, MA 01021
413-536-1200 or 800-642-5004

Spectrum Juvenile Products, Inc.
1974 Ohio Street
Lisle, IL 60532
312-852-9585

Squibb Corporation
P.O. Box 4000
Princeton, NJ 08543-4000
609-921-4279 or 800-332-2056

Stahlwood Toy Mfg. Co., Inc./Young
   Times
117 Franklin Park Avenue
Youngsville, NC 27596
919-556-8411

Stork Craft Ltd.
11511 No. 5 Road
Richmond, B.C. Canada V7A 4E8
604-274-5121

Stork-Mate, Inc.
R3 Box 85B
Warren, AR 71671
501-226-7263

Strawberry Patch
4519 Bankhead Highway
Douglasville, GA 30134
404-949-2123 or 800-662-2236

Strolee
21800 Oxnard Street, #700
Woodland Hills, CA 91367
818-346-5200

Suh & Lee International, Inc.
168 7th Street
Brooklyn, NY 11215
718-499-7733

Sumersault, Ltd.
P.O. Box 269
Scarsdale, NY 10583
914-472-5778

Summer Infant Products, Inc.
33 Meeting Street
Cumberland, RI 02864
401-725-8280

Sun-Diamond Growers of California
P.O. Box 1727
Stockton, CA 95201
209-466-4851

Sweet Pea of California
491 S. Arroyo Parkway
Pasadena, CA 91105
213-681-0617

Tabor International
8220 West 30th Court
Hialeah, FL 33016
305-557-1481

Tailored Baby, Inc.
500 Library Street
San Fernando, CA 91340
800-824-8147

Tandy Corporation/Radio Shack
1600 One Tandy Center
Fort Worth, TX 76102
817-390-3218

Teddy Tuckers, Inc.
Route 1, Box 47B
Friedens, PA 15541
814-443-3106

Tennessee Woolen Mills
218 N. Maple Street
Lebanon, TN 37088
615-391-4235

Texas Juvenile Products, Inc.
3503 Polk Street
Houston, TX 77003
713-222-8675

Thom McAn Shoe Co.
67 Millbrook Street
Worcester, MA 01606
508-791-3811

Three Marthas Inc.—Cuddle Dry Bath
   Apron
4323 Beverly Drive
Dallas, TX 75205
214-521-4455

Three Weavers
1206 Brooks Street
Houston, TX 77009
713-224-3165

TL Care, Inc.
P.O. Box 77087
San Francisco, CA 94107
415-626-3127

TLC Industries Inc.
712 Morse Avenue
Schaumburg, IL 60193
312-893-0456

Tonka Corporation
6000 Clearwater Drive
Minnetonka, MN 55343
612-936-3300 or 800-347-3628

Tot Inc.
P.O. Box 32239, 2262 Hall Place, NW
Washington, DC 20007
202-337-1177

Toy Time, Inc.
53 Melden Drive
Brunswick, ME 04011
207-725-9800

Toys "R" Us
395 West Passaic Street
Rochelle Park, NJ 07662
201-854-5033

Tracers Furniture, Inc.
612 Waverly Avenue
Mamaroneck, NY 10543
914-381-5777

Tradis Inc.
18600 NE 2nd Avenue
Miami, FL 33179
305-653-8141

Tri Industries, Inc.
412 Main Street
Hopkins, MN 55343
612-935-6110

Triboro Quilt Mfg. Corp.
172 South Broadway
White Plains, NY 10605
914-428-7551

Twin Panda
410 Madison Avenue, #806
New York, NY 10017
212-751-2850

Two Little Girls Inc.
617 Huntington Avenue
San Bruno, CA 94066
415-873-2229

Tyke Corporation
2750 W. 35th Street
Chicago, IL 60632
312-927-5599

U.S. Furniture Industries
P.O. Box 2127, 1200 Surrett Drive
High Point, NC 27261
919-884-7375

U.S. Shoe Corporation
One Eastwood Drive
Cincinnati, OH 45227
513-527-7590

Upjohn Company
7000 Portage Road
Kalamazoo, MI 49001
616-323-6004

W.B. Nod & Company
7000 Peachtree-Dunwoody Road,
Bldg. 6, #100
Atlanta, GA 39328
404-396-9493

Welsh Company
1535 South 8th Street
St. Louis, MO 63105
314-231-8822

Wheeler Enterprises, Inc.
12936 Beethoven Boulevard
Silver Spring, MD 20904
301-890-5568

Wiggle Wrap "C.J. Leachco, Inc."
124 E. 14th Street, #103
Ada, OK 74820
800-525-1050

Wimmer-Ferguson Child Products,
   Inc.
P.O. Box 10427/1073-A S. Pearl Street
Denver, CO 80210
800-747-2454

Wonder Products, Inc.
465 Hamilton Road
Bossier City, LA 71111
318-742-1100 or 800-537-8225

Woods by Hartco, Inc.
600 N. Meridian Road
Youngstown, OH 44509
216-792-1986

Young Generation Furniture Ltd.
4600 Thimens
St. Laurent, Quebec, Canada H9B 1B7
514-337-1100

Zookeedoo, Inc.
5848 Acacia Circle, #A-201
El Paso, TX 79912
915-833-7666

Day Care

Aupair Homestay USA
1522 K Street, N.W.
Suite 1100
Washington, DC 20077-1820
1-800-443-8178
>The Aupair Homestay USA program allows young adults in Europe to study in the United states while providing child care for their host family. Families pay the Aupair $100.00 a week and a maximum tuition subsidy of $300.00. Aupairs provide 45 hours a week of child care and light housework. Both parties pay a $500.00 refundable bond to Aupair Homestay USA.

Safe Sitter
Contact: Sally Herrholz
1500 North Ritter Avenue
Indianapolis, IN 46219
(317) 353-4888
1-800-255-4089
>Safe Sitter is a nationwide program designed to teach teenagers between 11 and 13 how to handle major or minor baby sitting emergencies. To be certified, the students must pass a rigorous written and practical exam that includes rescue breathing and care of a choking child.

Children's Foundation, The
1420 New York Avenue, N.W.
Suite 800
Washington, DC 20005
(202) 347-3300
>The Children's Foundation is a national advocacy organization for children and the people who care for them. Publications include materials on family day care, umbrella sponsorship for family day care homes, child care food programs in family day care homes, regulation of family day care, and child support.

Government Agencies

(See page 7-8 for a complete description of the Consumer Product Safety Commission, Food and Drug Adminstration and the National Highway Traffic Safety Adminstration.)

Consumer Information Center (CIC)
Pueblo, CO 81009

Department of Agriculture (USDA)

Food and Nutrition Service
3101 Park Center Drive
Alexandria, VA 22302
703-756-3276

Food Safety and Inspection
Service
Washington, DC 20250
(202) 472-4485

Human Nutrition Information
Service
6505 Belcrest Road, #360
Hyattsville, MD 20782
301-436-8617, 7725

Office of the Consumer Advisor
Administration Building
Washington, DC 20250
(202) 382-9681

Department of Education

Clearinghouse on the Handicapped
Washington, DC 20202
202-732-1241

Department of Health and Human
Services (HHS)

Centers for Disease Control
Atlanta, GA 30333

National Center on Child Abuse
and Neglect
P.O. Box 1182
Washington, DC 20013
202-245-0586

Office of Child Support and
Enforcement
Washington, DC 20201
202-252-5377

President's Council on Physical
Fitness and Sports
450 5th Street, N.W.
Washington, DC 20001
(202) 272-3430

Department of Labor

Women's Bureau
The Work and Family
Clearinghouse
Division of Information and
Publications
Washington, DC 20210
202-523-6652

Department of Transportation

Federal Aviation Administration
Washington, DC 20590

Office of Intergovernmental and
Consumer Affairs (I-25)
Washington, DC 20590
202-366-2220

United States Coast Guard
Washington, DC 20593
202-267-0972

Environmental Protection Agency
Office of Public Affairs
Washington, DC 20460
(202) 382-4355

Federal Communications Commission
Mass Media Bureau
Complaints and Investigations
2025 M Street, N.W., #8210
Washington, DC 20554
202-632-7048

United States Postal Service
Chief Postal Inspector
United States Postal Service
Washington, DC 20260
(202) 245-5445

Health Care Providers

American Academy of Pediatrics
1801 Hinman Avenue
Evanston, IL 60204

American Medical Association
535 North Dearborn Street
Chicago, IL 60610

American Dental Association
211 East Chicago Avenue
Chicago, IL 60611

Health Organizations

There are a great number of health organizations dedicated to assisting individuals and their families by providing information, referrals, offering support, and conducting research on diseases and health conditions affecting children and their families. Many of these organizations are specifically devoted to working with parents. We have included many of these organizations below, categorized by disease or health condition. In addition to assisting families with children with these medical problems, these organizations can provide you with information that will help you teach your child about medical conditions experienced by other family members, neighbors, and classmates.

Alzheimer's Disease

Alzheimer's Disease and Related Disorders Association, Inc. (ADRDA)
70 East Lake St.
Chicago, IL 60601
800-631-0379
(312) 853-3060

Arthritis

Arthritis Foundation/
American Juvenile Arthritis Organization (AJAO)
1314 Spring St., N.W.
Atlanta, GA 30309
(404) 872-7100

Autism

Autism Society of America
1234 Massachusetts Ave., N.W., Suite 1017
Washington, DC 20005-4599
(202) 783-0125

Birth Defects

March of Dimes Birth Defects Foundation
1275 Mamaroneck Avenue
White Plains, NY 10605
(914) 428-7100

Cancer

American Cancer Society, Inc.
3340 Peachtree Road, N.E.
Atlanta, GA 30026
(404) 320-3333

Candlelighters Childhood Cancer Foundation
1901 Pennsylvania Ave., N.W.
Suite 1011
Washington, DC 20006
(202) 659-5136

Leukemia Society of America, Inc.
733 Third Avenue
New York, NY 10017
(212) 573-8484

National Cancer Care Foundation (NCCF)
1180 Avenue of the Americas
New York, NY 10036
(212) 221-3300

Cardiovascular Disease

Council on Cardiovascular Disease in the Young
American Heart Association National Center
7320 Greenville Avenue
Dallas, TX 75231
(214) 373-6300

Cerebral Palsy

United Cerebral Palsy Associations, Inc.
UCP Research and Educational Foundation
66 East 34th St.
New York, NY 10016
800-USA-1UCP
(212) 481-6300

Cleft Lip and Palete

Prescription Parents, Inc.
P.O. Box 426
Quincy, MA 02269
(617) 479-2463

Cystic Fibrosis

Cystic Fibrosis Foundation
6931 Arlington Rd.
Bethesda, MD 20814
800-FIGHT CF
(301) 951-4422

Diabetes

American Diabetes Association, Inc.
1660 Duke St.
Alexandria, VA 22314
(703) 549-1500

Juvenile Diabetes Foundation International
432 Park Ave. South, 16th Fl.
New York, NY 10010
(212) 889-7575

Disabilities

National Easter Seal Society
2023 West Ogden Ave.
Chicago, IL 60612
(312) 243-8400

Sibling Information Network
University Affiliated Program on
  Developmental Disabilities
University of Connecticut
249 Glenbrook Road
Box U-64
Storrs, CT 06268
(203) 486-3783

TASH: The Association for Persons
  with Severe Handicaps
7010 Roosevelt Way, N.E.
Seattle, WA 98115
(206) 523-8446

Down's Syndrome

Association for Children with
  Down's Syndrome, Inc.
2626 Martin Avenue
Bellmore, Long Island, NY 11710
(516) 221-4700

National Down's Syndrome
  Congress
1800 Dempster St.
Park Ridge, IL 60068-1146
800-232-NDSC
(312) 823-7550

Dwarfism

Parents of Dwarfed Children
11524 Colt Terrace
Silver Spring, MD 20902
(301) 649-3275

Epilepsy

Epilepsy Foundation of America
  (EFA)
4351 Garden City Dr.
Landover, MD 20785
(301) 459-3700

Eyesight

American Foundation for the Blind,
  Inc.
15 West 16th St.
New York, NY 10011
(212) 620-2000

Blind Children's Fund
230 Central Street
Auburndale, MA 02166-2399
(617) 332-4014

National Association for Parents of
  the Visually Impaired
P.O. Box 180806
Austin, TX 78718
(512) 323-5710

Parents and Cataract Kids
179 Hunters Lane
Devon, PA 19333
(215) 293-1917
(215) 721-9131
(215) 352-0719

Hearing Impairment

Alexander Graham Bell Association
  for the Deaf
3417 Volta Place, N.W.
Washington, DC 20007
(202) 337-5220

American Society for Deaf Children
814 Thayer Avenue
Silver Spring, MD 20910
(301) 585-5400

Hemophilia

National Hemophilia Foundation
110 Greene St., Room 406
New York, NY 10012
(212) 219-8180

Hyperactivity

Center for Hyperactive Child   Information, Inc.
P.O. Box 66272
Washington, DC 20035-6272
(703) 920-7495

Kidney Disease

National Kidney Foundation, Inc.
Two Park Ave.
New York, NY 10016
(212) 889-2210

Learning Disabled

Association for Children and Adults
  with Learning Disabilities
4156 Liberty Road
Pittsburgh, PA 15234
(412) 341-1515

Liver Disease

American Liver Foundation
998 Pompton Ave.
Cedar Grove, NJ 07009
(201) 857-2626

Children's Liver Foundation, Inc.
76 South Orange Ave., Suite 202
South Orange, NJ 07079
(201) 761-1111

Mental Retardation

Association for Retarded Citizens of
  the United States
2501 Avenue J
Arlington, TX 76006
(817) 640-0204

Multiple Sclerosis

National Multiple Sclerosis Society
205 East 42nd St.
New York, NY 10017
(212) 986-3240

Muscular Dystrophy

Muscular Dystrophy Association
810 Seventh Avenue
New York, NY 10019
(212) 586-0808

Parkinson Disease

American Parkinson Disease
Association
116 John St., Suite 417
New York, NY 10038
800-223-2732
(212) 732-9550

Reye's Syndrome

National Reye's Syndrome
  Foundation
426 North Lewis
Bryan, OH 43506
(419) 636-2679

Scoliosis

Scoliosis Association, Inc.
P.O. Box 51353
Raleigh, NC 27609
(919) 846-2639

Sudden Infant Death Syndrome

National Sudden Infant Death Syndrome Foundation
2 Metro Plaza
Suite 205
8240 Professional Place
Landover, MD 20785
(301) 459-3388

Missing Children

National Center for Missing and
Exploited Children
2101 Wilson Boulevard, Suite 550
Arlington, VA 22201
(800) 843-5678
   This organization serves as a clearinghouse for information on missing and exploited children. Call
   their toll-free number for a list of
   publications, many of which are fee.

Adam Walsh Child Resource Center
1876 N. University Dr., Suite 306
Fort Lauderdale, FL 33322
(305) 475-4847

National Crime Prevention Council
The Woodward Building
733 15th St., N.W.
Washington, DC 20005
(202) 393-7141

Child Safety Program Handbook
(subj: missing children)
Consumer Information Center
Dept. 402N
Pueblo, CO 81009
(enclose .$50)

Parenting Publications

American Baby (magazine)
352 Evelyn Street
Paramus, NJ 07652
   A monthly magazine for expectant
   and new parents which covers a
   wide variety of topics associated
   with pregnancy, newborns, and
   toddlers. Free subscriptions are
   available for expectant parents.
   After a limited amount of time, free
   subscribers are offered the option
   to continue their subscription for a
   fee.

Baby Talk (magazine)
Blessings Corporation
185 Madison Avenue
New York, NY 10016
   This monthly magazine has been
   published since 1935 and is aimed
   at expectant parents and parents of
   infants and toddlers. It is often
   offered to expectant and new
   parents compliments of a local ven-
   dor of children's products or
   services (such as a diaper service).
   Subscriptions are available for
   $7.50/year.

Child Magazine
The New York Times Company Magazine Group
110 Fifth Avenue
New York, NY 10011
   Formerly a fashion oriented magazine for children's clothes, Child
   has evolved into a monthly
   parenting magazine which focuses
   on numerous issues facing parents.

Growing Child
22 North Second Street
P.O. Box 1200
Lafayette, IN 47902
   Growing Child is a monthly child
   development newsletter. Parents
   are sent newsletter issues that discuss babies and children the same
   age as their child. Topics include
   information on baby's growth and
   development, how children learn,
   and what babies are expected to do
   at certain ages. One year subscriptions (12 issues) cost $15.95. A
   special introductory offer is available which includes three free
   issues plus a year subscription for
   $12.95.

Parenting (magazine)
501 Second St.
San Francisco, CA 94107
  Published 10 times per year, *Parenting* offers a fresh approach to the usual magazine for Moms and Dads. Highlights include in-depth interviews of the experts, regular reviews of books and videos, and some really great photography.

Parents (magazine)
80 New Bridge Road
Bergenfield, NJ 07621
  A monthly magazine for parents which focuses on all aspects of parenting and children, from prenatal to age 13. Subscription price: $11.95/year.

Poison Prevention and Control

All of the following organizations supply information on poison prevention and control.

U.S. Food and Drug Administration
Poisoning Surveillance and
Epidemiology Branch (HFN-720)
5600 Fishers Lane
Rockville, MD 20857
(301) 443-6260

U.S. Consumer Product Safety
  Commission
Division of Poison Prevention and
  Scientific Coordination
Washington, DC 20207
(202) 634-7780

Poison Prevention Week Council
P.O. Box 1543
Washington, DC 20013
(301) 492-6477

American Association of Poison
  Control Centers
San Diego Regional Poison Control
  Center
University California at San Diego
  Medical Center
225 W. Dickinson Street
San Diego, CA 92103
(714) 294-6000

American Board of Medical
  Toxicology
Children's Orthopedic Hospital and
  Medical Center
P.O. Box 5371
Seattle, WA 98105
(206) 634-5252
800-732-6985

American College of Emergency
  Physicians
P.O. Box 61911
Dallas, TX 75261
(214) 659-0911

Safety Organizations

National Safety Council
444 North Michigan Avenue
Chicago, IL 60611
312-527-4800

I • N • D • E • X

T H E   A U T H O R S

Jack Gillis and Mary Ellen R. Fise are two of America's most respected child safety experts and consumer advocates. In addition to their professional qualifications, Gillis and Fise are themselves active and involved parents.

Jack Gillis is an author, columnist and Director of Public Affairs for the Consumer Federation of America, the nation's largest consumer advocacy group. He is a regular guest on NBC's "Today Show," has appeared on "Donahue," "Nightline," "Good Morning America," and numerous local and national talk shows. He is frequently quoted in the "Wall Street Journal," "Business Week," "The New York Times," and "USA Today."

He is author of *The Car Book, The Used Car Book,* and *How to Make Your Car Last Almost Forever;* co-author of *The Armchair Mechanic* and *How to Fly: Consumer Federation of America's Airline Survival Guide;* editor of *The Bank Book* and *The Product Safety Book.* He has two monthly columns in "Good Housekeeping," and is contributing editor to "Child Magazine." In 1985, the National Press Club cited Gillis as one of the best in consumer journalism. "Money Magazine" listed two of his books among the "10 Best Personal Finance Books of 1988" and he was selected by "Sylvia Porter's Personal Finance Magazine" as one of America's personal finance heroes. He and his wife, Marilyn, have three children, Katie, John and Brian.

Mary Ellen R. Fise is Director of Product Safety for the Consumer Federation of America. CFA is rated as one of the ten most influential lobbying organizations in the U.S. and Fise has been instrumental in lobbying the Consumer Product Safety Commission to ban lawn darts, and set safety standards for children's toys, bunk beds, and child resistant cigarette lighters. In addition, she is a consumer representative on several committees which develop safety standards for children's products. An attorney, Fise works closely on product safety issues with a number of consumer groups and serves as a member of the Danny Foundation Advisory Board, a crib safety group. She has taught consumer safety and law courses at the University of Maryland and Boston University. Fise is a contributing editor to "Child Magazine," the editor of the "Consumer Product Safety Network Newsletter," and is frequently quoted in the "Washington Post," "The New York Times," and the "Wall Street Journal" on product safety issues. She and her husband Tom, have a son, Peter.